MY KINGDOM SHALL ROLL FORTH

Readings in Church History

Published by
The Church of Jesus Christ of Latter-day Saints
Salt Lake City, Utah

CONTENTS

Message from the First Presidency   vi
Introduction   1

1 Joseph Smith   3
Preparation and Affliction   4
Humility and Integrity   4
Impressions of Joseph   5
"Always Good-natured"   5
"He Was a Man of God"   6
Administration and Teachings   6
Man's Relationship to God   7

2 Succession in the Presidency   10
Twelve Learn of the Martyrdom   10
Return to Nauvoo   10
The Mantle of the Prophet   11
The Keys of the Kingdom   12
A Day Long to Be Remembered   13
An Epistle to the Church   14

3 Brigham Young   16
Early Life   16
Salvation: The Practical to the Sublime   17
Work in the Ministry   18
Family Life   19
A Practical Religion   20

4 Exodus from Nauvoo   21
Building the Kingdom   21
A Proclamation to All the World   22
The Nauvoo Temple   23
General Conference in the Temple   24
Departure from Nauvoo   24
The Twelve's Counsel on the Exodus   25
The Fall of Nauvoo   26
The Miracle of the Quail   26

5 The Journey West   28
Coming to Zion   28
The Mormon Battalion   29
Colonel Cooke's Tribute   29
The Pioneers   30
Journal of Mary Ann Weston Maughan   30
First Presidency Epistles 1849–56   32
The Migration Continues   35
Ephraim K. Hanks and the Martin Handcart Company   36

6 Sanctuary in Utah   39
Auxiliaries Established   39
Priesthood Quorums Strengthened   40
The Priesthood and Its Functions   41
Strengthening the Church   41

7 John Taylor 46
Early Life 46
Work in the Ministry 47
The Martyrdom 47
A Decade of Persecution 49
Organizing the Priesthood 50
On the Organization of the Seventies 51

8 An Era of Persecution 53
Beginnings of Plural Marriage 53
Legal Persecution Begins 54
Prosecution vs. Persecution 55
Obedience to Law 56
"Naturalization Hearings" Revelation 58
The Lord Intervenes 58

9 Wilford Woodruff 61
Early Years 62
Administration 63
Salvation for the Dead 63
The Law of Adoption 64
Some Church Practices Modified 66

10 Lorenzo Snow 67
Receiving the Holy Ghost 67
The Nature of God 68
Inspirational Experiences 68
Administration 70
The Church's Worldwide Mission 71

11 Joseph F. Smith 73
Early Life 73
Gospel Doctrines 74
"The Origin of Man" 75
"A Warning Voice" 78
"The Father and the Son" 79

12 Heber J. Grant 85
Early Life 85
Integrity, Honesty, Industry 86
Arizona Revelation 87
Ministry 88
Statement on War 90
Missionary Work 92

13 The First Century: Some Reflections 93
Special Services 93
Additional Events 96
Histories of the Church 96
Historic Sites 97

14 That the Church May Stand Independent 98
The Lord's Plan Revealed 98
The Welfare Plan Inaugurated 99
Communism and the United Order 101
The Welfare Plan and the United Order 102

15 George Albert Smith 105
Early Ministry 105
Vision of Grandfather 106
Administration 107
A Visit with the President of the United States 107

Missionary Work   108
Other Developments   109

16 David O. McKay   110
Early Life   110
Mission, Marriage, and a Career   111
World Tour   112
Administration   113
First Presidency Statement on Birth Control   114

17 Priesthood Correlation   115
Beginnings of Priesthood Correlation   115
Announcement of New Correlation Program   117
The Unfolding of Priesthood Correlation   119
Family Home Evening   119
Destiny of Priesthood Correlation   122

18 Joseph Fielding Smith   123
Early Life   123
Strong Self-Discipline   124
A Defender of Truth   125
Oath and Covenant of the Melchizedek Priesthood   125
The Fall of Adam and Eve: A Blessing   126
A New President Is Sustained   127
Counsel to the Saints   127

19 Harold B. Lee   129
Early Life   129
A Polished Shaft   130
The Welfare Plan   131
Call to the Apostleship   132
Correlation   133
Counselor and President   134
The Home and the Family   135

20 The Expanding Worldwide Church   137
Phenomenal Growth   138
A Looming Crisis   140
A Time of Gathering   142

21 Spencer W. Kimball   143
Early Life   144
Service in the Quorum of the Twelve   144
Work with the Lamanites   145
Repentance and Forgiveness   147
Administration   148
"When the World Will Be Converted"   148
The Importance of Temple Work   153
Priesthood Blessings for All   154
A Warning Voice   155

22 Zion Will Yet Arise   157
The Nature of Zion   157
Establishing the Cause of Zion   158
Responsibility to Establish Zion   159
Zion in This Dispensation   162

Sources Cited and Suggested Readings   165

MESSAGE FROM THE FIRST PRESIDENCY

To Latter-day Saints throughout the world:

Since the time of Adam the Lord's prophets have foreseen our day—the dispensation of the fulness of times. One prophet, Daniel, foresaw that the kingdom of God in the last days would, from humble beginnings, roll forth to fill the entire earth (see Daniel 2:31–45).

Our solemn message to the world is that the ancient prophets' visions of the latter-day kingdom of God are literally fulfilled in the establishment and growth of The Church of Jesus Christ of Latter-day Saints.

Much of the remarkable unfolding of the Lord's plan for his Church and kingdom is traced on the pages of this volume, highlighting the continuing stream of revelation that has guided each of the Lord's living prophets in this last dispensation.

May our study of the lives and teachings of the prophets and other faithful Saints inspire each of us to greater devotion to the Lord's work as we prepare for his coming.

Faithfully your brethren,

Spencer W. Kimball

N. Eldon Tanner

Marion G. Romney

The First Presidency

INTRODUCTION

THE Lord has ever sought to prepare his children to return to his presence by sending prophets through whom he has given the blessings of the priesthood and the teachings of the gospel. In all ages Satan has countered these efforts, attempting to draw men and women away from God and make them "miserable like unto himself" (see 2 Nephi 2:27). Accordingly, as men have either accepted or rejected the gospel, they have lived in the light of the gospel or in the darkness of apostasy. A series of gospel dispensations and subsequent apostasies has resulted from these competing forces. In this last dispensation, however, the apostasy-restoration cycle has been broken, for the restoration of the gospel will end not in apostasy, but in the second coming of the Lord. Anciently, the prophet Daniel testified that in the last days "the God of heaven" would "set up a kingdom, which shall never be destroyed," but like "the stone . . . cut out of the mountain without hands," it will roll forth to "fill the whole earth" and "stand forever" (see Daniel 2:26–45).

Much of the unfolding drama of the Lord's dealings with his children on earth is found in the standard works, which contain the truths that will guide us to eternal life and which relate the trials and triumphs of faithful Saints in earlier times. The scriptures truly convey the message of the gospel, which is "the power of God unto salvation" (see Romans 1:16).

THE SCRIPTURE STUDY PROGRAM OF THE CHURCH

In 1972, under the direction of the First Presidency, the Saints commenced a new program by which they would study the standard works over an eight-year period. "The texts for the eight-year series," the Brethren announced, "will be the Standard Works them-selves, rather than secondary manuals." The goal was to learn the gospel "directly from basic sources" ("Adult Sunday School to Study Scriptures," *Church News,* 19 Aug. 1972, p. 4). Accordingly, members of the Church have studied the Old and New Testaments, Book of Mormon, Pearl of Great Price, and the Doctrine and Covenants.

PURPOSE OF THIS TEXT

Although the bulk of the Doctrine and Covenants was written before 1847, the Lord has not ceased since that time to give light and knowledge to his people. President Spencer W. Kimball has testified:

> There are those who would assume that with the printing and binding of these sacred records [in the Doctrine and Covenants], that would be the "end of the prophets." But again we testify to the world that revelation continues and that the vaults and files of the Church contain these revelations which come month to month and day to day. We testify also that there is, since 1830 when The Church of Jesus Christ of Latter-day Saints was organized, and will continue to be, so long as time shall last, a prophet, recognized of God and his people, who will continue to interpret the mind and will of the Lord. [In Conference Report, Apr. 1977, p. 115; or *Ensign,* May 1977, p. 78]

Hence the Lord's inspired guidance of his children did not end with the period covered in the Doctrine and Covenants. Many of the revelations and teachings guiding Presidents Brigham Young, John Taylor, Wilford Woodruff, Lorenzo Snow, Joseph F. Smith, Heber J. Grant, George Albert Smith, David O. McKay, Joseph Fielding Smith, Harold B. Lee, and Spencer W. Kimball are contained in the readings in this text. Revelation continues to guide the Lord's Church today.

ORGANIZATION OF THE TEXT

As the study of the Doctrine and Covenants is completed, *My Kingdom Shall Roll Forth* will serve as the Gospel Doctrine course text for the balance of the year. The chapters in this volume are divided into the following three major parts:

1. An introductory section includes (a) a synopsis of the events of the chapter, linking them with the material covered in previous chapters and (b) a "Highlights" section which lists many of the key dates covered in the chapter.

2. A "Historical Summary" section presents a brief chronological summary of the period. This is not intended to take the place of more thorough histories of the Church, so additional references for further study are provided in "Sources Cited and Suggested Readings" at the back of the book. It will also include published revelations, official statements by the First Presidency and other Church leaders, and selected teachings by the Presidents of the Church. Though not published as part of the standard works, "whatsoever they shall speak when moved upon by the Holy Ghost," the Lord has testified, "shall be scripture, shall be the will of the Lord, shall be the mind of the Lord, shall be the word of the Lord, shall be the voice of the Lord, and the power of God unto salvation" (D&C 68:4). He therefore has instructed the Saints to accept the prophets' words "as if from mine own mouth" (see D&C 21:4–5 and D&C 1:38). Excerpts from diaries and other records of historical value are also included.

3. Study questions found at the end of each chapter will help identify key ideas presented therein. They also

relate to the corresponding Gospel Doctrine class lessons, and will help guide preparation for class discussions.

It is especially relevant this year to study the history of the Church since 1980 marks the one hundred fiftieth anniversary of its organization in this dispensation. Though not exhaustive in scope, *My Kingdom Shall Roll Forth* captures many of the highlights of Church history as it outlines the progress of the Lord's kingdom in the latter days and enables Church members to celebrate this anniversary year with a sharpened historical perspective.

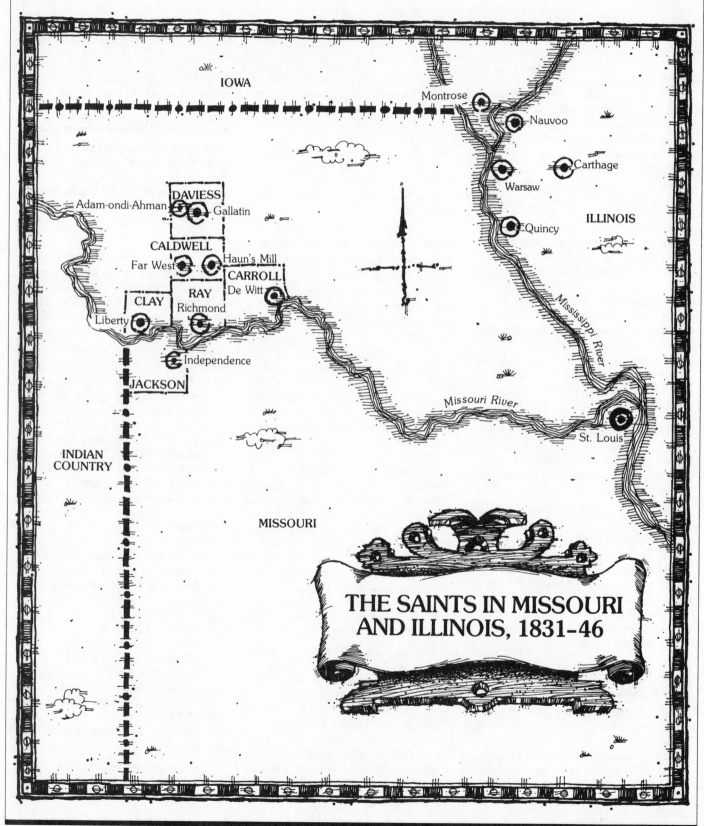

THE SAINTS IN MISSOURI AND ILLINOIS, 1831-46

JOSEPH SMITH

BORN of humble New England parentage shortly after the turn of the nineteenth century, Joseph Smith, Jr, became the divine instrument for the restoration of the Lord's kingdom to the earth for one last time before his coming in glory. Though short in years, Joseph Smith's life was filled with inspired accomplishments. He brought forth the Book of Mormon and other sacred records that had been hidden away to be revealed in the latter days. He sought out the revealed will of the Lord. He founded cities and towns, and when bitter persecution broke out, provided for their resettlement to Ohio, Missouri, and Illinois. He founded a great city that grew to tremendous size in a few short years, and supervised the gathering of thousands there. Amidst all this, he was bitterly persecuted but returned love for the malice given him. His prophetic mission encompassed the restoration of the saving truths and ordinances of the gospel of Jesus Christ, and he sought not only to prepare men for the Savior's coming millennial reign, but to prepare them to enter into his presence.

HIGHLIGHTS

1805 Dec. 23: Born in Sharon, Windsor County, Vermont.

1813 Contracts typhoid fever; undergoes an operation on his leg (7 years old).

1815 Moves with his family to New York (9 years old).

1820 Spring: Receives the First Vision (14).

1823 Sept. 21-22: Moroni visits him four times (17).

1827 Jan. 18: Marries Emma Hale (21).

Sept. 22: Receives the Book of Mormon plates (21).

1828 Loses 116 Book of Mormon manuscript pages (22).

June 15: His first child dies (22).

1829 May–June: The priesthood is restored (23).

1830 Mar.: Publishes the Book of Mormon (24).

Apr. 6: Organizes the Church (24).

June–Dec.: The Book of Moses is revealed (24–25).

Begins work on the "new translation" of the Bible (24).

1831 Moves to Kirtland, Ohio (25).

Feb. 9: Receives Doctrine and Covenants section 42 and introduces the law of consecration and stewardship (25).

Apr. 30: His twin boys die; adopts the Murdock twins (25).

1832 Feb. 16: Receives Doctrine and Covenants section 76, the revelation on the three degrees of glory (26).

Mar. 24: A mob tars and feathers him (26).

Mar. 29: His adopted son, Joseph, dies (26).

Nov. 6: His son, Joseph, is born (26).

1833 Feb. 27: Receives Doctrine and Covenants section 89, a revelation on the Word of Wisdom (27).

May–July: Publishes the Book of Commandments (27).

Oct.: Undertakes a mission to Canada (27).

1834 Leads Zion's Camp into Missouri (28).

1835–36 Studies Hebrew and Greek (29–30).

1835 Feb.: Publishes the Doctrine and Covenants; begins work on the Book of Abraham (29).

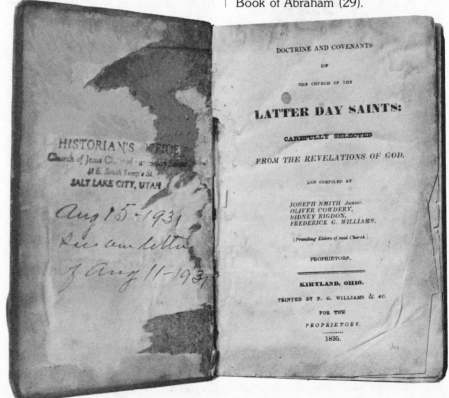

1836 Mar. 27: Dedicates the Kirtland Temple (30).

June 20: A son, Frederick G. Williams, is born (30).

1837 Extends missionary work to England; several leading brethren apostatize (31).

1838 Jan. 12: Forced to flee Kirtland (32).

June 2: A son, Alexander Hale, is born (32).

Missouri difficulties continue (32).

1838–39 Imprisoned in Liberty Jail (32–33).

1839 Mar. 20–25: Writes Doctrine and Covenants sections 121–23 (33).

Apr. 15: Escapes from custody (33).

Founds Nauvoo (33).

1839–40 Seeks redress at Washington, D.C. (34).

1840 A son, Don Carlos, is born (34).

1841: Feb. 4: Commissioned Lt. General of the Nauvoo Legion (35).

Joseph Smith, 1805–1844 (by Frederick Piercy)

Apr. 6: The Nauvoo Temple is begun (35).

Aug. 15: His son, Don Carlos, dies (35).

1842 Feb. 6: An infant child dies (36).

May 4: Temple endowment is first given to a select few in a room above his store (36).

May 19: Elected mayor of Nauvoo (36).

Aug: Arrested on false charges, is

Nauvoo and the temple, 1845

released, goes into hiding (36).

1843 July 12: Writes a revelation on marriage, Doctrine and Covenants section 132 (37).

1844 Becomes a candidate for United States president (38).

June 27: Dies at Carthage, Illinois (38).

Nov. 17: A son, David Hyrum, is born.

HISTORICAL SUMMARY

Preparation and Affliction

As the prophet of God, Joseph Smith was favored of God in a special way, but his divine calling did not spare him from hardship and affliction. In summarizing his labors in 1842 he said, "The envy and wrath of man have been my common lot all the days of my life; . . . deep water is what I am wont to swim in" (D&C 127:2). He testified in 1843, "If I had not actually got into this work and been called of God, I would back out. But I cannot back out: I have no doubt of the truth" (*History of the Church*, 5:336). Early in his life an angel had declared to him "that God had a work for [him] to do; and that [his] name should be had for good and evil among all nations, kindreds, and tongues" (Joseph Smith—History 1:33 [formerly Joseph Smith 2:33]). This proved to be a prophetic description of Joseph Smith's life.

Almost from the very beginning Joseph was the subject of violence. His mother records an assassination attempt on his life when he was only fourteen. Repeatedly, he was the object of mob violence and wrath. In Hiram, Ohio, in 1832 he was tarred and feathered. In 1838 in Missouri he was betrayed to his enemies and sentenced to be shot. When the sentence was not carried out, he subsequently languished in Missouri jails. "It is, I believe, now about five months and six days since I have been under the *grimmace* of a guard night and day, and within the walls grates and screeking of iron doors, of a lonesome, dark, dirty prison," he wrote his wife (Joseph Smith, Jr., to Emma Smith, 4 Apr. 1839, Historical Department, The Church of Jesus Christ of Latter-day Saints, Salt Lake City). He also suffered because of false brethren. Again, writing to his wife from Liberty Jail, he said, "A combination of things have conspired to place me where I am, and I know it is not my fault, and further if my voice and *council* had been heeded I should not have been here" (Joseph Smith, Jr., to Emma Smith, 4 Apr. 1839, Historical Department, The Church of Jesus Christ of Latter-day Saints, Salt Lake City). For weeks in 1842 the Prophet was separated from his family, hiding from unjust arrest.

Humility and Integrity

Joseph Smith did not become a rich man. The Lord told him in an early revelation, "Thou shalt devote all thy service in Zion; and in this thou shalt have strength. . . . And in temporal labors thou shalt not have strength, for this is not thy calling" (D&C 24:7, 9). Time and again, throughout his life, the Prophet lost almost everything he had of an earthly nature due, as he said, to the long imprisonments, the treachery of false brethren, the plunder and driving, and the vexatious and long-continued lawsuits. He was not at peace until he had paid his debts, for integrity was basic to his character: "My heart is full of desire today to be blessed of the God of Abraham with prosperity until I will be able to pay all my debts, for it is the delight of my soul to be honest. Oh Lord, that thou knowest right well!" (Joseph Smith, Jr., Diary, 23 Sept. 1835, Historical Department, The Church of Jesus Christ of Latter-day Saints, Salt Lake City; spelling and punctuation modernized).

Despite the abuse of those around him, love and forgiveness were prominent traits of his life. "I feel myself bound to be a friend to all the sons of Adam. Whether they are just or unjust, they have a degree of my compassion and sympathy" (*History of the Church,* 5:156–57). He felt that friendship was central to the gospel: "Friendship is one of the grand fundamental principles of 'Mormonism'; [it is designed] to revolutionize and civilize the world, and cause wars and contentions to cease and men to become friends and brothers....

"It is a time-honored adage that love begets love. Let us pour forth love—show forth our kindness unto all mankind, and the Lord will reward us with everlasting increase; cast our bread upon the waters and we shall receive it after many days, increased to a hundredfold" (*History of the Church,* 5:517).

His love for his family was unbounded. He was the father of nine children and adopted two others. Six died in infancy, and his last child was born after his own death. Typical of the feelings he had for his family are the words he wrote to them from Richmond Jail: "Oh God grant that I may have the privilege of seeing once more my lovely family, in the enjoyment of the sweets of liberty, and social life; to press them to my bosom and kiss their lovely cheeks would fill my heart with unspeakable gratitude" (Joseph Smith, Jr., to Emma Smith, 12 Nov. 1838, Historical Department, The Church of Jesus Christ of Latter-day Saints, Salt Lake City).

Impressions of Joseph

Many who associated with the Prophet knew him to be a man of God whose integrity and moral character were of the highest level. John Bernhisel knew Joseph Smith intimately in Nauvoo, having lived in his home many months. On 14 June 1844 he wrote a letter to Governor Thomas Ford of Illinois in which he said this of the Prophet:

Having been a boarder in General Smith's family for more than nine months, and having therefore had abundant opportunities of contemplating his character and observing his conduct, I have concluded to give you a few of my "impressions" of him.

General Joseph Smith is naturally a man of strong mental powers, and is possessed of much energy and decision of character, great penetration, and a profound knowledge of human nature. He is a man of calm judgment, enlarged views, and is eminently distinguished by his love of justice. He is kind and obliging, generous and benevolent, sociable and cheerful, and is possessed of a mind of a contemplative and reflective character. He is honest, frank, fearless and independent, and as free from dissimulation as any man to be found.

But it is in the gentle charities of domestic life, as the tender and affectionate husband and parent, the warm and sympathizing friend, that the prominent traits of his character are revealed, and his heart is felt to be keenly alive to the kindest and softest emotions of which human nature is susceptible; and I feel assured that his family and friends formed one of the greatest consolations to him while the vials of wrath were poured upon his head ... for worshiping God according to the dictates of his own conscience.

He is a true lover of his country, and a bright and shining example of integrity and moral excellence in all the relations of life. [*History of the Church,* 6:468]

"Always Good-natured"

Aroet Hale lived in Nauvoo and as a child knew the Prophet and associated with his children. He left the following reflections about Joseph Smith:

The Prophet was fond of children and frequently used to come out of the Mansion and play ball with us boys.... Joseph would always conform to the rules. He would catch till it came his turn to take the club. Then, being a very stout man, he would knock the ball so far that we used to holloa to the boy that was going for the ball to take his dinner. This used to make the Prophet laugh. Joseph was always good-natured and full of fun. I have seen him sit down on the carpet in his office in the Mansion and pull sticks with the Nauvoo Police.... The Prophet would ... pull the stoutest man up with one hand. ["First Book or Journal of the Life and Travels of Aroet L. Hale," Historical Department, The Church of Jesus Christ of Latter-day Saints, Salt Lake City, p. 24; spelling and punctuation modernized]

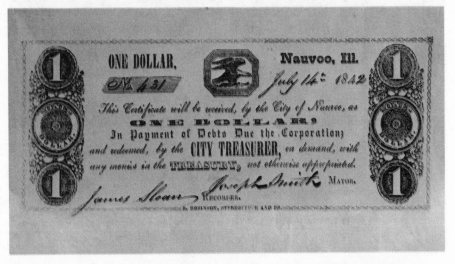

"He Was a Man of God"

Orson Pratt of the Quorum of the Twelve was associated closely with Joseph Smith for some fourteen years. He saw him not only in public, but also observed him in the confines of his home. In a speech given in Salt Lake City, 10 July 1859, Elder Pratt described the Prophet in these words:

I oftentimes reflect back upon the early period of my experience in this Church, having been baptized into the same only about five months after its first organization, when there were but a very few individuals numbered with the Saints. I presume that all who belonged to the Church at that time might occupy a small room about the size of fifteen feet by twenty. I then became intimately acquainted with the Prophet Joseph Smith, and continued intimately acquainted with him until the day of his death. I had the great privilege, when I was in from my missions, of boarding the most of the time at his house, so that I not only knew him as a public teacher, but as a private citizen, as a husband and father. I witnessed his earnest and humble devotions both morning and evening in his family. I heard the words of eternal life flowing from his mouth, nourishing, soothing, and comforting his family, neighbours, and friends. I saw his countenance lighted up as the inspiration of the Holy Ghost rested upon him, dictating the great and most precious revelations now printed for our guide. I saw him translating, by inspiration, the Old and New Testaments, and the inspired book of Abraham from Egyptian papyrus.

And what now is my testimony concerning that man, founded upon my own personal observations? It is the same to-day as it was when I first received the testimony that he was a Prophet. I knew that he was a man of God. It was not a matter of opinion with me, for I received a testimony from the heavens concerning that matter; and without such a testimony it is difficult for us always to judge; for no man can know the things of God but by the Spirit of God. I do not care how much education a man may have—how learned he may be—how much he has studied theology under the eyes of teachers that are uninspired; I do know there is no man living that can know the things of God for himself only by revelation. I could form some kind of an opinion about Joseph Smith as a natural man, without receiving any communication or revelation for myself. I could believe him to be a man of God from his conversation, from his acts, from his dealings; I could believe him to be a Prophet by seeing many things take place that he prophesied of: but all this would not give me that certain knowledge which is necessary for an individual to have, in order to bear testimony to the nations. . . .

. . . The testimony I have borne for twenty-nine years past upon this point is that the Lord revealed to me the truth of this work; and because the Lord revealed this fact to me, I have the utmost confidence in bearing testimony to it in all the world. [*Journal of Discourses,* 7:176–77]

Administration and Teachings

Joseph Smith's contributions to the temporal well-being of his fellowmen are impressive. He directed the settlement of the Latter-day Saints in three states. He revealed economic and social principles that have created unity and prosperity among all who have obeyed them. He was named the commanding officer of one of the largest bodies of trained militia in the United States. He served as a city councilman and mayor of Nauvoo. He also was editor of the *Times and Seasons,* established schools and places of recreation, and operated a store.

It was toward the salvation and spiritual well-being of mankind, however, that Joseph Smith made his greatest contribution. He was the instrument through which divine authority was restored to the earth and through which men received the true knowledge of God and man's relationship to him.

Gold-lettered on a black background, this broadside publicized the Book of Mormon in the 1830s

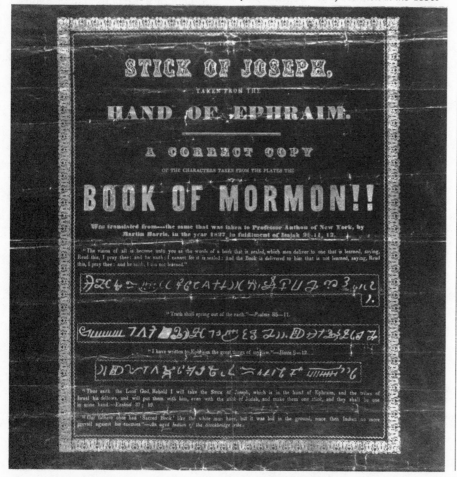

Joseph Smith reviewing the Nauvoo Legion (painting by C.C.A. Christensen, 1831–1912)

Man's Relationship to God

In his address at the conference of the Church in Nauvoo, Illinois, 7 April 1844, the Prophet Joseph revealed this about the nature of God and man's relationship to him:

> In the first place, I wish to go back to the beginning—to the morn of creation. There is the starting point for us to look to, in order to understand and be fully acquainted with the mind, purposes and decrees of the Great Eloheim, who sits in yonder heavens as he did at the creation of the world. It is necessary for us to have an understanding of God himself in the beginning. If we start right, it is easy to go right all the time; but if we start wrong we may go wrong, and it will be a hard matter to get right....
>
> If a man learns nothing more than to eat, drink and sleep, and does not comprehend any of the designs of God, the beast comprehends the same things. It eats, drinks, sleeps, and knows nothing more about God; yet it knows as much as we, unless we are able to comprehend by the inspiration of Almighty God. If men do not comprehend the character of God, they do not comprehend themselves. I want to go back to the beginning, and so lift your minds into more lofty spheres and a more exalted understanding than what the human mind generally aspires to....
>
> God himself was once as we are now, and is an exalted man, and sits enthroned in yonder heavens! That is the great secret. If the veil were rent today, and the great God who holds this world in its orbit, and who upholds all worlds and all things by His power, was to make himself visible,—I say, if you were to see him today, you would see him like a man in form—like yourselves in all the person, image, and very form as a man; for Adam was created in the very fashion, image and likeness of God, and received instruction from, and walked, talked and conversed with Him, as one man talks and communes with another.
>
> In order to understand the subject of the dead, for consolation of those who mourn for the loss of their friends, it is necessary we should understand the character and being of God and how He came to be so; for I am going to tell you how God came to be God. We have imagined and supposed that God was God from all eternity. I will refute that idea, and take away the veil, so that you may see.
>
> These are incomprehensible ideas to some, but they are simple. It is the first principle of the gospel to know for a certainty the character of God, and to know that we may converse with Him as one man converses with another, and that He was once a man like us; yea, that God himself, the Father of us all, dwelt on an earth, the same as Jesus Christ Himself did; and I will show it from the Bible....
>
> ...Here, then, is eternal life—to know the only wise and true God; and you have got to learn how to be gods yourselves, and to be kings and priests to God, the same as all gods have done before you, namely, by going from one small degree to another, and from a small capacity to a great one; from grace to grace, from exaltation to exaltation, until you attain to the resurrection of the dead, and are able to dwell in everlasting burnings, and to sit in glory, as do those who sit enthroned in everlasting power. [*History of the Church*, 6:303, 305–6]

In an essay he wrote sometime in 1842, the Prophet said that man's happiness depends on a harmonious relationship with God:

"Happiness is the object and design of our existence; and will be the end thereof, if we pursue the path that leads to it; and this path is virtue, uprightness, faithfulness, holiness, and keeping all the commandments of God. But we cannot keep all the commandments without first knowing them, and we cannot expect to know

Home of the Prophet in Harmony, Pennsylvania, where much of the Book of Mormon was translated, about 1890

all, or more than we now know unless we comply with or keep those we have already received" (*History of the Church,* 5:134–35).

The Prophet also left more than a hundred revelations and numerous important addresses that formed the foundation of the Church, both in its organizational structure and its doctrine. He inaugurated a vigorous missionary system to take the restored gospel to the nations of the earth. Through him, the Lord brought forth the Book of Mormon, the Doctrine and Covenants, and the Pearl of Great Price. In addition, Joseph made significant progress toward a revision of the Bible. As a capstone, he restored the highest knowledge and blessings of God available to man, knowledge that guarantees the perpetuation of the family unit and prepares men to meet God. He also taught the eternal nature of the marriage covenant and family life: "Except a man and his wife enter into an everlasting covenant and be married for eternity, while in this probation, by the power and authority of the Holy Priesthood, they will cease to increase when they die; that is, they will not have any children after the resurrection" (*History of the Church,* 5:391).

Toward the end of Joseph's life the Lord told him, "I am well pleased with your offering . . . for unto this end have I raised you up, that I might show forth my wisdom through the weak things of

the earth" (D&C 124:1). But his divine call did not mean that his spiritual experiences came without effort or preparation. As the Prophet himself declared, "The things of God are of deep import; and time, and experience, and careful and ponderous and solemn thoughts can only find them out" (*History of the Church,* 3:295). His mother recalled that as a youth Joseph "always seemed to reflect more deeply than common persons of his age upon everything of a religious nature," and was "much . . . given to reflection and deep study" (Lucy Smith, "Biographical Sketches of Joseph Smith,"

unpublished manuscript, Historical Department, The Church of Jesus Christ of Latter-day Saints, Salt Lake City, n.p.).

At a special family meeting on 9 December 1834 Joseph Smith, Sr., gave patriarchal blessings to members of his family. In the blessing to his son, Joseph, Jr., he made the following statement:

Joseph, my son, I lay my hands upon thy head in the name of the Lord Jesus Christ, to confirm upon thee a father's blessing. The Lord thy God has called thee by name out of the heavens: thou hast heard his voice from on high from time to time, even in thy youth. The hand of the angel of his presence has been extended toward thee by which thou hast been lifted up and sustained; yea, the Lord has delivered thee from the hands of thine enemies and thou hast been made to rejoice in his salvation: thou hast sought to know his ways, and from thy childhood thou hast meditated much upon the great things of his law. Thou hast suffered much in thy youth, and the poverty and afflictions of thy father's family have been a grief to thy soul. Thou hast desired to see them delivered from bondage, for thou hast loved them with a perfect love. Thou hast stood by thy father. . . . Thou hast been an

Joseph Smith's store in Nauvoo, where the endowment ordinances were first given (the only known photograph of the store, by B.H. Roberts, 1885)

obedient son: the commands of thy father and the reproofs of thy mother, thou hast respected and obeyed—for all these things the Lord my God will bless thee. [Joseph Smith, Sr., Patriarchal Blessing Book no. 1, Historical Department, The Church of Jesus Christ of Latter-day Saints, Salt Lake City, p. 3]

In an early account of the First Vision, the Prophet elaborated upon the struggle that preceded this event—the searching, the solemn and serious impressions, the concern for mankind, the study of scripture and the guidance of teachers, the years of pondering, the parental teachings, the sorrow for sin, the serious contemplations of the works of nature, and the yearning to God for mercy, because "there was none else to whom I could go" (see Joseph Smith, "A History of the Life of Joseph Smith," unpublished manuscript, Historical Department, The Church of Jesus Christ of Latter-day Saints, Salt Lake City, pp. 1–3).

Emma Hale Smith (painting by Lee Greene Richards, 1941)

Early in his life Joseph found that "God has created man with a mind capable of instruction, and a faculty which may be enlarged in proportion to the heed and diligence given to the light communicated from heaven to the intellect" (*The Evening and the Morning Star*, Feb. 1834, p. 135). His diary reveals frequent seasons of "reading and meditation," endeavors "to treasure up knowledge for the

The First Vision, from a stained glass window in the Salt Lake Seventeenth Ward chapel, 1907

benefit of [his] calling" (*History of the Church*, 2:287, 288, 344). While detained in Indiana for several weeks on one occasion, he wrote of his visit to "a grove which is just back of the town almost every day where I can be secluded from the eyes of any mortal and there give vent to all the feelings of my heart in meditation and prayer." He added, "I rejoice that [God] sendeth forth the Comforter unto as many as believe and humbleth themselves before him" (Joseph Smith, Jr., to Emma Smith, 6 June 1832, Historical Department, The Church of Jesus Christ of Latter-day Saints, Salt Lake City).

It is impossible to weigh the impact of Joseph Smith's life and mission upon the Church and the world. Perhaps *he* gave the best summary when he said, "I calculate to be one of the instruments of setting up the kingdom of Daniel by the word of the Lord, and I intend to lay a foundation that will revolutionize the whole world. . . . It will not be by sword or gun that this kingdom will roll on: the power of truth is such that all nations will be under the

necessity of obeying the Gospel" (*History of the Church*, 6:365).

STUDY QUESTIONS

1. What were some of the major qualities of Joseph Smith's character?

2. How did John Bernhisel view the way the Prophet Joseph Smith associated with his family?

3. How would you describe the Prophet's temperament and athletic ability?

4. What were Joseph Smith's contributions to the temporal and spiritual well-being of his fellowmen as a prophet of God?

5. What doctrine was revealed to the Prophet Joseph Smith regarding marriage?

6. What doctrine was revealed to the Prophet regarding man's relationship to God and the eternal potential of man?

7. What did the Prophet say was the objective of life and the way to obtain it?

SUCCESSION IN THE PRESIDENCY

OF the many challenges facing the Saints after Joseph's death, one critical queston stood above the rest: who was to lead the Church? Joseph had led the Church from its organization in 1830. Now he was gone, and the grief-stricken Saints were unsure about who should lead them. In the aftermath of the Martyrdom, many of the prominent men of the Church who had been away hurriedly returned to Nauvoo. Among them was Sidney Rigdon, the lone survivor of the First Presidency, with Joseph Smith and Frederick G. Williams dead; and Brigham Young, President of the Twelve. The question of succession finally led to a confrontation between these two parties—Sidney Rigdon and Brigham Young. In August 1844 the Saints resolved this question, following the Lord's manifestation of the course to take. From that time to the present, the Lord has called the Presidents of the Church by means of this divine pattern of succession.

HIGHLIGHTS

1844 June 27: Joseph Smith the Prophet is killed.

July 10: Parley P. Pratt returns to Nauvoo.

Aug. 3: Sidney Rigdon arrives from Pittsburgh, Pennsylvania.

Aug. 4: Sidney Rigdon preaches to the Nauvoo Saints, proposing he be appointed "guardian" for the Church.

Aug. 6: Brigham Young and others of the Twelve arrive back in Nauvoo.

Aug. 7: Brigham Young asks Sidney Rigdon to meet with the Twelve and explain his position.

Aug. 8: Brigham Young's transfiguration occurs as members of the Church sustain the Twelve's leadership of the Church in a special conference.

Aug. 15: The Twelve send an epistle to the Saints.

1847 Dec. 5: The Quorum of the Twelve sustains Brigham Young as President of the Church. He selects Heber C. Kimball and Willard Richards as his counselors.

Dec. 27: The Saints, assembled in general conference at Kanesville (Council Bluffs), Iowa, sustain Brigham Young as President of the Church.

HISTORICAL SUMMARY

Twelve Learn of the Martyrdom

All but two of the Twelve were away from Nauvoo serving missions when they learned that Joseph and Hyrum Smith had been murdered. Brigham Young and Orson Pratt were in Peterboro, New Hampshire, when they received a letter informing them of the Martyrdom. Brigham Young questioned for only a moment whether the

Brigham Young, 1850

keys of the kingdom had been taken from the earth with the Prophet Joseph Smith's death or whether they remained on the earth with the Quorum of the Twelve. He later recalled, "Bringing my hand down on my knee, I said 'the keys of the kingdom are right here with the Church'" ("History of Brigham Young," *Millennial Star,* June 1864, p. 359). After learning of the Martyrdom, Wilford Woodruff wrote to Brigham Young suggesting the Twelve meet in Boston, Massachusetts, to decide what course to take before returning to Nauvoo. Elder Woodruff clearly understood that Brigham Young, as President of the Twelve, was then head of the Church. He wrote to Brigham Young: "It is not for me to counsel you" (*History of the Church,* 7:194).

Return to Nauvoo

After a brief meeting of five of the Twelve in Boston, they issued an epistle calling all quorum presidents and others who were away from Church headquarters to gather to Nauvoo immediately. The first of the Twelve to return was Parley P. Pratt. As he neared Nauvoo, Elder Pratt earnestly sought for words with which he could comfort the sorrowing Saints. In response to his plea, the Spirit of the Lord said to him, "'Lift up your head and rejoice; for behold! it is well with my servants Joseph and Hyrum. . . . Go and say unto my people in Nauvoo, that they shall continue to pursue their daily duties and . . . make no movement in Church government to reorganize or alter anything until the return of the remainder of the Quorum of the Twelve'" (*Autobiography of Parley P. Pratt,* p. 333). Elder Pratt arrived in Nauvoo just two weeks following the Martyrdom, finding a weary Willard Richards and John Taylor, the only members of the Twelve to remain in Nauvoo. Most of the burden of Church leadership had fallen on Elder Richards since Elder Taylor was still recovering from wounds he had received in Carthage Jail.

A few days after Elder Pratt's homecoming (3 August), Sidney Rigdon also returned from his self-imposed exile in Pittsburgh, Pennsylvania. Spurning all efforts of the Twelve in Nauvoo to meet with him, Elder Rigdon presented himself to the Saints in their regular Sunday service 4 August and offered to take over the leadership of the Church as "guardian." He requested

Sidney Rigdon (by Charles B. Hall)

the stake president, William Marks, who supported the claim of Sidney Rigdon, to call a special meeting for 6 August to sustain a new leader. President Marks called a meeting for 8 August instead. This was providential, because on the night of 6 August, Brigham Young and other members of the Twelve arrived in Nauvoo. The next day, the Twelve, the high council, and the high priests met to hear Sidney Rigdon's claim. Rigdon maintained that "no man can be the successor of Joseph," but since he had been spokesman for Joseph Smith when he was alive, he proposed that he continue to speak for him (*History of the Church,* 7:229–30). Brigham Young then said: "I do not care who leads the church, . . . but one thing I must know, and that is what God says about it. . . .

"Joseph conferred upon our heads all the keys and powers belonging to the Apostleship which he himself held

before he was taken away, and no man or set of men can get between Joseph and the Twelve in this world or in the world to come.

"How often has Joseph said to the Twelve, 'I have laid the foundation and you must build thereon, for upon your shoulders the kingdom rests' " (*History of the Church,* 7:230).

The following day (8 August) at 10:00 A.M. in the grove near the temple, members of the Church listened to a long speech by Sidney Rigdon explaining his claims for leadership of the Church. The longer he spoke, the less impressed the Saints were. At the conclusion of his speech, Brigham Young spoke, and for many was transfigured to appear to be Joseph Smith, even to his voice. The Saints felt the Lord's acceptance of the leadership of Brigham Young and the Twelve. Doubt and uncertainty disappeared.

The Mantle of the Prophet

The following three eyewitness accounts corroborate Wilford Woodruff's testimony to the English Saints in February 1845: "It was evident to the Saints that the mantle of Joseph had fallen upon him [Brigham Young], the road that he pointed out could be seen so plainly, that none need err therein; the spirit of wisdom and counsel attended all his teachings, he struck upon a chord, with which all hearts beat in unison" (*Millennial Star,* Feb. 1845, p. 138).

Orson Hyde's Testimony:

We went among the congregation and President Young went on the stand. Well, he spoke, and his words went through me like electricity. "Am I mistaken?" said I, "or is it really the voice of Joseph Smith?" This is my testimony; it was not only the voice of Joseph, but there were the features, the gestures and even the *stature* of Joseph before us in the person of Brigham. And though it may be said that President Young is a complete *mimic,* and can mimic anybody, I would like to see the man who can mimic another in *stature* who was about *four or five inches higher than himself.* [*Journal of Discourses,* 13:181]

Benjamin F. Johnson's Testimony:

I sat in the assembly near to President Rigdon, closely attentive to his appeal to the conference to recognize and sustain his claim as "guardian for the Church." And I was, perhaps, to a degree, forgetful of what I knew to be the rights and duties of the apostleship. And as he closed his address and sat down, my back was partly turned to the seat occupied by Apostle Brigham Young and other Apostles, when suddenly, and as from heaven, I heard the voice of the Prophet Joseph. That thrilled my whole being, and quickly turning around, I saw in the transfiguration of Brigham Young, the tall, straight, and portly form of the Prophet

The grove where large meetings of the Nauvoo Saints were held, looking southwest to Nauvoo, about 1900 (from one block north of the temple site)

Joseph Smith, clothed in a sheen of light covering him to his feet. And I heard the real and perfect voice of the Prophet, even to the whistle, as in years past caused by the loss of a tooth, said to have been broken out by the mob at Hiram. This view or vision, although but for seconds, was to me as vivid and real as the glare of lightning or the voice of thunder from the heavens. And so deeply was I impressed with what I saw and heard in this transfiguration, that for years I dared not publicly tell what was given me of the Lord to see. But when in later years I did publicly bear this testimony, I found that others could testify to having seen and heard the same. But to what proportion of the congregation that were present, I could never know. But I do know that this, my testimony, is true. [Benjamin F. Johnson to George F. Gibbs, n.d., Historical Department, The Church of Jesus Christ of Latter-day Saints, Salt Lake City; spelling and punctuation modernized]

George Q. Cannon

George Q. Cannon's Testimony:

Who that was present on that occasion can ever forget the impression it made upon them! If Joseph had arisen from the dead and again spoken in their hearing, the effect could not have been more startling than it was to many present at that meeting. It was the voice of Joseph himself; and not only was it the voice of Joseph which was heard; but it seemed in the eyes of the people as though it was the very person of Joseph which stood before them. A more wonderful and miraculous event than was wrought that day in the presence of that congregation we never heard of. The Lord gave his people a testimony that left no room for doubt as to who was the man He had chosen to lead them. [*Juvenile Instructor*, 5:174–75]

The Keys of the Kingdom

Brigham Young, as President of the Quorum of the Twelve, then called another meeting for 2:00 P.M. where the two claims were to be voted on as directed by the Lord in Doctrine and Covenants 20:65. At this meeting Brigham Young spoke with great authority, telling the Saints that only God could fill the position of prophet, seer, and revelator for the Church:

For the first time in my life, for the first time in your lives, for the first time in the kingdom of God in the 19th century, without a Prophet at our head, do I step forth to act in my calling in connection with the Quorum of the Twelve, as Apostles of Jesus Christ unto this generation—Apostles whom God has called by revelation through the Prophet Joseph, who are ordained and anointed to bear off the keys of the kingdom of God in all the world.

This people have hitherto walked by sight and not by faith. You have had the Prophet in your midst. Do you all understand? You have walked by sight and without much pleading to the Lord to know whether things were right or not.

Heretofore you have had a Prophet as the mouth of the Lord to speak to you, but he has sealed his testimony with his blood, and now, for the first time, are you called to walk by faith, not by sight.

The first position I take in behalf of the Twelve and the people is, to ask a few questions. I ask the Latter-day Saints: do you, as individuals, at this time, want to choose a Prophet or a guardian? Inasmuch as our Prophet and Patriarch are taken from our midst, do you want some one to guard, to guide and lead you through this world into the kingdom of God, or not? All that want some person to be a guardian or a Prophet, a spokesman or something else, signify it by raising the right hand. (No votes).

When I came to this stand I had peculiar feelings and impressions. The faces of this people seem to say, we want a shepherd to guide and lead us through this world. *All that want to draw away a party from the church after them, let them do it if they can, but they will not prosper.*

If any man thinks he has influence among this people to lead away a party, let him try it, and he will find out that there is power with the Apostles which will carry them off victorious through all the world, and build up and defend the church and kingdom of God....

Here is President Rigdon, who was counselor to Joseph. I ask, where are Joseph and Hyrum? They are gone beyond the veil; and if Elder Rigdon wants to act as his counselor, he must go beyond the veil where he is.

There has been much said about President Rigdon being President of the Church, and leading the people, being the head, etc. Brother Rigdon has come 1,600 miles to tell you what he wants to do for you. If the people want President Rigdon to lead them they may have him; but I say unto you that the Quorum of the Twelve have the keys of the kingdom of God in all the world.

The Twelve are appointed by the finger of God. Here is Brigham, have his knees ever faltered? Have his lips ever quivered? Here is Heber and the rest of the Twelve, an independent body who have the keys of the priesthood—the keys of the kingdom of God to deliver to all the world: this is true, so help me God. They stand next to Joseph, and are as the First Presidency of the Church.

I do not know whether my enemies will take my life or not, and I do not care, for I want to be with the man I love.

You cannot fill the office of a prophet, seer and revelator: God must do this. You are like children without a father and sheep without a shepherd. You must not appoint any man at our head; if you should, the Twelve must ordain him. You cannot appoint a man at our head; but if you do want any other man or men to lead you, take them and we will go our way to build up the kingdom in all the world.

I know who are Joseph's friends, and who are his enemies. I know where the keys of the kingdom are, and where they will eternally be. You cannot call a man to be a prophet; you cannot take Elder Rigdon and place him above the Twelve; if so, he must be ordained by them. . . .

Now, if you want Sidney Rigdon or William Law to lead you, or anybody else, you are welcome to them; but I tell you, in the name of the Lord that no man can put another between the Twelve and the Prophet Joseph. Why? Because Joseph was their file leader, and he has committed into their hands the keys of the kingdom in this last dispensation, for all the world; don't put a thread between the priesthood and God.

I will ask, who has stood next to Joseph and Hyrum? I have, and I will stand next to him. We have a head, and that head is the Apostleship, the spirit and power of Joseph, and we can now begin to see the necessity of that Apostleship.

Brother Rigdon was at his side—not above. No man has a right to counsel the Twelve but Joseph Smith. Think of these things. You cannot appoint a prophet; but if you let the Twelve remain and act in their place, the keys of the kingdom are with them and they can manage the affairs of the church and direct all things aright.

Now, all this does not lessen the character of President Rigdon; let him magnify his calling, and Joseph will want him beyond the veil—let him be careful what he does, lest that thread which binds us together is cut asunder. May God bless you all. [*History of the Church,* 7:232–33, 35–36]

Later at the same meeting, Brigham Young again stood and said:

I do not ask you to take my counsel or advice alone, but every one of you act for yourselves; but if Brother Rigdon is the person you want to lead you, vote for him, but not unless you intend to follow him and support him as you did Joseph. Do not say so without you mean to take his counsel hereafter.

And I would say the same for the Twelve, don't make a covenant to support them unless you intend to abide by their counsel; and if they do not counsel you as you please, don't turn round and oppose them.

I want every man, before he enters into a covenant, to know what he is going to do; but we want to know if this people will support the priesthood in the name of Israel's God. . . .

I will ask you as quorums, Do you want Brother Rigdon to stand forward as your leader, your guide, your spokesman. President Rigdon wants me to bring up the other question first, and that is, Does the church want, and is it their only desire to sustain the Twelve as the First Presidency of this people?

Here are the Apostles, the *Bible,* the *Book of Mormon,* the *Doctrine and Covenants*—they are written on the tablet of my heart. If the church want the Twelve to stand as the head, the First Presidency of the Church, and at the head of this kingdom in all the world, stand next to Joseph, walk up into their calling, and hold the keys of this kingdom, every man, every woman, every quorum is now put in order, and you are now the sole controllers of it.

All that are in favor of this, in all the congregation of the saints, manifest it by holding up the right hand. (There was a universal vote). If there are any of the contrary mind, every man and every woman who does not want the Twelve to preside, lift up your hands in like manner. (No hands up). This supersedes the other question, and trying it by quorums. [*History of the Church,* 7:239–40]

A Day Long to Be Remembered

Brigham Young wrote in his journal the following account of the 8 August 1844 meeting, giving credit to the Lord for being able to speak by the "power of the Holy Ghost, even the spirit of the prophets."

This day is long to be remembered by me; it is the first time I have met with the Church at Nauvoo since Brother Joseph and Hyrum were killed—and the occasion on which the Church was called was somewhat painful to me. Brother Rigdon had come from Pittsburgh to see the brethren and find out if they would sustain him as the leader of the Saints. I perceived a spirit to hurry business, to get a trustee in trust and a presidency over the Church—priesthood or no priesthood, right or wrong—and this grieved my heart. Now Joseph is gone, it seemed as though many wanted to draw off a party and be leaders, but this cannot be; the Church must be one or they are not the Lord's. The Saints looked as though they had lost a friend that was able and willing to counsel them in all things. In this time of sorrow, my heart was filled with compassion. After Brother Rigdon had made a long speech to the Saints (I should think five thousand), I arose and spoke to the people. My heart was swollen with compassion toward them, and by the power of the Holy Ghost, even the spirit of the prophets, I was enabled to comfort the hearts of the Saints. In the afternoon, according to my request, the people assembled by thousands. I laid before them the order of the Church and the power of the priesthood. After a long and laborious talk of about two hours in the open air with the wind blowing, the Church was of one heart and one mind. They wanted the Twelve to lead the Church as Brother Joseph had done in his day. Brother Rigdon was called upon to make some remarks but refused to do so. I called upon the Church to express their wishes by vote if they wanted Brother Rigdon for their President, on which motion Brother Rigdon objected and wanted the vote called to see if the Church wanted the Twelve to preside, and it was done. And the Church with one heart and voice lifted up their hands for the Twelve to preside. In this meeting, the quorums were organized, the high council, high priests, seventies, elders, and etc. [Diary of Brigham Young, 8 Aug. 1844, Historical Department, The Church of Jesus Christ of Latter-day Saints, Salt Lake City; spelling and punctuation modernized]

Thus the Twelve were sustained to lead the Church with Brigham Young as President. In an act of unity and brotherly love following the sustaining, President Young asked the Saints to sustain Elder Rigdon in the place he occupied and as "one with us and we with him," which was done (see *History of the Church,* 7:242). However, within a few weeks, Sidney Rigdon demonstrated that he did not sustain the Quorum of the Twelve as the presidency of the Church but in fact secretly asserted that he held authority superior to that of the Twelve. On 8 September 1844, he was excommunicated from the Church. Upon returning to Pittsburgh, Sidney Rigdon established his own church, ordaining men prophets, priests, and kings to the gentiles, but his organization was short-lived.

One week following the historic 8 August meeting, the Quorum of the Twelve, over the signature of President Brigham Young, sent an epistle to members of the Church throughout the world, giving comfort and direction to them.

An Epistle to the Church

The epistle stresses that the Twelve were the proper successors to Joseph Smith because they held the keys (1) "to seal on earth that which shall be sealed in heaven" and (2) "to preside over all the affairs of the Church in all the world."

> *To the Church of Jesus Christ of Latter Day Saints, in Nauvoo and all the world: . . . GREETING.*
>
> BELOVED BRETHREN:—Forasmuch as the Saints have been called to suffer deep affliction and persecution, and also to mourn the loss of our beloved Prophet and also our Patriarch, who have suffered a cruel martyrdom for the testimony of Jesus, having voluntarily yielded themselves to cruel murderers who had sworn to take their lives, and thus like good shepherds have laid

The First Presidency and the Quorum of the Twelve, 1850 (by Frederick Piercy)

> down their lives for the sheep, therefore it becomes necessary for us to address you at this time on several important subjects.
>
> You are now without a prophet present with you in the flesh to guide you; but you are not without apostles, who hold the keys of power to seal on earth that which shall be sealed in heaven, and to preside over all the affairs of the church in all the world; being still under the direction of the same God,
>
> and being dictated by the same spirit, having the same manifestations of the Holy Ghost to dictate all the affairs of the church in all the world, to build up the kingdom upon the foundation that the prophet Joseph has laid, who still holds the keys of this last dispensation, and will hold them to all eternity, as a king and priest unto the most high God, ministering in heaven, on earth, or among the spirits of the departed dead, as seemeth good to him who sent him.

Let no man presume for a moment that his place will be filled by another; for, *remember he stands in his own place,* and always will; and the Twelve Apostles of this dispensation stand in their own place and always will, both in time and in eternity, to minister, preside and regulate the affairs of the whole Church. . . .

On the subject of the gathering, let it be distinctly understood that the City of Nauvoo and the Temple of our Lord are to continue to be built up according to the pattern which has been commenced, and which has progressed with such rapidity thus far. . . .

The United States and adjoining provinces will be immediately organized by the Twelve into proper districts, in a similar manner as they have already done in England and Scotland, and high priests will be appointed over each district, to preside over the same, and to call quarterly conferences for the regulation and representation of the branches included in the same, and for the furtherance of the gospel; and also to take measures for a yearly representation in a general conference. This will save the trouble and confusion of the running to and fro of elders; detect false doctrine and false teachers, and make every elder abroad accountable to the conference in which he may happen to labor. Bishops will also be ap-

Joseph and Hyrum Smith

pointed in the larger branches, to attend to the management of the temporal funds, such as tythings, and funds for the poor, according to the revelations of God, and to be judges in Israel.

The gospel in its fulness and purity, must now roll forth through every neighborhood of this wide-spread country, and to all the world; and millions will awake to its truths and obey its precepts; and the kingdoms of this world will become the kingdoms of our Lord and of his Christ. . . .

Now, dear brethren, to conclude our present communication, we would exhort you in the name of the Lord Jesus Christ, to be humble and faithful before God, and before all the people, and give no occasion for any man to speak evil of you; but preach the gospel in its simplicity and purity, and practice righteousness, and seek to establish the influence of truth, peace and love among mankind, and in so doing the Lord will bless you, and make you a blessing to all people.

You may expect to hear from us again. [*Times and Seasons,* 5:618–20]

The Quorum of the Twelve presided over the Church until 5 December 1847, when the Twelve sustained Brigham Young as President of the Church. He selected Heber C. Kimball and Willard Richards as his counselors. On 27 December 1847, Brigham Young was sustained as President of the Church by the Saints assembled in general conference at Kanesville (Council Bluffs), Iowa.

Thus the divinely revealed plan of succession in the Church operated for the first time, the President of the Quorum of the Twelve, by virtue of his office, being the presiding officer of the Church upon the death of the prophet. He is then sustained as President of the Church by the Quorum of the Twelve and by the Saints in a general conference. (See Joseph Fielding Smith, *Doctrines of Salvation,* 3:155–56.)

The Carthage Jail, 1971

STUDY QUESTIONS

1. How did Brigham Young demonstrate his understanding of the question of succession in the Church?

2. Why wasn't Sidney Rigdon chosen to lead the Church?

3. For what purpose did Brigham Young's transfiguration take place?

4. In what ways are the eyewitness accounts of Brigham Young's transfiguration, as well as his own account of that day's events, valuable to Church members today?

5. Suppose the present prophet died today. Who would be the next President of the Church and why?

BRIGHAM YOUNG

FOR over three years Brigham Young and the Twelve guided the Church. Then in a special conference at Winter Quarters, 27 December 1847, the Saints sustained Brigham Young as President of the Church, with Heber C. Kimball and Willard Richards as his counselors. In this capacity, President Young led the Church for over twenty-nine years, longer than any other man. During that time, he directed the missionary labors and emigration efforts that brought thousands of Saints from all parts of the world to the western United States.

Brigham Young, 1801–1877

He also oversaw the development of a far-flung sanctuary in the Rocky Mountains and the reorganization of the wards and stakes of the Church (see chapters 4–5). He was prepared for these labors by such experiences as the march of Zion's Camp, the tribulations at Kirtland, the removal from Missouri, and the Twelve's mission to the British Isles.

HIGHLIGHTS

1801 June 1: Born in Whittingham, Widdham County, Vermont.

1814–21 Mother dies; Brigham begins to earn his own way in life, eventually becoming a carpenter (14).

1824 Marries Miriam Works (23).

1832 Baptized into the Church and ordained an elder. Wife dies (31).

1834 Marries Mary Ann Angell. Acts as captain in march of Zion's Camp (33).

1835 Feb. 14: Ordained as one of the original members of the Quorum of the Twelve (34).

1839–41 Serves a mission to Great Britain (38–40).

1844–47 Joseph Smith is martyred. Brigham Young leads Church as President of the Quorum of the Twelve (43–46).

1846 Receives section 136 of the Doctrine and Covenants. Sees Joseph Smith in vision and is given valuable instruction (45).

1846–47 Leads the exodus to Salt Lake City and returns to Winter Quarters (45–46).

1847 Dec. 27: Sustained as President of the Church at Kanesville (Council Bluffs), Iowa (46).

1851 Becomes governor of the Territory of Utah (49).

1853 Apr. 6: Lays the cornerstone for the Salt Lake Temple (52).

Discourses on the redemption of fallen beings (52).

1857–58 Utah War. Released as governor after eight-year term (56–57).

1867 The tabernacle is completed. Reorganizes Relief Society (66).

1869 Railroad comes to Utah. The young men's and young women's mutual improvement associations organized (68).

1877 Apr. 6: Dedicates the St. George Temple. Gives new emphasis to the proper organization of the priesthood (75).

Aug. 29: Dies in Salt Lake City, Utah (76).

HISTORICAL SUMMARY

Early Life

Brigham Young brought to his responsibilites as President of the Church a background filled with the kind of experience that can either build or break men and women. Brigham Young spent his early years helping his father clear timber off new land and cultivate the ground. He remembered "logging and driving team, summer and winter, not half clad, and with insufficient food until [his] stomach would ache" (*Journal of Discourses* 12:287). When he was fourteen years

President Young, about 1844

old, his mother died, leaving the numerous domestic responsibilites of the home to the father and the children.

Shortly after this tragedy, John Young moved his family to Tompkins County, New York, where they settled on one hundred acres of timberland fifteen miles from any settlement (see James A. Little, "Biography of Lorenzo Dow Young," *Utah Historical Quarterly* 14:130). Here, in addition to "picking up brush, chopping down trees, rolling logs, and working amongst the roots," Brigham did his share of the housework: "I learned how to make bread, wash the dishes, milk the cows, and make butter;...Those are about all the advantages I gained in my youth. I know how to economize, for my father had to do it" (*Journal of Discourses* 5:97).

When his mother died, he was apprenticed to a furniture maker and house painter to help out the family and learned well, excelling at the craft. At twenty-one, he was in business for himself, and at the age of twenty-three, a successful young man, he married Miriam Works.

He was honest in his business. For example, he refused to dilute the linseed oil he used for making paint in order to compete with those who did. Instead, he sold out and moved to Mendon, New York, just fifteen miles from the home of Joseph Smith. There, his second daughter was born to him, and his wife contracted tuberculosis. Each day before and after work Brigham saw to his wife's comfort and his children's needs. He buried his lovely wife there in Mendon.

Brigham and Miriam had joined the Church after two years of cautious, sincere study. Brigham would not be hurried into anything. His conversion was total, and he served mission after mission in Ohio, Pennsylvania, Vermont, New Hampshire, and cities of southeastern Canada. Then formal missionary calls sent him to additional states and to England. He was blessed with gifts of the Spirit—revelation, prophecy, and speaking in tongues—but his first attempts at preaching were painful. Yet as he shared what he knew to be true, he eventually became a master in declaring the mind and will of God.

Salt Lake City, looking northwest to the tabernacle, 1865

Salvation: The Practical to the Sublime

The following discourse, delivered in the Salt Lake Tabernacle 16 January 1853, is an example of his spiritual insight and power.

The plan of salvation, or in other words, the redemption of fallen beings, is a subject that should occupy the attention of all intelligence that pertains to fallen beings. I do not like the term fallen beings, but I will say, subjected intelligence, which term suits me better—subjected to law, order, rule, and government....

How difficult it is to teach the natural man, who comprehends nothing more than that which he sees with the natural eye! How hard it is for him to believe! How difficult would be the task to make the philosopher, who, for many years, has argued himself into the belief that his spirit is no more after his body sleeps in the grave, believe that his intelligence came from eternity, and is as eternal, in its nature, as the elements, or as the Gods. Such doctrine by him would be considered vanity and foolishness, it would be entirely beyond his comprehension. It is difficult, indeed, to remove an opinion or belief into which he has argued himself from the mind of the natural man. Talk to him about angels, heavens, God, immortality, and eternal lives, and it is like sounding brass, or a tinkling cymbal to his ears; it has no music to him; there is nothing in it that

charms his senses, soothes his feelings, attracts his attention, or engages his affections, in the least; to him it is all vanity....If the Lord does not speak from heaven, and touch the eyes of their understanding by His Spirit, who can instruct or guide them to good? who can give them words of eternal life? It is not in the power of man to do it; but when the Lord gives His Spirit to a person, or to a people, they can then hear, believe, and be instructed. An Elder of Israel may preach the principles of the Gospel, from first to last, as they were taught to him, to a congregation ignorant of them; but if he does not do it under the influence of the Spirit of the Lord, he cannot enlighten that congregation on those principles, it is impossible. Job said that "There is a spirit in man, and the inspiration of the Almighty giveth them understanding." Unless we enjoy that understanding in this probation, we cannot grow or increase, we cannot be made acquainted with the principles of truth and righteousness so as to become exalted....

We are the temples of God, but when we are overcome of evil by yielding to temptation, we deprive ourselves of the privilege of the Father, the Son, and the Holy Ghost, taking up their abode and dwelling with us. We are the people, by our calling and profession, and ought to be by our daily works, of whom it should be truly said, "Ye are the temples of our God." Let me ask, what is there to prevent any person in this congregation from being so blessed, and becoming a holy temple fit for the in-dwelling of the Holy Ghost? Has any being in heaven or on earth done aught to prevent you from becoming so blessed? No, but why the people are not so privileged I will leave you to judge....

When will the people realize that this is the period of time in which they should commence to lay the foundation of their exaltation for time and eternity, that this is the time to conceive, and bring forth from the heart fruit to the honor and glory of God, as Jesus did—grow as he did from the child, become perfect, and be prepared to be raised to salvation? You will find that this probation is the place to increase upon every little we receive, for the Lord gives line upon line to the children of men. When He reveals the plan of salvation, then is the time to fill up our days with good works....

A few words more upon the subject of the eternal existence of the soul. It is hard for mankind to comprehend that principle. The philosophers of the world will concede that the elements of which you and I are composed are eternal, yet they believe that there was a time when there was no God. They cannot comprehend how it is that God can be eternal. Let me ask this congregation, Can you realise the eternity of your own existence? Can you realise that the intelligence which you receive is eternal? I can comprehend this, just as well as I can that I am now in possession of it. It is as easy for me to comprehend that it will exist eternally, as that anything else will. I wish to impress upon your minds the reality that when the body which is organized for intelligence to dwell in, dies, and returns to its mother earth, all the feelings, sensibilities, faculties, and powers of the spirit are still alive, they never die, but in the absence of the body are more acute. They are organized for an eternal existence. If this congregation could comprehend that the intelligence that is

in them is eternal in its nature and existence; if they could realize that when Saints pass through the vail, they are not dead, but have been laying the foundation in these tabernacles for exaltation, laying the foundation to become Gods, even the sons of God, and for crowns which they will yet receive—they would receive the truth in the love of it, live by it, and continue in it, until they receive all knowledge and wisdom, until they grow into eternity, and have the vail taken from before their eyes, to behold the handiworks of God among all people, His goings forth among the nations of the earth, and to discover the rule and law by which He governs. [*Journal of Discourses,* 1:1–5]

Work in the Ministry

Brigham was given leadership positions early, and his responsibilities, which continually increased, included being a captain in Zion's Camp, a confidant of the Prophet Joseph, a member of the Council of the Twelve, the organizer of the Missouri exodus, the President of the Twelve, and the presiding elder of the English mission. His loyalty to the Prophet was complete. During the dark days of Kirtland, when apostasy was rampant even in the high circles of Church leadership, his unyielding firmness became a strength to the loyal Saints: "During this siege of darkness I stood close by Joseph, and, with all the wisdom and power

God bestowed upon me, put forth my utmost energies to sustain the servant of God and unite the Quorums of the Church" ("History of Brigham Young," *Millennial Star,* Aug. 1863, p. 487). The Prophet Joseph Smith could testify that Brigham Young had never lifted a heel against him.

Later, Brigham led six of the Twelve three hundred miles into hostile Missouri, so that they could leave on their mission to England as the Lord had appointed (see D&C 118). He was supported again by a loving wife, Mary Ann Angell, whom he had married in 1834.

The mission in England was a great trial for the Twelve as they struggled against considerable opposition. Through it all Elder Young assisted Wilford Woodruff in the mass conversions of Herefordshire, and, preaching throughout the country with other members of the Twelve, spoke in tongues, healed the sick and the lame, compiled a book of hymns, published the Book of Mormon, established the British Mission, and organized a system for transporting thousands of converts to America.

Later in Nauvoo, as President of the Twelve, he presided over meetings and councils, and with increasing frequency, the Saints referred to him as "President Young." Free from any self-seeking or self-aggrandizement, he sought only to sustain the Prophet he

The Kimball grist mill on north State Street, Salt Lake City

loved. After the Martyrdom (as will be covered in the next two chapters), he led the Saints west and under his leadership the Saints explored and settled vast areas; founded towns and cities; started schools; established roadways, transportation systems, railroads and telegraph lines; began irrigation, farming, industry, and mercantile institutions; made the desert blossom as the rose; and expanded the missionary system. In addition, he served as the first territorial governor of Utah. To the end of his life, President Young worked with amazing confidence and energy towards establishing the kingdom of God and Zion both in the West and throughout the world.

Family Life

That which he loved most was home and family. When united at last with his wife and children at Nauvoo after his long mission to England, he confided in his journal, "This evening I am with my wife alone by my fireside for the first time for years. We enjoy it and feel to praise the Lord" (Journal of Brigham Young, 18 Jan. 1842, Historical Department, The Church of Jesus Christ of Latter-day Saints, Salt Lake City; spelling and punctuation modernized).

Brigham Young entered into plural marriage only after a period of great inward struggle. Mary Ann Angell, his second wife, related that his feelings were so intense that after attending a funeral he reported wishing it had been his own. Nevertheless, he and Mary Ann accepted the practice as coming from God. Their faithfulness rewarded them with a rich home life. (See Clarissa Young Spencer with Mabel Harmer, *Brigham Young at Home,* p. 68.)

Brigham Young had fifty-seven children by sixteen of his wives (see Dean C. Jessee, ed., *Letters of Brigham Young to His Sons,* p. xxiii). Other women were sealed to him in order to have his care and protection. Of his wives, Clarissa Young Spencer, a daughter, wrote: "I believe that a finer group of women never lived together than my father's wives. They cooperated with one another to a remarkable degree, and to each one of us children the 'aunts' were almost as dear as our own mothers were"

Ten of President Young's teenage daughters about 1865 (courtesy of the Utah Historical Society)

(Young and Harmer, *Brigham Young at Home,* p. 64).

The success of the Young family home life is also reflected in statements made by two of President Young's daughters. One said, " 'Home was as beautiful to me as love and happiness could make it.' " Another remembered her childhood as " 'one long round of happiness' " (Jessee, *Letters,* pp. xxiii–xiv).

President Young's interest in his family's welfare did not confine itself to home alone. As his sons traveled to faraway places as missionaries and students, he kept in touch with them and offered fatherly counsel in letter after letter. "Be prudent in your choice of companions," he wrote to Don Carlos and Ferramorz Young, who were in New York studying.

Choose those whose characters are established for truthfulness and honor, whose pursuits are honorable, whose lives are temperate, and whose expenses are moderate. Studiously avoid all those whose lives are tinctured with looseness, prodigality or profanity, and even among the very best of your associates be sure and only imitate their virtues. Remember that however bright any character may be, however much he may shine mentally or intellectually, that if he has vices

they are blemishes and should not be copied. It would be as foolish, yes more so, to copy a man's moral blemishes because he has the reputation of being a gentleman, a student, or a good fellow, as it would be to make an artificial wart upon one's face because some very handsome man had the misfortune to have a natural one on his. We all of us are subject to the influence of others, especially of those for whom we have regard, and from our companions both our character and disposition we'll receive a tincture, as water passing through minerals partakes of their taste and efficacy. How careful then ought we to be to associate only with the upright, the good, and the pure. [Jessee, *Letters,* p. 278]

"Amongst the pleasures of my life at the present time," he wrote to Willard, who was serving in the military,

is the thought that so many of my sons are acquiring experimental and practical knowledge that will fit them for lives of great usefulness. And with this thought I associate the hope that by God's mercy that knowledge will be applied in striving to save the souls of men, and building up the kingdom of heaven on the earth. This knowledge and this work will prove your happiness, for every human being will find that his happiness very greatly depends upon the work he does, and the doing of it well. Whoever wastes his life in idleness, either because he need not work in order to live, or because he will not live to work, will be a wretched creature, and at the close of a listless existence, will regret the loss of precious gifts and the neglect of great opportunities. Our daily toil, however humble it may be, is our daily duty, and by doing it well we make it a part of our daily worship. But, whatever be our labor, calling, or profession, we should hold our skill, knowledge, and talents therein, subservient to the accomplishment of the purposes of Jehovah, that our entire lives, day by day, may be made to praise Him, and our individual happiness secured by the consciousness that we are fulfilling the purpose and design of our presence here on the earth. [Jessee, *Letters,* pp. 190–91]

Indeed, any time President Young could be at home, he enjoyed it. He declared, "The father should be full of kindness, and endeavour to happify and cheer the mother, that her heart may be comforted and her affections unimpaired in her earthly protector, that her love for God and righteousness may vibrate throughout her whole being, that she may bear and bring forth offspring impressed and endowed with all the qualities necessary to a being designed to reign king of kings and lord of lords" (*Journal of Discourses,* 8:62). His application of such principles toward his wives and children indeed made home life joyous.

A Practical Religion

Throughout his life, Brigham Young was a practical man. He continually stressed to the Saints the need for a practical application of the gospel through which men could gain a present salvation:

I am decidedly in favor of practical religion—of everyday useful life. And if I today attend to what devolves upon me to do, and then do that which presents itself tomorrow, and so on, when eternity comes I will be prepared to enter on the things of eternity. But I would not be prepared for that sphere of action, unless I could manage the things that are now within my reach. You must all learn to do this. . . .

If you cannot provide for your natural lives, how can you expect to have wisdom to obtain eternal lives? God has given you your existence—your body and spirit, and has blest you with ability, and thereby laid the foundation of all knowledge, wisdom, and understanding, and all glory and eternal lives. If you have not attained ability to provide for your natural wants, and for a wife and a few children, what have you to do with heavenly things? . . .

It is present salvation and the present influence of the Holy Ghost that we need every day to keep us on saving ground. When an individual refuses to comply with the further requirements of Heaven, then the sins he had formerly committed return upon his head; his former righteousness departs from him, and is not accounted to him for righteousness; but if he had continued in righteousness and obedience to the requirements of Heaven, he is saved all the time, through baptism, the laying on of hands, and obeying the commandments of the Lord and all that is required of him by the heavens—the living oracles. He is saved now, next week, next year, and continually, and is prepared for the celestial kingdom of God whenever the time comes for him to inherit it. . . .

The work of building up Zion is in every sense a practical work; it is not a mere theory. A theoretical religion amounts to very little real good or advantage to any person. To possess an inheritance in Zion or in Jerusalem only in theory—only in imagination—would be the same as having no inheritance at all. It is necessary to get a deed of it, to make an inheritance practical, substantial and profitable. Then let us not rest contented with a mere theoretical religion, but let it be practical, self-purifying, and self-sustaining, keeping the love of God within us, walking by every precept, by every law, and by every word that is given to lead us. [*Discourses of Brigham Young,* sel. John A. Widtsoe, pp. 11–13, 15]

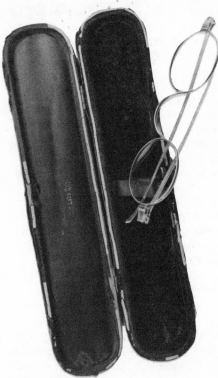

President Young's glasses

For twenty-nine years, President Brigham Young led the Church. He knew the meaning of the Savior's words: "Blessed are ye, when men shall revile you, and persecute you, and shall say all manner of evil against you falsely, for my sake" (Matthew 5:11). From the foundation he laid, the kingdom would go forth to encompass the world. He knew the Saints and the power of God would affect the whole of it, and he willingly and successfully led them on the second leg of that journey.

STUDY QUESTIONS

1. Why did Brigham Young stress the need for a practical religion?

2. For what purpose has man been blessed with a spirit and a body?

3. In order for man to obtain "present salvation," what is essential?

4. What is absolutely necessary in order for a man to effectively teach the natural man the things of God?

5. In what way is man the temple of God?

6. According to Brigham Young, what would be the result if the Saints really understood that when they pass through the veil they are not dead?

EXODUS FROM NAUVOO

AS Brigham Young and the Twelve assumed the leadership of the Church in August 1844, they put into effect plans previously outlined by Joseph Smith for the building of the kingdom, Focusing at first on setting the leadership of the Church in order, expanding missionary work, settling other gathering places, and completing the Nauvoo Temple, they did not concern themselves until later with the evacuation of the Saints from their much-loved city on the banks of the Mississippi River. Through 1845, however, anti-Mormon sentiment in the Illinois communities surrounding Nauvoo forced Church leaders to consider when, how, and where they would remove the entire Church membership to a new place of refuge. They were faced with the challenge of building up the Church community and organization in Nauvoo and at the same time preparing to transplant it to the West.

The Mansion House in Nauvoo, 1971

HIGHLIGHTS

1844 Sept. 24: Seventy presidents are called to preside over all seventies.

1845 Jan. 3: Wilford Woodruff and other missionaries arrive in Liverpool, England.

Jan. 24: The Illinois state legislature repeals the Nauvoo City Charter.

Apr. 6: The Council of the Twelve issues a "Proclamation" to world rulers and to all people.

May 30: Jury at Carthage, Illinois, acquits mob members responsible for martyrdom of Joseph and Hyrum.

June 26: The first stone of the baptismal font for the Nauvoo Temple is laid, a temporary font having been in use up to this time.

Sept. 10: Mobs burn Saints' homes in Hancock County, Illinois.

Sept. 22–24: The Saints are asked to announce their plans for leaving Illinois.

Oct. 6–8: The Saints hold general conference in the nearly completed Nauvoo Temple.

Dec. 10: The endowment is given for the first time in a Latter-day Saint temple. (The endowment was previously given to a select few.)

1846 Jan.: Mob pressure for expulsion of the Saints increases.

Feb. 4: The first Saints leave Nauvoo, crossing the Mississippi River; the ship *Brooklyn* leaves New York Harbor with Saints going to the western United States by ocean route.

Feb. 15: Brigham Young leaves Nauvoo and organizes the Saints into camps.

Apr. 24: The Saints establish their first temporary settlement at Garden Grove, Iowa.

May 1: Orson Hyde publicly dedicates the Nauvoo Temple though most of the Saints have already left.

May 18: The Saints establish a temporary settlement at Mount Pisgah, Iowa.

June 14: The Saints establish a temporary settlement at Council Bluffs, Iowa.

July 13: The Mormon Battalion enlists at Mount Pisgah.

Sept.: The Saints establish Winter Quarters in Nebraska.

Sept. 10–17: Mobs attack the Saints remaining in Nauvoo, and, in what is known as the "Battle of Nauvoo," drive them out.

Oct. 9: Quail are miraculously sent to the poor camp of Nauvoo.

HISTORICAL SUMMARY

Building the Kingdom

During the autumn of 1844, the Twelve filled the priesthood quorums and offices and better defined their duties in order to strengthen the Church's

leadership. The number of seventies increased as sixty-three members of the first quorum became presidents over nine new quorums. The first seven presidents created additional quorums and by January 1846, thirty quorums were functioning, enough to push to completion Nauvoo's Seventies Hall where a preparatory school for missionaries was to be held. In May 1845, Amasa M. Lyman became a member of the Council of the Twelve, filling the vacancy left when William Smith, brother of the Prophet Joseph, was ordained Patriarch to the Church. Members of the Aaronic Priesthood were encouraged to visit the homes of members regularly, and the deacons were instructed to assist bishops in caring for the poor.

A Proclamation to All the World

The Twelve also sought to carry out their obligation to spread forth the restored gospel. In April 1845, they issued a "Proclamation . . . to the Rulers and People of all Nations," calling upon all to make their lives ready for the coming of the Lord.

PROCLAMATION *of the Twelve Apostles of the Church of Jesus Christ of Latter-day Saints.*

To all the Kings of the World;

To the President of the United States of America;

To the Governors of the several States;

And to the Rulers and People of all Nations:

GREETING:

KNOW YE:—

That the kingdom of God has come: as has been predicted by ancient prophets, and prayed for in all ages; even that kingdom which shall fill the whole earth, and shall stand for ever.

The great Eloheem Jehovah* has been pleased once more to speak

*The distinctions that we are accustomed to today in the use of the exalted name-titles *Elohim* and *Jehovah* were very likely not as clear in the 1840s. Moreover, this passage does not confuse the Father with the Son, for in many things the Son speaks for the Father, and in some ways is our Father. For a full discussion of the relationship of the Father and the Son, see "The Father and the Son: A Doctrinal Exposition by the First Presidency and the Twelve," pp. 79–84 of this book.

from the heavens: and also to commune with man upon the earth, by means of open visions, and by the ministration of HOLY MESSENGERS.

By this means the great and eternal High Priesthood, after the Order of his Son, even the Apostleship, has been restored; or, returned to the earth.

This High Priesthood, or Apostleship, holds the keys of the kingdom of God, and power to bind on earth that which shall be bound in heaven; and to loose on earth that which shall be loosed in heaven. And, in fine, to do, and to administer in all things pertaining to the ordinances, organization, government and direction of the kingdom of God.

Being established in these last days for the restoration of all things spoken by the prophets since the world began; and in order to prepare the way for the coming of the Son of Man.

And now we bear witness that his coming is near at hand; and not many years hence, the nations and their kings shall see him coming in the clouds of heaven with power and great glory.

In order to meet this great event there must needs be a preparation.

Therefore we send unto you with authority from on high, and command you all to repent and humble yourselves as little children, before the majesty of the Holy One; and come unto Jesus with a broken heart and a contrite spirit; and be baptized in his name, for the remission of sins (that is, be buried in the water in the likeness of his burial and rise again to newness of life, in the likeness of his resurrection), and you shall receive the gift of the Holy Spirit, through the laying on of the hands of the Apostles and elders, of this great and last dispensation of mercy to man.

This Spirit shall bear witness to you, of the truth of our testimony; and shall enlighten your minds, and be in you as the spirit of prophecy and revelation. It shall bring things past to your understanding and remembrance; and shall show you things to come.

It shall also impart unto you many great and glorious gifts; such as the gift of healing the sick, and of being healed, by the laying on of hands in the name of Jesus; and of expelling Demons; and even of seeing visions, and conversing with Angels and spirits from the unseen world.

By the light of this Spirit, received through the ministration of the ordinances—by the power and authority of the Holy Apostleship and Priesthood, you will be enabled to understand, and to be the children of light; and thus be prepared to escape all the things that are coming on the earth, and so stand before the Son of Man.

We testify that the foregoing doctrine is the doctrine or gospel of Jesus Christ, in its fulness; and that it is the only true, everlasting, and unchangeable gospel; and the only plan revealed on earth whereby man can be saved. . . .

A great, a glorious, and a mighty work is yet to be achieved, in spreading the truth and kingdom among the Gentiles—in restoring, organizing, instructing and establishing the Jews—in gathering, instructing, relieving, civilizing, educating and administering salvation to the remnant of Israel on this continent; in building Jerusalem in Palestine; and the cities, stakes, temples, and sanctuaries of Zion in America; and in gathering the Gentiles into the same covenant and organization—instructing them in all things for their sanctification and preparation; that the whole Church of the Saints, both Gentile, Jew and Israel, may be prepared as a bride, for the coming of the Lord. . . .

As this work progresses in its onward course, and becomes more and more an object of political and religious interest and excitement, no king, ruler, or subject, no community or individual, will stand *neutral*. All will at length be influenced by one spirit or the other; and will take sides either for or against the kingdom of God, and fulfilment of the prophets, in the great restoration and return of his long dispersed covenant people.

The Nauvoo Temple from a daguerrotype, about 1845

Some will act the part of the venerable Jethro, the father-in-law of Moses; or the noble Cyrus; and will aid and bless the people of God; or like Ruth, the Moabitess, will forsake their people and their kindred and country, and will say to the Saints, or to Israel: "*This people shall be my people, and their God my God.*" While others will walk in the footsteps of a Pharaoh, or a Balak, and will harden their hearts, and fight against God, and seek to destroy his people. These will commune with priests and prophets who love the wages of unrighteousness; and who, like Balaam, will seek to curse, or to find enchantments against Israel.

You cannot therefore stand as idle and disinterested spectators of the scenes and events which are calculated in their very nature to reduce all nations and creeds to *one* political and religious *standard,* and thus put an end to Babel forms and names, and to strife and war. You

will, therefore, either be led by the good Spirit to cast in your lot, and to take a lively interest with the Saints of the Most High, and the covenant people of the Lord, or on the other hand, you will become their inveterate enemy, and oppose them by every means in your power....

Therefore, again we say to all people, Repent, and be baptized in the name of Jesus Christ, for remission of sins; and you shall receive the Holy Spirit, and shall know the truth, and be numbered with the house of Israel.

And we once more invite all the kings, presidents, governors, rulers, judges, and people of the earth, to aid us, the Latter-day Saints; and also, the Jews, and all the remnants of Israel, by your influence and protection, and by your silver and gold, that we may build the cities of Zion and Jerusalem, and the temples and sanctuaries of our God; and may accomplish the great restoration of all

things, and bring in the latter-day glory.

That knowledge, truth, light, love, peace, union, honor, glory, and power, may fill the earth with eternal life and joy.

That death, bondage, oppression, wars, mourning, sorrow, and pain, may be done away for ever, and all tears be wiped from every eye. [James R. Clark, comp., *Messages of the First Presidency of The Church of Jesus Christ of Latter-day Saints,* 1:252–64]

The concern of the Twelve to set the missions in order was evidenced by their sending Elder Wilford Woodruff to England to preside over the Church throughout Europe. Three other members of the Council—Brigham Young, Heber C. Kimball and Willard Richards—were called to supervise the affairs of the Church in North America. They set up an early system of districts presided over by high priests and branches administered by bishops or presiding elders.

The Nauvoo Temple

Even before Joseph Smith's death, Church leaders had considered expanding the gathering places by colonizing a new settlement for Saints in the West, beyond what was then the United States boundary. Lyman Wight and George Miller had been authorized by Joseph Smith to establish a stake in Texas. James Emmett had been part of an 1844 California-Oregon exploring party that had left Nauvoo under the Prophet's direction. After the death of the Prophet, these brethren abused their callings and tried to draw members away from the main body of the Saints to their own locations. Though the Twelve sought to counsel them, the advice went unheeded and the erring brethren were disfellowshipped. Committed to keeping the Saints at a central gathering place until the temple and other buildings were completed in Nauvoo, the Twelve did not want to disperse the Church's growing strength.

The Nauvoo Temple was given priority above all other building projects. Brigham Young and the Twelve stressed the importance of the temple to all the Saints, not just those living in

Nauvoo. All were expected to contribute labor and means. Relief Society sisters supported the temple through donating a penny a week per member for glass and nails. The Saints knew they soon planned to abandon Nauvoo, but, strong in their faith, they were still desirous of fulfilling the Lord's command and receiving the promised blessing (see D&C 124:25–48).

General Conference in the Temple

Though completion of the temple was not scheduled until April 1846, a general conference was held there in October 1845. The week following, a circular describing the proceedings was prepared for all the Saints throughout the world.

CIRCULAR *to the whole Church of Jesus Christ of Latter-day Saints.*

FIRST MEETING IN THE TEMPLE.

On Sunday the 5th day of October, through the indefatigable exertions, unceasing industry, and heaven blessed labors, in the midst of trials, tribulations, poverty, and worldly obstacles, solemnized in some instances by death, about five thousand saints had the inexpressible joy and great satisfaction to meet for the first time in the House of the Lord in the city of Joseph. From mites and tithing, millions had risen up to the glory of God, as a Temple where the children of the last kingdom, could come together and praise the Lord.

It certainly afforded a holy satisfaction to think that since the 6th of April, 1841, when the first stone was laid, amidst the most straitened circumstances, the Church of Jesus Christ of Latter Day Saints had witnessed their bread cast upon waters, or more properly, their obedience to the commandments of the Lord, appear in the tangible form of a Temple, entirely enclosed, windows in, with temporary floors, pulpits, and seats to accommodate so many persons preparatory to a General Conference: no General Conference having been held for three years past, according to the declaration of our martyred prophet:

"There shall be no more baptisms for the dead, until the ordinance can be attended to in the font of the Lord's House; and the church shall not hold another general conference until they can meet in said house. For thus saith the Lord."

President Young opened the services of the day in a dedicatory prayer, presenting the Temple, thus far completed, as a monument of the saints' liberality, fidelity, and faith,—concluding, "Lord we dedicate this house and ourselves unto thee." The day was occupied most agreeably in hearing instructions and teachings, and offering up the gratitude of honest hearts, for so great a privilege, as worshipping God, *within* instead of *without* an edifice, whose beauty and workmanship will compare with any house of worship in America, and whose motto is: "*Holiness to the Lord.*" [Clark, *Messages*, 1:281–82]

The attic story of the temple was completed and dedicated at the end of November 1845, and the first endowment work was administered in the temple 10 December. Sessions for small companies continued steadily into the night and on Saturdays until by 7 February 1846, more than five thousand six hundred ordinances—including endowments, sealings and marriages—had been administered.

Hundreds of Saints received their endowments just previous to leaving Nauvoo, though the temple in its entirety was not dedicated until May 1846—long after most of them were gone.

Departure from Nauvoo

A number of circumstances led to the removal of the Saints early in 1846. In 1844, a few weeks following the martyrdom of Joseph and Hyrum Smith, an August election gave the Saints virtual control of the government of Hancock County, which included Nauvoo. Members of the Illinois legislature who were determined to remove the Mormons' hold on political power in the county proposed legislation to repeal the Nauvoo City Charter. On 24 January 1845, the proposal passed, leaving Nauvoo without a government.

The loss of their city government left the Saints without police and courts. To protect the community from harassment, Nauvoo's militia officers organized a quasi-legal protective force under the structure of the priesthood, with bishops supervising quorums of twelve deacons who patrolled the streets. Part of the city was reorganized as a town in April, which allowed for justices of the peace, a council of

Architect's drawing of the Nauvoo House

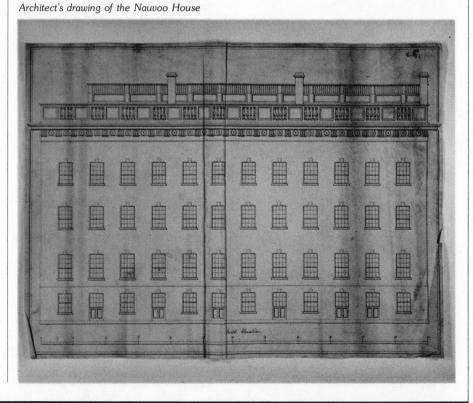

Brigham Young's home in Nauvoo, interior

trustees, the Nauvoo Legion and other officers. But the reorganization of Nauvoo government brought more antagonism from local newspapers who again opposed Mormon officeholders.

In September 1845, mobs began burning homes in the outlying settlements, forcing the Saints to leave their farms. Jacob B. Backenstos, the Hancock County sheriff who had long been friendly towards Mormons, tried to preserve order, but his life was threatened because of his sympathetic actions. Illinois Governor Thomas Ford finally sent in the state militia to halt the violence that was spreading on both sides, despite Brigham Young's caution to the Saints against retaliation.

By the time these activities were occurring, Church leaders had been considering for several months where they might move the Church membership. A committee had searched and evaluated possible settlement sites, including Texas, upper California, and the American Northwest. They did not make these considerations public, however, until 24 September 1845, when a group of citizens from Quincy, Illinois, requested that Mormon leaders make definite their plans for removal from the state. Among the Saints, opposition arose against abandoning the city and the nearly completed temple,

but at October conference the Twelve assured them leaving Nauvoo was the Lord's will.

The departure was to be unified and orderly. Two emigration companies of one hundred families each began forming before the conference. Now twenty-three additional companies would be created with captains over tens, fifties, and hundreds. The conference voted to move the entire membership of the Church to the West. The poor would be aided as they had been when the Saints left Missouri. An epistle from the Twelve informed the Saints unable to attend the meeting of these plans.

The Twelve's Counsel on the Exodus

The epistle from the Twelve included the following summary of the October 1845 conference:

In the afternoon Elder P. P. Pratt addressed the conference on the subject of our present situation and prospects. He referred to the great amount of expense and labor we have been at to purchase lands, build houses, the Temple &c.; we might ask, why is it that we have been at all this outlay and expense, and then are called to leave it? He would answer that the people of God always were required to make sacrifices, and if we have a sacrifice to make, he is in favor of its being something worthy of the people of God. We do not want to leave a desolate place, to be a reproach to us but something that will be a monument of our industry and

Parley P. Pratt

virtue. Our houses, our farms, this Temple and all we leave will be a monument to those who may visit the place of our industry, diligence and virtue. There is no sacrifice required at the hands of the people of God but shall be rewarded to them an hundred fold, in time or eternity.

The Lord has another purpose to bring about and to fulfil. We know that the great work of God must all the while be on the increase and grow greater. The people must enlarge in numbers and extend their borders; they cannot always live in one city, nor in one county; they cannot always wear the yoke; Israel must be the head and not the tail. The Lord designs to lead us to a wider field of action, where there will be more room for the saints to grow and increase, and where there will be no one to say we crowd them, and where we can enjoy the pure principles of liberty and equal rights. . . .

One small nursery may produce many thousands of fruit trees, while they are small. But as they expand towards maturity, they must needs be transplanted, in order to have room to grow and produce the natural fruits. It is so with us. We want a country where we have room to expand, and to put in requisition all our energies and the enterprise and talents of a numerous, intelligent and increasing people.

In short, this people are fast approaching that point which ancient prophets have long since pointed out as the destiny of the saints of the last days.

After many other spirited remarks touching similar points, he was succeeded by Elder George A. Smith, on the same subject. Elder Smith observed that a revelation was given in Missouri in regard to the saints consecrating their property which was not understood at the time; but they were soon brought to their understanding, for the Lord in his providence caused it all to be consecrated, for they were compelled to leave it.

He is glad of the prospect of leaving this county and seeking a place where we can enjoy the fruits of our

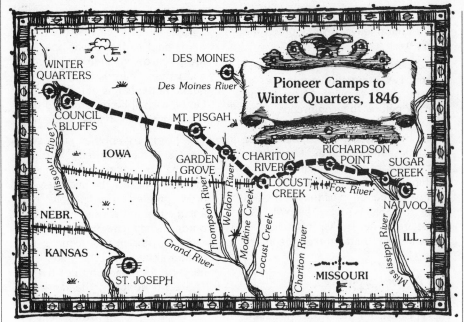

Pioneer Camps to Winter Quarters, 1846

labors and God himself be the sole proprietor of the elements.

Here is one principle in which he wants this whole people to unite. When we were to leave Missouri the saints entered into a covenant not to cease their exertions until every saint who wished to go was removed, which was done.

We are better off now than we were then, and he wants to see the same principle carried out now, that every man will give all to help to take the poor; and every honest industrious member who wants to go. He wants to see this influence extend from the West to the East sea.

On motion, it was unanimously resolved that this people move, en masse, to the West.

On motion, it was unanimously resolved that we take all of the saints with us to the extent of our ability, that is, our influence and property.

The Conference then adjourned to Tuesday at 10 o'clock A.M. [Clark, *Messages,* 1:283–84]

The Fall of Nauvoo

Through the autumn and early winter of 1845, the Saints busied themselves preparing for their westward journey. One sister wrote, "The fall of 1845 found Nauvoo as it were one vast mechanic shop, as nearly every family was engaged in making wagons" (Autobiography of Bathsheba W. Smith, His-

torical Department, The Church of Jesus Christ of Latter-day Saints, Salt Lake City, p. 8). Members of the Twelve read John C. Fremont's report of explorations in California and studied other maps of the regions west of the Rocky Mountains. In January 1846, an official circular announced that the Saints expected to depart in March seeking a good valley in the Rocky Mountains. Eastern Saints were encouraged to go west via the five-month ocean voyage to San Francisco. Though the Nauvoo Saints had planned to leave in the spring when water and grass would be available for their teams, anti-Mormon pressure prompted their early departure on 4 February 1846, the same day the ship *Brooklyn* sailed out of New York harbor with a load of eastern Saints bound also for the West.

Threats of possible interference in the spring had caused the Twelve to begin the removal of Saints earlier than planned. In February 1846, they decided that the two thousand emigrants who were prepared to go should leave immediately, with thousands to follow within weeks as they completed their preparations. The evacuation began 4 February 1846, and continued slowly and steadily until 24 February, when the Mississippi River providentially froze and many more Saints were able to cross. By mid-February Brigham Young had joined the Saints at Sugar Creek, Iowa, and organized them into camps. Within several weeks

the Saints were assembled in temporary camps across Iowa, making their way to scattered winter quarters. Many of them spent the winter in Nebraska at a settlement known as Winter Quarters.

By mid-May 1846, nearly twelve thousand Saints had crossed the river, leaving about six hundred in Nauvoo. To anti-Mormon forces it seemed that the Saints intended to keep some hold on the city and a final confrontation at Nauvoo resulted. Attacks on Mormons in outlying areas continued and in June mobbers marched to Nauvoo and demanded surrender of the city itself. City residents organized under the direction of Nauvoo Legion officers and prevented the invasion, but by September the anti-Mormon forces had returned eight hundred strong and armed with cannon. They demanded that Mormons and Mormon sympathizers leave the city.

Residents united and armed themselves as best they could and then engaged in a two-day exchange of gunfire with the forces stationed on the outskirts of Nauvoo. On 12 September, men on both sides were killed as invaders attacked the city. Mormons and anti-Mormons then sought a truce, with a committee from Quincy mediating the terms. In exchange for a promise of safety as they crossed the river, the Saints surrendered their arms and the city. Those who were able left immediately in safety, while in direct violation of this agreement, those who had to remain to get ready for the journey were forcibly driven from the city.

The Miracle of the Quail

Some six hundred forty destitute Latter-day Saints crossed the river that September. Having little food, clothing, or shelter, they were ill-prepared for travel. Many contracted chills and fever as they crowded into makeshift tents near the river bottoms. Relief in the form of provisions, tents and wagons was sent to this "poor camp" by the Twelve, and on 9 October 1846, the group was organized for the journey west. That same day, quail, weary from a long flight, miraculously settled near the travelers, providing them with much needed food, as this diarist recorded (the spelling and punctuation have been modernized):

The miracle of the quail (from a painting by C.C.A. Christensen, 1831–1912)

9 October 1846. This morning we had a direct manifestation of the mercy and goodness of God in a miracle being performed in the camp. A large (or rather several large) flock of quails flew into camp. Some fell on the wagons, some under, some on the breakfast tables. The boys and brethren ran about after them and caught them alive with their hands. Men who were not in the Church marvelled at the sight. The brethren and sisters praised God and glorified his name, that what was showered down upon the children of Israel in the wilderness is manifested unto us in our persecution. The boys caught about twenty alive, and as to the number that were killed—every man, woman, and child had quails to eat for their dinner. After dinner the flocks increased in size. Captain Allen ordered the brethren not to kill when they had eaten and were satisfied. A steamboat passed down within five or six rods of our wagons at the time we were catching the quails with our hands. Not a gun was afterwards fired, and the quails flew round the camp. Many alighted in it, then all the flock would arise, fly round our camp again a few rods off, and then would alight again, in and close to the camp. This was repeated more than half a dozen times during the afternoon. About three P.M. the trustees arrived and deeded out shoes, clothing, molasses, salt, and salt pork; and at half past four, Captain Allen called out my wagon to take up the line of march for the West, when I left the banks of the Mississippi, my property, Nauvoo, and the mob forever and started merrily over a level prairie, amid the songs of quails and blackbirds, the sun shining smilingly upon us, the cattle lowing, pleased at getting their liberty. The scene was delightful, the prairie surrounded on all sides by timber. All things conspired for us to praise the Lord. [Diary of Thomas Bullock, 9 Oct. 1846, Historical Department, The Church of Jesus Christ of Latter-day Saints; Salt Lake City]

Thus did the Saints leave Nauvoo. Under the direction of the Twelve they had acquired new strength through the temple endowment so many received before departing. The Saints had wanted to expand their gathering places, and however harried their westward travel, they must have known they were fulfilling that dream.

STUDY QUESTIONS

1. Read carefully Doctrine and Covenants 124:25–48 and then answer the following questions:
   a. Why did the Lord want the Saints to build the Nauvoo Temple?
   b. What blessings were promised if they did?
   c. What problems were promised if they didn't?
   d. Why do you suppose the Twelve were so anxious to build the temple even though they would shortly abandon it?
   e. How could the temple endowment prepare the Saints for their future journey?

2. Knowing how most leaders of the world would react to the Twelve's "Proclamation," why do you think the Twelve wrote it as they did?

3. From our historical perspective, why was it wise for the Saints to leave their "city beautiful" and move west?

4. In addition to the miracle of the quail, what other parallels do you see between the exodus of the pioneers and the exodus of ancient Israel?

The exodus from Nauvoo, February 1846 (from a painting by Lynn Fausett, 1958, located in the visitors' center, Pioneer Trails State Park, Salt Lake City)

THE JOURNEY WEST

D URING the Mormon pioneer period, 1846–68, nearly eighty thousand Saints crossed the plains. Unlike others who had crossed the Great American Desert, the Saints were religiously motivated and took entire families in their westward trek. Men, women, and children walked over one thousand miles to the Great Salt Lake Valley. During this time the Mormon Battalion was formed, company after company of pioneers left Winter Quarters and subsequent gathering points for the West, and the Saints established their sanctuary in the Rocky Mountains. Their diaries and journals reveal in eloquent simplicity a faith born of the sacrifice of all they possessed for the kingdom of God.

HIGHLIGHTS

1846 Feb. 4: The first group of Saints leaves Nauvoo and crosses the Mississippi. The ship *Brooklyn* sets sail from New York Harbor.

July 15–16: The Mormon Battalion enlists at Winter Quarters.

July 29: The *Brooklyn* arrives at Yerba Buena Harbor (San Francisco Bay).

Aug. 12: The Battalion leaves Fort Leavenworth for Sante Fe, New Mexico.

Nov. 17: The Battalion's sick detachment arrives at Pueblo, Colorado, where it spends the winter.

1847 Jan. 29: The battalion arrives at San Diego.

Apr. 16: The pioneer company begins the trek west.

July 16: Part of the battalion discharged at San Diego.

July 19: (Monday) Orson Pratt and John Brown see the Great Salt Lake Valley.

July 21: (Wednesday) Orson Pratt and Erastus Snow enter the valley.

July 22: (Thursday) A small scouting party enters the valley.

July 23: (Friday) The advance group enters the valley and camps. Orson Pratt dedicates the land to the Lord and the brethren begin plowing and planting.

July 24: (Saturday) Brigham Young and the main camp enter the valley.

July 29: The Battalion's sick detachment and the Mississippi Saints arrive in the valley.

Aug. 27: Brigham Young and 107 men leave the Great Salt Lake Valley for Winter Quarters.

Dec. 23: The Twelve issue a general epistle.

1848 Jan. 24: Battalion members participate in gold discovery in California.

Sept. 20: President Young arrives at Great Salt Lake Valley.

1849 Apr. 4: The first of the fourteen general epistles is issued.

1856 June 9: The first handcart company leaves Florence, Nebraska and arrives in Salt Lake 26 September.

Dec. 10: The last of the fourteen general epistles issued.

1860 July 10: The last handcart company leaves Florence, Nebraska, and arrives in Salt Lake 24 September.

1861 The first Church train, comprising two hundred wagons, leaves with flour to sell in the East and returns with immigrant Saints in the fall.

1868 The last Church-sponsored wagon train, comprising two hundred wagons, leaves with flour to sell in the East, returning with four thousand immigrant Saints in the fall.

1869 Mar. 8: The Union Pacific Railroad reaches Ogden, Utah.

HISTORICAL SUMMARY

Coming to Zion

The Saints employed five basic means of travel to reach the Great Basin: ship, wagon train, handcart, "Church trains," and railroad transportation. "Church trains" were essentially the same as the earlier wagon trains except that the Church called men to a summer mission, and wards in Salt Lake City and vicinity outfitted wagons, teams and provisions to ferry the immigrants across the plains.

Some Saints traveled via ocean from New York to California; one ship, the *Brooklyn,* left New York Harbor 4 February 1846 with 238 passengers bound for California with the intent of joining the Nauvoo pioneers after they reached the West. Interestingly, both poineer groups began their journey the same day. The *Brooklyn* sailed via Cape Horn to the Sandwich (Hawaiian) Islands, finally arriving at Yerba Buena (San Francisco) on 29 July 1846. During the nearly six-month voyage, ten Latter-day Saints lost their lives. The Saints who booked passage aboard the *Brooklyn* were primarily American farmers and mechanics from the eastern states. They took with them tools necessary to continue their lifestyle in the West: plows and other farm implements, blacksmith tools, equipment for a saw mill, a printing press, and school books. After their arrival at Yerba Buena, the group moved inland a short distance, founded their own colony, naming it New Hope, and there awaited for over a year the arrival of the Nauvoo Saints, who had settled temporarily at Winter Quarters along the Missouri River.

At Winter Quarters the Nauvoo Saints surveyed a town of eight hundred twenty lots and constructed a large stockade and seven hundred log homes before Christmas of 1846, pro-

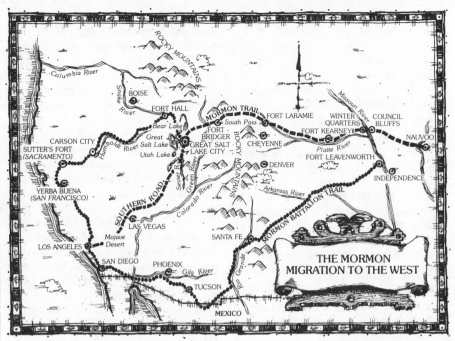

THE MORMON MIGRATION TO THE WEST

viding shelter for over three thousand five hundred Saints. A high council presided over the ecclesiastical, municipal, and educational needs of the community, while a police force maintained order. Tragically, many of the Saints were near destitute, and poor diets contributed to the deaths of over six hundred. John R. Young described Winter Quarters as "the Valley Forge of Mormondom" (John R. Young, *Memoirs of John R. Young, Utah Pioneer, 1847,* p. 41).

The Mormon Battalion

While the Saints were gathering to Winter Quarters in 1846, the United States government sought their help in the war with Mexico, asking them to raise a battalion to march to California. In the middle of July 1846, 549 men enlisted in the United States Army, forming the Mormon Battalion. These men, along with 33 women and 51 children, left Winter Quarters for California on 20 July. They traveled from Winter Quarters to Fort Leavenworth, Kansas, where the battalion was officially outfitted for their trip west, and thence to Santa Fe, Tucson, and finally to San Diego, 29 January 1847. At least three sick detachments left the battalion between Santa Fe and Tucson and made their way to Pueblo, Colorado, where they

The Mormon Battalion enlists

spent the winter of 1846–47 and joined the pioneers in the Salt Lake Valley in the summer of 1847.

While the battalion did not formally engage in fighting in the Mexican War, its members experienced many hardships and moments of intrigue that proved their mettle. For example, when the battalion reached the Rio Grande 10 November 1846, they continued following the road that led south into Mexico for the next several days. The men feared that they would continue on course to Mexico instead of continuing on to California and subsequently would not be able to rejoin their families. Levi Hancock, a member of the First Council of Seventy, and David Pettegrew visited each tent and encouraged each soldier to fast, praying to the Lord that he change the route of travel toward California, and soon the battalion was heading west again. Another incident occurred just prior to the battalion's arrival in Tucson, Arizona, where they were attacked by a group of wild bulls. During the fight, the bulls wounded two men and the soldiers killed from thirty to sixty bulls.

Colonel Cooke's Tribute

Weary and greatly emaciated, the battalion finally arrived 29 January 1847 at San Diego, California. The next day Colonel Philip St. George Cooke, commander of the group, commended the Saints for their devotion and fortitude:

Headquarters "Mormon" Battalion Mission of San Diego, January 30, 1847.

ORDERS NO. 1.

The Lieutenant-Colonel commanding congratulates the battalion on their safe arrival on the shore of the Pacific Ocean, and the conclusion of their march of over two thousand miles.

History may be searched in vain for an equal march of infantry. Half of it has been through a wilderness where nothing but savages and wild beasts are found, or deserts where, for want of water, there is no living creature. There, with almost hopeless labor we have dug deep wells, which the future traveler will enjoy. Without a guide who had traversed them, we have ventured into trackless tablelands where water was not found for several marches. With crowbar and pick and axe in hand, we have worked our way over mountains, which seemed to defy aught save the wild goat, and hewed a passage through a chasm of living rock more narrow than our wagons. To bring these first wagons to the Pacific, we have preserved the strength of our mules by herding them over large tracts, which you have laboriously guarded without loss. The garrison of four presidios of Sonora concentrated within the walls of Tucson, gave us no pause. We drove them out, with their artillery, but our intercourse with the citizens was unmarked by a single act of injustice. Thus, marching half naked and half fed, and living upon wild animals, we have discovered and made a road of great value to our country.

Arrived at the first settlement of California, after a single day's rest, you cheerfully turned off from the route to this point of promised repose, to enter upon a campaign, and meet, as we supposed, the approach of the enemy; and this too, without even salt to season your sole subsistence of fresh meat.

Lieutenant A. J. Smith and George Stonemen, of the First Dragoons, have shared and given valuable aid in all these labors.

Thus, volunteers, you have exhibited some high and essential qualities of veterans. But much remains undone. Soon, you will turn your attention to the drill, to system and order, to forms also, which are all necessary to the soldier. [Philip St. George Cooke, *The Conquest of New Mexico and California,* p. 197]

Once in San Diego, battalion members diffused into two areas: some remaining there, others being stationed in Los Angeles. As their enlistments expired, the men were encouraged to reenlist for another year, which some did. Others journeyed directly to Salt Lake Valley, while others sought employment and remained in California another year before they went to Salt Lake or returned to Winter Quarters. Members of this last-named group participated in the discovery of gold in California.

The Pioneers

While the battalion experienced its hardships in crossing what has become the southwestern United States, the Saints at Winter Quarters began to prepare for the trek west as soon as spring arrived. On 14 January 1847, Brigham Young received a revelation from the Lord relative to the Saints' westward journey (see D&C 136). In this revelation, the Lord required his people to keep his commandments and statutes (see verse 2). He com-

manded that the traveling camps of Zion be organized with captains of groups of one hundred, fifty, and ten, and that travel proceed under the direction of the Twelve. The Lord commanded the Saints to provide for themselves food, clothing, provisions, teams, wagons, and other necessities (see verse 5). When they were organized, the Lord commanded the "captains and presidents" to decide how many Saints would go west the next spring (verses 6–7). Each company received its share of responsibilities to bear the burden of "the poor, the widows, the fatherless and the families" of those men who had enlisted in the army (verses 8–9). The Lord gave the Saints rules of conduct, commanded them not to fear their enemies, and told them that he would prove them in all things (verses 20–42).

Following this revelation, the pioneers organized themselves and on 16 April 1847 began to move west. This advance company, led by President Young and consisting of 143 men, 3 women, and 2 children, traveled fast and founded a settlement in the Great Basin, arriving at their destination 21–24 July 1847. Families made up the majority of the other ten companies that came in 1847 and the companies that came in the ensuing years. The Saints came by the thousands,

young and old, sick and healthy. Women walked by the side of their husbands and on occasion drove their own teams. Children walked by their parents, suffering fatigue, hunger, starvation, and even death with them.

Journal of Mary Ann Weston Maughan

One such pioneer family was Mary Ann Weston Maughan's. The following excerpt from the journal account of her family's 1850 migration to the West well illustrates the sacrifices and the spirit of the pioneers.

[June] 19th. This morning we had a powerful rain; commenced at breakfast time and continued till near noon. Started in the afternoon. On the way passed the grave of Bro. Warren, who died of cholera. This is the 1st grave we have seen. Traveled 8 miles. Camped on a small stream.

21st. We were called to bury 2 of our company who died of cholera this morning, a man named Brown and a child. There are more sick in camp. Have been in sight of the Platte river all day. Traveled 15 miles, camped on Salt Creek. Soon some of our company came up with another child dead. They buried it at twilight on the bank of the creek. There are more sick. It makes us feel sad thus to bury our friends by the way. Weather very hot.

The pioneers crossing the Platte River in Nebraska (painting by C.C.A. Christensen, 1831–1912)

22nd. This morning before starting we were called to bury 3 more children. They all belonged to one family. We started late and before all had crossed the creek it commenced to rain very hard. We were detained till noon. Traveled 9 miles, camped on the Paria without wood or water, or some that is very poor. This is the worst time we have had since we crossed the Missouri river. Every thing wet and several sick in camp. Very little fire.

23rd. We buried 3 more this evening. Traveled 8 miles.

24th. This morning is wet and uncomfortable. It was thought best to remain in camp. Some are washing and baking, all were busy. About noon it cleared up and we had a public meeting in camp. Some fasted and humbled themselves before the Lord and prayed that He would remove disease from us. Brother Crandall said in four days five of his family had been taken from their midst and requested the Brethren to pray that the other members of his family might be spared.

25th. The mother of the three children spoke of yesterday died this afternoon. She will be buried this evening. We are camped on a creek which we call Pleasant Point. Here we buried Sister Spafford, the mother of nine children. There are no more sick in camp and we hope the worst is over. Traveled 10 miles. . . .

July 12th. About noon as we were traveling along on a good plain road, my little Peter, about three years old, was sitting in the front of the wagon between his brother Charles and his sister Mary Ann. They were looking at a cow that had lost one horn. He leaned forward, lost his balance, and fell before the wheels. The first passed over him and he tried to escape the other one. But alas the wagon stopped just as the hind wheel stood on his dear little back. The Brethren from behind ran up and lifted the wheel and took him from under it. He was bruised internally so that it was impossible for him to live long. We done all that was possible for him, but no earthly power could save

An odometer of the type used by the pioneers to measure the distance they traveled

him. He did not suffer much pain, only twice for a very little time. The people left their wagons and gathered around mine, and all wept for the dear little boy that we knew must soon leave us. I had talked to him many times to be careful and not fall out of the wagon, or he might be hurt very bad. He only spoke twice. I said to him, "Pete, did you fall?" and he said, "Yes," and seemed to know that he would leave us, and asked for his father. I did not know that his father had fainted, for the Brethren stood to hide him from my sight. On my asking for him, they said he would come soon. As soon as he was able he came to the wagon, covered with dust. But his little boy could not speak to him. He opened his eyes and looked so lovingly at us, then gently closed them and passed peacefully away, and left us weeping around his dear little bruised body. Then loving hands tenderly dressed him in a suit of his own white linen clothes. He looked so lovely. I emptied a dry goods box and Bro. Wood made him a nice coffin; and it even was a mournful satisfaction, for we had seen our brothers and sisters bury their dear ones without a coffin to lay them in. We buried him on a little hill on the North side of the road. The grave was consecrated and then they laid him to rest. Some one had made a nice headboard, with his name printed on, also his age and date of death. This was all we could do, and many prayers were offered to our heavenly Father, that he might rest in peace and not be disturbed by

wolves. We turned away in sorrow and grief. A few days after, we heard that his grave had not been touched, but another little one made beside it, and afterwards some more were buried by them. This was a great satisfaction to us, to know that he remained as we left him. Our dear one's name was Peter Weston Maughan, born in New Diggings, Wisconsin Territory, May 20th, 1847. . . .

[August] 8th. I was very sick this morning with the Mountain fever. As I lay in my wagon today I thought the wheels went over every rock there was in the road. Camped in the Black Hills. After camping, Mr. Maughan laid my bed in the shade of the wagon. On the outside, chains were fastened across the wheels to keep some sheep in. Thinking my bed would stop them, my wagon wheels were not chained. Seeing a open place, the sheep darted through and every one sprang over me. I clasped my baby close to me, lay still and was not hurt, not even touched by one of them. I think the sheep were worse frightened than I was.

10th. Today we came up with Bennett's Company. They have the whooping cough among them. We drove off the road while they passed. . . .

17th. This morning we entered the canyon and traveled on the most dreadful road imaginable. Some places we had to make the road before we could pass. Passed the toll gate and paid for passing over the road we had made. We had a

A pioneer wagon train between Echo Head and Hanging Rock, Utah, 1867

view of the Valley, and it delighted me much to think I was near my long journey's end. The road today has been the worst we ever saw, but we came safely through without any accident. Camped at dusk 1 mile past the toll house. Here is no food or wood.

18th. We rose at day break and all are happy because our long journey is so near done. When we came near the city we met Bro. Blackhurst, a friend of Mr. Maughan's. On arriving in the city we soon found many kind friends. We camped in the street in front of Bro. Peart's house. I think this is destined to be a great place. There are stores and houses going up in all directions. We stayed in Salt Lake City one week and enjoyed the Society of our friends. Then we were counseled to settle in Tooele, 35 miles west of Salt Lake City. This Valley was then being settled. Here I found 2 old friends from England, Bro. and Sister Rowberry, and some of our friends from Nauvoo. Here we camped in tent and wagon on our city lot until we built a nice large double log house. We moved into our house in the middle of November, 1850. I had not eaten or slept in a house since we left our own home in New Diggings, Wisconsin Territory. [Kate B. Carter, comp., "Journal of Mary Ann Weston Maughan," *Our Pioneer Heritage* 2:374–80]

Strict order and discipline were observed in the pioneer camps. At Winter Quarters Parley P. Pratt and Bishop George Miller were charged by President Young with the spirit of dissension and insubordination. Elder Pratt felt that their motives were honorable. He learned, however, that President Young had reproved in the correct spirit, for Bishop Miller's influence had resulted in unnecessary hardship for three pioneer companies. Soon afterward, Miller, refusing to acknowledge the counsel of the Twelve, departed and later apostatized. Elder Pratt wrote: "Although my own motives were pure, so far as I could know my own heart, yet I thank God for this timely chastisement; I profited by it, and it caused me to be more watchful and careful ever after" (*Autobiography of Parley P. Pratt*, pp. 341–42).

First Presidency Epistles 1849–56

Between 4 April 1849 and 10 December 1856 fourteen "General Epistles" were issued by the First Presidency. These epistles informed the Saints "scattered abroad" of developments in the Church (primarily in the Utah territory) and gave "such counsel" as the Holy Spirit might indicate. Each epistle summarized the historical events, emphasizing the happenings in Zion that had transpired since the previous epistle, and contained the admonitions that the First Presidency felt inspired to give. Together they provide an excellent commentary on the progress of the Church during those first several critical years in the Rocky Mountains. The following is a series of extracts from these epistles focusing on the gathering and

one of its major purposes—temple building.

The Purpose of the General Epistles

Many events have transpired, interesting in their nature as pertaining to the advancement of the church preparatory to the coming of the Son of Man; and we cheerfully improve this, the earliest opportunity, to communicate to you a brief history of these events, together with such counsel as the Holy Spirit shall indite. [From the First General Epistle, 4 Apr. 1849, in James R. Clark, comp., *Messages of the First Presidency of The Church of Jesus Christ of Latter-day Saints,* 1:350]

Feeling impelled by the Spirit of our God to write unto you concerning the things of the kingdom, and having greater boldness therein by reason of the faith and testimony of the Lord Jesus and the Holy Ghost, of which we have received and bear record unto the whole world, we proceed to manifest unto you such intimations of the Spirit pertaining unto the Church and kingdom of God as are or may be presented unto us, trusting that they may prove instructive and beneficial unto the Saints. [From the Fourteenth General Epistle, 10 Dec. 1856, in Clark, *Messages,* 2:193]

Why the Saints Need to Gather

Our holy religion brings us in contact with long established error, and the traditions of centuries, which are prevalent throughout the world; hence are we necessarily a peculiar and separate people, whose best interests and preservation depend upon union and self-dependence, upon practising virture, industry, and sobriety, and manifesting our faith by our works in magnifying our Priesthood, and in serving our God by keeping ourselves pure and unspotted in this wicked and adulterous generation.

For this cause we gather out from the world, and for this cause we should rely upon our own skill and ability to produce, from the native elements, every article of food and raiment necessary for our use or comfort. [From the Twelfth General Epistle, 25 Apr. 1855, in Clark, *Messages,* 2:162]

Sustain the government of the nation wherever you are, and speak well of it, for this is right, and the government has a right to expect it of you, so long as that government sustains you in your civil and religious liberty, in those rights which inherently belong to every person born on the earth; and if you are persecuted in your native land, and denied the privilege of worshiping the true God in spirit and in truth, flee to the land of Zion, to America—to the United States, where constitutional rights and freedoms are not surpassed by any nation—where God saw fit, in these last days, to renew the dispensation of salvation, by revelations from the heavens, and where all, by the consitution and laws of the land, when executed in righteousness, are protected in all the civil and religious freedom that man is capable of enjoying on earth; and our national institutions will never fail, unless it be through the wickedness of the people, and the designs of evil men in brief authority; for those rights were ordained of God on this land, for the establishment of the principles of truth on the earth; and our national organization originated in the heavens. [From the Seventh General Epistle, 18 Apr. 1852, in Clark, *Messages,* 2:98]

Let the Saints take courage and avail themselves of the privilege of gathering to this place while the way is open before them, for the time will come when whoso would gather to Zion must needs flee with his budget upon his shoulder, or under his arm. Verily, they will come like flocks of doves to the windows, comparatively bare and naked, without food or clothing, escaping, as it were by the skin of their teeth, from the righteous indignation of an offending Deity poured out upon and passing over a wicked and adulterous generation. [From the Fourteenth General Epistle, 10 Dec. 1856, in Clark, *Messages,* 2:199]

The Perpetual Emigration Fund

About one month since we suggested the propriety of creating a perpetual fund for the purpose of helping the poor Saints to emigrate to this place, agreeably to our cov-

enants in the Temple that we would "never cease our exertions, by all the means and influence within our reach, till all the Saints who were obliged to leave Nauvoo should be located at some gathering place of the Saints." The Council approved of the suggestion, and a committee was immediately appointed to raise a fund by voluntary contribution to be forwarded east next mail. The October Conference sanctioned the doings of the committee, and appointed Brother Edward Hunter, a tried, faithful, and approved Bishop, a general agent to bear the perpetual emigrating funds to the States, to superintend the direction and appropriation thereof, and return the same to this place with such poor brethren as shall be wisdom to help.

We wish all to understand, that this fund is PERPETUAL, and is never to be diverted from the object of gathering the poor to Zion while there are Saints to be gathered, unless He whose right it is to rule shall otherwise command. Therefore we call upon President Orson Hyde and all the Saints, and all benevolent souls everywhere, to unite their gold, their silver, and their cattle, with ours in this perpetual fund, and cooperate with Bishop Hunter in producing as many teams as possible, preparatory for next spring's emigration, and let the poor who are to be helped, go to work with their might, and prepare wagons of wood for their journey.

Such wagons, without any iron, now exist in this valley, that have come from the states, having done good business; and so great has been the influx of wagons this season, that they are cheap, and iron comparatively plentiful. [From the Second General Epistle, 12 Oct. 1849, in Clark, *Messages,* 2:34–35]

Every possible exertion will be made on our part, and that of the Emigrating Company, to extend the usefulness of the Perpetual Fund in gathering the Saints; and it is important that those who anticipate help therefrom, should understand that the means sent forth are, and will be designed to furnish teams, almost or quite exclusively; and even the cases in which wagons will be furnished will be rare. The poor who can live in the States with little clothing, and little or no groceries, &c., can live equally as cheap on the road; and when once here, can procure the comforts of life by their industry. Souls are the articles for the Perpetual Fund to gather home, and that, too, as many as possible; and other things will be attended to in their time and place.

We are under obligation by covenant, firstly to apply the Perpetual Funds, gathered in this country, to bring home the poor Saints who were driven from Nauvoo; and as soon as this shall be accomplished, we shall be ready to extend our exertions to other places and countries. Let the European Saints continue to add to their Perpetual Funds, which we doubt not they have commenced according to our previous counsel; and as soon as sufficient shall be collected to remove a suitable company, we will give instructions concerning its application, and emigration will commence. [From the Fourth General Epistle, 27 Sept. 1850, in Clark, *Messages,* 2:60–61]

This ever rising, ever increasing desire for the gathering of the remnants of Israel pertains unto all the Saints of God, who live their religion and enjoy the rich blessings of the Holy Ghost. It is in the heart of every faithful Saint, their constant prayer to the Almighty Father to enable them, not only to promulgate the Gospel of Christ to those who sit in darkness, but to gather out the honest in heart, even the Israel of God, from their long dispersion and to aid them in returning to a knowledge of the Lord God of their Fathers, that they may participate in the society of the Saints and a peaceful inheritance in these sequestered vales. To this end, and the further accomplishment of this object, are continually directed the efforts of the Perpetual Emigrating

Fund Company for the emigration of the honest and worthy poor—those who desire to serve God and keep His commandments, being full of virtue and integrity towards God and their brethren. These are those we wish to deliver from the oppression of wicked Babylon, whose vital energies the proud and powerful are crushing out; upon whom the despotism, bigotry, ignorance and superstition of the world hang like an incubus, and to bring them to a land where manhood though found in poverty is respected, and where the God of Heaven can receive the homage due from man to his Maker; where freedom and liberty of conscience can enjoy protection, honest and faithful labour meet a just equivalent, and where the light of revelation and power of the Holy and Eternal Priesthood hold the adversary of truth in abeyance and roll back the curtains of error and darkness, sin, and death which have so long enveloped the earth. [From the Fourteenth General Epistle, 10 Dec. 1856, in Clark, *Messages,* 2:198]

The Work on the Temple

We contemplate erecting a wall around the Temple block this season, preparatory to laying the foundation of the Temple the year following; and this we will be sure to do, if all the Saints shall prove themselves as ready to pay their tithing, and sacrifice and consecrate of their substance, as freely as we will: and if the Saints do not pay their tithing, we can neither build nor prepare for building; and if

Quarrying the granite blocks for the Salt Lake Temple

there shall be no Temple built, the Saints can have no endowments; and if they do not receive their endowments, they can never attain unto that salvation they are anxiously looking for. So far as the Saints in the United States and Canada desire to see the work of the Lord prosper, let them arise as one man, and come to Deseret, where they can do more for Zion in one year than they can in many years where they are. [From the Fifth General Epistle, 7 Apr. 1851, in Clark, *Messages,* 2:71]

After the opening of the Conference by singing and prayer in the Tabernacle, the general authorities of the Church, surrounded by escorts, guards, police, martial music, instrumental bands, and choir, with the National Flag unfurled from its topmost staff, the ensigns of the various bands and escorts floating in the breeze, and the banner of "Zion's Workmen" towering aloft, proceeded to the Temple ground, and after singing by the choir, the First Presidency laid the South East Corner Stone of the Temple....

The Corner Stones now rest in their several positions, about sixteen feet below the surface of the eastern bank, beneath the reach of mountain floods, when the edifice shall be completed, and so deep beneath

The foundation of the temple, the "old" (left) and "new" (right) tabernacles looking west

the surface, that it will cost robbers and mobs too much labour to raze it to its foundation, leaving not one stone upon another, as they did with the Temple at Jerusalem.

The work for the redemption and salvation of Israel has commenced, as it were, anew on the earth, which makes Satan mad, and causes devils to howl. But their doleful moans are not heeded by the Saints in the mountains, their hearts are cheered to press forward with all their energies, to complete the Lord's House, as speedily as possible. . . .

The Holy Spirit has been in our midst, and the revelations of Jesus have guided His Apostles and Prophets, in laying the Corner Stones of the Temple, and ministering unto the Saints, during Conference, in an unusual degree, which has caused much gladness of heart, and great joy and rejoicing. And that same Spirit will accompany this our Epistle, and be felt, and experienced to the joy of your hearts, even by all who will receive our testimony, and practice those precepts which we inculcate. [From the Ninth General Epistle, 13 Apr. 1853, in Clark, *Messages*, 2:115, 117]

During the General Conference, just closed, the youngerly people were counselled to obtain their endowments and marry; hence we wish it understood that we are prepared to give the Saints their endowments in the House of the Lord, which has been built and dedicated expressly for that purpose; therefore, let parents, guardians, and Bishops take this matter properly in hand, and counsel freely with the young people, and prepare them to receive their endowments and sealings. Young men, take unto yourselves wives of the daughters of Zion, and come up and receive your endowments and sealings, that you may raise up a holy seed unto the God of Abraham, even a holy and royal Priesthood who shall be born legal heirs thereunto, having a right to the keys thereof, and to administer in all the ordinances pertaining to the House of the Lord. Cease your folly and become men of God;

act wisely and righteously before Him, and His choice blessings will attend you.

We exhort all the Saints to live righteously, to remember and keep their covenants with their God and with each other, to pay their tithing and make their consecrations in the spirit of liberality and in all good conscience, nothing doubting. [From the Thirteenth General Epistle, 29 Oct. 1855, in Clark, *Messages*, 2:186–87]

The Migration Continues

By 1856 the cost of outfitting a team, a wagon, and provisions in the East had more than doubled because of the heavy migration resulting from the discovery of gold in California and the announcement of free land in Oregon. Responding to the increased costs, Brigham Young suggested that the Saints travel across the plains pulling handcarts.

LeRoy Hafen explains what the handcarts were like:

The handcarts used by the different companies varied in size and construction, but the general pattern was uniform. The carts resembled those used by porters and street sweepers in the cities of the United States. They were constructed with little or no iron. The axles of many consisted of a single pole of hickory, without iron skeins. Some of the wheels were hooped with thin iron tires, others were not. Many of the

carts, made in a hurry and of unseasoned wood, shrank, warped, and cracked as they were drawn across the dry plains through the summer heat.

J. Rogerson, a veteran of the handcart emigration, gives the following description: "The open handcart was made of Iowa hickory or oak, the shafts and side pieces of the same material, but the axles generally of hickory. In length the side pieces and shafts were about six or seven feet, with three or four binding cross bars from the back part to the fore part of the body of the cart; then two or three feet space from the latter bar to the front bar or singletree for the lead horse or lead man, woman or boy of the team.

"The carts were the usual width of the wide track wagon. Across the bars of the bed of the cart we generally sewed a strip of bed ticking or a counterpane. On this wooden cart of a thimbleless axle, with about 2½ inch shoulder and 1 inch point, were often loaded 400 to 500 pounds of flour, bedding, extra clothing, cooking utensils and a tent. How the flimsy yankee hickory structure held up the load for the hundreds of miles has been a wonder to us since then.

"The covered or family cart was similar in size and construction with the exception that it was made stronger, with an iron axle. It was surmounted by a small wagon box 3

The handcart pioneers (painting by C.C.A. Christensen, 1831–1912)

or 4 feet long with side and end pieces about 8 inches high. Two persons were assigned to the pulling of each open cart, and where a father and son of age and strength were found in one family, with smaller children, they were allotted a covered cart, but in many instances the father had to pull the covered cart alone." [LeRoy R. Hafen and Ann W. Hafen, *Handcarts to Zion,* pp. 53–55]

The first Mormon handcart company left Iowa City, 9 June 1856, and arrived in Salt Lake City 26 September 1856. Three companies crossed the plains without incident in 1856, but the last two companies led by James G. Willie and Edward Martin, leaving Iowa City in late July 1856, were caught by early snows in the heart of the Rocky Mountains. Their suffering and privation, reflected in the following two accounts, are unsurpassed in the annals of western migration.

Ephraim K. Hanks and the Martin Handcart Company

Ephraim Hanks, "one of the greatest of Mormon scouts" (Hafen, *Handcarts to Zion,* p. 135), recalled the rescue of the Martin handcart company:

In the fall of 1856, I spent considerable of my time fishing in Utah Lake; and in traveling backward and forward between that Lake and Salt Lake City, I had occasion to stop once over night with Gurney Brown,

in Draper, about nineteen miles south of Salt Lake City. Being somewhat fatigued after the day's journey, I retired to rest quite early, and while I still lay wide awake in my bed I heard a voice calling me by name, and then saying, "The handcart people are in trouble and you are wanted; will you go and help them?" I turned instinctively in the direction from whence the voice came and beheld an ordinary sized man in the room. Without any hesitation I answered, "Yes, I will go if I am called." I then turned around to go to sleep, but had laid only a few minutes when the voice called a second time, repeating almost the same as before. This was repeated a third time.

When I got up the next morning I said to Brother Brown, "The handcart people are in trouble, and I have promised to go out and help them;" but I did not tell him of my experience during the night.

I now hastened to Salt Lake City, and arrived there on the Saturday, preceding the Sunday on which the call was made for volunteers to go out and help the last hand-cart companies in. When some of the brethren responded by explaining that they could get ready to start in a few days; I spoke out at once saying, "I am ready now!" The next day I was wending my way eastward over the

mountains with a light wagon all alone.

The terrific storm which caused the immigrants so much suffering and loss overtook me near the South Pass, where I stopped three days with Reddick N. Allred, who had come out with provisions for the immigrants. The storm during these three days was simply awful. In all my travels in the Rocky Mountains both before and afterwards, I have seen no worse. When the snow at length ceased falling, it lay on the ground so deep that for many days it was impossible to move wagons through it.

Being deeply concerned about the possible fate of the immigrants, and feeling anxious to learn of their condition, I determined to start out on horseback to meet them; and for this purpose I secured a pack-saddle and two animals, (one to ride and one to pack), from Brother Allred, and began to make my way slowly through the snow, alone. After traveling for some time I met Joseph A. Young and one of the Garr boys, two of the relief company which had been sent out from Salt Lake City to help the companies. They had met the immigrants and were now returning with important dispatches from the camps to the head-quarters of the Church, reporting the awful condition of the companies.

In the meantime I continued my lonely journey, and the night after meeting Elders Young and Garr, I camped in the snow in the mountains. As I was preparing to make a bed in the snow with the few articles that my pack animal carried for me, I thought how comfortable a buffalo robe would be on such an occasion, and also how I could relish a little buffalo meat for supper, and before lying down for the night I was instinctively led to ask the Lord to send me a buffalo. Now, I am a firm believer in the efficacy of prayer, for I have on many different occasions asked the Lord for blessings, which He in his mercy has bestowed upon me. But when I, after praying as I did on that lonely night in the South Pass, looked around me and spied a buffalo bull within fifty yards of my camp, my surprise was complete; I

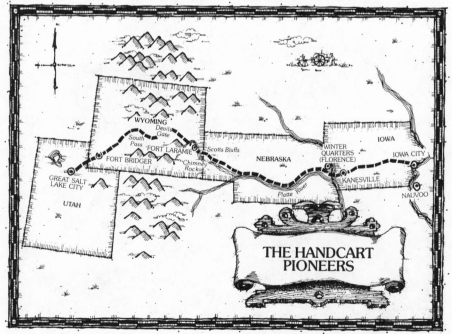

THE HANDCART
PIONEERS

"Handcart company in a snowstorm" (from Harald Jensen Kent, Danske Mormoner *[N. P.: Udvalget for Utah-missionen, 1913, p. 11)*

had certainly not expected so immediate an answer to my prayer. However, I soon collected myself and was not at a loss to know what to do. Taking deliberate aim at the animal, my first shot brought him down, he made a few jumps only, and then rolled down into the very hollow where I was encamped. I was soon busily engaged skinning my game; finishing which, I spread the hide on the snow and placed my bed upon it. I next prepared supper, eating the tongue and other choice parts of the animal I had killed, to my heart's content. After this I enjoyed a refreshing night's sleep, while my horses were browsing on the sage brush.

Early the next morning I was on my way again, and soon reached what is known as the Ice Springs Bench. There I happened upon a herd of buffalo and killed a nice cow. . . . I reached the ill-fated train just as the immigrants were camping for the night. The sight that met my gaze as I entered their camp can never be erased from my memory. The starved forms and haggard countenances of the poor sufferers, as they moved about slowly, shivering with cold, to prepare their scanty evening meal, was enough to touch the stoutest heart. When they saw me coming, they hailed me with joy inexpressible, and when they further

beheld the supply of fresh meat I brought into their camp, their gratitude knew no bounds. Flocking around me, one would say, "Oh, please give me a small piece of meat;" Another would exclaim, "My poor children are starving, do give me a little;" and children with tears in their eyes would call out, "Give me some, give me some." At first I tried to wait on them and handed out the meat as they called for it; but finally I told them to help themselves. Five minutes later both my horses had been released of their extra burden—the meat was all gone, and the next few hours found the people in camp busily engaged cooking and eating it, with thankful hearts.

A prophecy had been made by one of the brethren that the company should feast on buffalo meat, when their provisions might run short; my arrival in their camp, loaded with meat, was the beginning of the fulfillment of that prediction; but only the beginning, as I afterwards shot and killed a number of buffalo for them as we journeyed along. ["Church Emigration," *Contributor,* Mar. 1893, pp. 202–3]

Traveling with the Martin handcart company was a thirteen-year-old English girl, Mary Goble Pay, who, with her parents and five brothers and sisters,

had emigrated from England that spring. She gives this vivid description of the ordeal of the company:

We traveled from 15 to 25 miles a day. We used to stop one day in the week to wash. On Sunday we would hold our meetings and rest. Every morning and night we were called to prayers by the bugle. . . .

We traveled on till we got to the Platt River. That was the last walk I ever had with my mother. We caught up with Handcart companies that day. We watched them cross the river. There were great lumps of ice floating down the river. It was bitter cold. The next morning there were fourteen dead in camp through the cold. We went back to camp and went to prayers. We sang the song "Come, Come, Ye Saints, No Toil Nor Labor Fear." I wondered what made my mother cry. That night my mother took sick and the next morning my little sister was born. It was the 23rd of September. We named her Edith and she lived six weeks and died for want of nourishment.

We had been without water for several days, just drinking snow water. The captain said there was a spring of fresh water just a few miles away. It was snowing hard, but my mother begged me to go and get her a drink. Another lady went with me. We were about half way to the spring when we found an old man who had fallen in the snow. He was frozen so stiff, we could not lift him, so the lady told me where to go and she would go back to camp for help for we knew he would soon be frozen if we left him. When she had gone I began to think of the Indians and looking and looking in all directions. I became confused and forgot the way I should go. I waded around in the snow up to my knees and I became lost. Later when I did not return to camp the men started out after me. It was 11:00 p.m. o'clock before they found me. My feet and legs were frozen. They carried me to camp and rubbed me with snow. They put my feet in a bucket of water. The pain was so terrible. The frost came out of my legs and feet but did not come out of my toes. We traveled in the snow from the last crossing of the Platt River. We had orders not to pass the handcart companies. We had to keep close to them to help them if we could. We began to get short of food and our cattle gave out. We could only travel a few miles a day. When we started out of camp in the morning the brethren would shovel the snow to make a track for our cattle. They were weak for the want of food as the buffaloes were in large herds by the road and ate all the grass.

When we arived at Devil's Gate it was bitter cold. We left lots of our things there. There were two or three log houses there. . . . My brother James ate a hearty supper was as well as he ever was when he went to bed. In the morning he was dead.

My feet were frozen also my brother Edwin and my sister Caroline had their feet frozen. It was nothing but snow. We could not drive the pegs in the ground for our tents. Father would clean a place for our tents and put snow around to keep it down. We were short of flour but father was a good shot. They called him the hunter of the camp. So that helped us out. We could not get enough flour for bread as we got only a quarter of a pound per head a day, so we would make it like thin gruel. We called it "skilly."

There were four companies on the plains. We did not know what would become of us. One night a man came to our camp and told us there would be plenty of flour in the morning for Bro. Young had sent men and teams to help us. There was rejoicing that night. We sang songs, some danced and some cried. His name was Ephriam Hanks. We thought he was a living Santa Claus.

We traveled faster now that we had horse teams. My mother had never got well, she lingered until the 11 of December, the day we arrived in Salt Lake City 1856. She died between the Little and Big Mountain. She was buried in the Salt Lake City Cemetery. She was 43 years old. She and her baby lost their lives gathering to Zion in such a late season of the year. My sister was buried at the last crossing of the Sweet Water.

We arrived in Salt Lake City nine o'clock at night the 11th of December 1856. Three out of four that were living were frozen. My mother was dead in the wagon.

Bishop Hardy had us taken to a home in his ward and the brethren and the sisters brought us plenty of food. We had to be careful and not eat too much as it might kill us we were so hungry.

Early next morning Bro. Brigham Young and a doctor came. The doctor's name was Williams. When Bro. Young came in he shook hands with us all. When he saw our condition—our feet frozen and our mother dead—tears rolled down his cheeks.

The doctor amputated my toes using a saw and a butcher knife. Brigham Young promised me I would not have to have any more of my feet cut off. The sisters were dressing mother for the last time. Oh how did we stand it? That afternoon she was buried. ["Autobiography of Mary Goble Pay," in *A Believing People: Literature of the Latter-day Saints,* comp. Richard H. Cracroft and Neal E. Lambert, pp. 143–45]

In spite of the tragedies of the Willie and Martin handcart companies, handcart migration continued until 1860. Between 1856 and 1860 ten companies with 2,962 immigrants walked and pushed their small carts across the plains. Then President Brigham Young announced in 1860 that missionaries would be called to travel east with flour and other provisions to sell on eastern markets and that immigrants would return with them in the fall. Following a call from the prophet, 293 men went east in 1861 with 200 wagons containing nearly 72 tons of flour. They were organized into ten companies and returned in the fall with the immigrant Saints who desired to come to Zion that year. In 1863, 488 men with 384 wagons and 118 tons of flour went east and brought immigrants west. In 1868, the Perpetual Emigration Fund raised $70,000 and sent men and teams to Laramie City, Wyoming, since the Union Pacific Railroad had reached that far west. Four thousand immigrants returned with the wagons. On 8 March 1869, the Union Pacific Railroad arrived at Ogden, Utah, and formally ended the necessity of Church trains.

Even though immigration continued, the coming of the railroad marked the end of the pioneer period. Between the years 1847 and 1887, when immigration was no longer formally encouraged, over seventy-eight thousand men, women, and children came to Zion with the help of the Perpetual Emigration Fund. The pioneers experienced extreme hardship, suffering, and death; but they paid the price willingly to follow the prophet of the living God. They were human beings with human frailties. Very few of them ever realized any material rewards in this life from the great sacrifice they made, but they sought far more than physical comfort and prosperity. Vilate C. Raile immortalized their efforts in her centennial tribute to them:

> They cut desire into short lengths
> And fed it to the hungry fires of courage.
> Long after, when the flames had died,
> Molten gold gleamed in the ashes.
> They gathered it into bruised palms
> And handed it to their children
> And their children's children forever.
> [As quoted in T. Edgar Lyon, "Some Uncommon Aspects of the Mormon Migration," *Improvement Era,* Sept. 1969, p. 33]

STUDY QUESTIONS

1. Why were the pioneers willing to sacrifice everything for the gospel, even their own lives?

2. What were their earthly rewards? Their eternal rewards?

3. Why was the Perpetual Emigration Fund such an important part of the gathering?

4. Why did the pioneer Saints feel a need to gather?

5. Why was the building of temples such an integral part of the gathering?

6. How do the challenges faced by us differ from those faced by our pioneer Saints? How are they the same?

SANCTUARY IN UTAH

THE growth of the Church and its establishment in permanent communities in the American West between 1847 and 1877 necessitated a restructuring of the Church organization to provide strength for the future progress of the kingdom of God on the earth. This need was largely met by the establishment of important new auxiliary organizations, the revamping of already-existing priesthood and auxiliary functions, and a strengthening of the priesthood. Following their one-thousand-mile migration to the valleys of the Rocky Mountains, the Saints, renewed in their faith in their divine mission and destiny, established within thirty years a commonwealth of more than three hundred settlements. In addition they carried the message of the gospel to other lands and brought thousands of people to modern Zion. The stone of Daniel's prophecy, which the Lord had cut from the mountain through the instrumentality of Joseph Smith, now received important impetus under the guidance of Brigham Young.

HIGHLIGHTS

1861–62: The Saints settle in the Rio Virgin area of southwestern Utah and in southern Idaho.

1861 Oct. 18: The overland telegraph is completed to Salt Lake City.

1863–64 The Saints settle in Bear Lake Valley of Utah and Idaho.

1865 The Saints settle along the Muddy River in Nevada.

1866 The *Juvenile Instructor* begins publication. The Parent Sunday School Union is organized.

1867 Oct. 6: General conference convenes in the almost-completed Salt Lake Tabernacle.

Autumn: President Young revives the Relief Society, calling Eliza R. Snow as president.

Dec.: The School of the Prophets is organized again.

1868 Zion's Cooperative Mercantile Institution (ZCMI), the first department store west of the Mississippi River, is organized.

1869 May 10: The transcontinental railroad is completed at Promontory, Utah.

Nov: The young ladies' Cooperative Retrenchment Association (later YWMIA) begins.

1870 Feb. 12: A woman's suffrage law is enacted in Utah.

1872 Aug. 2: The Parent Sunday School Union becomes the Deseret Sunday School Union, with Elder George Q. Cannon as general superintendent.

1873 Cooperative settlements are established in various locations.

1875 Brigham Young inaugurates the YMMIA.

Brigham Young Academy opens in Provo, Utah.

1876 The Saints settle on the Little Colorado River in Arizona.

1877 Apr. 6: President Young dedicates the St. George Temple.

The Brethren define duties of the priesthood and restructure stakes.

Aug. 29: President Brigham Young dies in Salt Lake City.

HISTORICAL SUMMARY

Auxiliaries Established

In 1849 Richard Ballantyne organized the first Sunday school in the Salt Lake Valley, which children of leading Church families attended. This led to the start of other such schools. For many years, however, Sunday school work did not have a central direction and was left to the efforts of interested individuals. Impressed with the value of this means of teaching the Saints' children, George Q. Cannon, a secretary to President Young, began publication of the *Juvenile Instructor* magazine in 1866, directing it to the young people involved in the Sunday school movement. On 4 November of that same year, a central organization, called the Parent Sunday School Union (since 1872 the Deseret Sunday School Union) was organized, and Elder

Eliza R. Snow

Cannon was chosen as president. Although established by the Prophet Joseph Smith in Nauvoo in 1842, the Women's Relief Society had not flourished in an organized, general capacity during the exodus from Nauvoo and the early years of colonization in Utah. However, in 1866 Brigham Young appointed Eliza R. Snow, who had been the secretary in the original Nauvoo organization, to preside over the sisters of the Church as Relief Society president and rekindle the spark of that organization. Within a few years, hundreds of ward and branch Relief Society organizations were functioning throughout the Church. The involvement of the sisters in home manufacturing and the buying, storing, and selling of grain provided them with thousands of dollars for the poor, for missionaries, and for temple building. This new Church involvement also provided sisters with opportunities for personal growth, especially as leaders. Women trained in the Relief Society later helped organize and lead the associations for young women (1869) and the Primary Association for children (1878).

Sister Snow was present when President Young called his daughters together on 28 November 1869 to start a movement toward "retrenchment" (the abandonment of extremes in dress, speech, and social activity). He appointed a married daughter, Ella Young Empey, to preside over the association, with six of her sisters as counselors. Sister Snow was to assist in expanding the Cooperative Retrenchment Association beyond President Young's family by helping women organize the association in the wards of Salt Lake City and other towns in Utah.

President Young then turned his attention to the young men of the Church. In June 1875 he called Junius F. Wells, a twenty-year-old returned missionary and son of his counselor Daniel H. Wells, to organize the young men of the Church into associations for self- and mutual improvement. For some time in the 1850s and 60s independent literary societies, debating clubs, and young men's clubs had sprung into existence in the Church, but this move by President Young marked the beginning of the Young Men's Mutual Improvement Association. In a letter dated 6 November 1875, President Young told Brother Wells: "Each member will find that happiness in this world mainly depends on the work he does, and the way in which he does it. It now becomes the duty of these institutions to aid the holy priesthood in instructing the youth of Israel in all things commendable and worthy of the acceptance of saints of the Most High God" (B. H. Roberts, *A Comprehensive History of the Church,* 5:481). The first YMMIA was formed in

the Salt Lake City Thirteenth Ward, and then in December 1875 a central committee was organized with Junius Wells as president. After the YMMIA was underway, the young women's Cooperative Retrenchment Association officially called itself the Young Women's Mutual Improvement Association. Both organizations published literary journals, the young men the *Contributor* and the young women the *Young Woman's Journal.* In 1897 the *Contributor* became the *Improvement Era* and in 1929 the *Journal* merged with it.

Priesthood Quorums Strengthened

During the last year of his life President Young felt strongly compelled to bring the priesthood organization of the Church more closely in line with the revelations. Previously, conditions such as the constant movement of the Church from one place to another, a limited population, poor communication, and the difficulty of settling and colonizing a new country had combined to limit or alter the organizational structure that had been revealed. For example, as colonization spread to more than three hundred communities throughout the western United States, members of the Quorum of Twelve were appointed to act as overseers of groups of settlements located long distances from Church headquarters. The preoccupation of the Twelve with problems of settlement and colonization

prevented them from exercising their full responsibility to the nations of the earth. Furthermore, several seventies quorums had been established at Nauvoo whose members had been ordained into specific quorums. By the 1860s the members of these quorums had become widely scattered, creating problems with quorum communication and activity. In addition, men had been appointed to oversee local communities or congregations without the benefit of proper ordination or assistance of counselors. In some instances elders and seventies were serving as bishops, and bishops were functioning with only one counselor or none at all. The function of stake organizations as well had not been adequately defined for the maximum strength of the overall Church organization. The Salt Lake Stake functioned more or less as a center stake that gave direction and guidance and had jurisdiction over other stakes. When quorum leaders in outlying areas needed new officers they sent a list of nominees to the Salt Lake Stake quorum presidencies for selection and appointment. In addition, during the early years, Aaronic Priesthood responsibilities were primarily assigned to adult men; but the large turnover that came to Aaronic Priesthood quorums because of the advancement of men to Melchizedek Priesthood offices resulted in the lesser priesthood quorums being staffed from Melchizedek Priesthood

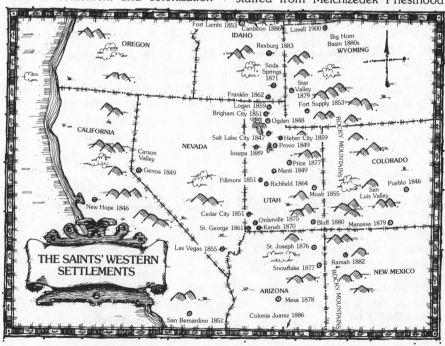

THE SAINTS' WESTERN SETTLEMENTS

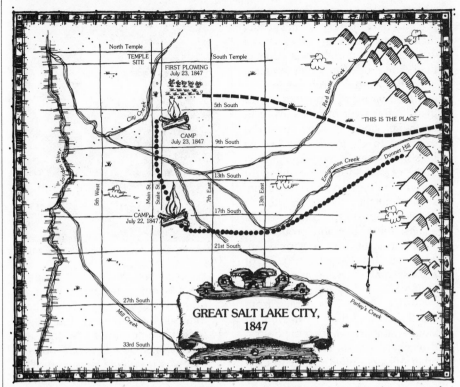

GREAT SALT LAKE CITY, 1847

quorums with men serving as "acting" deacons, teachers, or priests.

The Priesthood and Its Functions

At a special conference in the Salt Lake Tabernacle on 13 May 1877, Orson Pratt spoke to the Saints about the function of the priesthood, describing the reorganization that was then taking place in the stakes of the Church.

In the early days of this church, the Lord, through a revelation, set forth the various appendages of the higher priesthood, the duties of its several offices and their callings; also how they should officiate, and what ordinances they were permitted to administer, and what was not permitted to be administered by those holding it.

It seems that since these revelations were given, the church, during its history, has passed through a variety of circumstances, wherein a perfect organization according to the rules and laws, as laid down by modern revelation, has not been entered into. Circumstances always did more or less to alter the condition of the people. Some, by virtue of their priesthood have officiated, without being set apart, in certain callings that pertain to those who

should be selected and set apart for that purpose....

We might refer to persons in some few of our settlements, both north and south, who have acted as bishops by virtue of appointment only, and not ordination.

I understand now that the Spirit of the Lord has manifested unto the President of the Chruch, who is the proper authority, for the Twelve to go forth and set in order and organize more perfectly the various branches that are located throughout all the Territory, and in the adjoining territories. And no doubt those few who are acting in the bishoprick without being ordained will receive their ordination, and there may be many changes, in order to introduce, in all its perfection, as far as we have knowledge and understanding, a more perfect organization throughout the Church in these mountains.

The object of this perfect organization is that we may be entitled to greater blessings therefrom; that we may be entitled to a greater fulness of the Holy Spirit; that everything may be dictated according to the mind and will of God, not only in spiritual things, but also in regard to our temporal matters; and also that

every person may know his place, that his duties may be assigned to him, and by knowing what is required, that all may the more diligently seek after the Holy Ghost to direct them in their positions and callings, and have more faith, more assurance before God, to obtain confidence before the heavens, and before the brethren, in order that their ministry may benefit the people. You are well aware that we have been taught, for these many years, the great necessity of establishing a union in the midst of this people. Although we are the most united people upon the face of the earth, of which we have any knowledge, yet we are far from that perfection of unity which should characterize the Saints of the Most High God....

We declare to all men, wherever our missionaries go, that this is the grand preparation for the coming of our Lord and Saviour to reign on the earth. [*Deseret News,* 30 May 1877, p. 258]

Strengthening the Church

In July of that same year, a circular formally announcing the reorganization was sent to all the priesthood leaders in the Church. It is a very important document in Church history, for it marked a turning point in the organizational pattern of The Church of Jesus Christ of Latter-day Saints.

CIRCULAR *of The First Presidency of the Church of Jesus Christ of Latter-day Saints to the Presidency of the Various Stakes of Zion, to the Bishops of the different Wards and to all the Officers and Members of the Church; Greeting:*

BELOVED SAINTS:

As we are now organizing the Stakes of Zion in these mountains and setting in order the quorums of the priesthood, we think it proper to give some general instructions to secure uniformity and concert of action in the church.

Under the direction of the First Presidency and the Twelve Apostles the presidency of the various Stakes will have the general supervision of all matters pertaining to the church within the limits of their Stakes; and every one of the seventies, of the high priests, the elders and the lesser priesthood, as well as the members, within those limits should be governed in all righteousness by that presidency. It is the duty of those who preside over Stakes to seek for and receive counsel from the First Presidency and the Twelve Apostles, and, under their direction, to see that every Ward is thoroughly organized with a bishop and two counselors—who must be high priests and set apart to preside as the bishop and counselors—and with the priests, teachers and deacons assigned their duties by the bishops as ministers to the Wards; also, that every family, no matter how far removed from settlements, is recognized and numbered with the people of the nearest Ward. It is expected that every member of the church will have his name enrolled in the church record of the Ward and Stake in which he lives, or else he will not be recognized as a member of the church. Many persons have claimed fellowship in the church who have not lived according to the requirements of the gospel; but this should no longer be permitted. The laws of the Lord must be more strictly enforced, and such persons must repent and bring forth the fruits of righteousness in their lives, or be severed from the church. If persons professing to be members of the church be guilty of lying,

drunkenness, sabbath-breaking, profanity, defrauding or backbiting their neighbors, or any other kind of wickedness or unrighteous dealing, they should be visited by the teachers of the Ward in which they reside, and their wrongs be pointed out to them in the spirit of meekness and brotherly kindness, and they be exhorted to repent. If they should persist in their wrong-doing, then their cases should be brought before the bishop and his counselors, and they should be cited to appear to answer the charges made against them. If, upon proper and sufficient testimony, it should appear that they have been guilty of acts which are in violation of the law of God, and they will not repent, then they should be expelled from the church, and their names be no longer numbered among the Saints. If teachers, priests and bishops, or other officers, suffer iniquity to exist in the church, in districts where they preside, without taking action against it, they become partakers of other men's sins and they are unworthy of their positions. If an officer of the church will not perform his duty faithfully, he should be removed and another be appointed in his stead.

There are small settlements where only a few families reside—too few to be organized as a Ward. For such a settlement the bishop, to whose Ward it belongs, should appoint a

Missionaries at the mouth of Echo Canyon, Utah, 1867

priest to preside, if there is one; if there is not, a teacher can be appointed to take charge of the church affairs in the settlement. But if there is neither a priest nor a teacher, and there should be a high priest or seventy who is suitable he can be called upon to act for the time being in the capacity of a priest. In every settlement, however small, meetings and Sunday schools should be strictly maintained.

In organizing the various Stakes, there will be a president and two counselors selected in each Stake to preside over the high priests who reside there. There is no limit to the number that shall compose a quorum of high priests. They may number but a few, or they may number thousands; therefore one presidency in a Stake is sufficient for them, and in holding quorum meetings they should meet in a Stake capacity and not in Wards.

The seventies can meet with the high priests, or with the elders, as they may choose, they being a traveling ministry; but when it is necessary for the transaction of business of a missionary character, they can meet in the capacity of a quorum, otherwise they are like any other elders or members of the church, and are under the direction of their bishops.

The elders should be organized in quorums each numbering ninety-six, and where there are more than enough for one quorum and not enough for two they can continue to meet as one quorum until the nec-

Salt Lake Fourteenth Ward chapel

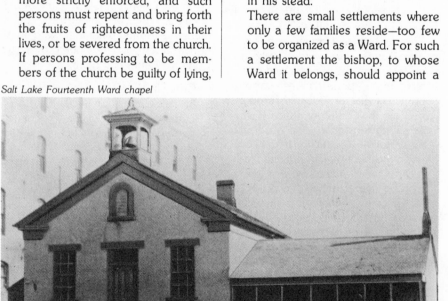

essary number to organize another quorum are ordained.

When forty-eight priests are ordained they should be organized as a quorum; twenty-four teachers constitute a quorum, and twelve deacons. Should there be an excess of these numbers in any place, and yet not sufficient to form another quorum, they will meet, as in the case of the elders, with their brethren as one quorum until there are enough to form another quorum.

In the work of organizing, the Stakes and Wards should first receive attention. After their general presiding officers have been selected and ordained, and the lists of the various officers in the Stake have been collected and the number of each kind in each Ward is known, then the quorums should be organized. In organizing them, if there should not be a sufficient number for a quorum in one Ward, then they should be taken from others contiguous to it and most convenient for communication and meetings. The officers who are designed to form a quorum should be called together and the most suitable men should be selected for

presidents and counselors. In organizing a quorum of priests a bishop is the proper person to preside over them. In organizing quorums of teachers and deacons the presidents and their counselors should be selected from their own number. Seventies, high priests and elders who are called to act in the offices of the lesser priesthood should not be numbered in the quorums of that priesthood; but their names should be recorded in their own quorums, though when called upon by the bishops they should be willing to act in the offices of the lesser priesthood until priests, teachers and deacons of the necessary experience are found. When priests and teachers visit the Saints, according to the instructions in the Book of Doctrine and Covenants, the experienced priest or teacher should have as a companion a young man, so that the latter may have the opportunity of learning the duties of his calling, and becoming thoroughly wise and efficient in the discharge thereof.

Once in every three months a conference of the officers and members of each Stake will be held, and it will

be the duty of the Apostles to attend these as often as practicable. The Twelve have been relieved from presiding over districts, and they will devote themselves to traveling and preaching the gospel to the people, and see that the officers in the several Stakes do their duty. To prevent loss of time, and to save unnecessary labor in traveling, the dates upon which conferences will be held should be so arranged that one will succeed another in a manner most convenient for visiting, which will be attended to in due time. At these quarterly conferences reports should be made, giving the number of members and officers, with the offices the latter hold, the number of families, the number of ordinations, of baptisms, of excommunications and births and deaths, with the sex and age of both the latter, and a report of the condition and ability, with regard to temporal affairs, of the members of the Ward, and the percentage or amount of tithing which they pay, and such other information as shall make the record of each Stake a complete one. In each Ward a record of all these matters must be kept, and before the holding of each quarterly conference, a transcript of these records should be handed to the president of the Stake, whose duty it will be to compile the same for record. A report from each quarterly conference should be made by the president of each Stake to the First Presidency.

In each Ward there should be kept a record of all cases brought before the bishop's court for trial and adjudication, with a copy of the complaint and the decision. The proceedings of each case as recorded should be read by the clerk, after the trial, to the bishop and his counselors, so that they may be satisfied of their correctness. Should an appeal be taken from the bishop's court to the High Council, a transcript of the proceedings can be sent to that council.

No member who moves from one Ward to another should be received into fellowship and be recognized as a member in good standing in the Ward to which he moves, without he

"Bird's eye view of Salt Lake City, Utah Territory, 1870" (courtesy of the Geography and Map Division, Library of Congress)

brings with him a letter of recommendation from the presiding authorities in the Ward where he has resided.

It has been the practice in many places for the presidents of high priests and seventies to take members of other quorums, and sometimes persons who held no priesthood, and ordain them into their quorums, and this too very frequently without consulting any one in authority, not even the presidents of the quorums to which these persons rightfully belonged. Because of this practice it has been a difficult thing to keep young men in the elders' quorum or in any of the quorums of the lesser priesthood; and when deacons, teachers and priests have been wanted it has generally been the case that seventies and high priests have had to be taken to act in those offices. It would be excellent training for the young men if they had the opportunity of acting in the offices of the lesser priesthood. They would thereby obtain very valuable experience, and when they obtain the Melchisedec priesthood they would be likely to place a higher value upon it. We desire to be distinctly understood, therefore, that hereafter when seventies and high priests are to be ordained, it must be under the direction of the First Presidency or the Twelve. Whenever it may be deemed proper to ordain men to these offices the proper authority can be consulted respecting their ordination. The presidents will see that this counsel is observed in their respective Stakes.

In consequence of it having been thought more convenient in some of the Stakes for the tithing to be concentrated in one place, and for one bishop to receive reports from others and keep charge of the tithing, &c., the idea has grown up that such a bishop is a presiding bishop, and in many places he has been so regarded. This idea is an incorrect one. Brother Edward Hunter is the only one who acts as presiding bishop in the church.

It is designed, as we have already said, that under the direction of the First Presidency and the Twelve, the

Salt Lake City, looking south, 1877

presidents of each Stake will preside over the High Council and have general charge of the affairs of the Stake, and through the proper officers will see that the members of the Stake do their duty. But we do not expect them to take personal charge of the tithing, unless especially appointed to do so, as the duties of their calling will require too much of their attention to have them perform this duty. They should, however, instruct the Saints respecting the payment of tithing and impress upon them the necessity of being punctual and strict in performing this duty, as well as in bringing forward their offerings to the poor. The bishops in each Ward will act under their direction and counsel, and they will see that they do their duty and take proper care of the tithing and that no waste of this property shall occur in places under their jurisdiction; for this is the duty of a bishop, to receive and care for the tithing. Respecting the management of tithing and in the various Stakes we shall give instruction from time to time as may be needed. . . .

Among the many duties which devolve upon us, there is none that should receive more careful and constant attention than the education of our children. They are numerous, and if properly trained will become a great blessing to the in-

habitants of the earth. Parents should take time—if not every day, at least as often as they can and not allow many days to elapse—to call their families together and interrogate them respecting their associations, their words, actions, &c., and teach them the principles of the gospel. They should send them regularly to day and sunday schools and furnish them every possible facility for gaining a sound and thorough education, and especially in the principles of the gospel and the history of the church. The teachers to whom we entrust our children for education should be faithful Latter-day Saints, sound in doctrine and thoroughly imbued with a love of Zion. In this way we can rear up a generation of men and women who shall love and maintain truth and righteousness in the earth. . . .

In order that children may have the opportunity to partake of the sacrament, and be taught the value and importance of that ordinance, we desire the bishops and their counselors in the various Wards to administer the sacrament every Sunday morning in the Sunday Schools. In settlements where there are Meeting Houses sufficiently spacious to admit of children attending the public meetings on Sunday afternoon, we suggest that they be encouraged to go there. If it should not require too much walking, they might assemble first at the place where the Sunday School is held, and from there walk, under the guidance of their superintendents and teachers, to the meeting. But whether this be done or not, they should have seats set apart for them to occupy in the Meeting House, and while there they should be in charge of their teachers. These seats should be made very comfortable, so that the children will not get uneasy; the children should be waited upon with water to drink. This need not interfere with the administration of the sacrament in the schools; for though some of the children may partake of it there and at meeting also, there others would miss it altogether if they did not partake of it in the school room. The proper observance of the Lord's day would be greatly increased among the rising generation if this were to become a custom in all our settlements. At the present time this day is not properly respected by old and young. Too many look upon it as a day for the enjoyment of worldly pleasure, and not for the worship of God. Many children who attend Sunday schools in the morning think they have the right to play the remainder of the day, and they act accordingly, frequently to the annoyance of the well-disposed.

Children who are capable of repentance should be baptized when they reach the proper age, ac-

Pioneer Day celebration in Salt Lake City, about 1889

cording to the revelations. Up to that age they are entitled to the sacrament.

It is very desirable that the children in the Sunday schools should be taught the art of singing. The cultivation of this art will make the schools more attractive to the children themselves and add greatly to the pleasure of parents and all connected with the schools. And if in our Ward meetings and conferences congregational singing were encouraged and practised more than it is, our worship would be no less acceptable to the Lord, to his angels and to the Saints themselves. . . .

Finally, the presidents of the different Stakes should make arrangements to travel and visit as frequently as possible the various Wards under their jurisdiction, and elders, sound in doctrine and full of the Spirit of the Lord, should be appointed to preach from time to time, that our meetings may be more interesting and instructive. And all the officers of the church should constantly keep in mind, and in the exercise of the duties of their offices in the midst of the people act upon, the teachings and counsel of the Prophet Joseph Smith, contained in Sec. CXXI, pages 386–7, in the new edition of the Book of Doctrine and Covenants. [James R. Clark, *Messages of the First Presidency of The Church of Jesus Christ of Latter-day Saints,* 2:283–95]

When, several months earlier, President Young had announced to a meeting of bishops in Salt Lake City on 19 October 1876 that all stakes of Zion were independent of other stakes, he created some surprise; those present had believed that the Salt Lake Stake "had jurisdiction over all [the] quorums throughout the land" (Diary of Frederick Kesler, 19 Oct. 1876, Special Collections Department, Manuscripts, Marriott Library, University of Utah; spelling and punctuation modernized).

"[The] work of setting in order the stakes of Zion began at the general conference at St. George, and was continued through all the settlements" (Roberts, *Comprehensive History,* 5:508). By the time of Brigham

Young's death in August, 1877, twenty stakes had been organized or reorganized. Where the Church had been organized in one stake and thirteen wards in 1844, in 1877 there were twenty stakes and two hundred and sixty wards. George Q. Cannon summarized Brigham Young's work to strengthen the Church organization when he spoke at the President's funeral: "He released all of the twelve from presiding over local places; . . . all were released from presiding over the stakes of Zion, and were told by the president that their mission had a larger field than a stake of Zion. He set the priesthood in order as it had never been since the first organization of the church upon the earth. He defined the duties of the apostles, he defined the duties of the seventies, he defined the duties of the high priests, the duties of the elders and those of the lesser priesthood, with plainness and distinctness and power—the power of God—in a way that it is left on record in such unmistakable language that no one need err who has the Spirit of God resting down upon him" (Roberts, *Comprehensive History,* 5:507–8).

Today the approximately one thousand stakes all over the world attest to the benefits of President Young's inspired vision.

STUDY QUESTIONS

1. List the major factors in Brigham Young's administration that helped establish Zion firmly in the Rocky Mountains and produce a thriving and healthy church. How has this affected the Church in the years since then?

2. What justifies us in calling such organizations as the Young Men or Young Women auxiliaries and gives the basis for all auxiliaries?

3. How have the change in the relationship of the Twelve with the stakes and the change in the function of the stakes influenced the growth and development of the Church?

4. How could the First Presidency circular on p. 41 be thought of as the first of the official Church handbooks prepared for its leaders? How does it serve such a purpose?

JOHN TAYLOR

JOHN Taylor guided the Church through one of its greatest trials. As never before, journalists, pastors, congressmen, and presidents combined to eradicate the "evil" of polygamy, and, in the case of the Church's enemies, to actually destroy the Church itself. John Taylor's experiences as a missionary both in the United States and in the British Isles and Europe, as an editor of Church newspapers in Nauvoo and in New York City, as a member of the Utah legislature for over twenty years, and as a witness of the Martyrdom—all contributed to the skill and the conviction with which he guided the Church in the 1870s and 80s. His administration saw the organization of the Primary Association and the celebration of a jubilee year, the disenfranchisement of faithful Saints and the disincorporation of the Church. Through this period of growth and trial he remained committed deeply to the vision of the kingdom of God he had shared with both Joseph Smith and Brigham Young.

HIGHLIGHTS

1808 Nov. 1: Born in Milnthorpe, Westmoreland, England.

1832 Immigrates to Toronto, Upper Canada (24).

1836 Baptized; called to preside over the Church in Canada (27).

1838 Dec. 19: Becomes a member of the Quorum of the Twelve (30).

1839 Aug. 8: Departs on his first mission to the British Isles (31).

1842–46 Serves as editor of the *Times and Seasons* (34–37).

1843–46 Serves as editor of the *Nauvoo Neighbor* (35–37).

1844 June 27: Severely wounded by a mob in the Carthage Jail (35).

1846–47 Serves a second mission to Great Britain (37–38).

1850–54 Fills a mission to France and Germany and writes *The Government of God* (41–45).

1855–57 Publishes the *Mormon* in New York City (47–49).

1857–76 Serves as a member of the Utah Territorial Legislature (49–68).

1877 Aug. 29: Upon Brigham Young's death, leads the Church as President of the Twelve (69).

1878 Aug. 11: Organizes the Primary Association (70).

1880 Celebrates a jubilee year, the fiftieth anniversary of the organization of the Church (71).

Oct. 10: Sustained as President of the Church (71).

1882 *The Mediation and Atonement of Our Lord and Savior Jesus Christ* is published (73).

1882–83 Special revelations given (73–74).

1884 May 17: Dedicates the Logan Temple (75).

1885 Feb. 1: Delivers his last public sermon and goes into "retirement" (76).

1887 July 25: Passes away peacefully in Kaysville, Utah (78).

HISTORICAL SUMMARY

Early Life

John Taylor was born on 1 November 1808, in western England. His maturing years were devoted to learning a trade and to many acts of religious service. From his youth, he was keenly sensitive to spiritual matters, and he spent many hours in prayer and contemplation of the scriptures. While in his teens, he joined the Methodist church and labored to bring others to worship God. Many spiritual experiences foreshadowed his future ministry as a special witness for the Savior. As a small child, he saw in a vision an angel with a trumpet, proclaiming a message to the nations. In his seventeenth year, he was inspired to state that he would one day preach the gospel in America.

John Taylor, 1808–1887 (by Frederick Piercy)

In 1832 John Taylor immigrated to Toronto, Canada, where his parents had moved two years earlier, established a successful business, and reaffiliated with the Methodist church. While serving as a Sunday school teacher there, he met and married Leonora Cannon, a refined and gracious young Englishwoman. Convinced from their Bible studies that no denomination of their acquaintance resembled the Savior's New Testament church, the Taylors and their friends fasted and prayed for the Lord to send a representative with the truth. Obedient to a divine directive, Elder Parley P. Pratt traveled from Kirtland, Ohio, to Toronto, where he met and taught the questing group. The Taylors were subsequently baptized. After John received the Melchizedek Priesthood he was called to preside over the Church in Canada.

Work in the Ministry

In 1838 Elder Taylor was called by the Lord to fill a vacancy in the Quorum of the Twelve (see D&C 118). Assigned to assist the persecuted Saints in Missouri, he demonstrated great skill in drafting petitions, seeking relief and restitution from the state for mob-inflicted damages. When the governor subsequently issued his extermination order, John Taylor took a prominent part in relocating the stricken Saints to Illinois.

In the summer of 1839, the Twelve left to preach the gospel in Great Britain. During this highly productive period, Elder Taylor preached, debated, and baptized throughout England and Scotland, and he introduced the gospel in Ireland and the Isle of Man. He also wrote several tracts and assisted Brigham Young in publishing a hymnal and the Book of Mormon for the British Saints.

Returning to Nauvoo, Elder Taylor was called to edit two newspapers, the *Times and Seasons* and the *Nauvoo Neighbor,* important voices of communication and counsel for the Saints. His editorials and otherwise outspoken defense of the Church both in Kirtland and Nauvoo earned him the title "Champion of Liberty."

Once home from their missionary labors, the Twelve were taught the doctrine of celestial marriage, including plural wives, by Joseph Smith. Of his feelings John Taylor wrote: " 'I had always entertained strict ideas of virtue, and I felt as a married man that this was to me, outside of this principle, an appalling thing to do.... Hence, with the feelings I had entertained, nothing but a knowledge of God, and the revelations of God, and the truth of them, could have induced me to embrace such a principle as this' " (B. H. Roberts, *The Life of John Taylor*, p. 100).

The Martyrdom

One of John Taylor's saddest experiences was the martyrdom of Joseph and Hyrum Smith at Carthage Jail. He said of the Martyrdom: "Was there anything surprising in all this? No. If they killed Jesus in former times, would

not the same feeling and influence bring about the same results in these times? I had counted the cost when I first started out, and stood prepared to meet it" (*Journal of Discourses,* 25:91–92).

The afternoon of 27 June 1844 was hot and sultry. The four men incarcerated in Carthage Jail all suffered from depression. To cheer Joseph, in his vibrant and melodious voice, John Taylor sang "A Poor Wayfaring Man of Grief," a song recently introduced in Nauvoo which the Prophet had quite enjoyed.

Late in the afternoon the jailor came in and suggested that for their own safety they should be moved from the jailor's bedroom to the cells. Joseph agreed to go right after supper. Then he turned to the fourth man in the room, Willard Richards, who acted as his personal scribe, and said, "If we go into the cell, will you go with us?"

To which Elder Richards replied: "Brother Joseph, you did not ask me to cross the river with you [referring to the time when they crossed the Mississippi, en route for the Rocky Mountains]—you did not ask me to come to Carthage—you did not ask me to come to jail with you—and do you think I would forsake you now? But I will tell you what I will do; if you are condemned to be hung for 'treason,' I will be hung in your stead, and you shall go free."

Joseph replied, "But you cannot."

Elder Richards said, "I will."

John Taylor was of a different though no less heroic mind. Considering the whole affair a legal farce, if not a flagrant violation of the liberty of innocent men, he proposed that he slip past the guards, go to Nauvoo, and get a sufficient force to rescue the Prophet: "If you permit it, and say the word, I will have you out of this prison in five hours, if the jail has to come down to do it." This idea Joseph refused. Hyrum asked John Taylor to again sing the song. Initially he refused, stating he just didn't feel like singing, but Hyrum was not to be dissuaded, stating, "Oh, never mind: commence singing and you will get the spirit of it." Once again John Taylor's strong voice filled the prison.

Soon after finishing the song, Elder Taylor saw from the front window of the bedroom a number of men with painted faces rush up to the jail. The guards good-naturedly pretended to resist them but were soon hustled away. The mob rushed up the stairs to the second story bedroom. The four men inside secured the door as best they could. In the meantime, other members of the mob surrounded the building. Those on the stairwell managed to burst open the door and fire within, while those outside began to shoot through the windows. (See B. H. Roberts, *A Comprehensive History of the Church,* 2:282–84.)

The Carthage Jail (by Frederick Piercy, from Route from Liverpool to the Great Salt Lake Valley, *ed. James Linforth [Liverpool: Franklin D. Richards, 1855])*

The Carthage Jail, interior (photo by Don O. Thorpe)

What followed, John Taylor recorded:

After parrying the guns for some time, which now protruded thicker and farther into the room, and seeing no hope of escape or protection there, as we were now unarmed, it occurred to me that we might have some friends outside, and that there might be some chance of escape in that direction, but here there seemed to be none. As I expected them every moment to rush into the room—nothing but extreme cowardice having thus far kept them out—as the tumult and pressure increased, without any other hope, I made a spring for the window which was right in front of the jail door, where the mob was standing, and also exposed to the fire of the Carthage Greys, who were stationed some ten or twelve rods off. The weather was hot, we all of us had our coats off, and the window was raised to admit air. As I reached the window, and was on the point of leaping out, I was struck by a ball from the door about midway of my thigh, which struck the bone, and flattened out almost to the size of a quarter of a dollar, and then passed on through the fleshy part to within about half an inch of the outside. I think some prominent nerve must have been severed or injured for, as soon as the ball struck me, I fell like a bird when shot, or an ox when struck by a butcher, and lost entirely and instantaneously all power of action or locomotion. I fell upon the window-sill, and cried out, "I am shot!" Not possessing any power to move, I felt myself falling outside of the window, but immediately I fell inside, from some, at that time, unknown cause. When I struck the floor my animation seemed restored, as I have seen it sometimes in squirrels and birds after being shot. As soon as I felt the power of motion I crawled under the bed, which was in a corner of the room, not far from the window where I received my wound. While on my way and under the bed I was wounded in three other places; one ball entered a little below the left knee, and never was extracted; another entered the forepart of my left arm, a little above the wrist, and, passing down by the joint, lodged in the fleshy part of my hand, about midway, a little above the upper joint of my little finger; another struck me on the fleshy part of my left hip, and tore away the flesh as large as my hand, dashing the mangled fragments of flesh and blood against the wall.

My wounds were painful, and the sensation produced was as though a ball had passed through and down the whole length of my leg. I very well remember my reflections at the time. I had a very painful idea of becoming lame and decrepid, and being an object of pity, and I felt as though I would rather die than be placed in such circumstances.

It would seem that immediately after my attempt to leap out of the window, Joseph also did the same thing, of which circumstance I have no knowledge only from information. The first thing that I noticed was a cry that he had leaped out of the window. A cessation of firing followed, the mob rushed downstairs, and Dr. Richards went to the window. [*History of the Church,* 7:104–5]

Within three minutes from its start, the Martyrdom was over. Fearing the mob, which had left the interior of the jail, might return, Willard Richards carried John Taylor into a cell and covered him with bedding in such a way as to conceal him from any returning mobbers. But before Elder Richards could leave for help, a company of mobbers again rushed up the stairs. They entered the bedroom but found only the body of Hyrum. Before they could search for Elders Richards and Taylor, mobbers outside cried in alarm, "The Mormons are coming!" This idea was false, but the panic which ensued caused the members of the mob to instantly flee, leaving the two elders safe.

Word was sent by Willard Richards to Nauvoo telling the Saints what had happened. In this communication, John Taylor insisted that Elder Richards play down his wounds so that his family would not be worried. Nonetheless, his wounds were too serious to allow him to accompany Willard Richards to Nauvoo the next day. After a few days recovering in Carthage, Elder Taylor was moved to Nauvoo, where he eventually healed from his wounds. Not until he had arrived home in Nauvoo did he discover the reason why he had not fallen out of the window of the jail when first shot. When his family examined his watch, they

were not a little startled to find that my watch had been struck with a ball. I sent for my vest, and, upon examination, it was found that there was a cut as if with a knife, in the vest pocket which had contained my watch. In the pocket the fragments

John Taylor's watch

of the glass were found literally ground to powder. It then occurred to me that a ball had struck me at the time I felt myself falling out of the window, and that it was this force that threw me inside. I had often remarked to Mrs. Taylor the singular fact of finding myself inside the room, when I felt a moment before after being shot, that I was falling out, and I never could account for it until then; but here the thing was fully elucidated, and was rendered plain to my mind. I was indeed falling out, when some villain aimed at my heart. The ball struck my watch, and forced me back; if I had fallen out I should assuredly have been killed, if not by the fall, by those around, and this ball, intended to dispatch me, was turned by an overruling Providence into a messenger of mercy, and saved my life. I shall never forget the feelings of gratitude that I then experienced towards my heavenly Father; the whole scene was vividly portrayed before me, and my heart melted before the Lord. I felt that the Lord had preserved me by a special act of mercy; that my time had not yet come, and that I had still a work to perform upon the earth. [*History of the Church,* 7:119–20]

John Taylor returned to Europe twice more during his ministry as one of the Twelve. As the Saints arrived at Council Bluffs in 1846, Elders Taylor, Hyde, and Orson Pratt were dispatched by President Young to resolve problems facing the Church in England. Upon their return to America in 1847, Elders Taylor and Pratt led two companies of pioneers to the Salt Lake Valley. In October of 1849, John Taylor was called by Brigham Young to open France for missionary labor. While in Europe this last time, he directed the translation and publication of the Book of Mormon into French and German. He also wrote *The Goverment of God,* a classic work comparing and contrasting the inferior political systems of mankind with the harmony and grandeur of the Lord's kingdom.

Elder Taylor returned home in 1852. Two years later, President Young called him to publish a newspaper, the *Mormon,* in New York City to counter-

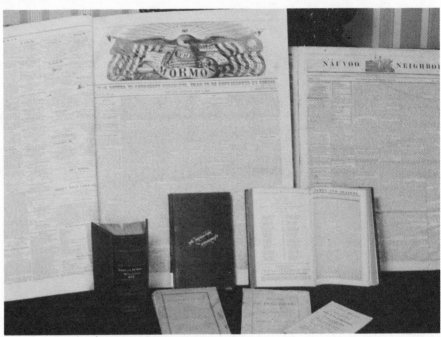
Publications written or edited by John Taylor (photo by Don O. Thorpe)

act the rising swell of criticism against the Church's practice of plural marriage. Of Elder Taylor's labors, President Young said, "With regard to the labors of Brother Taylor in editing the paper called *The Mormon,* published in the city of New York, I have heard many remarks concerning the editorials in that paper, not only from the Saints, but from those who do not profess to believe the religion we have embraced; and it is probably one of the strongest edited papers that is now published" (Roberts, *John Taylor,* p. 271).

A naturalized United States citizen, Elder Taylor was a strong advocate of electing government officials who were responsive to the righteous will of the people. He was actively involved in civic affairs and served with distinction in the Utah Territorial Legislature for nearly twenty years.

A Decade of Persecution

At the death of President Young, the Quorum of the Twelve lead the Church for three years, with John Taylor as its presiding officer. The Church made great strides forward, President Taylor continuing Brigham Young's colonization programs and vigorously implementing the changes in Church government President Young had inaugurated (see chapter 6). Weekly ward and monthly stake priesthood meetings were firmly established.

Quarterly stake conferences were standardized, with President Taylor or other General Authorities in attendance, and the auxiliaries were adopted throughout the Church.

This progress was further enhanced during the Church's 1880 jubilee year, when President Taylor proposed at April conference that the Church forgive the worthy poor any debt to the Perpetual Emigration Fund as well as any delinquent tithing they owed the Church. In addition, President Taylor and the Twelve suggested that one thousand cows and five thousand head of sheep be given to the worthy poor. This was approved unanimously by the conference. In the same spirit, the sisters of the Relief Society approved loaning thirty-four thousand bushels of wheat that had been stored to the needy until after the harvest. Citing these examples of generosity, President Taylor then urged the Saints to forgive debts owed one another: "We respectfully remind those who have the riches of this world more abundantly bestowed upon them, that they have a fitting opportunity of remembering the Lord's poor. If you hold their notes and they are unable to pay, forgive the interest and the principal, or as much thereof as you might desire them to forgive were their and your circumstances reversed; thus doing unto others as you would that others should do unto you. For upon this hang the law and the prophets" (James R. Clark, comp., *Messages of the First Presidency of The Church of Jesus Christ of Latter-day Saints,* 2:329).

The First Presidency was reorganized on 10 October 1880. The Saints sustained John Taylor as President, with George Q. Cannon and Joseph F. Smith as counselors. President Taylor asked that Aaronic and Melchizedek Priesthood bearers sustain the First Presidency quorum by quorum in a solemn assembly, a practice that continues to this day.

In 1881, persecution against the Church began to intensify. Congress passed a series of laws that disenfranchised, fined, and/or imprisoned all Saints who believed in or practiced plural marriage. Saints in some areas were so greatly abused that President Taylor advised them to relocate to Canada or Mexico. Several hundred families eventually formed colonies in these countries.

Organizing the Priesthood

On 13 October 1882, in Salt Lake City, President Taylor received a revelation directing the appointment of certain brethren to fill vacancies in the Quorum of the Twelve and the First Seven Presidents of the Seventy. The Lord also instructed priesthood bearers concerning their responsibilities and issued a call for the Saints to purify themselves in order to be found worthy of his blessings and protection.

> Thus saith the Lord to the Twelve, and to the Priesthood and people of my Church: Let my servants George Teasdale and Heber J. Grant be appointed to fill the vacancies in the Twelve, that you may be fully organized and prepared for the labors devolving upon you, for you have a great work to perform; and then proceed to fill up the presiding quorum of Seventies, and assist in organizing that body of my Priesthood who are your co-laborers in the ministry. You may appoint Seymour B. Young to fill up the vacancy in the presiding quorum of Seventies, if he will conform to my law; for it is not meet that men who will not abide my law shall preside over my Priesthood; and then proceed forthwith and call to your aid any assistance that you may require from among

The First Presidency and the Quorum of the Twelve in the 1880s

the Seventies to assist you in your labors in introducing and maintaining the Gospel among the Lamanites throughout the land. And then let High Priests be selected, under the direction of the First Presidency, to preside over the various organizations that shall exist among this people; that those who receive the Gospel may be taught in the doctrines of my Church and in the ordinances and laws thereof, and also in the things pertaining to my Zion and my Kingdom, saith the Lord, that they may be one with you in my Church and my Kingdom.

Let the Presidency of my Church be one in all things; and let the Twelve also be one in all things; and let them all be one with me as I am one with the Father.

And let the High Priests organize themselves, and purify themselves, and prepare themselves for this labor, and for all other labors that they may be called upon to fulfil.

And let the Presidents of Stakes also purify themselves, and the Priesthood and people of the Stakes over which they preside, and organize the Priesthood in their various Stakes according to my law, in all the various departments thereof, in the High Councils, in the Elders Quorums, and in the Bishops and their Councils, and in the Quorums of Priests, Teachers and Deacons; that every Quorum may be fully organized according to the order of my Church; and, then, let them inquire into the standing and fellowship of all that hold my Holy Priesthood in their several Stakes; and if they find those that are unworthy let them remove them, except they repent; for my Priesthood, whom I have called and whom I have sustained and honored, shall honor me and obey my laws, and the laws of my Holy Priesthood, or they shall not be considered worthy to hold my Priesthood, saith the Lord. And let my Priesthood humble themselves before me, and seek not their own will but my will; for if my Priesthood whom I have chosen, and called, and endowed with the spirit and gifts of their several callings, and with the powers thereof, do not acknowledge me I will not acknowledge them, saith the Lord; for I will be honored and obeyed by my Priesthood. And, then, I call upon my Priesthood, and upon all of my people to repent of all their sins and shortcomings, of their covetousness and pride and self will, and of all their iniquities wherein they sin against me; and to seek with all humility to fulfil my law, as my Priesthood, my Saints, and my people; and I call upon the heads of families to put their houses in order according to the law of God, and attend to the various duties and responsibilities associated therewith, and to purify themselves before me, and to purge out iniquity from their households. And I will bless and be with you, saith the Lord; and ye shall gather together in your holy places wherein ye assemble to call upon me, and ye shall ask for such things as are right, and I will hear your prayers, and my Spirit and power shall be with you, and my blessing shall rest upon you, upon your families, your dwellings and your households, upon your flocks and herds and fields, your orchards and vineyards, and upon all that pertains to you; and you

shall be my people and I will be your God; and your enemies shall not have dominion over you, for I will preserve you and confound them, saith the Lord, and they shall not have power nor dominion over you; for my word shall go forth, and my work shall be accomplished, and my Zion shall be established, and my rule and my power and my dominion shall prevail among my people, and all nations shall yet acknowledge me. Even so, Amen. [Clark, *Messages,* 2:347–49]

On the Organization of the Seventies

At a meeting of the First Presidency of the Church and the councils of the Twelve Apostles and the First Seven Presidents of the Seventies, on Saturday, 14 April 1883, President Taylor presented some organizational changes for the seventies quorums as outlined in a letter addressed to the two latter quorums the previous day:

In the organization of these quorums in October, 1844, there were ten quorums, each provided with seven presidents, which presidents constituted the First Quorum of Seventies, and of which the First Seven Presidents of the Seventies

were members, and over which they presided. But as the Seventies have greatly increased, these regulations will not apply to the present circumstances; and furthermore, the First Quorum, according to the present organization, has not acted in a quorum capacity, but it would seem there are duties devolving upon its members, as a quorum, that may require their official action.

The First Quorum of Seventies may be composed of the First Seven Presidents of the Seventies, and the senior president of the first sixty-four quorums. These may form the Seventy referred to in the Book of Doctrine and Covenants, and may act in an official capacity as the First Quorum of Seventies.

The senior presidents of the other quorums, over and above the sixty-four, may meet with the First Quorum in their assemblies in any other than an official capacity; but in case of the absence of any of the members of the First Quorum, they can act in the place of such members with the First Quorum during such absence, in any cases of importance that may arise. [Clark, *Messages,* 2:353]

The First Presidency, 1880, left to right: George Q. Cannon, John Taylor, and Joseph F. Smith

John Taylor's Salt Lake City home

His recommendations were unanimously approved by all present.

Then in answer to President Taylor's prayer, "Show unto us Thy will, O Lord, concerning the organization of the seventies" (Clark, *Messages,* 2:354), the following revelation was received:

> What ye have written is my will, and is acceptable unto me: and furthermore,
>
> Thus saith the Lord unto the First Presidency, unto the Twelve, unto the Seventies and unto all my holy Priesthood, let not your hearts be troubled, neither be ye concerned about the management and organization of my Church and Priesthood and the accomplishment of my work. Fear me and observe my laws and I will reveal unto you, from time to time, through the channels that I have appointed, everything that shall be necessary for the future development and perfection of my Church, for the adjustment and rolling forth of my kingdom, and for the building up and the establishment of my Zion. For ye are my Priesthood and I am your God. Even so. Amen. [Clark, *Messages,* 2:354]

The following year, 1884, on 17 May, President Taylor dedicated the Logan Temple, one of his few public appearances during this period. Persecution had increased so greatly since 1881 that the First Presidency felt it wise to withdraw from public view to continue their labors. In his last public address on 1 February 1885, President Taylor urged the Saints "to fear God, to observe His laws, and keep His commandments, and the Lord will manage all the rest" (*Journal of Discourses,* 26:156). (This era of persecution will be discussed in greater detail in the next chapter.)

For the next two and one-half years, President Taylor directed the affairs of the Church from the homes of Saints in Salt Lake and Davis Counties. He died in Kaysville, 25 July 1887, at the age of seventy-eight. His passing was a cause of great sorrow for the Saints. The ordeal of the Martyrdom—having shed his blood with Joseph and Hyrum—and the circumstances of his death—in hiding, a reward posted for his capture—caused the Saints to consider him a "double martyr" (see Roberts, *Comprehensive History,* 6:188). On one occasion he stated: "So far as I am concerned, I say, let everything come as God has ordained it. I do not desire trials; I do not desire affliction.... But if the earthquake bellows, the lightnings flash, the thunders roll, and the powers of darkness are let loose, and the spirit of evil is permitted to rage, and an evil influence is brought to bear on the Saints, and my life, with theirs, is put to the test; let it come, for we are the Saints of the most High God, and all is well, all is peace, all is right, and we be, both in time and in eternity" (*Journal of Discourses,* 5:114–15).

STUDY QUESTIONS

1. How did John Taylor's youth help him prepare for his ministry?

2. Why were John and Leonora Taylor successful in their quest for truth?

3. What helped to make John Taylor a "champion of liberty"?

4. How has the Lord's promise in the 1883 revelation about the seventies been fulfilled in recent years?

The Logan Temple

AN ERA OF PERSECUTION

THE years between Brigham Young's death in 1877 and Utah's statehood in 1896 were marked by important events that have had a lasting influence upon the Church. Presidents John Taylor and Wilford Woodruff, continuing President Young's efforts, established more than a hundred settlements in Utah, Wyoming, Nevada, Arizona, Mexico, and Canada; organized the first Primary; added the Pearl of Great Price to the canon of Church scripture; began a weekday religious instruction program; founded Church academies; and completed the Salt Lake Temple. Overshadowing these events, however, a national legislative and judicial crusade against the Church sought to end the Saints' practice of plural marriage. Before it ran its course, this crusade abolished the Latter-day Saints' right to self-government and destroyed the Church's ability to function as a legal organization, with much of its property confiscated by the government. These measures at first greatly slowed its temporal and spiritual progress and ultimately threatened its destruction. Only the intervention of the Lord saved the Church.

HIGHLIGHTS

1877 Aug. 29: Brigham Young dies.

1878 Aug. 11: Aurelia S. Rogers organizes a Primary at Farmington, Utah. Zion's Central Board of Trade is established.

1876–79 The Saints establish more than one hundred settlements in Utah, Wyoming, Nevada, and Arizona.

1879 Jan. 6: The United States Supreme Court decision in the Reynolds case upholds the constitutionality of the Morrill Anti-Bigamy Act of 1862.

1880 Apr.: The Council of the Twelve announces a jubilee year.

Oct.: The First Presidency is reorga-

nized: John Taylor, George Q. Cannon, and Joseph F. Smith.

The Pearl of Great Price is accepted as one of the standard works at general conference.

1882 Mar. 22: The Edmunds Act, making "unlawful cohabitation" a crime, is signed into law.

1884 The Cane Creek Massacre in Tennessee occurs; two missionaries are killed.

1885 The Saints establish a colony in the state of Chihuahua, Mexico.

1885 John Taylor goes into "retirement."

1886 The Saints found a settlement in Alberta, Canada.

1887 Mar. 3: The Edmunds-Tucker Act, disincorporating the Corporation of the President, becomes law without the president's signature.

July 25: President John Taylor dies at Kaysville, Utah.

1888 Stake boards of education are established.

1889 Apr.: The First Presidency is reorganized: Wilford Woodruff, George Q. Cannon, Joseph F. Smith.

1890 Sept. 24: The "Manifesto" announces discontinuation of the practice of plural marriage.

Oct. 25: Weekday religion classes are instituted.

1893 Apr. 6: President Woodruff dedicates the Salt Lake Temple.

1896 Utah achieves statehood.

HISTORICAL SUMMARY

Beginnings of Plural Marriage

The practice of plural marriage could have been revealed as early as 1831 while the Prophet Joseph Smith revised the Bible. While reading the biblical account of the lives of Abraham, Isaac, and Jacob, the young Prophet may have wondered why

some of the ancient patriarchs were permitted to have more than one wife. Certainly a question such as this one prompted the Lord's reply in Doctrine and Covenants 132: "Because this was the law... and in nothing did they sin save in those things which they received not of me" (verses 34, 38). Although the revelation that introduced the principle was not recorded until July 1843, plural marriage was practiced in a limited way some time prior to that. Strong prejudice from within and the prospect of increased persecution from without the Church dictated a policy of secrecy when the practice was first introduced. However, as rumors spread, self-aggrandizing men took advantage of the situation to commit adultery. The issue became the source of much bitterness when some prominent men in Nauvoo—John C. Bennett, William and Wilson Law, Charles and Francis Higbee, and Charles Foster—were severed from the Church for immorality. Antagonism over this issue led to the publication and subsequent destruction of the *Nauvoo Expositor* and contributed directly to Joseph Smith's last imprisonment and death.

The Church publicly announced plural marriage as a practice on 29 August 1852. The practice received increasing opposition from the non-Mormon population of the United States. Along with false charges of political wrongdoing by Brigham Young and the Latter-day Saints, plural marriage became the focal point of an intense legislative campaign against the Church. In 1856, one of the planks in the platform of the newly formed Republican Party promised to eradicate "those twin relics of barbarism—Polygamy, and Slavery" (quoted in Richard D. Poll, "The Mormon Question Enters National Politics, 1850–56," *Utah Historical Quarterly*, 25:127).

Legal Persecution Begins

Although preoccupied with the slavery question for several years, Congress passed the first antipolygamy legislation, the Morrill Anti-Bigamy Act, in 1862. This bill defined bigamy as the act of remarrying when one already had a living husband or wife. The Morrill law punished bigamy with a five-hundred-dollar fine and five-year imprisonment. However, inadequate provisions for enforcement made the law ineffectual. Most Latter-day Saints considered the law to be an interference with their free exercise of religion and therefore unconstitutional.

After the Civil War, the Latter-day Saint practice of plural marriage received increasing attention. In 1874, Congress enacted the Poland Act, which removed the probate courts in Utah from local jurisdiction (most polygamy cases had been tried in the probate courts, and many of the probate judges were bishops and thus sympathetic to plural marriage), abolished the offices of territorial marshal and attorney general, and assigned their duties to federally appointed officers. Although the bill placed much of the legal machinery for prosecuting polygamy cases in the hands of non-Mormons, so long as juries were composed of Latter-day Saints, the law proved ineffective.

Throughout these years, Church leaders remained confident that the Supreme Court of the United States would find the antipolygamy legislation in violation of the religious guaranties of the Constitution. However, on 6 January 1879, in a case involving the late President Young's secretary, George Reynolds, the high court ruled that every government has a right to determine the form of marriage within its jurisdiction and that the laws enacted against the practice of plural marriage were constitutional. As a result of that decision Elder Reynolds was sent to prison.

The Supreme Court decision in the Reynolds case gave opponents of Mormonism renewed vigor, and more radical legislation against the Church followed. In 1882, the Edmunds Act was signed into law. This bill defined polygamy as a crime and made it easier to prosecute an individual by declaring that the mere act of living

Looking southeast along Main Street, Salt Lake City, about 1880

with more than one wife (termed "unlawful cohabitation") was illegal and punishable by fine and imprisonment. Further, anyone who practiced plural marriage or even believed in it was excluded from jury duty, and the right to vote or hold public office was denied him. One of the things particularly galling to the Saints was the fact that this law applied only in the territories of the United States and not in the states themselves. This legislation was obviously aimed only at the Mormons and not motivated by any real commitment to moral issues.

After the Edmunds Act was declared constitutional by the Supreme Court in a monumental decision in March 1885, prosecution of the Latter-day Saints who practiced polygamy began in earnest. Known as the period of "the raid," the next several years saw more than one thousand Latter-day Saints imprisoned on charges of polygamy and unlawful cohabitation. At times, law enforcement became a complete farce. Novel ways of interpreting the Edmunds Law were employed. Persons were convicted of crime for ordinary acts of association and courtesy, and it appeared that nothing short of complete abandonment of one's family would satisfy the law. At one point, single instances of living with one's plural wife were "segregated" as separate offenses, each of which drew the full penalty of the law—a three-hundred-dollar fine and six months' imprisonment. By this means, it became possible for federal officers to imprison a person for life and require a continual payment of fines to satisfy the law. Furthermore, constitutional guarantees protecting a person from unreasonable searches and seizures were violated. Hunting "cohabs" (those involved in "unlawful cohabitation") became a lucrative employment in Utah. Children were stopped by strangers and questioned about the activities of their parents. Under the guise of peddlers, tramps, or tourists, deputies flooded the countryside, and at night prowlers peered in people's windows or lurked in the shadows to gather convicting information. In the face of this onslaught, many family men went into hiding rather than submit to the unprincipled enforcement of the law. President John Taylor went into "retirement" on 1 February 1885, and was not seen again publicly by the Saints before he died in July 1887. During this time, general conferences were held away from Salt Lake City, and messages of the First Presidency were read in their absence.

Prosecution vs. Persecution

The following First Presidency letter, dated 4 April 1885, was read to the Saints assembled in general conference on that same date. For reasons set forth in the letter, members of the Presidency were not present at the conference. In it is the eloquent defense of why the Church was resisting the law seemingly in contradiction to the twelfth article of faith.

BELOVED BRETHREN AND SISTERS: It is eminently proper under the circumstances, not being able to be with you in person at our Annual Conference, that we should address you a few lines and express to you our faith, feelings and hopes concerning the great work of our God in which we are mutually interested. Never at any time in our lives have we had more joy and satisfaction in

the Gospel, and in the labors thereof, than we have at the present time. Profoundly grateful to our God for His kindness to us in permitting us to have a name and a place among His people, and to be the bearers of His everlasting Priesthood, we are determined with His help to press forward with increased diligence and zeal in doing our part towards the carrying on of His purposes and work. We see His hand marvelously manifested in behalf of His people. We know that His power is with us, that His angels have charge concerning us, and that no affliction can fall upon any one, however humble, without it being fully known to Him. This knowledge that God is near to us and hears and answers our prayers, is an unceasing cause of thankfulness and praise. For a wise purpose in His providence He permits the wicked, in the exercise of their agency, from time to time to afflict His followers. Since the days of our father Adam this has always been the case, and it will continue to be, so long as Satan has any power over the hearts of the children of men. We are all children of the same Great Parent, and each one has the opportunity and privilege granted to him or her to exercise his or her agency. We have chosen to serve the God of Israel. We have

submitted to His laws, have obeyed His Gospel, and have chosen the path which He assures us will bring us into His presence. Others of His children prefer a different course. They yield to a different influence, and under its power, they seek to destroy the work of God and all who are connected with it. This they can do in the exercise of the agency which the Father has given unto them. Not only in times past, but in our own day, the wicked have persecuted, tormented and murdered the Saints of God. But, while in so doing, they bring upon themselves everlasting condemnation, their acts are overruled for the glory and exaltation of His faithful people, and the accomplishment of His purposes in the redemption of the earth.

For a few months past we have seen in these valleys an exhibition of this deadly hostility against the Latter-day Saints. We need not enumerate to you all these acts of oppression and wrong. You are familiar with them. But the best men in the community, men of pure lives, men who have set an example to the people ever since they came to these mountains, and in all their days, who have led in works of righteousness, who have been citizens of the highest type of character, have been selected as victims of a

A polygamous family

vile persecution, and been assailed and denounced as criminals of the lowest grade. Juries have been selected for the express purpose of convicting men who are prominent in the Church; and their partisan bias has become so thoroughly known in the community, that the common expression is, that an accusation in the courts, as now constituted, is equivalent to a conviction. The rule of jurisprudence which has come down for ages past has been, that the accused shall be deemed innocent until proved guilty. In our courts, we are sorry to say, this has been reversed. The burden of proof has rested upon the accused in almost every instance—the judge, the jury, equally with the prosecution, appearing to view him as guilty, and that it was his duty to furnish all the proof necessary to exculpate him from the accusation of guilt....

... Indictments have been found against different parties upon the flimsiest evidence, and in some instances upon evidence which would have no weight with any fair-minded jury. The result has been that a reign of terror has prevailed and still prevails in these valleys. Seeing no prospect of fair trial, men have deemed it better to avoid arrest for a season, or until there was a prospect of receiving impartial treatment by the courts and juries. Prosecution has degenerated into persecution. A law which is in and of itself, as we believe, unconstitutional, and aimed at the practice of religion, and so viewed by a number of our leading statesmen in Congress, is taken advantage of and carried to lengths probably never dreamed of by many of the men who voted for it. We have sometimes thought that it was impossible for men to indulge in such vindictive feelings as have been manifested here; but in searching for a cause we have been forced to the conclusion that these violent prosecutions were only intended to provoke the people to commit some overt act whereby the incoming administration might be embarrassed....

The question has been asked us, how long we intend to pursue this course. In answer we say, that at no time during our existence have we ever shrunk from the investigation of our conduct, our utterances or of our lives by any fair tribunal. We have lived under the gaze of the public, and where every act and expression could be scrutinized. We are as ready today, as ever, to submit our cases to a properly organized court and jury of our peers, to decide upon. So confident are we of our innocence of alleged wrongdoing, that we entertain no fears of the result of such a trial. We are willing to meet the issue at any moment. We are fully conscious of our innocence of all violation of the laws of God or of Constitutional laws enacted by man. But if there are laws made to entrap us, because of our belief in and practice of the revelations which God has given to His Church, which a court and jury shall decide we have violated, we desire at least that it shall be upon what all the world calls good evidence and substantial proof, and not upon religious prejudice, and through a determination to convict and punish, evidence or no evidence. We ought, at least, to have the same rights that burglars, thieves and murderers are accorded under the law. In that case, should conviction follow, we should submit to it as martyrs have submitted in every age when God has had a people upon the earth as persecution inflicted upon us for our adherence to His laws....

In conclusion, we solemnly testify to the Latter-day Saints and to the world, as we have done so often in the past, that God has established His Zion, and His work will roll forth, and that all those who fight against it will perish. You have seen this fulfilled to the letter in the past.

We pray God, the Eternal Father, to bless you in your families, in your fields, and flocks and herds, and in your business and in all your righteous undertakings, and to preserve you from the hands of all your enemies, and to eventually save and exalt you in His Celestial Kingdom, in the name of Jesus Christ, our Savior and Redeemer. Amen. [James R. Clark, comp., *Messages of the First Presidency of The Church of Jesus Christ of Latter-day Saints*, 3:4–8, 12]

Obedience to Law

This First Presidency letter, read in their absence to the general conference of the Church, 6 October 1885, presented another justification for the

The old Utah State Prison, located in Sugarhouse, about 1880 (by C. R. Savage)

Church's stand against the anti-polygamy laws. As the letter points out, even when the statutes were out of harmony with the Constitution, the Church was willing to submit to these laws and have them tested in fair and impartial councils. Such impartiality was lacking in the persecutors' treatment of the Saints, however.

Speaking concerning law, the Lord, in a revelation given through the Prophet Joseph, Aug. 6, 1833, says:

4. And now, verily, I say unto you concerning the laws of the land, it is my will that my people should observe to do all things whatsoever I command them;

5. And the law of the land which is constitutional, supporting that principle of freedom in maintaining rights and privileges, belongs to all mankind, and is justifiable before me;

6. Therefore I, the Lord, justify you, and your brethren of my church, in befriending that law which is the constitutional law of the land;

7. And as pertaining to law of man, whatsoever is more or less than these cometh of evil.

8. I, the Lord God, make you free, therefore ye are free indeed; and the law also maketh you free;

9. Nevertheless, when the wicked rule the people mourn.

10. Wherefore, honest men and wise men should be sought for diligently, and good men and wise men ye should observe to uphold otherwise; whatsoever is less than these cometh of evil.

11. And I give unto you a commandment, that ye shall forsake all evil and cleave unto all good, that ye shall live by every word which proceedeth forth out of the mouth of God;

12. For he will give unto the faithful line upon line, precept upon precept; and I will try you and prove you herewith;

13. And whoso layeth down his life in my cause, for my name's sake, shall find it again, even life eternal;

14. Therefore be not afraid of your enemies, for I have decreed in my heart, saith the Lord, that I will prove you in all things, whether you will abide in my covenant even unto death, that you may be found worthy;

15. For if ye will not abide in my covenant, ye are not worthy of me.

Fifty-two years have passed since this was given to the Church, and we are now witnessing its fulfillment. The Saints are required to do whatsoever the Lord commands them, to live by every word which proceedeth forth out of the mouth of God. They are also instructed to befriend every constitutional law of the land; for such laws support the principle of freedom; they maintain rights and privileges. This, as a people, we have striven to do from the beginning of our organization. We have ever been a law-abiding people. Times without number we have suffered the most grievous wrong without resenting them. We have ever thought it better to suffer wrong than to do wrong. . . .

We are expressly commanded, and it becomes our duty, to uphold and sustain every law of the land which is constitutional; we have always had a strong desire to obey such laws, and to play ourselves in harmony with all the institutions of the country. . . .

Nor have we the least desire to shun the consequences of our acts in their relationship to the laws to which we refer, providing there were any assurance that our cases would be submitted to a fair and just adjudication. Events of the past few months give no ground for hope that such treatment would be accorded. It must be contended, however, that as stated elsewhere, connected with this disposition to have our conduct passed upon as provided by law administered in the genius of justice, there never can be any hope of our yielding up, under any circumstances, a principle of conscientious or religious conviction. Were we to make such a surrender, our conduct in that respect would not be in harmony with the guaranties of the Constitution, which we are in duty bound to uphold. . . .

Notwithstanding all that we are now passing through, our hearts are filled with joy and peace. We can truly say, Hosannah to God in the highest. We know that Zion will not be overthrown or be made desolate. Every promise made concerning Zion by the Almighty will be fulfilled. The only thing which ever disturbs our serenity is the report of wrongdoing by those who are called Latter-day Saints. [Clark, *Messages*, 3:28–30, 41]

In 1887, Congress enacted the Edmunds-Tucker Act, which added further to the plight of the Church. This law dissolved the Church as a legal corporation, abolished women's suffrage in Utah, provided that a test oath rejecting plural marriage be administered to all voters as a condition for voting, and provided for a federal receiver to confiscate Church property in excess of $50,000 not used exclusively for worship.

A direct effort to destroy the temporal power of the Church, the enactment of the Edmunds-Tucker Act brought added pressure to an already difficult situation. Almost every Mormon male of any distinction was in prison or hiding, and many women were also forced to flee their homes. The economy stagnated and businesses were abandoned or limped along under inexperienced management. The Church, which had always been a central factor in the stimulation of the Saints' economy, was forced out of this activity when it was needed most. In addition, the expenses of the Church were now greater than usual, and income was much less. Under the mounting debt, the Church found it increasingly difficult to fulfill its missionary, educational, charitable, and business responsibilities. Twice during these years, antagonism against the Saints in America flared into violence, resulting in the deaths of three missionaries and two investigators. It appeared that the warning of one of the judges would be fulfilled: "The will of the American people is expressed, (severely) and this law will go on and grind you and your institution to powder" (quoted in *Deseret News Weekly*, 21 Oct. 1885, p. 625).

"Naturalization Hearings" Revelation

During the political struggle between the Liberal (anti-Mormon) and People's (Mormon) parties for control of the municipal governments of Ogden and Salt Lake City in the election of 1890, both sides sought to increase their ranks by the naturalization of aliens. In cases involving Latter-day Saint aliens before the United States Third District Court, questions were raised regarding the endowment ceremony and the loyalty of Church members. In the hearings that ensued, Church attorneys asked the First Presidency how proper it would be to make statements in court about the endowment ceremony and about instructions that had been given discontinuing the solemnization of plural marriages. The

President Wilford Woodruff

question was taken to President Woodruff, who made it a matter of prayer, and on 24 November 1889, he dictated the following revelation to his clerk, L. John Nuttall:

Thus saith the Lord to my servant Wilford, I the Lord have heard thy prayer and thy request, and will answer thee by the voice of my Spirit. Thus saith the Lord, unto my servants, the Presidency of my Church, who hold the keys of the Kingdom of God on the earth. I the Lord hold the destiny of the Courts in your midst, and the destiny of this nation, and all other nations of the earth in mine own hands; all that I have

revealed, and promised and decreed concerning the generation in which you live, shall come to pass, and no power shall stay my hand. Let not my servants who are called to the Presidency of my Church, deny my word or my law, which concerns the salvation of the children of men. Let them pray for the Holy Spirit, which shall be given them, to guide them in their acts. Place not yourselves in jeopardy to your enemies by promise; your enemies seek your destruction and the destruction of my people. If the Saints will hearken unto my voice, and the counsel of my servants, the wicked shall not prevail. Let my servants, who officiate as your Counselors before the Courts, make their pleadings as they are moved upon by the Holy Spirit, without any further pledges from the Priesthood, and they shall be justified. I the Lord will hold the Courts, with the officers of government, and the nation responsible for their acts towards the inhabitants of Zion. I, Jesus Christ, the savior of the world, am in your midst. I am your advocate with the Father. Fear not little flock, it is your Father's good pleasure to give you the Kingdom. Fear not the wicked and ungodly. Search the Scriptures, for they are they which testify of me; also those revelations which I have given to my Servant Joseph, and to all my Servants since the world began, which are recorded in the records of divine truth. Those revelations contain the judgments of God, which are to be poured out upon all nations under the heavens, which include great babylon. These judgments are at the door, they will be fulfilled as God lives. Leave judgment with me, it is mine saith the Lord. Watch the signs of the times, and they will show the fulfillment of the words of the Lord. Let my servants call upon the Lord in mighty prayer, retain the Holy Ghost as your constant companion, and act as you are moved upon by that spirit, and all will be well with you. The wicked are fast ripening in iniquity, and they will be cut off by the judgments of God. Great events await you and this generation, and are nigh at your doors. Awake, O

The First Presidency at the dedication of the Salt Lake Temple, 1893, left to right: George Q. Cannon, Wilford Woodruff, and Joseph F. Smith (courtesy of the Utah Historical Society)

Israel, and have faith in God, and His promises, and He will not forsake you. I, the Lord will deliver my Saints from the dominion of the wicked, in mine own due time and way. I cannot deny my word, neither in blessings nor judgments. Therefore let mine anointed gird up their loins, watch and be sober, and keep my commandments. Pray always and faint not; exercise faith in the Lord and in the promises of God; be valiant in the testimony of Jesus Christ. The eyes of the Lord and the Heavenly Hosts are watching over you and your acts. Therefore be faithful until I come. I come quickly, to reward every man according with deeds done in the body. Even so, Amen. [Clark, *Messages*, 3:175–76]

The Lord Intervenes

In July 1887, upon President Taylor's death, Wilford Woodruff and the Twelve presided over the Church. In April 1889, he was sustained as President of the Church. For weeks and months, President Woodruff "wrestled mightily" over the problems facing the Church. Then, on 25 September 1890, four months after the Supreme Court had upheld the constitutionality of the Edmunds-Tucker Act, President Woodruff submitted for publication to the world the "Official Declaration," which proclaimed the end of plural marriage by the Church (see Official Declaration – 1, which follows the last section of the Doctrine and Covenants). He wrote that day in his diary, "I have arrived at a point in the history of my life as the President of The Church of Jesus Christ of Latter-day Saints where I am under the necessity of acting for the temporal salvation of the Church. The United States government has taken a stand and passed laws to destroy the Latter-day Saints on the subject of polygamy or patriarchal order of marriage, and after praying to the Lord and feeling inspired by his spirit, I have issued the following proclamation, which is sustained by my counselors and the Twelve Apostles" (Diary of Wilford Woodruff, 25 September 1890, Historical Department, The Church of Jesus Christ of Latter-day Saints, Salt Lake City; spelling and punctuation modernized). This action brought relief from the oppression that weighed so heavily upon the Church.

Some of the Saints expressed surprise that the Lord would be influenced by the pressures and persecutions of evil men. President Woodruff, speaking on the subject of revelation at the Cache Stake conference, in Logan, Utah, on 1 November 1891, gave more detail about how he had come to issue the Manifesto. After referring to the inspiration that attended Brigham Young, he continued:

"And whatsoever they shall speak when moved upon by the Holy Ghost shall be Scripture, shall be the will of the Lord, shall be the mind of the Lord, shall be the word of the Lord, shall be the voice of the Lord, and the power of God unto salvation." [D&C 68:4]

It is by that power that we have led Israel. By that power President Young presided over and led the Church. By the same power President John Taylor presided over and led the Church. And that is the way I have acted, according to the best of my ability, in that capacity. I do not want the Latter-day Saints to understand that the Lord is not with us, and that He is not giving revelation to us; for He is giving us revelation, and will give us revelation until this scene is wound up.

I have had some revelations of late, and very important ones to me, and I will tell you what the Lord has said to me. Let me bring your minds to what is termed the manifesto. The

Lord has told me by revelation that there are many members of the Church throughout Zion who are sorely tried in their hearts because of that manifesto, and also because of the testimony of the Presidency of this Church and the Apostles before the Master in Chancery. Since I received that revelation I have heard of many who are tried in these things, though I had not heard of any before that, particularly. Now, the Lord has commanded me to do one thing, and I fulfilled that commandment at the conference at Brigham City last Sunday, and I will do the same here today. The Lord has told me to ask the Latter-day Saints a question, and He also told me that if they would listen to what I said to them and answer the question put to them, by the spirit and power of God, they would all answer alike with regard to this matter. The question is this: Which is the wisest course for the Latter-day Saints to pursue—to continue to attempt to practice plural marriage with the laws of the nation against it and the opposition of sixty millions of people, and at the cost of the confiscation and loss of all the Temples, and the stopping of all the ordinances therein, both for the living and the dead, and the imprisonment of the First Presidency and Twelve and the head of families in the Church, and the confiscation of personal property of the people (all

of which of themselves would stop the practice), or after doing and suffering what we have through our adherence to this principle to cease the practice and submit to the law, and through doing so leave the Prophets, Apostles, and fathers at home, so that they can instruct the people and attend to the duties of the Church, and also leave the Temples in the hands of the Saints, so that they can attend to the ordinances of the Gospel, both for the living and the dead?

The Lord showed me by vision and revelation exactly what would take place if we did not stop this practice. If we had not stopped it, you would have had no use for Brother Merrill, for Brother Edlefsen, for Brother Roskelley, for Brother Leishman, or for any of the men in this temple at Logan; for all ordinances would be stopped throughout the land of Zion. Confusion would reign throughout Israel, and many men would be made prisoners. This trouble would have come upon the whole Church, and we should have been compelled to stop the practice. Now, the question is, whether it should be stopped in this manner, or in the way the Lord has manifested to us, and leave our Prophets and Apostles and fathers free men, and the temples in the hands of the people, so that the dead may be redeemed. A large

President Joseph F. Smith and his family

number has already been delivered from the prison house in the spirit world by this people, and shall the work go on or stop? This is the question I lay before the Latter-day Saints. You have to judge for yourselves. I shall not answer it; but I say to you that that is exactly the condition we as a people would have been in had we not taken the course we have.

I know there are a good many men, and probably some leading men, in this Church who have been tried and felt as though President Woodruff had lost the Spirit of God and was about to apostatize. Now, I want you to understand that he has not lost the Spirit, nor is he about to apostatize. He has told me exactly what to do, and what the result would be if we did not do it. I have been called upon by friends outside of the Church and urged to take some steps with regard to this matter. They knew the course which the Government were determined to take. This feeling has also been manifested more or less by members of the Church. I saw exactly what would come to pass if there was not something done. I have had this spirit upon me for a long time. But I want to say this: I should have let all the temples go out of our hands; I should have gone to prison myself, and let every other man go there, had not the God of heaven commanded me to do what I did do; and when the hour came that I was commanded to do that, it was all clear to me. I went before the Lord, and I wrote what the Lord told me to write. I laid it before my brethren—such strong men as Brother Geo. Q. Cannon, Brother Jos. F. Smith, and the Twelve Apostles. I might as well undertake to turn an army with banners out of its course as to turn them out of a course that they considered to be right. These men agreed with me, and ten thousand Latter-day Saints also agreed with me. Why? Because they were moved upon by the Spirit of God and by the revelations of Jesus Christ to do it. [Clark, *Messages*, 3:225–27]

Ever since the Lord's revelation to President Wilford Woodruff, the Presi-

dents of the Church have consistently admonished the Saints not to engage in plural marriage. On this subject, President Smith submitted the following statement to the April 1904 general conference of the Church:

Inasmuch as there are numerous reports in circulation that plural marriages have been entered into contrary to the official declaration of President Woodruff, of September 26, 1890, commonly called the Manifesto, which was issued by President Woodruff and adopted by the Church at its general conference, October 6, 1890, which forbade any marriages violative of the law of the land; I, Joseph F. Smith, President of the Church of Jesus Christ of Latter-day Saints, hereby affirm and declare that no such marriages have been solemnized with the sanction, consent or knowledge of the Church of Jesus Christ of Latter-day Saints, and

I hereby announce that all such marriages are prohibited, and if any officer or member of the Church shall assume to solemnize or enter into any such marriage he will be deemed in transgression against the Church and will be liable to be dealt with, according to the rules and regulations thereof, and excommunicated therefrom. [In Conference Report, Apr. 1904, p. 75]

President Francis M. Lyman, President of the Council of the Twelve, presented a resolution of endorsement to the conference, which carried unanimously (see Conference Report, Apr. 1904, p. 76).

In his opening address at the October 1974 conference, President Kimball declared:

We warn you against the so-called polygamy cults which would lead you astray. Remember the Lord brought an end to this program many decades ago through a prophet who proclaimed the revelation to the world. People are abroad who will deceive you and bring you much sorrow and remorse. Have nothing to do with those who would lead you astray. It is wrong and sinful to ignore the Lord when he speaks. He has spoken—strongly

and conclusively. [In Conference Report, Oct. 1974, p. 5; or *Ensign*, Nov. 1974, p. 5]

With the announcement of the "Manifesto" the persecution against the Latter-day Saints began to ease. At first federal officials were still suspicious of the Church's motives for ending the practice of plural marriage, but time proved the sincerity of the Saints' action. In January 1893 Benjamin Harrison, United States president, issued amnesty to all who had complied with the law since the "Manifesto," and President Grover Cleveland issued a more general amnesty in September 1894. In 1896 Utah finally became a state in the Union, allowing the citizens of Utah to govern themselves and thus eliminating many of the problems associated with unsympathetic federally-appointed territorial officials.

The Church financial problems began to ease when the Church property confiscated under the Edmunds-Tucker Act was returned in 1896. The Saints' weighty financial problems were not fully resolved, however, until the administrations of Presidents Lorenzo Snow and Joseph F. Smith.

STUDY QUESTIONS

1. Why could the First Presidency say during these times of terrible persecution for polygamy, "Never at any time in our lives have we had more joy and satisfaction in the Gospel, and in the labors thereof, than we have at the present time"? (p. 55).

2. Why did the Church feel justified in resisting the antipolygamy laws passed by Congress during this time? What is the standard given by the Lord?

3. What specifically did President Woodruff counsel the Saints to do in the "Official Declaration" (see immediately following the last section of the Doctrine and Covenants)? Why?

4. Did the Church suspend plural marriage because the leaders did not have the courage to face persecution?

WILFORD WOODRUFF

UPON the death of John Taylor in 1887, the leadership of the Church fell upon the Council of the Twelve Apostles, with eighty-year-old Wilford Woodruff presiding. At the time he became President of the Church in 1889, Wilford Woodruff had been in the quorum of the Twelve nearly fifty years, having been ordained an Apostle in 1839. He was baptized in 1833 by missionaries tracting in New York. His own commitment to missionary work was lifelong; he served missions in the United States and in England, where in 1840 he and his fellow missionaries brought some eighteen hundred people into the Church over an eight-month period. His interest in the salvation of both the living and the dead led to a manifestation from the spirit world while he served as president of the Saint George Temple in 1877. The work of the temples pressed more and more upon him while President of the Church: the potential loss of the temples under the provisions of the Edmunds-Tucker Act led to the revelation of the "Manifesto" in 1890; the great Salt Lake Temple, the work of forty years, was dedicated in 1893; his questions about the re-

Wilford Woodruff, 1807–1898

demption of the dead brought a change in the policy of sealing or "adopting" in 1894; and that same year the Genealogical Society was organized. His administration would also see Utah's admission to the Union in 1896 and the government's return of the confiscated Church properties, but President Woodruff's overriding concern would still be the salvation of mankind.

HIGHLIGHTS

1807 Mar. 1: Born in Farmington, Hartford County, Connecticut.

1821 Begins work, learning the trade of a miller (14).

1830 Learns from Robert Mason of the restoration of the gospel (23).

1832 Reads of Mormonism in a newspaper article (25).

1833 Baptized into the Church (26).

1834 Participates in the march of Zion's Camp (27).

1834–36 Serves a mission to the southern states (27–29).

1837 Marries Phoebe Carter (30).

1837–38 Serves a mission to the eastern states and to the Fox Islands (30–31).

1839 Becomes a member of the Council of the Twelve (32).

1839–41 Serves a mission to Great Britain (32–34).

1842 Acts as the business manager of the *Times and Seasons* (35).

1843–44 Embarks on a mission to eastern states to raise money for the building of the Nauvoo Temple (36–37).

1844 Serves a mission to the eastern states; learns of the martyrdom of Joseph and Hyrum Smith (37).

1844–46 Presides over the European Mission (37–39).

1847 July 24: Enters the Great Salt Lake Valley with Brigham Young (40).

1848–50 Presides over the Church in the eastern states (41–43).

1850 Appointed to the territorial legislature, serving one term in the lower house and twenty sessions in the upper house (43).

1856 Appointed Church historian (49).

1858–77 Becomes president of the Deseret Agricultural and Manufacturing Society (later the Utah State Fair Board; 51–70).

1867 Participates in the reestablishment of the School of the Prophets (60).

1877 Appointed president of the St. George Temple; sees prominent people of history in vision (70).

1879 Performs missionary work among the Indians while in hiding (72).

1880 Receives two visions while in Arizona (72).

Oct.: Becomes President of the Quorum of the Twelve when the First Presidency is reorganized (73).

1881 Becomes superintendent of the YMMIA (74).

1885–87 Goes into self-imposed exile in St. George, due to plural marriage persecution (78–80).

1887 Sustained again as President of the Quorum of the Twelve upon the death of President John Taylor (80).

1888 May 17: Dedicates the Manti Temple in private services; the temple is publicly dedicated May 21 by Lorenzo Snow (81).

1889 Sustained as President of the Church (82).

1890 Issues the Official Declaration ("Manifesto") on plural marriage (83).

1893 Dedicates the Salt Lake Temple (86).

1894 Announces that practice of "adoption" is discontinued (87).

1896 Utah achieves statehood; fast day is changed from the first Thursday to the first Sunday of each month (89).

1898 Sept. 2: Dies in San Francisco, California (91).

HISTORICAL SUMMARY

Early Years

For more than sixty years Wilford Woodruff kept a careful record of his daily life, often spending an hour or more each day writing journal entries.

In his journal he records a chapter of accidents which gives us an insight into his record keeping:

Evidently I have been numbered with those who are apparently the marked victims of misfortunes. It has seemed to me at times as though some invisible power were watching my footsteps in search of an opportunity to destroy my life. I, therefore, ascribe my preservation on earth to the watchcare of a merciful Providence, whose hand has been stretched out to rescue me from death when I was in the presence of the most threatening dangers. Some of these dangers from which I so narrowly escaped I shall here briefly describe:

When three years of age, I fell into a caldron of scalding water and although instantly rescued, I was so badly burned that it was nine months before I was thought to be out of the danger of fatal consequences. My fifth and sixth years were interwoven with many accidents. On a certain day, in company with my elder brothers, I entered the barn, and chose the top of a hay mow for a place of diversion. We had not been there long before I fell from the great beam upon my face on the bare floor. I was severely hurt, but recovered in a short time, and was again at play.

One Saturday evening, with my brothers Azmon and Thompson, while playing in the chamber of my father's house, contrary to his instructions, I made a misstep and fell to the bottom of the stairs, breaking one of my arms in the fall. So much for disobedience. I suffered intensely, but soon recovered, feeling that whatever I suffered in the future, it would not be for disobedience to parents. The Lord has commanded children to obey their parents; and Paul says, "This is the first commandment with promise."

It was only a short time after this that I narrowly escaped with my life. My father owned a number of horned cattle, among which was a surly bull. One evening I was feeding pumpkins to the cattle, and the bull leaving his own took the pumpkin I had given to a cow which I called mine. I was incensed at the selfishness of this male beast, and promptly picked up the pumpkin he had left, to give it to the cow. No sooner had I got it in my arms than the bull came plunging toward me with great fury. I ran down the hill with all my might, the bull at my heels. My father, seeing the danger I was in, called to me to throw down the pumpkin, but (forgetting to be obedient) I held on, and as the bull was approaching me with the fierceness of a tiger, I made a misstep and fell flat upon the ground.

Elder Woodruff's journal entry, 24 July 1847, the day the pioneers entered the Salt Lake Valley

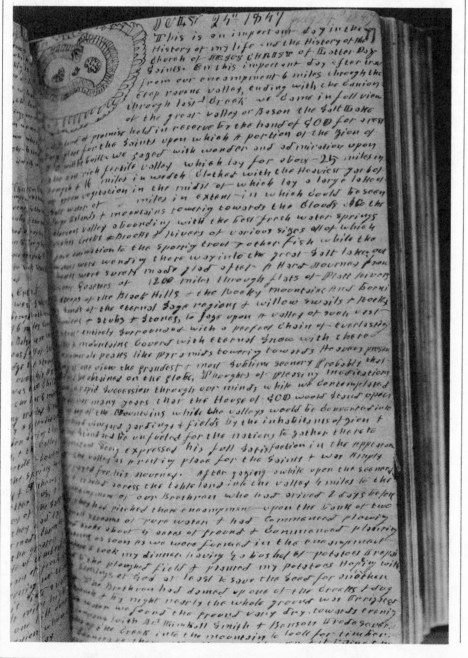

The pumpkin rolled out of my arms, the bull leaped over me, ran his horns into the pumpkin and tore it to pieces. Undoubtedly he would have done the same thing to me if I had not fallen to the ground. This escape, like all others, I attribute to the mercy and goodness of God. . . .

A summary of what is here given may be briefly stated thus: I have broken both legs, one of them in two places; both arms, both ankles, my breastbone, and three ribs; I have been scalded, frozen, and drowned; I have been in two water wheels while turning under a full head; I have passed through a score of other hairbreadth escapes. The repeated deliverances from all these remarkable dangers I ascribe to the mercies of my Heavenly Father. In recalling them to mind I always feel impressed to render the gratitude of my heart, with thanksgiving and joy, to the Lord. I pray that the remainder of my days may pass in His service, in the building up of His kingdom. [Quoted in Matthias F. Cowley, *Wilford Woodruff*, pp. 5–6, 12]

Over several generations, President Woodruff's voluminous diaries have served as an important source of the history of the Church.

Administration

In 1889 the First Presidency was reorganized and President Woodruff was officially sustained as President of the Church, with George Q. Cannon and Joseph F. Smith as counselors. It was the last time that the Council of the Twelve would preside over the Church for an extended period following a President's death. After President Woodruff prayerfully considered the possible problems in continuing this practice, he instructed Church leaders that it was the Lord's will that upon the death of a Church President the First Presidency be reorganized without delay.

As fourth President of the Church, Wilford Woodruff led the Latter-day Saints through a period of transition. Chiefly due to the "Manifesto," conflict with the federal government over plural marriage, politics, and economics began to ease during his administration and the Church resumed activi-

The First Presidency on President Woodruff's eighty-seventh birthday, 1894, left to right: George Q. Cannon, Wilford Woodruff, and Joseph F. Smith (by C.R. Savage)

ties interrupted by the intense persecution of the 1880s. Missionary work, for example, expanded significantly, over six thousand missionaries being called and set apart from 1890 to 1900, three times as many as had been called the previous decade. The flow of new converts into Utah declined, however, partly because the Perpetual Emigration Fund Company had been dissolved by the 1887 Edmunds-Tucker Law, and partly because Church leaders encouraged the Saints to build up Zion in places other than Utah.

Educational programs for auxiliary leaders were set up during this period. The Relief Society and the Primary began annual conferences in 1889 and the Sunday School started holding special training conferences in each stake in 1893. At the same time the Church began to sponsor religion classes for children to be held after school

in ward meetinghouses now that the teaching of religion in the public schools was forbidden by Utah law. In addition, from 1888 to 1891 some thirty-one individual stakes, drawing financial support from the Church, set up academies or high schools in Utah, Idaho, Arizona, Canada, and Mexico.

Salvation for the Dead

Following the January 1877 dedication of the St. George Temple, Wilford Woodruff was called to preside over the only temple then completed. While there it was revealed to him that the Saints could perform ordinances for the dead who were not their ancestors. Accordingly, on 21 August 1877, he and others participated in ordinance work for several prominent men and women of history. The following record of that occasion is taken from his diary (spelling and punctuation have been modernized):

I, Wilford Woodruff, went to the temple of the Lord this morning and was baptized for 100 persons who were dead including the signers of the Declaration of Independence all except John Hancock[1] and [blank]. I was baptized for the following names [The list of names which follows includes, among others, Thomas Jefferson, Benjamin Franklin, Charles Louis Napoleon Bonaparte, Christopher Columbus, Johann Wolfgang Goethe and William Wordsworth].

When Brother McAllister had baptized me for the preceding, I baptized him for 21, including Gen. Washington and his forefathers and all the presidents of the United States that were not in my list except Buchanan, Van Buren, and Grant.[2] It was a very interesting day. I felt thankful that we had the privilege and the power to administer for the worthy dead, especially for the signers of the Declaration of Independence, that inasmuch as they had laid the foundation of our government that we could do as much for them as they had done for us. Sister Lucy Bigelow Young went forth into the font and was baptized for Martha Washington and her family and seventy (70) of the eminent women of the world. I called upon all the brethren and sisters who were present to assist in getting endowments for these that we had been baptized for today. [Diary of Wilford Woodruff, 21 Aug. 1877, Historical Department, The Church of Jesus Christ of Latter-day Saints, Salt Lake City]

Four generations of Woodruffs

One month after Elder Woodruff performed the above temple ordinances, he explained to the Saints assembled in general conference how he had come to do this work:

I feel to say little else to the Latter-day Saints wherever and whenever I have the opportunity of speaking to them, than to call upon them to build these Temples now under way, to hurry them up to completion. The dead will be after you, they will seek after you as they have after us in St. George. They called upon us, knowing that we held the keys and power to redeem them.

I will here say, before closing, that two weeks before I left St. George, the spirits of the dead gathered around me, wanting to know why we did not redeem them. Said they, "You have had the use of the Endowment House for a number of years, and yet nothing has ever been done for us. We laid the foundation of the government you now enjoy, and we never apostatized from it, but we remained true to it and were faithful to God." These were the signers of the Declaration of Independence, and they waited on me for two days and two nights. I thought it very singular, that notwithstanding so much work had been done, and yet nothing had been done for them. The thought never entered my heart, from the fact, I suppose, that heretofore our minds were reaching after our more immediate friends and relatives. I straightway went into the baptismal font and called upon brother McAllister to baptize me for the signers of the Declaration of Independence, and fifty other eminent men, making one hundred in all, including John Wesley, Columbus, and others; I then baptized him for every President of the United States, except three; and when their cause is just, somebody will do the work for them. [*Journal of Discourses,* 19:229].

President Woodruff also presided over the dedication of the Salt Lake Temple in April 1893 and conducted the special dedicatory services held daily for twelve days following to accommodate those eager to witness the event. In 1894 he announced that Latter-day Saints should trace their genealogies back as far as they could and seal their own family groups together rather than seal or "adopt" family groups to prominent Church leaders as had been the practice for many years.

The Law of Adoption

The ordinance for the redemption of the dead had been revealed to Joseph Smith in the 1840s. However, up to 1894, few members had been sealed to their parents. After President Wilford Woodruff made the following pronouncement in general conference, genealogy and temple work greatly increased as members performed the sealing ordinances for their ancestors.

The St. George Temple in the late 1800s

---

1. John Hancock's work had already been done by his descendant, Levi Hancock.

2. President Buchanan sent the troops into Utah in 1857, in the "Utah War." President Martin Van Buren was the president who had turned down the appeals for redress for the wrongs committed upon the Saints when they were driven from the state of Missouri. Joseph Smith wrote in his diary: "During my stay I had an interview with Martin Van Buren, the President, who treated me very insolently, and it was with great reluctance he listened to our message, which, when he had heard, he said: 'Gentlemen, your cause is just, but I can do nothing for you;' and 'If I take up for you I shall lose the vote of Missouri'" (*History of the Church,* 4:80). President Ulysses S. Grant was still alive when this work was performed.

Joseph Smith, instead of living to be nearly a thousand years of age as Adam did, lived to be about thirty-eight years of age. He brought forth the record of the stick of Joseph in the hands of Ephraim—the history of the ancient inhabitants of this continent. By the power of God he translated that, and it has been published in many languages. Besides this, he organized the Church of Jesus Christ of Latter-day Saints upon the foundation of apostles and prophets, Christ Jesus being the chief corner stone. Men were ordained to the Priesthood and sent forth, from the various occupations of life, to carry this Gospel to the world. God informed Joseph Smith that he was called to prune the vineyard once more for the last time before the coming of the Son of Man. Since that, thousands of Elders of Israel have been sent into the world to preach the Gospel. Joseph Smith did all this during the fifteen years he held the Priesthood. Let any man read the revelations in the Book of Doctrine and Covenants, which were given through him during the little time he spent here in the flesh. It is one of the greatest records that any man ever gave to the human family. Not only this, but he organized the endowments and did a great deal of other work. Who could expect him, during the short time he lived in the flesh, to do more than he did? I received my endowments from under his hands. He brought forth all these ordinances that have been given unto the Latter-day Saints. In fact, it is a marvel and a wonder that he performed as much as he did.

I want to say, as the President of the Church of Jesus Christ of Latter-day Saints, that we should now go on and progress. We have not got through revelation. We have not got through the work of God. But at this period we want to go on and fulfill this commandment of God given through Malachi—that the Lord should send Elijah the prophet, "and he shall turn the heart of the fathers to the children, and the heart of the children to their fathers, lest I come and smite the earth with a curse."

President Woodruff's home in Salt Lake City, 1892

Ye sons of men, I say unto you, in the name of Israel's God, those very pinciples that God has revealed are what have stayed the judgments of the Almighty on the earth. Were it not for these principles, you and I would not be here today. We have had prophets and apostles. President Young, who followed President Joseph Smith, led us here. He organized these Temples and carried out the purposes of his calling and office. He laid the foundation of this great Temple on this block, as well as others in the mountains of Israel. What for? That we might carry out these principles of redemption for the dead. He accomplished all that God required at his hands. But he did not receive all the revelations that belong to this work; neither did President Taylor, nor has Wilford Woodruff. There will be no end to this work until it is perfected.

I want to lay before you what there is for us to do at the present time; and in doing this I desire particularly the attention of President Lorenzo Snow, of the Salt Lake Temple; President M. W. Merrill, of the Logan Temple; President J. D. T. McAllister, of the Manti Temple,

and President D. H. Cannon, of the St. George Temple, and those associated with them. You have acted up to all the light and knowledge that you have had; but you have now something more to do than what you have done. We have not fully carried out those principles in fulfillment of the revelations of God to us, in sealing the hearts of the fathers to the children and the children to the fathers. I have not felt satisfied, neither did President Taylor, neither has any man since the Prophet Joseph who has attended to the ordinance of adoption in the temples of our God. We have felt that there was more to be revealed upon this subject than we had received. Revelations were given to us in the St. George Temple, which President Young presented to the Church of God.

Changes were made there, and we still have more changes to make, in order to satisfy our Heavenly Father, satisfy our dead and ourselves. I will tell you what some of them are. I have prayed over this matter, and my brethren have. We have felt as President Taylor said, that we have got to have more revelation concerning sealing under the law of adoption. Well, what are these changes? One of them is the principle of adoption.

In the commencement of adopting men and women in the Temple at Nauvoo, a great many persons were adopted to different men who were not of the lineage of their fathers, and there was a spirit manifested by some in that work there that was not of God. Men would go out and electioneer and labor with all their power to get men adopted to them.... Now, what are the feelings of Israel? They have felt that they wanted to be adopted to somebody. President Young was not satisfied in his mind with regard to the extent of this matter; President Taylor was not. When I went before the Lord to know who I should be adopted to (we were then being adopted to prophets and apostles,) the Spirit of God said to me, "Have you not a father, who begot you?" "Yes, I have." "Then why not honor him? Why not be adopted to him?" "Yes," says I, "that is right." I was adopted to my father, and should have had my father sealed to his father, and so on back; and the duty that I want every man who presides over a Temple to see performed from this day henceforth and forever, unless the Lord Almighty commands otherwise, is, let every man be adopted to his father. When a man receives the endowments, adopt him to his father; not to Wilford Woodruff, nor to any other man outside the lineage of his fathers. That is the will of God to this people. I want all men who preside over these temples in these mountains of Israel to bear this in mind. What business have I to take away the rights of the lineage of any man? What right has any man to do this? No; I say let every man be adopted to his father; and then you will do exactly what God said when he declared He would send Elijah the prophet in the last days. Elijah the prophet appeared unto Joseph Smith and told him that the day had come when this principle must be carried out. Joseph Smith did not live long enough to enter any further upon these things. His soul was wound up with this work before he was martyred for the word of God and testimony of Jesus Christ.

He told us that there must be a welding link of all dispensations and of the work of God from one generation to another. This was upon his mind more than most any other subject that was given to him. In my prayers the Lord revealed to me, that it was my duty to say to all Israel to carry this principle out, and in fulfillment of that revelation I lay it before this people. I say to all men who are laboring in these temples, carry out this principle, and then we will make one step in advance of what we have had before. Myself and counselors conversed upon this and were agreed upon it, and afterwards we laid it before all the Apostles who were here (two were absent—Brothers Thatcher and Lund, the latter being in England,) and the Lord revealed to every one of these men—and they would bear testimony to it if they were to speak—that that was the word of the Lord to them. I never met with anything in my life in this Church that there was more unity upon than there was upon that principle. They all feel right about it, and that it is our duty. That is one principle that should be carried out from this time henceforth. "But," says one, "suppose we come along to a man who perhaps is a murderer." Well, if he is a murderer, drop him out and connect with the next man beyond him. But the Spirit of God will be with us in this matter. We want the Latter day Saints from this time to trace their genealogies as far as they can, and to be sealed to their fathers and mothers. Have children sealed to their parents, and run this chain through as far as you can get it. [*Deseret Weekly*, 21 Apr. 1894, pp. 542–43]

The Genealogical Society of Utah was formed in May 1894 to provide Latter-day Saints with encouragement and assistance in tracing their family lines.

Some Church Practices Modified

Other practices were reconsidered at this time. Rebaptism as a means of personal rededication was phased out beginning in 1893, as Church leaders began to teach the Saints that after they had been baptized initially, it was the process of repentance and faithful service to the higher ordinances that would save them from their sins, not rebaptism. Also, up to that time the first Thursday of each month had been set apart as a fast day, and fast and testimony meetings had been held on that day. In 1896 the First Presidency changed fast day to the first Sunday of each month so as to minimize the conflict with the employment of the Saints.

The Saints had entered Utah in 1847 with the hope that they could establish themselves as a political and economic entity apart from the rest of the world, but through the 1880s it became increasingly clear that they could not. Though the base of Zion had been firmly established, Latter-day Saints in Utah and throughout the world now had to live *in* the world without being *of* the world. The responsibility for leading the Church through this adjustment period had fallen to President Wilford Woodruff, who recognized that though the political kingdom of God would not yet be realized, the spiritual kingdom could be built up to prepare the way for the coming of the Lord.

STUDY QUESTIONS

1. To what did President Woodruff ascribe his long life on earth?

2. How had Wilford Woodruff been prepared to lead the Church?

3. How did Wilford Woodruff's experience in the St. George Temple accelerate the rate at which persons in the spirit world could receive temple ordinances?

4. The Lord called the framers of the United States Constitution "wise men" whom he "raised up" (see D&C 101:80). What additional evidence is there that these founding fathers were wise men concerned about the principles leading to salvation?

5. How similar should our earthly lineage be to the lineage we are attempting to establish for the eternities?

6. Did President Woodruff claim to have received the final word about sealing or other aspects of temple work?

LORENZO SNOW

THE life of Lorenzo Snow was characterized by his spirituality, his teachings on the nature of God and man, the importance he placed on tithing, and his stress on the worldwide mission of the Church. As he said to the Quorum of the Twelve when he became President of the Church: "I don't want this administration to be known as Lorenzo Snow's administration, but as God's, in and through Lorenzo Snow" (quoted in Orson F. Whitney, "Lives of Our Leaders— The Apostles — Lorenzo Snow" *Juvenile Instructor,* Jan. 1900, p. 3).

HIGHLIGHTS

1814 Apr. 3: Born at Mantua, Portage County, Ohio.

1831 His mother and his sister, Leonora, join the Church; hears Joseph Smith speak at Hiram, Ohio (17).

1835 Enters Oberlin College; his sister, Eliza R., joins the Church (21).

1836 Attends Hebrew school in Kirtland; baptized (22).

1837 Serves a mission in Ohio (23).

1838–39 Moves to Far West; serves a mission to southern Missouri, Illinois, Kentucky, and Ohio (24–25).

1840 Receives a revelation on the nature of God and man (26).

1840–43 Serves a mission to Great Britain; presents a copy of the Book of Mormon to Queen Victoria (26–29).

1844 Learns of the martyrdom of Joseph Smith while in Ohio on a campaigning mission for Joseph's candidacy for the United States presidency (30).

1845 Marries Charlotte Squires and Mary Adaline Goddard (31).

1846–48 Crosses the plains; presides over the Saints in Mount Pisgah (32–34).

1849 Becomes a member of the Council of the Twelve; helps organize the Perpetual Emigration Fund (35).

1849–52 Serves a mission to Europe (35–38).

1852 Organizes the Polysophical Society, a cultural refinement group somewhat similar to the later Mutual Improvement Association (38).

1853 Called to preside over the colonization of Brigham City (39).

1854 Participates in the organization of the Philosophical Society, later called the Universal Scientific Society (40).

1864 Completes a short-term mission to Hawaii (50).

1872–82 Serves as president of Utah Territorial Legislative Council (58–68).

1872–73 Tours Europe and Asia Minor; participates in the second dedication of Palestine for the return of the Jews (58–59).

1873–77 Serves as one of seven counselors to President Brigham Young (59–63).

1873–80 Organizes the united order in Brigham City (59–66).

1885 Fills a short-term mission to the Lamanites in the northwestern United States (71).

1886–87 Serves an eleven-month prison term for a plural marriage charge (72–73).

1888 May 21: Offers public dedicatory prayers at the Manti Temple, the temple having been privately dedicated May 17 by Wilford Woodruff (65).

1889 Becomes President of the Quorum of the Twelve (75).

1893 Becomes President of the Salt Lake Temple (79).

1898 Sees the Savior in the Salt Lake Temple (84).

Sustained as President of the Church (84).

1899 Initiates a drive to reemphasize the law of tithing, beginning in southern Utah (85).

1901 Serves as general superintendent of the Sunday School; Elder Heber J. Grant is sent to open the Japanese Mission (87).

Oct. 10: Dies at Salt Lake City, Utah (87).

HISTORICAL SUMMARY

Receiving the Holy Ghost

Young Lorenzo's great spirituality was evidenced shortly after his decision to join the Church. He later wrote of that experience:

Some two or three weeks after I was baptized, one day while engaged in my studies, I began to reflect upon the fact that I had not obtained a *knowledge* of the truth of the work— that I had not realized the fulfilment of the promise "he that doeth my will shall know of the doctrine," and I began to feel very uneasy. I laid aside my books, left the house, and wandered around through the fields under the oppressive influence of a gloomy, disconsolate spirit, while an indescribable cloud of darkness seemed to envelop me. I had been accustomed, at the close of the day, to retire for secret prayer, to a grove a short distance from my lodgings, but at this time I felt no inclination to do so. The spirit of prayer had departed and the heavens seemed like brass over my head. At length, realizing that the usual time had come for secret prayer, I concluded I would not forego my evening service, and, as a matter of formality, knelt as I was in the habit of doing, and in my accustomed retired place, but not feeling as I was wont to feel.

I had no sooner opened my lips in an effort to pray, than I heard a sound, just above my head, like the rustling of silken robes, and immediately the Spirit of God descended upon me, completely enveloping my whole person, filling me, from the crown of my head to the soles of my feet, and O, the joy and happiness I felt! No language can describe the almost instantaneous transition from a dense cloud of mental and spiritual darkness into a refulgence of light and knowledge, as it was at that time imparted to my understanding. I then received a perfect knowledge that God lives, that Jesus Christ is the Son of God, and of the restoration of the holy Priesthood, and the fulness of the Gospel. It was a complete baptism—a tangible immersion in the heavenly principle or element, the Holy Ghost; and even more real and physical in its effects upon every

Young Lorenzo Snow (by Frederick Piercy)

part of my system than the immersion by water; dispelling forever, so long as reason and memory last, all possibility of doubt or fear in relation to the fact handed down to us historically, that the "Babe of Bethlehem" is truly the Son of God; also the fact that He is now being revealed to the children of men, and communicating knowledge, the same as in the Apostolic times. I was perfectly satisfied, as well I might be, for my expectations were more than realized, I think I may safely say in an infinite degree.

I cannot tell how long I remained in the full flow of the blissful enjoy-

ment and divine enlightenment, but it was several minutes before the celestial element which filled and surrounded me began gradually to withdraw. On arising from my kneeling posture, with my heart swelling with gratitude to God, beyond the power of expression, I felt—I *knew* that He had conferred on me what only an omnipotent being can confer—that which is of greater value than all the wealth and honors worlds can bestow. That night, as I retired to rest, the same wonderful manifestations were repeated, and continued to be for several successive nights. The sweet remembrance of those glorious experiences, from that time to the present, bring them fresh before me, imparting an inspiring influence which pervades my whole being, and I trust will to the close of my earthly existence. [In Eliza R. Snow, *Biography and Family Record of Lorenzo Snow*, pp. 7–9]

The Nature of God

Early in his life, Lorenzo Snow developed a remarkable understanding about the nature of God and man. In Kirtland, Ohio, he met Joseph Smith, Sr., the first patriarch to the Church, who promised him that he would soon be baptized into the Church and then said, "You will become as great as you can possibly wish—EVEN AS GREAT AS GOD, and you cannot wish to be greater" (Snow, *Biography,* p. 10).

Four years later, in 1840, Lorenzo received a personal revelation that clarified Father Smith's mysterious saying: "The Spirit of the Lord rested mightily upon me—the eyes of my understanding were opened, and I saw as clear as the sun at noonday, with wonder and astonishment, the pathway of God and man. I formed the following couplet which expresses the revelation, as it was shown to me, and explains Father Smith's dark saying to me at a blessing meeting in the Kirtland Temple, prior to my baptism, . . . 'As man now is, God once was: As God now is, man may be" (Snow, *Biography,* p. 46). At first, he shared this revelation with no one except his sister Eliza. Then he privately related it to Brigham Young, who wisely told him: "Brother Snow, that is

Lorenzo's sister Eliza introduced him to the Church

a new doctrine; if true, it has been revealed to you for your own private information, and will be taught in due time by the Prophet to the Church; till then I advise you to lay it upon the shelf and say no more about it" (Whitney, *Juvenile Instructor,* Jan. 1900, p. 4). This Lorenzo did until the Prophet Joseph delivered the King Follett discourse and taught the same doctrine publicly for the first time (see p. 7). Thereafter, Lorenzo Snow felt free to teach it.

Inspirational Experiences

Through a long life of service and dedication to the Church, Lorenzo Snow had numerous spiritual experiences. In 1850 he was an instrument in the miraculous healing of a young boy in Italy, which helped open doors to missionary work in that country. During a special mission to Hawaii in 1864, Elder Snow drowned when the small boat in which he was riding capsized. After fifteen or twenty minutes his lifeless body was finally found and taken from the water. His companions were impressed to apply mouth-to-mouth resuscitation, a life saving technique not commonly known at that time, and his life was restored. These experiences were climaxed by a marvelous manifestation following the death of President Wilford Woodruff, 2 September 1898. The day Lorenzo Snow was informed of President Woodruff's death, he went to the Salt

Lake Temple, dressed in his temple robes, and went to the Holy of Holies, where he knelt at the altar to pray. He reminded the Lord how he had pleaded for a long life for President Woodruff so that the heavy responsibility of the leadership of the Church would not fall upon him. Nevertheless he accepted the will of the Lord and now asked for the Lord to show him what to do:

After finishing his prayer he expected a reply, some special manifestation from the Lord. So he waited,—and waited—and waited. There was no reply, no voice, no visitation, no manifestation. He left the altar and the room in great disappointment. Passing through the Celestial room and out into the large corridor a glorious manifestation was given President Snow which I relate in the words of his grand-daughter, Allie Young Pond, now the wife of Elder Noah S. Pond, recently president of the Northern States Mission:

"One evening while I was visiting grandpa Snow in his room in the Salt Lake Temple, I remained until the door keepers had gone and the night-watchmen had not yet come in, so grand-pa said he would take me to the main front entrance and let me out that way. He got his bunch of keys from his dresser. After we left his room and while we were still in the large corridor leading into the celestial room, I was walking several steps ahead of grand-pa when he stopped me and said: 'Wait a moment, Allie, I want to tell you something. It was right here that the Lord Jesus Christ appeared to me at the time of the death of President Woodruff. He instructed me to go right ahead and reorganize the First Presidency of the Church at once and not wait as had been done after the death of the previous presidents, and that I was to succeed President Woodruff.'

"Then grand-pa came a step nearer and held out his left hand and said: 'He stood right here, about three feet above the floor. It looked as though He stood on a plate of solid gold.'

"Grand-pa told me what a glorious personage the Savior is and de-scribed His hands, feet, countenance and beautiful white robes, all of which were of such a glory of whiteness and brightness that he could hardly gaze upon Him.

"Then he came another step nearer and put his right hand on my head and said: 'Now, grand-daughter, I want you to remember that this is the testimony of your grand-father, that he told you with his own lips that he actually saw the Savior, here in the Temple, and talked with Him face to face' " (LeRoi C. Snow, "An Experience of My Father's," *Improvement Era*, Sept. 1933, p. 677).

Following the appearance of the Savior to President Snow, he met in a special council meeting 13 September 1898 with the other members of the Quorum of the Twelve. The following are excerpts of that meeting:

At 10 o'clock this morning the Council of the Apostles met at the President's office, according to appointment. . . .

Elder Lyman, speaking to this question [of a new Trustee-in-trust for the Church] said he was reminded of the time when the Council was together after the death of President Taylor, and the feeling of President Woodruff at that time; he was also reminded of President Woodruff's feelings, as expressed on different occasions during his administration, to the effect that when-ever he died, the First Presidency of the Church should be organized without delay. "And if the Lord should manifest to you, President Snow, that it was the proper thing to do now, I am prepared to not only vote for a Trustee-in-trust, but for the President of the Church." . . .

Brother Grant remarked that the present time was just as opportune as any other, and that he could sustain Pres. Snow with all his heart as President of the Church.

Bro. Young remarked that Bro. Grant had expressed his feelings exactly. He felt that this was the way out.

Bro. Teasdale said that he was in perfect harmony and accord with the feelings of [the] brethren.

Jos. F. Smith: "I move that that be the sense of this meeting."

President Snow asked if there were any further remarks. Several of the brethren called for the question, whereupon Pres. Snow asked Elder Jos. F. Smith to put the motion. This being done, it was carried unanimously, and Lorenzo Snow was thus sustained by the Council of the Apostles, as President of The Church of Jesus Christ of Latter-day Saints.

Pres. Snow then arose and said: There was no use in his making excuses as to inability, etc., to assume

President Snow (third from left, seated), his counselors, George Q. Cannon and Joseph F. Smith (to his right), and the Council of the Twelve, September 1898

Lorenzo Snow, 1814–1901

the vast responsibilities involved in the position to which he had been elected. He felt that it was for him to do the very best he could and depend upon the Lord. He knew the action taken by the Council was according to the mind and will of the Lord, who had shown and revealed to him several days ago that the First Presidency should be organized before the next conference. He had been feeling a little gloomy, and perhaps a little discouraged at the prospect, and the vast responsibility that would naturally fall upon him as President of the Twelve Apostles, and with this feeling he went before the Lord, offered up the signs of the Holy Priesthood and called upon Him to let light come to his mind. His prayer was answered, the Lord manifesting unto him clearly what he should do; also in regard to the counselors he should select when he became President of the Church, "And," said he, "In accordance with the light given me, I now present to you the name of Geo. Q. Cannon as my first counselor, and that of Joseph F. Smith as my second

counselor." . . .

Pres. Snow, before calling for the vote, said, "I have not mentioned this matter to any person, either man or woman. I wanted to see what the feelings of the brethren were. I wanted to see if the same spirit which the Lord manifested to me was in you. I had confidence in you that the Lord would indicate to you that this was proper and according to his mind and will." [Journal History of the Church, 13 Sept. 1898, Historical Department, The Church of Jesus Christ of Latter-day Saints, Salt Lake City]

Administration

President Snow is probably best remembered for his teaching concerning tithing. For a number of years the Church had suffered under great financial bondage, partly due to the provisions of the 1887 Edmunds-Tucker Act (see chapter 8) that authorized the United States government's confiscation of much of the Church's property. It was under these conditions that President Wilford Woodruff wrote in his diary on 30 December 1896, less than two years before his death: "The

presidency of the church are so overwhelmed in financial matters it seems as though we shall never live to get through with it unless the Lord opens the way in a marvelous manner. It looks as though we shall never pay our debts" (James R. Clark, comp., *Messages of the First Presidency of The Church of Jesus Christ of Latter-day Saints,* 3:304). When Lorenzo Snow became President of the Church, he stated it was his "prayer and labor" to get the Church out of debt. Francis M. Lyman as well said that this was the great work of President Snow's administration (see Albert R. Lyman, *Francis Marion Lyman, 1840–1916,* p. 149). A short time later he received divine guidance on which direction the Church should take.

One morning in 1899, the Spirit directed President Snow to travel with several other General Authorities to drought-stricken St. George, Utah, to hold a special conference on Thursday, 8 May 1899. As he sat in the conference with the Saints he was not yet sure why the Lord had directed him to come. Then as he spoke to them, the Lord revealed to him the necessity for every Latter-day Saint to pay a full and honest tithe, and he gave the now famous instructions for paying tithing:

The Latter-day Saints have done wonders; but they cannot cease from doing wonders in the future. There will be greater things demanded of the Latter-day Saints than has ever been demanded since the organization of the Church. The Lord has determined in His heart that He will try us until He knows what He can do with us. He tried His Son Jesus. Thousands of years before He came upon earth the Father had watched His course and knew that He could depend upon Him when the salvation of worlds should be at stake; and He was not disappointed. So in regard to ourselves. He will try us, and continue to try us, in order that He may place us in the highest positions in life and put upon us the most sacred responsibilities. When we were placed in certain circumstances with our wives and children, and the nation was pursuing us with the intention of destroying us, the Lord opened our way in a manner that we never expected. Very few indeed thought our deliverance would come in the way which the Lord saw proper to bring it. A sacrifice had to be made—a greater one than had ever been made before. The Church itself depended upon the Saints acting in a wise and prudent manner, and making the sacrifice that was required at that time. The word of the Lord came to President Woodruff. When that Manifesto was issued, you knew what it meant. Some were alarmed. They thought the Church would go to pieces; thought they were breaking their covenants; thought the Lord had withdrawn from them. But that Manifesto was issued by the command of the Lord; and the Saints humbled themselves before the Lord and bowed to the requirement. The heavens rejoiced and God smiled upon us. He blessed His people, and delivered us from our enemies, and they were brought to shame and disgrace. They thought to destroy the Latter-day Saints, but they failed in their attempt. Nevertheless, we had to make the sacrifice, and it was right that we should. The Lord could have delivered us in some other way, had He so wished; but He knew best, and that was the course He required us to pursue and the sacrifice He desired us to make. We made it, and He has blessed us wonderfully from that time to the present. He has given us power among the nations, and in various ways the people have been raised in the estimation of the world. Men of great wisdom have looked upon us, though they may have been silent, and they have honored the course we have taken. The Lord required that of us.

I come here now with my brethren that you may understand what is required of you as a people under the peculiar conditions in which the Church is now placed. It is the word of the Lord to you, my brethren and sisters, that you should conform to that which is required of you as a people who have these glorious prospects of exaltation and glory before you. What is it? Why, it is something that has been drummed into your ears from time to time until you perhaps have got tired of hearing it. I need the faith and prayers of every Latter-day Saint; no man needs them any more than I do; and it is unpleasant for me to say things that would in any way diminish the exercise of your faith and prayers in my behalf. But the Lord requires me to say something to you, and since I commenced to labor in His interest, I have never failed, thank the Lord, to do that which He has required at my hands; and I shall not do it today, nor any other day, the Lord being my helper. The word of the Lord to you is not anything new; it is simply this: THE TIME HAS NOW COME FOR EVERY LATTER-DAY SAINT, WHO CALCULATES TO BE PREPARED FOR THE FUTURE AND TO HOLD HIS FEET STRONG UPON A PROPER FOUNDATION, TO DO THE WILL OF THE LORD AND TO PAY HIS TITHING IN FULL. That is the word of the Lord to you, and it will be the word of the Lord to every settlement throughout the land of Zion. After I leave you and you get to thinking about this, you will see yourselves that the time has come when every man should stand up and pay his tithing in full. The Lord has blessed us and has had mercy upon us in the past; but there are times coming when the Lord requires us to stand up and do that which He has commanded and not leave it any longer. What I say to you in this Stake of Zion I will say to every Stake of Zion that has been organized. There is no man or woman that now hears what I am saying who will feel satisfied if he or she fails to pay a full tithing.

I could reason with you upon this, but what need is there of showing why we should do these things. We receive from the different Stakes of Zion requests for help, some to build meeting houses and some for other purposes. Well, we feel that we ought to help them, because they are deserving of help; but we cannot do it. I do not think I will say much about the financial condition of the Church. The Church, of course, is very much in debt. And I do not know that anybody is to blame for it being in debt. It has been partially explained to-day by the brethren, and I will leave it in that way. But we are going into debt no longer. All the enterprises that we have gone into, have been for the benefit of the people. Well, I do not care to talk about this. It is sufficient to say to the Latter-day Saints that we must now pay our tithing. I have scarcely ever talked about tithing. I have said it was the duty of the Latter-day Saints to pay tithing, but I have never made it a business like some of my brethren have. You will not hear much from me now in regard to tithing. I simply tell you the truth straight out; and I have faith in the Latter-day Saints to believe and know that they will respond to this.

Brethren and sisters, I feel and know that you are a good people. I do not flatter you when I say this. I simply tell the facts. The Lord has helped you, as He has helped other portions of the people in Zion. He has done this, not because they have done right under all circumstances, not because they have paid their tithing properly, but because they have paid it partially and have done some good. But when the voice of the Lord comes to us and His will is expressed, then is the time for us to act. [*Millennial Star*, 24 Aug. 1899, pp. 532–33; 31 Aug. 1899, pp. 545–46]

After the Saint George conference, the General Authorities went to all the stakes of the Church calling upon the Saints to pay a full tithing.

The Church's Worldwide Mission

As he neared the end of his life, President Snow spoke frequently about the worldwide mission of the Church. Up to that point, much of the General Authorities' time was spent in administering the needs of the Church locally in the wards and stakes of the western United States. President Snow possessed a much wider perspective, as can be seen from the following remarks to the General Authorities on 28 September 1901.

I want to say, here are the Apostles and the Seventies, their business is to warn the nations of the earth and prepare the world for the coming of the Savior. They have been engaged in this more or less. Now we find ourselves in a compact, gathered condition, the Church divided into stakes, and we come together from time to time in a council capacity to consider the interests of the cause generally, and make appointments for brethren to visit the stakes when holding their conferences. It looks to me that our minds ought to extend somewhat, and we get out of the beaten track, and a little change be made. For instance, we have started in this direction by sending Brother Grant over to Japan, but this is only a start. Things seem to be going on favorably with him; but whether he will accomplish much or not matters not in one sense; it is for the Apostles to show to the Lord that they are His witnesses to all the nations, and that they are doing the best they can. [Quoted in Joseph F. Smith, "The Last Days of President Snow," *Juvenile Instructor,* Nov. 1901, p. 690]

Just over a week after the above remarks, President Snow left this vision of the Church in his last conference address before he died:

This Church is now nearly seventy two years of age, and we are not expected to do the work of the days of our youth, but to do greater, larger and more extensive work. The Lord is coming one of these days, and He is interested in the work that you ought to be doing, and anxious to be doing. You ought to do all that you possibly can, and leave everything in your business affairs that you wisely can do and attend to these matters. The presidents of these fifty Stakes should consider the people in their respective Stakes, in their various dominions. They should regard them as their own family, as their sons and daughters; and take as deep an interest in them as they ought to take in their own wives and children. It should be their thought by day and by night, how and in what way they can be most serviceable to their respective charges. Oh! brethren, do remember these things that I am now talking about; do not forget them. You presidents, when you re-

tire to your rest, you probably can spend half an hour before you go to sleep, and let your thoughts run over your several jurisdictions. See wherein, either physically, financially or spiritually, you can help, and what can be done best in advancing the interests of your official family. These Bishops, however wise and energetic they may think themselves—and the most of them certainly are very wise and energetic—need to be looked after. It is not the duty of the Apostles to look after them.

The Apostles have a work that is in another direction altogether. I want the Presidents of Stakes hereafter to realize that it is their business, not the business of the Apostles; it is the business of the High Priests, the Elders, the Bishops, Priests, Teachers and Deacons to look after these things. Do not lay this duty upon the shoulders of the Apostles. It is not in their line, at least only occasionally. There is a certain channel by and through which the Lord intends to exalt His sons and daughters, to remove wickedness from the earth and to establish righteousness, and that channel is the Priesthood, which God has established and shown clearly the nature and character of the various officers and duties thereof. The Apostles and the Seventies, it is their business by the appointment of the Almighty, to look after the interests of the world. The Seventies and the Twelve Apostles are special witnesses unto the nations of the earth. The business of the High Priests, the Elders and the Bishops is to look after the interests of these various organizations that I have mentioned. You presiding officers of the various Stakes of Zion, the time is coming when you will not have to call and depend so much upon the Twelve Apostles. They will be directed in other channels, and I want you to distinctly understand it; and do not seek to throw responsibilities that belong to you upon these Twelve Apostles and upon the Seventies.

I wanted to say this, and to speak it with energy and in a way that you will not forget it, that you cannot

forget it. It is a wonderful responsibility, and the Lord expects it of you. [In Conference Report, Oct. 1901, pp. 60–61]

It was at this time that President Snow sent Elder Heber J. Grant to open a mission in Japan and began investigating the possibility of missionary work in other parts of the world, including Russia and Australia. Shortly thereafter President Snow died. Though President Snow's administration was relatively short, the many contributions, among them the Church's strengthened economic condition and its worldwide growth, have had a lasting influence on the Saints. As the nineteenth century drew to a close, the Church saw an end to many of its intense struggles and looked forward to a bright future in the twentieth century.

STUDY QUESTIONS

1. How did the blessing of Joseph Smith, Sr., start Lorenzo Snow on an important search for knowledge? How was his search fulfilled, and what significance does his answer have for us today?

2. Joseph Smith said "It is the first principle of the Gospel to know for a certainty the Character of God, and to know that we may converse with him" (*Teachings of the Prophet Joseph Smith,* pp. 345–46). How and why are President Lorenzo Snow's insights on the nature of God and man important to us?

3. What occasion brought the Savior to Lorenzo Snow in the Salt Lake Temple? What significance does this appearance have for Church members today?

4. Why was the Church in financial bondage when President Snow came to office? How had President Snow's early life and leadership prepared him for this crisis?

5. Why did the Lord give this revelation on tithing?

6. Why should one pay tithing?

7. According to President Snow, what is one of the primary duties of the Quorum of Twelve, the Quorum of Seventy, and the members of the Church?

JOSEPH F. SMITH

PRESIDENT Joseph F. Smith led the Church during most of the first two decades of the twentieth century. His administration as well as his personal life represented important links with the past as well as with the future. A son of the martyred Patriarch, Hyrum Smith, he participated in the pioneer migration and before his sixteenth birthday left Utah to serve a mission to Hawaii. By the time he was twenty-eight years old, he had served three missions, had married, and had been elected to the territorial legislature. Then at twenty-eight he was ordained an Apostle by President Brigham Young, though he did not serve in the quorum until a vacancy occurred one year later. He later served as a counselor to Presidents Brigham Young, John Taylor, Wilford Woodruff, and Lorenzo Snow. He lived through the trying days before and after the "Manifesto" and later issued what many termed the second manifesto in 1904. He saw the financial ruin brought upon the Church during President Woodruff's administration by the Edmunds-Tucker Act, the inspiration that attended President Snow's emphasis on the law of tithing, and the end of indebtedness while he was President in 1906. At the same time, his emphasis on family home evening and correlation of priesthood and auxiliary activities foreshadowed the future development of these programs.

HIGHLIGHTS

1838 Nov. 13: Born in Far West, Caldwell County, Missouri.

1844 His father, Hyrum Smith, is martyred with the Prophet Joseph Smith (5).

1846–48 Drives an ox team across the plains from Nauvoo to Salt Lake (8–10).

1852 Becomes an orphan at the death of his mother, Mary Fielding Smith (14).

1854–57 Serves a mission to Hawaii (15–19).

1857 Serves in the Echo Canyon campaign of the Utah War (19).

1859 Marries Levira A. Smith; called to the Salt Lake Stake high council (21).

1860–63 Serves a mission to Great Britain (22–25).

1864 Serves on a special mission to Hawaii (26).

1865–74 Serves as a member of the territorial legislature (27–36).

1866 Ordained an Apostle and a counselor to the First Presidency (28).

1867 Sustained in general conference as a member of the Quorum of the Twelve Apostles (29).

1874–77 Serves as president of the European Mission (36–37).

1877 Serves a second term as president of the European Mission (39).

1878 Serves a short-term mission to the eastern United States in the interest of the history of the Church (40).

1880 Becomes the Second Counselor to John Taylor in the First Presidency (42).

1884–91 Goes into voluntary exile because of plural marriage persecution (46–53).

1890 "Manifesto" is issued on plural marriage (52).

1893 Acts as a member of the constitutional convention for the state of Utah (55).

1901 Sustained as the general superintendent of the Sunday School and as President of the Church (63).

1904 Called as a witness in Smoot hearings (66).

Joseph F. Smith, 1857

1906 Tours Europe; first President to do so during his administration (68).

1909 First Presidency issues a statement on the doctrine of the origin of man (71).

1913 First Presidency issues a warning about false revelation (75).

1914 World War I begins (76).

1916 First Presidency issues a "doctrinal exposition" on the Father and the Son (78).

1918 Oct. 3: Has a vision of the redemption of the dead (79).

Nov. 19: Dies in Salt Lake City, Utah (80).

HISTORICAL SUMMARY

Early Life

Joseph F. Smith was born in the midst of the northern Missouri persecutions and spent his early boyhood in Nauvoo, Illinois. When he was only five years old, his father, Hyrum Smith, and his uncle, the Prophet Joseph, were cruelly murdered in nearby Carthage.

During the trek to the Rocky Mountains, young Joseph F. had to assume

Salt Lake City, looking southeast along Main Street, 1904

a good deal of responsibility. From his mother's example he learned the important lesson of depending on the Lord in complete faith during times of need. Unfortunately, Mary Fielding Smith died not long after they arrived in Utah, leaving her son Joseph an orphan. Yet he did not have time to feel sorry for himself; when he was only fifteen, he accepted a mission call to Hawaii. From that time onward Joseph F. Smith was almost constantly in the work of the Lord, serving as a member of the Quorum of the Twelve and as a counselor to Presidents John Taylor, Wilford Woodruff, and Lorenzo Snow, which climaxed his preparation for becoming President of the Church in 1901.

During the first years of the twentieth century, the Saints saw sensational demands, especially in the press, for reforming social ills. In this climate, magazines directed attacks against alleged plural marriages and Church influence in politics. These misconceptions were largely cleared up, however, during a series of hearings conducted by a hostile committee following the election of Elder Reed Smoot of the Council of the Twelve to the United States Senate in 1903. Even President Joseph F. Smith was called to Washington to testify. The seating of Elder Smoot marked the beginning of a day of better feelings toward the Latter-day Saints. This feeling of good will was further enhanced as the Saints demonstrated loyalty to their respective governments during the crisis of World War I.

As the Saints continued to pay their tithing faithfully, the Church was able to pay all its debts by 1906. This paved the way for a new era of prosperity and growth. Under President Smith's direction, the Church embarked on an expanded building program. Important structures begun at this time include the Church Administration Building in Salt Lake City as well as the Hawaii and Alberta Temples. The Church began purchasing key historic sites, including Joseph Smith's birthplace in Vermont; the Smith home and Sacred Grove near Palmyra, New York; the Carthage Jail in Illinois; and twenty-five acres in Independence, Missouri. Following the pattern inaugurated on Temple Square in Salt Lake City, a bureau of information was established at several of these sites in order to help interested visitors more fully appreciate the Church and its people. These efforts further helped to enhance the Saints' increasingly favorable image.

The administration of Joseph F. Smith also saw a substantial expansion of Church activities, particularly among the auxiliaries. While he presided over the Sunday School as general superintendent from 1901 to 1918, for example, that organization and the Relief Society inaugurated lesson work for adults. The auxiliaries also began publishing such well-known magazines as the *Improvement Era,* the *Children's Friend,* and the *Relief Society Magazine.* To coordinate the work of these organizations, President Smith appointed a correlation committee. In the midst of this surge of auxiliary activity, President Smith declared at general conference in April 1906: "We expect to see the day . . . when every council of the Priesthood . . . will understand its duty, will assume its own responsibility, will magnify its calling, and fill its place in the Church. . . . When that day shall come, there will not be so much necessity for work that is now being done by the auxiliary organizations, because it will be done by the regular quorums of the Priesthood" (in Conference Report, Apr. 1906, pp. 2–3). President Smith and his counselors also recognized the need for increased activity in the home. This emphasis on the priesthood and the home anticipated the achievements of priesthood correlation that began in the 1960s.

Gospel Doctrines

President Joseph F. Smith was an outstanding expounder of gospel truth; his sermons and writings have been compiled into the well-known volume entitled *Gospel Doctrine.* His clear definitions were particularly important during this time of unprecedented controversy throughout the world concerning the extent to which scriptural teachings could be accepted. During his administration, the First Presidency

President Smith and Hawaiian Saints while he was in Hawaii to dedicate the site for the Hawaii Temple, 1915

issued doctrinal expositions on such topics as man's origin and the nature of the Father and the Son.

The First Presidency also warned Latter-day Saints against false teachings and spurious revelations.

"The Origin of Man"

The first of the two doctrinal expositions by the First Presidency, this explanation of revealed truth issued in November 1909 came in the midst of a time when ideas advanced in the theory of evolution generated widespread controversy about the origin of man.

Inquiries arise from time to time respecting the attitude of the Church of Jesus Christ of Latter-day Saints upon questions which, though not vital from a doctrinal standpoint, are closely connected with the fundamental principles of salvation. The latest inquiry of this kind that has reached us is in relation to the origin of man. It is believed that a statement of the position held by the Church upon this important subject will be timely and productive of good.

In presenting the statement that follows we are not conscious of putting forth anything essentially new; neither is it our desire so to do. Truth is what we wish to present, and truth—eternal truth—is fundamentally old. A restatement of the original attitude of the Church relative to this matter is all that will be attempted here. To tell the truth as God has revealed it, and commend it to the acceptance of those who need to conform their opinions thereto, is the sole purpose of this presentation.

"God created man in his own image, in the image of God created he him; male and female created he them." In these plain and pointed words the inspired author of the book of Genesis made known to the world the truth concerning the origin of the human family. Moses, the prophet-historian, "learned," as we are told, "in all the wisdom of the Egyptians," when making this important announcement, was not voicing a mere opinion, a theory derived from his researches into the occult lore of that ancient people.

He was speaking as the mouthpiece of God, and his solemn declaration was for all time and for all people. No subsequent revelator of the truth has contradicted the great leader and law-giver of Israel. All who have since spoken by divine authority upon this theme have confirmed his simple and sublime proclamation. Nor could it be otherwise. Truth has but one source, and all revelations from heaven are harmonious with each other. The omnipotent Creator, the maker of heaven and earth—had shown unto Moses everything pertaining to this planet, including the facts relating to man's origin, and the authoritative pronouncement of that mighty prophet and seer to the house of Israel, and through Israel to the whole world, is couched in the simple clause: "God created man in his own image" (Genesis 1:27; Pearl of Great Price—Book of Moses; 1:27–41.)

Joseph F. Smith, 1838–1918

The creation was two-fold—firstly spiritual, secondly temporal. This truth, also, Moses plainly taught—much more plainly than it has come down to us in the imperfect translations of the Bible that are now in use. Therein the fact of a spiritual creation, antedating the temporal creation, is strongly implied, but the proof of it is not so clear and conclusive as in other records held by the Latter-day Saints to be of equal authority with the Jewish scriptures. The partial obscurity of the latter upon the point in question is owing,

no doubt, to the loss of those "plain and precious" parts of sacred writ, which, as the Book of Mormon informs us, have been taken away from the Bible during its passage down the centuries (I Nephi 13:24–29). Some of these missing parts the Prophet Joseph Smith undertook to restore when he revised those scriptures by the spirit of revelation, the result being that more complete account of the creation which is found in the book of Moses, previously cited. Note the following passages:

"And now, behold I say unto you, that these are the generations of the heaven and the earth, when they were created in the day that I, the Lord God, made the heaven and the earth,

"And every plant of the field before it was in the earth, and every herb of the field before it grew.

"For I, the Lord God, created all things of which I have spoken, spiritually, before they were naturally upon the face of the earth. For I, the Lord God, had not caused it to rain upon the face of the earth.

"And I, the Lord God, had created all the children of men, and not yet a man to till the ground; for in heaven created I them, and there was not yet flesh upon the earth, neither in the water, neither in the air.

"But I, the Lord God, spake, and there went up a mist from the earth, and watered the whole face of the ground.

"And I, the Lord God, formed man from the dust of the ground, and breathed into his nostrils the breath of life; and man became a living soul, the first flesh upon the earth, the first man also.

"Nevertheless, all things were before created, but spiritually were they created and made, according to my word" (Pearl of Great Price—Book of Moses, 3:4–7. See also chapters 1 and 2, and compare with Genesis 1 and 2).

These two points being established, namely, the creation of man in the image of God, and the two-fold character of the creation, let us now inquire: What was the form of man, in the spirit and in the body, as originally created? In a general way the answer is given in the words chosen as the text of this treatise, "God created man in his own image." It is more explicitly rendered in the Book of Mormon thus: "All men were created in the beginning after mine own image" (Ether 3:15). It is the Father who is speaking.* If, therefore, we can ascertain the form of the "Father of spirits," "The God of the spirits of all flesh," we shall be able to discover the form of the original man.

Jesus Christ, the Son of God, is "the express image" of His Father's person (Hebrews 1:3). He walked the earth as a human being, as a perfect man, and said, in answer to a question put to Him: "He that hath seen me hath seen the Father" (John 14:9). This alone ought to solve the problem to the satisfaction of every thoughtful, reverent mind. The conclusion is irresistible, that if the Son of God be the express image (that is, likeness) of His Father's person, then His Father is in the form of man; for that was the form of the Son of God, not only during His mortal life, but before His mortal birth, and after His resurrection. It was in this form that the Father and the Son, as two personages, appeared to Joseph Smith, when, as a boy of fourteen years, he received his first vision. Then if God made man—the first man—in His own image and likeness, he must have made him like unto Christ, and consequently like unto men of Christ's time and of the present day. That man was made in the image of Christ, is positively stated in the Book of Moses: "And I, God, said unto mine Only Begotten, which was with me from the beginning, Let us make man in our image, after our likeness; and it was so. . . . and I, God, created man in

mine own image, in the image of mine Only Begotten created I him, male and female created I them" (2:26, 27).

The Father of Jesus is our Father also. Jesus Himself taught this truth, when He instructed His disciples how to pray: "Our Father which art in heaven," etc. Jesus, however, is the first-born among all the sons of God—the first begotten in the spirit, and the only begotten in the flesh. He is our elder brother, and we, like Him, are in the image of God. All men and women are in the similitude of the universal Father and Mother, and are literally the sons and daughters of Deity.

"God created man in His own image." This is just as true of the spirit as it is of the body, which is only the clothing of the spirit, its complement; the two together constituting the soul. The spirit of man is in the form of man, and the spirits of all creatures are in the likeness of their bodies. This was plainly taught by the Prophet Joseph Smith (Doctrine and Covenants, 77:2).

Here is further evidence of the fact. More than seven hundred years before Moses was shown the things pertaining to this earth, another great prophet, known to us as the brother of Jared, was similarly favored by the Lord. He was even permitted to behold the spirit-body of the foreordained Savior, prior to His incarnation; and so like the body of a man was His spirit in form and appearance, that the prophet thought he was gazing upon a being of flesh and blood. He first saw the

*It is clear from the context of this verse that Jesus Christ is speaking, not the Father. But as the First Presidency later made plain in "The Father and the Son: A Doctrinal Exposition by the First Presidency and the Twelve" (see pp. 79–84 in this chapter), the Savior often does speak for the Father and as the Father.

The First Presidency, 1901–10, left to right: John R. Winder, Joseph F. Smith, and Anthon H. Lund

finger and then the entire body of the Lord—all in the spirit. The Book of Mormon says of this wonderful manifestation:

"And it came to pass that when the brother of Jared had said these words, behold, the Lord stretched forth His hand and touched the stones one by one with His finger; and the veil was taken from off the eyes of the brother of Jared, and he saw the finger of the Lord; and it was as the finger of a man, like unto flesh and blood; and the brother of Jared fell down before the Lord, for he was struck with fear.

"And the Lord saw that the brother of Jared had fallen to the earth; and the Lord said unto him, Arise, why hast thou fallen?

"And he saith unto the Lord, I saw the finger of the Lord, and feared lest he should smite me: for I knew not that the Lord had flesh and blood.

"And the Lord said unto him, Because of thy faith thou hast seen that I shall take upon me flesh and blood; and never has man come before me with such exceeding faith as thou hast; for were it not so, ye could not have seen my finger. Sawest thou more than this?

"And he answered, Nay, Lord, show thyself unto me.

"And the Lord said unto him, Believest thou the words which I shall speak?

"And he answered, Yea, Lord, I know that thou speakest the truth, for thou art a God of truth and canst not lie.

"And when he had said these words, behold, the Lord showed himself unto him, and said, Because thou knowest these things ye are redeemed from the fall; therefore ye are brought back into my presence; therefore I show myself unto you.

"Behold, I am He who was prepared from the foundation of the world to redeem my people. Behold, I am Jesus Christ, I am the Father and the Son. In me shall all mankind have light, and that eternally, even they who shall be-lieve on my name; and they shall become my sons and my daughters.

"And never have I shewed myself unto man whom I have created, for never hath man believed in me as thou hast. Seest thou that ye are created after mine own image? Yea, even all men were created in the beginning after mine own image.

"Behold, this body, which ye now behold, is the body of my spirit, and man have I created after the body of my spirit; and even as I appear unto thee to be in the spirit, will I appear unto my people in the flesh " (Ether, 3:6–16).

What more is needed to convince us that man, both in spirit and in body, is the image and likeness of God, and that God Himself is in the form of man?

When the divine Being whose spirit-body the brother of Jared beheld, took upon Him flesh and blood, He appeared as a man, having "body, parts and passions," like other men, though vastly superior to all other, because He was God, even the Son of God, the Word made flesh: in Him "dwelt the fulness of the Godhead bodily." And why should He not appear as a man? That was the form of His spirit, and it must needs have an appropriate covering, a suitable tabernacle. He came into the world as He had promised to come (III Nephi, 1:13), taking an infant tabernacle, and developing it gradually to the fulness of His spirit stature. He came as man had been coming for ages, and as man has continued to come ever since. Jesus, however, as shown, was the only begotten of God in the flesh.

Adam, our great progenitor, "the first man," was, like Christ, a pre-existent spirit, and like Christ he took upon him an appropriate body, the body of a man, and so became a "living soul." The doctrine of the pre-existence,—revealed so plainly, particularly in latter days, pours a wonderful flood of light upon the otherwise mysterious problem of man's origin. It shows that man, as a spirit, was begotten and born of heavenly parents, and reared to maturity in the eternal mansions of the Father, prior to coming upon the earth in a temporal body to undergo an experience in mortality. It teaches that all men existed in the spirit before any man existed in the flesh, and that all who have inhabited the earth since Adam have taken bodies and become souls in like manner.

It is held by some that Adam was not the first man upon this earth, and that the original human being was a development from lower orders of the animal creation. These, however, are the theories of men. The word of the Lord declares that Adam was "the first man of all men" (Moses 1:34), and we are therefore in duty bound to regard him as the primal parent of our race. It was shown to the brother of Jared that all men were created in the *beginning* after the image of God; and whether we take this to mean the spirit or the body, or both, it commits us to the same conclusion: Man began life as a human being, in the likeness of our heavenly Father.

True it is that the body of man enters upon its career as a tiny germ or embryo, which becomes an infant, quickened at a certain stage by the spirit whose tabernacle it is, and the child, after being born, develops into a man. There is nothing in this, however, to indicate that the original man, the first of our race, began life as anything less than a man, or less than the human germ or embryo that becomes a man.

Man, by searching, cannot find out God. Never, unaided, will he discover the truth about the beginning of human life. The Lord must reveal Himself, or remain unrevealed; and the same is true of the facts relating to the origin of Adam's race—God alone can reveal them. Some of these facts, however, are already known, and what has been made known it is our duty to receive and retain.

The Church of Jesus Christ of Latter-day Saints, basing its belief on divine revelation, ancient and modern, proclaims man to be the direct and lineal offspring of Deity. God Himself is an exalted man, perfected, enthroned, and supreme. By His almighty power He organized the earth, and all that it contains, from spirit and element, which exist co-eternally with Himself. He formed every plant that grows, and every animal that breathes, each after its own kind, spiritually and temporally—"that which is spiritual being in the likeness of that which is temporal, and that which is temporal in the likeness of that which is spiritual." He made the tadpole and the ape, the lion and the elephant; but He did not make them in His own image, nor endow them with Godlike reason and intelligence. Nevertheless, the whole animal creation will be perfected and perpetuated in the Hereafter, each class in its "distinct order or sphere," and will enjoy "eternal felicity." That fact has been made plain in this dispensation (Doctrine and Covenants, 77:3).

Man is the child of God, formed in the divine image and endowed with divine attributes, and even as the infant son of an earthly father and mother is capable in due time of becoming a man, so the undeveloped offspring of celestial parentage is capable, by experience through ages and aeons, of evolving into a God. [*Improvement Era,* Nov. 1909, pp. 75–81]

"A Warning Voice"

Four years later, on 2 August 1913, the First Presidency issued a letter of warning to the officers and members of the Church, about certain individuals who claimed to have learned the location of precious metals by means of dreams and were urging others to accept these purported revelations rather than the counsel of regularly acknowledged Church leaders.

From the days of Hiram Page (Doc. and Cov., Sec. 28), at different periods there have been manifestations from delusive spirits to members of the Church. Sometimes these have come to the men and women who because of transgression became easy prey to the Arch-Deceiver. At other times people who pride themselves on their strict observance of the rules and ordinances and ceremonies of the Church are

led astray by false spirits, who exercise an influence so imitative of that which proceeds from a Divine source that even these persons, who think they are "the very elect," find it difficult to discern the essential difference. Satan himself has transformed himself to be apparently "an angel of light."

When visions, dreams, tongues, prophecy, impressions or any extraordinary gift or inspiration conveys something out of harmony with the accepted revelations of the Church or contrary to the decisions of its constituted authorities, Latter-day Saints may know that it is not of God, no matter how plausible it may appear. Also they should understand that directions for the guidance of the Church will come, by revelation, through the head. All faithful members are entitled to the inspiration of the Holy Spirit for themselves, their families, and for those over whom they are appointed and ordained to preside. But anything at discord with that which comes from God through the head of the Church is not to be received as authoritative or reliable. In secular as well as spiritual affairs, Saints may receive Divine guidance and revelation affecting themselves, but this does not convey authority to direct others, and is not to be accepted when contrary to Church covenants, doctrine or discipline, or to known facts, demonstrated truths, or good common sense. No

person has the right to induce his fellow members of the Church to engage in speculations or take stock in ventures of any kind on the specious claim of Divine revelation or vision or dream, especially when it is in opposition to the voice of recognized authority, local or general. The Lord's Church "is a house of order." It is not governed by individual gifts or manifestations, but by the order and power of the Holy Priesthood as sustained by the voice and vote of the Church in its appointed conferences.

The history of the Church records many pretended revelations claimed by imposters or zealots who believed in the manifestations they sought to lead other persons to accept, and in every instance, disappointment, sorrow and disaster have resulted therefrom. Financial loss and sometimes utter ruin have followed. We feel it our duty to warn the Latter-day Saints against fake mining schemes which have no warrant for success beyond the professed spiritual manifestations of their projectors and the influence gained over the excited minds of their victims. We caution the Saints against investing money or property in shares of stock which bring no profit to anyone but those who issue and trade in them. Fanciful schemes to make money for the alleged purpose of "redeeming Zion" or providing means for "the salvation of the dead" or other

The Alberta Temple, begun during President Joseph F. Smith's administration

seemingly worthy objects, should not deceive anyone acquainted with the order of the Church, and will result only in waste of time and labor, which might be devoted now to doing something tangible and worthy and of record on earth and in heaven.

Be not led by any spirit or influence that discredits established authority, contradicts true scientific principles and discoveries, or leads away from the direct revelations of God for the government of the Church. The Holy Ghost does not contradict its own revealings. Truth is always harmonious with itself. Piety is often the cloak of error. The counsels of the Lord through the channel he has appointed will be followed with safety. Therefore, O! ye Latter-day Saints, profit by these words of warning. [Clark, *Messages*, 4: 284–86]

"The Father and the Son"

The traditional doctrine of the Trinity held that the Father, Son, and Holy Ghost were somehow all one being. During the early years of the twentieth century, liberal theologians increasingly rejected the fact that Jesus Christ was the Son of God. The following doctrinal exposition by the First Presidency and the Council of the Twelve, given 30 June 1916, sets forth revealed doctrine respecting these matters and explains how the titles *Father* and *Son* may be applied to members of the Godhead.

The scriptures plainly and repeatedly affirm that God is the Creator of the earth and the heavens and all things that in them are. In the sense so expressed the Creator is an Organizer. God created the earth as an organized sphere; but He certainly did not create, in the sense of bringing into primal existence, the ultimate elements of the materials of which the earth consists, for "the elements are eternal" (Doc. and Cov. 93:33).

So also life is eternal, and not created; but life, or the vital force, may be infused into organized matter, though the details of the process have not been revealed unto man. For illustrative instances see Genesis 2:7; Moses 3:7; and Abraham

President Joseph F. Smith and his wife, Julina Lambson, on their golden wedding anniversary, 5 May 1916

5:7. Each of these scriptures states that God breathed into the body of man the breath of life. See further Moses 3:19, for the statement that God breathed the breath of life into the bodies of the beasts and birds. God showed unto Abraham "the intelligences that were organized before the world was"; and by "intelligences" we are to understand personal "spirits" (Abraham 3:22, 23); nevertheless, we are expressly told that "Intelligence" that is, "the light of truth was not created or made, neither indeed can be" (Doc. and Cov. 93:29).

The term "Father" as applied to Deity occurs in sacred writ with plainly different meanings. Each of the four significations specified in

the following treatment should be carefully segregated.

1. "Father" as Literal Parent

Scriptures embodying the ordinary signification—literally that of Parent—are too numerous and specific to require citation. The purport of these scriptures is to the effect that God the Eternal Father, whom we designate by the exalted name-title "Elohim," is the literal Parent of our Lord and Savior Jesus Christ, and of the spirits of the human race. Elohim is the Father in every sense in which Jesus Christ is so designated, and distinctively He is the Father of spirits. Thus we read in the Epistle to the Hebrews: "Furthermore we have had fathers of our flesh which corrected us, and we gave them reverence: shall we not much rather be in subjection unto the Father of spirits, and live?" (Hebrews 12:9). In view of this fact we are taught by Jesus Christ to pray: "Our Father which art in heaven, Hallowed be thy name."

Jesus Christ applies to Himself both titles, "Son" and "Father." Indeed, He specifically said to the brother of Jared: "Behold, I am Jesus Christ. I am the Father and the Son" (Ether 3:14). Jesus Christ is the Son of Elohim both as spiritual and bodily offspring; that is to say, Elohim is literally the Father of the spirit of Jesus Christ and also of the body in which Jesus Christ performed His mission in the flesh, and which body died on the cross and was afterward taken up by the process of resurrection, and is now the immortalized tabernacle of the eternal spirit of our Lord and Savior. No extended explanation of the title "Son of God" as applied to Jesus Christ appears necessary.

2. "Father" as Creator

A second scriptural meaning of "Father" is that of Creator, e.g. in passages referring to any one of the Godhead as "The Father of the heavens and of the earth and all things that in them are" (Ether 4:7; see also Alma 11:38, 39 and Mosiah 15:4).

God is not the Father of the earth as one of the worlds in space, nor of the heavenly bodies in whole or in part, nor of the inanimate objects and the plants and the animals upon the earth, in the literal sense in which He is the Father of the spirits of mankind. Therefore, scriptures that refer to God in any way as the Father of the heavens and the earth are to be understood as signifying that God is the Maker, the Organizer, the Creator of the heavens and the earth.

With this meaning, as the context shows in every case, Jehovah, who is Jesus Christ the Son of Elohim, is called "the Father," and even "the very eternal Father of heaven and of earth" (see passages before cited, and also Mosiah 16:15). With analogous meaning Jesus Christ is called "The Everlasting Father"

The First Presidency and the Council of the Twelve, 1917 (President Smith fourth from left, seated)

(Isaiah 9:6; compare 2 Nephi 19:6). The descriptive titles "Everlasting" and "Eternal" in the foregoing texts are synonymous.

That Jesus Christ, whom we also know as Jehovah, was the executive of the Father, Elohim, in the work of creation is set forth in the book "Jesus the Christ" Chapter 4. Jesus Christ, being the Creator, is consistently called the Father of heaven and earth in the sense explained above; and since His creations are of eternal quality He is very properly called the Eternal Father of heaven and earth.

3. Jesus Christ the "Father" of Those Who Abide in His Gospel

A third sense in which Jesus Christ is regarded as the "Father" has reference to the relationship between Him and those who accept His Gospel and thereby become heirs of eternal life. Following are a few of the scriptures illustrating this meaning.

In the fervent prayer offered just prior to His entrance into Gethsemane, Jesus Christ supplicated His Father in behalf of those whom the Father had given unto Him, specifically the apostles, and, more generally, all who would accept and abide in the Gospel through the ministry of the apostles.

Read in our Lord's own words the solemn affirmation that those for whom He particularly prayed were His own, and that His Father had given them unto Him: "I have manifested thy name unto the men which thou gavest me out of the world: thine they were, and thou gavest them me; and they have kept thy word. Now they have known that all things whatsoever thou hast given me are of thee. For I have given unto them the words which thou gavest me; and they have received them, and have known surely that I came out from thee, and they have believed that thou didst send me. I pray for them: I pray not for the world, but for them which thou hast given me; for they are thine. And all mine are thine, and thine are mine; and I am glorified in them. And now I am no more in the world, but these are in the world, and I come to thee. Holy Father, keep through thine own name those whom thou hast given me, that they may be one as we are. While I was with them in the world, I kept them in thy name: those that thou gavest me I have kept, and none of them is lost, but the son of perdition; that the scripture might be fulfilled" (John 17:6–12).

And further: "Neither pray I for these alone, but for them also which shall believe on me through their word; That they all may be one; as thou, Father, art in me, and I in thee, that they also may be one in us: that the world may believe that thou hast sent me. And the glory which thou gavest me I have given them; that they may be one, even as we are one: I in them, and thou in me, that they may be made perfect in one; and that the world may know that thou hast sent me, and hast loved them, as thou hast loved me. Father, I will that they also, whom thou hast given me, be with me where I am; that they may behold my glory, which thou hast given me: for thou lovedst me before the foundation of the world'' (John 17:20–24).

To His faithful servants in the present dispensation the Lord has said: "Fear not, little children; for you are mine, and I have overcome the world, and you are of them that my Father hath given me" (Doc. & Cov. 50:41).

Salvation is attainable only through compliance with the laws and ordinances of the Gospel; and all who are thus saved become sons and daughters unto God in a distinctive sense. In a revelation given through Joseph the Prophet to Emma Smith the Lord Jesus addressed the woman as "My daughter," and said: "for verily I say unto you, all those who receive my gospel are sons and daughters in my kingdom" (Doc. & Cov. 25:1). In many instances the Lord has addressed men as His sons (e.g. Doc. & Cov. 9:1; 34:3; 121:7).

That by obedience to the Gospel men may become sons of God, both as sons of Jesus Christ, and, through Him, as sons of His Father, is set forth in many revelations given in the current dispensation. Thus we read in an utterance of the Lord Jesus Christ to Hyrum Smith in 1829: "Behold, I am Jesus Christ, the Son of God. I am the life and the light of the world. I am the same who came unto my own and my own received me not; But verily, verily, I say unto you, that as many as receive me, to them will I give power to become the sons of God, even to them that believe on my name.

Amen." (Doc. & Cov. 11:28–30). To Orson Pratt the Lord spoke through Joseph the Seer, in 1830: "My son Orson, hearken and hear and behold what I, the Lord God, shall say unto you, even Jesus Christ your Redeemer; The light and the life of the world; a light which shineth in darkness and the darkness comprehendeth it not; Who so loved the world that he gave his own life, that as many as would believe might become the sons of God: wherefore you are my son" (Doc. & Cov. 34:1–3). In 1830 the Lord thus addressed Joseph Smith and Sidney Rigdon: "Listen to the voice of the Lord your God, even Alpha and Omega, the beginning and the end, whose course is one eternal round, the same today as yesterday, and for ever. I am Jesus Christ, the Son of God, who was crucified for the sins of the world, even as many as will believe on my name, that they may become the sons of God, even one in me as I am in the Father, as the Father is one in me, that we may be one" (Doc. & Cov. 35:1–2). Consider also the following given in 1831: "Hearken and listen to the voice of him who is from all eternity to all eternity, the Great I AM, even Jesus Christ, The light and the life of the world; a light which shineth in darkness and the darkness comprehendeth it not: The same which came in the meridian of time unto my own, and my own received me not; But to as many as received me, gave I power to become my sons, and even so will I give unto as many as will receive me, power to become my sons" (Doc. & Cov. 39:1–4). In a revelation given through Joseph Smith in March, 1831 we read: "For verily I say unto you that I am Alpha and Omega, the beginning and the end, the light and the life of the world—a light that shineth in darkness and the darkness comprehendeth it not. I came unto my own, and my own received me not; but unto as many as received me, gave I power to do many miracles, and to become the sons of God, and even unto them that believed on my name gave I power to obtain eternal life" (Doc. & Cov. 45:7–8).

A forceful exposition of this

relationship between Jesus Christ as the Father and those who comply with the requirements of the Gospel as His children was given by Abinadi, centuries before our Lord's birth in the flesh: "And now I say unto you, who shall declare his generation? Behold, I say unto you, that when his soul has been made an offering for sin, he shall see his seed. And now what say ye? And who shall be his seed? Behold I say unto you, that whosoever has heard the words of the prophets, yea, all the holy prophets who have prophesied concerning the coming of the Lord; I say unto you, that all those who have hearkened unto their words, and believed that the Lord would redeem his people, and have looked forward to that day for a remission of their sins; I say unto you, that these are his seed, or they are the heirs of the kingdom of God: For these are they whose sins he has borne; these are they for whom he has died, to redeem them from their trangressions. And now, are they not his seed? Yea, and are not the prophets, every one that has opened his mouth to prophesy, that has not fallen into trangression; I mean all the holy prophets ever since the world began? I say unto you that they are his seed" (Mosiah 15:10–13).

In tragic contrast with the blessed state of those who become children of God through obedience to the Gospel of Jesus Christ is that of the unregenerate, who are specifically called the children of the devil. Note the words of Christ, while in the flesh, to certain wicked Jews who boasted of their Abrahamic lineage: "If ye were Abraham's children, ye would do the works of Abraham. . . . Ye do the deeds of your father. . . . If God were your Father, ye would love me. . . . Ye are of your father the devil, and the lusts of your father ye will do" (John 8:39, 41, 42, 44). Thus Satan is designated as the father of the wicked, though we cannot assume any personal relationship of parent and children as existing between him and them. A combined illustration showing that the righteous are the children of God and the wicked the children of the devil appears in the parable of the Tares: "The good seed are the children of the kingdom; but the tares are the children of the wicked one" (Matt. 13:38).

Men may become children of Jesus Christ by being born anew—born of God, as the inspired word states: "He that committeth sin is of the devil; for the devil sinneth from the beginning. For this purpose the Son of God was manifested, that he might destroy the works of the devil. Whosoever is born of God doth not commit sin; for his seed remaineth in him: and he cannot sin, because he is born of God. In this the children of God are manifest, and the children of the devil: Whosoever doeth not righteousness is not of God, neither he that loveth not his brother" (1 John 3:8–10).

Those who have been born unto God through obedience to the Gospel may by valiant devotion to righteousness obtain exaltation and even reach the status of Godhood. Of such we read: "Wherefore, as it is written, they are Gods, even the sons of God" (Doc. & Cov. 76:58; compare 132:20, and contrast paragraph 17 in the same section; see also paragraph 37). Yet, though they be Gods they are still subject to Jesus Christ as their Father in this exalted relationship; and so we read in the paragraph following the above quotation: "and they are Christ's and Christ is God's" (76:59).

By the new birth—that of water and the Spirit—mankind may become children of Jesus Christ, being

through the means by Him provided "begotten sons and daughters unto God" (Doc. & Cov. 76:24). This solemn truth is further emphasized in the words of the Lord Jesus Christ given through Joseph Smith in 1833: "And now, verily I say unto you, I was in the beginning with the Father, and am the firstborn; And all those who are begotten through me are partakers of the glory of the same, and are the church of the firstborn" (Doc. & Cov. 93:21, 22). For such figurative use of the term "begotten" in application to those who are born unto God see Paul's explanation: "for in Christ Jesus I have begotten you through the gospel" (I Cor. 4:15). An analogous instance of sonship attained by righteous service is found in the revelation relating to the order and functions of Priesthood, given in 1832: "For whoso is faithful unto the obtaining these two Priesthoods of which I have spoken, and the magnifying their calling, are sanctified by the Spirit unto the renewing of their bodies: They become the sons of Moses and of Aaron and the seed of Abraham, and the church and kingdom, and the elect of God" (Doc. & Cov. 84:33, 34).

If it be proper to speak of those who accept and abide in the Gospel as Christ's sons and daghters—and upon this matter the scriptures are explicit and cannot be gainsaid nor denied—it is consistently proper to speak of Jesus Christ as the Father of the righteous, they having become His children and He having been made their Father through the second birth—the baptismal regeneration.

4. Jesus Christ the "Father" By Divine Investiture of Authority

A fourth reason for applying the title "Father" to Jesus Christ is found in the fact that in all His dealings with the human family Jesus the Son has represented and yet represents Elohim His Father in power and authority. This is true of Christ in His preexistent, antemortal, or unembodied state, in the which He was known as Jehovah; also during His embodiment in the flesh; and during His labors as a disembodied

President Joseph F. Smith and his family

spirit in the realm of the dead; and since that period in His resurrected state. To the Jews He said: "I and my Father are one" (John 10:30; see also 7:11, 22); yet He declared "My Father is greater than I" (John 14:28); and further, "I am come in my Father's name" (John 5:43; see also 10:25). The same truth was declared by Christ Himself to the Nephites (see 3 Nephi 20:35 and 28:10), and has been reaffirmed by revelation in the present dispensation (Doc. & Cov. 50:43). Thus the Father placed His name upon the Son; and Jesus Christ spoke and ministered in and through the Father's name; and so far as power, authority and Godship are concerned His words and acts were and are those of the Father.

We read, by way of analogy, that God placed His name upon or in the Angel who was assigned to special ministry unto the people of Israel during the exodus. Of that Angel the Lord said: "Beware of him, and obey his voice, provoke him not; for he will not pardon your transgressions; for my name is in him" (Exodus 23:21).

The ancient apostle, John, was visited by an angel who ministered and spoke in the name of Jesus Christ. As we read: "The Revelation of Jesus Christ, which God gave unto him, to shew unto his servants things which must shortly come to pass; and he sent and signified it by his angel unto his servant John" (Revelation 1:1). John was about to worship the angelic being who spoke in the name of the Lord Jesus Christ, but was forbidden: "And I John saw these things, and heard them. And when I had heard and seen, I fell down to worship before the feet of the angel which shewed me these things. Then saith he unto me, See thou do it not: for I am thy fellowservant, and of thy brethren the prophets, and of them which keep the sayings of this book: worship God" (Rev. 22:8, 9). And then the angel continued to speak as though he were the Lord Himself: "And, behold, I come quickly; and my reward is with me, to give every man according as his work shall be. I am Alpha and Omega, the beginning and the end, the first and the last" (verses 12, 13). The resurrected Lord, Jesus Christ, who had been exalted to the right hand of God His Father, had placed His name upon the angel sent to John, and the angel spoke in the first person, saying "I come quickly," "I am Alpha and Omega," though he meant that Jesus Christ would come, and that Jesus Christ was Alpha and Omega.

None of these considerations, however, can change in the least degree the solemn fact of the literal relationship of Father and Son between Elohim and Jesus Christ. Among the spirit children of Elohim the firstborn was and is Jehovah or Jesus Christ to whom all others are juniors. Following are affirmative scriptures bearing upon this great truth. Paul, writing to the Colossians, says of Jesus Christ: "Who is the image of the invisible God, the firstborn of every creature: For by him were all things created, that are in heaven, and that are in earth, visible and invisible, whether they be thrones, or dominions, or principalities, or powers; all things were created by him, and for him: And he is before all things, and by him all things consist. And he is the head of the body, the church: who is the beginning, the firstborn from the dead; that in all things he might have the preeminence. For it pleased the Father that in him should all fullness dwell" (Colossians 1:15–19). From this scripture we learn that Jesus Christ was "the firstborn of every creature" and it is evident that the seniority here expressed must be with respect to antemortal existence, for Christ was not the senior of all mortals in the flesh. He is further designated as "the firstborn from the dead" this having reference to Him as the first to be resurrected from the dead, or as elsewhere written "the first fruits of them that slept" (I Corinthians 15:20, see also verse 23); and "the first begotten of the dead" (Revelation 1:5; compare Acts 26:23). The writer of the Epistle to the Hebrews affirms the status of Jesus Christ as the firstborn of the spirit children of His Father, and extols the preeminence of the Christ when tabernacled in flesh: "And again, when he bringeth in the firstbegotten into the world, he saith, And let all the angels of God worship him" (Hebrews 1:6; read the preceding verses). That the spirits who were juniors to Christ were predestined to be born in the image of their Elder Brother is thus attested by Paul: "And we know that all things work together for good to them that love God, to them who are the called according to his purpose. For whom he did foreknow, he also did predestinate to be conformed to the image of his Son, that he might be the firstborn among many brethren" (Romans 8:28,29).

John the Revelator was commanded to write to the head of the Laodicean church, as the words of the Lord Jesus Christ: "These things saith the Amen, the faithful and true witness, the beginning of the creation of God" (Revelation 3:14). In the course of a revelation given through Joseph Smith in May, 1833, the Lord Jesus Christ said as before cited: "And now, verily I say unto you, I was in the beginning with the Father, and am the firstborn" (Doc. & Cov. 93:21). A later verse makes plain the fact that human beings generally were similarly existent in spirit state prior to their embodiment in the flesh: "Ye were also in the beginning with the Father; that which is Spirit, even the Spirit of truth (verse 23).

There is no impropriety, therefore, in speaking of Jesus Christ as the Elder Brother of the rest of human kind. That He is by spiritual birth Brother to the rest of us is indicated in Hebrews: "Wherefore in all things it behoved him to be made like unto his brethren, that he might be a merciful and faithful high priest in things pertaining to God, to make reconciliation for the sins of the people" (Hebrews 2:17). Let it not be forgotten, however, that He is essentially greater than any and all others, by reason (1) of His seniority as the oldest or firstborn; (2) of His unique status in the flesh as the offspring of a mortal mother and of an immortal, or resurrected and glorified, Father; (3) of His selection and foreordination as the one and only Redeemer and Savior of the race; and (4) of His transcendent sinlessness.

Jesus Christ is not the Father of the spirits who have taken or yet shall take bodies upon this earth, for He is one of them. He is The Son, as they are sons or daughters of Elohim. So far as the stages of eternal progression and attainment have been made known through divine revelation, we are to understand that only resurrected and glorified beings can become parents of spirit offspring. Only such exalted souls have reached maturity in the appointed course of eternal life; and the spirits born to them in the eternal worlds will pass in due sequence through the several stages or estates by which the glorified parents have attained exaltation. [Clark, *Messages*, 5:26–34]

Just six weeks before his death, President Smith was privileged to witness a vision of the Savior's ministry in the spirit world. This great revelation, added to the standard works in 1976, seems a fitting climax to his gospel teachings (see D&C 138, originally placed in the Pearl of Great Price as Joseph F. Smith—Vision of the Redemption of the Dead).

STUDY QUESTIONS

1. How had Joseph F. Smith been prepared to lead the Church?

2. What contributed to the change in popular attitude toward the Church during the early years of the twentieth century?

3. In what ways do developments during Joseph F. Smith's administration still affect Church programs and activities today?

4. What evidence is there in the scriptures that man did not descend from lower forms of life? What are some essential differences between man and God's other creations? Since all men and women are the children of God, what is our ultimate potential?

5. What specific added insights concerning the nature of God and man are contained in President Smith's doctrinal discourses?

6. Who might be deceived by spurious revelations? How can Church members detect these false claims? Why should they be avoided?

7. In what specific ways is Christ the "Son of God"? In what distinct senses may the title *Father* be applied to Elohim and Jesus Christ respectively?

8. According to President Joseph F. Smith's 1918 vision, to whom did the Savior go and what did he do during the period between his death and his resurrection?

President Smith at the dedication of the Hyrum Smith Memorial, Salt Lake City Cemetery, 27 June 1918

HEBER J. GRANT

HEBER J. Grant learned early that persistence is a prerequisite to success, and his life became an example of what can be accomplished through such discipline. He adopted the following as his motto: "That which we persist in doing becomes easy to do, not that the nature of the task has changed, but that our capacity to do has increased." His persistence led to early business success and helped prepare him for the ministry he was called to at the age of twenty-six, when he became a member of the Quorum of the Twelve Apostles. While one of the Twelve, he opened Japan for the preaching of the gospel. He became President of the Church just twelve days after the close of the First World War in 1918, and he led the Church through the global depression that followed and the Second World War, dying just six days after the conclusion of the war in Europe in 1945. Amidst all of this turmoil, President Grant directed the growing missionary program, dedicated three temples, presided over the centennial celebration in 1930, and vigorously affirmed and reaffirmed such principles as the law of tithing, the Word of Wisdom, and industry and thrift. He well remembered President Joseph F. Smith's last charge to him, given the day President Smith died: "The Lord bless you, my boy, the Lord bless you, you have got a great responsibility. Always remember that this is the Lord's work, and not man's. The Lord is greater than any man. He knows whom He wants to lead His Church, and never makes any mistake. The Lord bless you" (quoted in *Improvement Era,* Nov. 1936, p. 692).

HIGHLIGHTS

1856 Nov. 22: Born in Salt Lake City, Utah; his father dies eight days later.

1871 Employed as a bank clerk, begins a career in the business world (15).

1875 Becomes superintendent of the first ward YMMIA (19).

1876 Elected assistant cashier with Zion's Savings Bank and Trust Co. (20).

1877 Marries Lucy Stringham; President Brigham Young dies (21).

1880 Called as president of the Tooele Stake (23).

1882 Becomes a member of the Quorum of the Twelve (25).

1883–84 Serves a mission to the Indians (26–28).

1884 Marries Augusta Winters and Emily Harris Wells (27).

1896 Considered as a candidate for first governor of Utah (40).

1897 Becomes a member of the General Superintendency of YMMIA (41).

1901–3 Opens the Japanese Mission and presides over it (45–47).

1904–6 Presides over the British and European Missions (47–50).

1918 Becomes President of the Church (62).

1919 Dedicates Hawaii Temple. Church membership reaches a half million (63).

1923 Dedicates Alberta Temple. Speaks on first radio broadcast of general conference (67).

1926 The Church purchases the Hill Cumorah and the Whitmer farm in upstate New York (70).

1927 Dedicates the Arizona Temple at Mesa (71).

1930 The Church celebrates its one-hundredth anniversary (74).

1933 The twenty-first Amendment to the Constitution ends prohibition of liquor (77).

1936 The Church welfare plan is established (80).

1937 Visits the missions in Europe (81).

1939 Missionaries are withdrawn from Europe as World War II begins (83).

1941 Assistants to the Quorum of the Twelve are called (85).

1945 May 14: Dies in Salt Lake City (88).

HISTORICAL SUMMARY

Early Life

Heber J. Grant was the first President of the Church born after the Saints settled in the Salt Lake Valley. His life paralleled the growth of the western United States from its pioneer beginnings through the Second World War. His father, Jedediah M. Grant, was the first mayor of Salt Lake City and a counselor to President Brigham Young when Heber was born 22 November 1856. Great Salt Lake City was not yet ten years old. Heber was given his father's nickname, "Jeddy," as a middle

Jedediah M. Grant

name. When the boy was only eight days old, his father died, leaving his mother a widow after only one year of marriage.

During the years after her husband's death, she supported herself and her young son by sewing and taking in boarders. Rachel Ridgeway Ivins Grant was a self-reliant, courageous woman. She had known and loved the Prophet Joseph Smith (having been sealed to him), and she transmitted that love to her son. Her goal in life was to rear Heber to realize his fullest potential. When Heber was a small boy, Heber C. Kimball stood him on a table one day, looked into his eyes, and prophesied that he would be an Apostle and become a greater man in the Church than his own father, Jedediah. Knowing this, his mother reminded him regularly to "behave himself." A thread of faith and confidence runs through her relationship with her son.

The home where Heber was born

Rachel Ivins Grant

When others thought the boy lazy for practicing so many hours with his baseball, she saw instead a persistence and a determination to be nurtured and developed. "Deprived of a father's companionship, President Grant appreciated all the more deeply the transforming power of a mother's love. It was she who changed his timidity to courage; his self-depreciation to self-confidence; impetuousness to self-control; lack of initiative to perseverance" (David O. McKay, "President Heber J. Grant," *Improvement Era*, June 1945, p. 334).

Heber first entered the business world as a messenger boy in an insurance office. His efforts to learn banking led to his securing the position of assistant cashier in a bank, and he became president of the State Bank of Utah at age thirty-four. Most of the organizations he created as a businessman survived the economic shocks of his time.

Integrity, Honesty, Industry

He was scrupulously honest and expected all whom he dealt with to be just as honest. He told of receiving a letter when he became a member of the Council of the Twelve from a prominent businessman who was not a member of the Church. The letter read, "I never thought very much of the leaders of the Mormon people, in fact I thought they were a very bright, keen, designing lot of fellows, getting rich from the tithes that they gathered from a lot of ignorant, superstitious, and over-zealous religious people, but now that you are one of the fifteen men at the head of the Mormon Church, I apologize to the other fourteen. I know that if there were anything crooked in the management of the Mormon Church you would give it all away" (*Relief Society Magazine*, Oct. 1937, pp. 625–26). Though some men disagreed with his beliefs, none questioned his integrity. Elder John A. Widtsoe said of President Grant in 1936:

Once convinced of the rightness of a cause he defends it at any cost. One need only recall his life-long advocacy of the Word of Wisdom. Knowing how dear the appetites are to most people; in the face of anti-prohibition sentiment; regardless of a nation's cancellation of the prohibition experiment—he has urged upon his people and the world to observe the Word of Wisdom.... One expression of this fearlessness is his outspokenness. There is no masking of meaning when the battle is on! He cannot understand why truth should be hidden by idle words. Traditional diplomacy is foreign to him. Yet, as he bides his time, for he can wait, his direct use of truth is more effective in obtaining results than would be the long-drawn-out subtle methods of idle negotiation. And it should be said that the outspoken opinions of President Grant carry no rancour with them. They but express the truth as he understands it. This characteristic attracts the honest, makes the dishonest hesitant. ["President Grant the Man," *Improvement Era*, Nov. 1936, pp. 663–64]

Joseph Anderson, President Grant's secretary of many years, recalled, "If he had a piece of property to sell and there was something about it of an undesirable nature he would not think of withholding that information from the prospective buyer" (*Prophets I Have Known*, p. 28)

He became a wealthy man, but as he accumulated riches he gave them away. He was a user of things, not a collector only. He believed in service. "Let every man feel that he is the architect and builder of his own life, and that he proposes to make a success of it by working. 'Six days shalt thou labor and do all thy work,' and rest on the seventh, and do not be willing to labor four or five days and then only half labor. Let every Latter-day Saint give value received for everything he gets, whether it be in work, or whatever he does" (Heber J. Grant, in Conference Report, Oct. 1936, p. 13).

"The real secret of happiness in life and the way in which to prepare ourselves for the hereafter is service, and it is because we give service more than any other people in the world, that we are happy. . . . I realize that it requires a constant effort on the part of each and every one of us to make a success of our lives. It requires no effort at all to roll down the hill, but it does require an effort to climb the hill to the summit" (Bryant S. Hinckley, *Heber J. Grant: Highlights in the Life of a Great Leader* p. 179).

Young Heber

Once, when offered a position at ten times his present salary Heber refused, explaining, "I can only sleep in one bed and wear one suit of clothes at a time." He felt money was to be used for good purposes. He loved to tell the story of one five-dollar bill that went the rounds as five people paid a five-dollar debt, each paying another until

the five dollars had come back to its original owner, having cancelled out twenty-five dollars worth of debt. He encouraged the Saints during the Great Depression years to use their money on locally made items, to keep the money at home so that all would profit.

As he foresaw the breakdown in families, President Grant watched over and cared for his own with particular concern. He fathered ten daughters and two sons, both of whom died as young children. He was always interested in his eternal family—his children, grandchildren, parents, grandparents. That concern led to a weekly temple session which he attended regularly with his children, even during the nearly twenty-seven years he was President of the Church. One daughter remembered his great love and regard for her when she was recovering from an illness. She had become so weak she lost the use of her legs so her father began teaching her to walk. She stated: "as I took the few uncertain steps and was gathered into his sheltering arms I was content. Those arms have always been my shelter. His great heart has understood my needs" (Lucy Grant Cannon, "A Father Who Is Loved and Honored," *Improvement Era,* Nov. 1936, p. 680).

When asked if he would leave a fortune to his children he often replied, "I want *my* children to be sorry when I die!" and asked them to join him in service in the Church. He bequeathed to them more than money. His daughter, Dessie, recorded, "He taught us to love life, but not to fear death; to be happy in the face of trials and to make our Heavenly Father our best friend" (Improvement Era, Nov. 1936, p. 704).

Arizona Revelation

Heber J. Grant devoted many years to serving the Church. For sixty-three years he was a General Authority. At age twenty-three he was a stake president, and at twenty-five, a member of the Quorum of the Twelve. He served as President of the Church for twenty-six and one-half years. A revelation in the Arizona desert after his call to the Quorum of the Twelve led him to the assurance that his call to serve as an Apostle was divinely inspired. In his

own words, President Grant later told of the circumstances surrounding that call and the struggle he had to fill it at such a young age.

There are two spirits striving with us always, one telling us to continue our labor for good, and one telling us that with the faults and failings of our nature we are unworthy. I can truthfully say that from October, 1882, until February, 1883, that spirit followed me day and night telling me that I was unworthy to be an Apostle of the Church, and that I ought to resign. When I would testify of my knowledge that Jesus is the Christ, the Son of the Living God, the Redeemer of mankind, it seemed as though a voice would say to me: "You lie! You lie! You have never seen Him."

While on the Navajo Indian reservation with Brigham Young, Jr., and a number of others, six or eight, on horseback, and several others in "white tops,"—riding along with Lot Smith at the rear of that procession, suddenly the road veered to the left almost straight, but there was a well beaten path leading ahead. I said: "Stop, Lot, stop. Where does this trail lead? There are plenty of foot marks and plenty of horses' hoof marks here." He said, "It leads to an immense gully just a short distance ahead, that it is impossible to cross with a wagon. . . ."

"I want to be all alone. Go ahead and follow the crowd." . . .

As I was riding along to meet them on the other side I seemed to see, and I seemed to hear, what to me is one of the most real things in all my life, I seemed to see a Council in Heaven. I seemed to hear the words that were spoken. I listened to the discussion with a great deal of interest. The First Presidency and the Council of the Twelve Apostles had not been able to agree on two men to fill the vacancies in the Quorum of the Twelve. There had been a vacancy of one for two years, and a vacancy of two for one year, and the Conferences had adjourned without the vacancies being filled. In this Council the Savior was present, my father was there, and the Prophet Joseph Smith was there. They discussed the question that a mistake had been made in not filling those two vacanices and that in all probability it would be another six months before the Quorum would be completed, and they discussed as to whom they wanted to occupy those positions, and decided that the way to remedy the mistake that had been made in not filling these vacancies was to send a revelation. It was given to me that the Prophet Joseph Smith and my father mentioned me and requested that I be called to that position. I sat there and wept for joy. It was given to me that I had done nothing to entitle me to that exalted position, except that I had lived a clean, sweet life. It was given to me that because of my father having practically sacrificed his life in what was known as the great Reformation, so to speak, of the people in early days, having been practically a martyr, that the Prophet Joseph and my father desired me to have that position, and it was because of their faithful labors that I was called, and not because of anything I had done of myself or any great thing that I had accomplished. It was also given to me that that was all these men, the Prophet and my father, could do for me; from that day it depended upon me and upon me alone as to whether I made a success of my life or a failure. . . .

No man could have been more

Heber J. Grant, 1856–1945

Elder Grant, his first wife, Lucy, and children, 1887 (by C.R. Savage)

unhappy than I was from October 1882, until February, 1883, but from that day I have never been bothered, night or day, with the idea that I was not worthy to stand as an Apostle, and I have not been worried since the last words uttered by Joseph F. Smith to me [in 1918]: "The Lord bless you, my boy, the Lord bless you; you have got a great responsibility. Always remember this is the Lord's work and not man's. The Lord is greater than any man. He knows whom He wants to lead His Church, and never makes any mistake. The Lord bless you." [In Conference Report, Apr. 1941, pp. 4–5]

Ministry

President Grant's contributions to the Saints were many. He helped found the *Improvement Era* (the forerunner of the *Ensign* and the *New Era*). He dedicated the Hawaii, Alberta, and Arizona temples. He lived through Prohibition (of liquor) and then its repeal, fearlessly preaching the Word of Wisdom throughout his life.

I believe honestly and conscientiously that we ought in the future to be more diligent, more faithful, more energetic . . . than we have been in the past, for fear of the temptations that are coming to our young people, and be sure to set examples before them that will be worthy of their imitation, because

example is the finest way to preach in all the world. Children notice the example of their parents, their friends, and their teachers. Upon one occasion, in one of the southern countries, when some missionaries were stopping at a brother's home and they had prayers, a little child said: "Papa, we never pray, do we, unless we have company?" [James H. Wallis, "President Grant—Defender of the Word of Wisdom," *Improvement Era*, Nov. 1936, p. 698]

I would like it known that if we as a people never used a particle of tea or coffee or of tobacco or of liquor, we would become one of the most wealthy people in the world. Why? Because we would have increased vigor of body, increased vigor of mind; we would grow spiritually; we would have a more direct line of communication with God, our Heavenly Father." [President Heber J. Grant, "Safeguard," *Improvement Era*, Feb. 1941, p. 73]

I believe beyond the shadow of a doubt that there are hundreds and thousands of Latter-day Saints, who but for the obeying of the Word of Wisdom, would not be here today. When they have been attacked by serious diseases and have been in a critical condition physically, having obeyed that law, having fulfilled an irrevocable law of God, he was bound to bestow the promised blessings, and they have come to the afflicted ones. [Wallis, *Improvement Era,* Nov. 1936, p. 697]

There is absolutely no benefit to any human being derived from breaking the Word of Wisdom, but there is everything for his benefit, morally, intellectually, physically, and spiritually, in obeying it. [Quoted in Emerson R. West, *Profiles of the Presidents,* p. 232].

Characteristic of his commitment to integrity, President Grant also counseled the Saints to be scrupulously honest with the Lord in their payment of tithes:

I heard a very splendid illustration given by a Sunday School teacher of the Primary class. She brought to her school ten beautiful red apples. She explained that everything we have in the world came to us from the Lord, and she said, "Now, children, if I gave one of you these ten apples, will you give me one back again? Now, any one of you children that will do that, hold up your hand." And of course they all held up their hands. Then she said, "That is what the Lord does for us. He gives us the ten apples, but He requests that we return one to Him to show our appreciation of that gift."

The great trouble with the majority of people is that when they get the ten apples, they eat up nine of them and then they cut the other in two and give the Lord half of what is left. Some of them cut the apple in two and eat up one-half of it and then hold up the other half and ask the Lord to take a bite. That is about as near as they see fit to share properly and show their gratitude to the Lord.

The payment of our tithing in the season thereof—when we get our income—makes it come easy. I find that those who pay tithing every month have very much less difficulty in paying it than those who postpone payment to the end of the year, when they have eaten the nine apples, so to speak; but if they pay the minute they get the apples in their possession, there is no hardship; their hearts are full of grati-

tude, and they are willing to express their gratitude; but after the nine apples are eaten, they think the Lord is very hard to want all they have left. . . .

The Lord, you know, does not send collectors around once a month to collect bills; He does not send us our account once a month; we are trusted by the Lord; we are agents; we have our free will; and when the battle of life is over, we have had the ability and the power and the capacity to have done those things which the Lord required us to do and we cannot blame anybody else. . . .

I have found a great many people who do not know what their tithing is. I have never met people of that kind but what I believe if I were in partnership with them and they had a tenth interest in that partnership, they would know pretty well what part their tenth was. I do not think they would have any difficulty whatever in finding how much I owed them. So, I am inclined to think that if we wanted to, we would have no difficulty in finding out what is one-tenth of our income, and that is what we owe to the Lord—no difficulty whatever.

Now, I believe that people are blessed in proportion to their liberality. I am not saying that they

always make more dollars, perhaps, than the other man, but so far as an increase in the faith and in the testimony and the knowledge of the divinity of the work in which we are engaged, men that are honest with the Lord in the payment of their tithing grow as men never grow that are not honest; there is no question in my mind. Moreover, I am just foolish enough to believe that the Lord magnifies those who do pay their tithing and that they are more prosperous, on the average, than the men who do not. I believe that to those who are liberal the Lord gives ideas, and they grow in capacity and ability more rapidly than those that are stingy. I have that faith, and I have had it from the time I was a boy. ["Settlement" *Improvement Era,* Jan. 1941, pp. 9, 56]

He spoke on the first church radio broadcast in 1922. He celebrated the centennial anniversary of the organization of the Church in 1930 and led them through the Great Depression years from 1929 through the 1930s. His business sense was invaluable when he established the Church welfare plan in 1936. The Church gained added respect during the years of the Depression for taking care of its own (see chapter 14). President Grant also lived through two world wars and

President Grant speaking on the first radio broadcast of the Church-owned station KZN, later KSL, in 1922

The First Presidency, 1925–31, left to right: Anthony W. Ivins, Heber J. Grant, and Charles W. Nibley

comforted his people around the world in the loss of their sons in those hostilities.

Statement on War

In 1939, war broke out in Europe. On 7 December 1941, the Japanese attacked Pearl Harbor. The following day, the United States officially entered World War II. At the next general conference, 6 Apr. 1942, President J. Reuben Clark, Jr., read the following official statement of the Latter-day Saint position on war:

In these days of trial and sorrow, when Satan is "seeking to destroy the souls of men" (D.&C. 10:27) we send to the righteous everywhere our greetings with prayers for their blessing; to the Saints in all lands and on the islands of the seas, we renew our testimonies and pledge our unselfish service, exhorting them to lives obedient to the gospel and the commandments of the Lord; we extend to them the hand of true and faithful fellowship, with deep and abiding love and blessing. . . .

Hate can have no place in the souls of the righteous. We must follow the commands of Christ Himself which declare the true life: "Love your enemies, bless them that curse you, do good to them that hate you, and pray for them which despitefully use you, and persecute you; That ye may be the children of your Father which is in heaven." (Matthew 5:44–45.)

These principles must be instilled into the hearts of our children, taught to our youth, given by way of instruction to our vigorous manhood and womanhood, lived in very fact and deed by the aged, ripened in experience and wisdom. These are the principles which God enjoins upon all who teach, in whatever capacity or in whatever place. The Lord has declared that those who teach not their "children light and truth, according to the commandments" shall be afflicted, the wicked one shall have power over them (D.&C. 93:42), and the sin shall be upon their heads (D.&C. 68:25). Woe will be the part of those who plant hate in the hearts of the youth, and of the people, for God will not hold them guiltless; they are sowing the wind, their victims will reap the whirlwinds. Hate is born of Satan; love is the offspring of God. We must drive out hate from our hearts, every one of us, and permit it not again to enter. . . .

Today, more than ever before in the history of the Church, we must bring the full force of the righteous living of our people and the full influence of the spiritual power and responsibility of the holy Priesthood, to combat the evil forces which Satan has let loose among the peoples of the earth. We are in the midst of a desperate struggle between Truth and Error, and Truth will finally prevail.

The state is responsible for the civil control of its citizens or subjects, for their political welfare, and for the carrying forward of political policies, domestic and foreign, of the body politic. For these policies, their success or failure, the state is alone responsible, and it must carry its burdens. All these matters involve and directly affect Church members because they are part of the body politic, and members must give allegiance to their sovereign and render it loyal service when called thereto. But the Church, itself, as such, has no responsibility for these policies, as to which it has no means of doing more than urging its members fully to render that loyalty to their country and to free institutions which the loftiest patriotism calls for.

Nevertheless, as a correlative of the principle of separation of the church and the State, themselves, there is an obligation running from every citizen or subject to the state. This obligation is voiced in that Article of Faith which declares:

"We believe in being subject to kings, presidents, rulers, and magistrates, in obeying, honoring, and sustaining the law." . . .

Obedient to these principles, the members of the Church have always felt under obligation to come to the defense of their country when a call to arms was made; on occasion the Church has prepared to defend its own members. . . .

When, therefore, constitutional law, obedient to these principles, calls the manhood of the Church into the armed service of any country to which they owe allegiance, their highest civic duty requires that they meet that call. If, harkening to that call and obeying those in command over them, they shall take the lives of those who fight against them, that will not make of them murderers, nor subject them to the penalty that God has prescribed for those who kill, beyond the principle to be mentioned shortly. For it would be a cruel God that would punish His children as moral sinners for acts done by them as the innocent instrumentalities of a sovereign whom He had told them to obey and whose will they were powerless to resist.

The whole world is in the midst of a war that seems the worst of all time.

This Church is a worldwide Church. Its devoted members are in both camps. They are the innocent war instrumentalities of their warring sovereignties. On each side they believe they are fighting for home, and country, and freedom. On each side, our brethren pray to the same God, in the same name, for victory. Both sides cannot be wholly right; perhaps neither is without wrong. God will work out in His own due time and in His own sovereign way the justice and right of the conflict, but He will not hold the innocent instrumentalities of the war, our brethren in arms, responsible for the conflict. This is a major crisis in the world-life of man. God is at the helm. . . .

In this terrible war now waging, thousands of our righteous young men in all parts of the world and in many countries are subject to a call into the military service of their own countries. Some of these, so serving, have already been called back to their heavenly home; others will almost surely be called to follow. But "behold," as Moroni said, the righteous of them who serve and are slain "do enter into the rest of the Lord their God," and of them the Lord has said "those that die in me shall not taste of death, for it shall be sweet unto them." (D.&C. 42:46) Their salvation and exaltation in the world to come will be secure. That in their work of destruction they will be striking at their brethren will not be held against them. That sin, as Moroni of old said, is to the condemnation of those who "sit in their places of power in a state of thoughtless stupor," those rulers in the world who in a frenzy of hate and lust for unrighteous power and dominion over their fellow men, have put into motion eternal forces they do not comprehend and cannot control. God, in His own due time, will pass sentence upon them.

"Vengeance is mine; I will repay, saith the Lord." (Romans 12:19)

To our young men who go into service, no matter whom they serve or where, we say live clean, keep the commandments of the Lord, pray to Him constantly to preserve you in truth and righteousness, live as you pray, and then whatever betides you the Lord will be with you and nothing will happen to you that will not be to the honor and glory of God and to your salvation and exaltation. There will come into your hearts from the living of the pure life you pray for, a joy that will pass your powers of expression or understanding. The Lord will be always near you; He will comfort you; you will feel His presence in the hour of your greatest tribulation; He will guard and protect you to the full extent that accords with His all-wise purpose. Then, when the conflict is over and you return to your homes, having lived the righteous life, how great will be your happiness—whether you be of the victors or of the vanquished—that you have lived as the Lord commanded. You will return so disciplined in righteousness that thereafter all Satan's wiles and stratagems will leave you untouched. Your faith and testimony will be strong beyond breaking. You will be looked up to and revered as having passed through the fiery furnace of trial and temptation and come forth unharmed. Your brethren will look to you for counsel, support, and guidance. You will be the anchors to which thereafter the youth of Zion will moor their faith in man. [In Conference Report, Apr. 1942, pp. 88, 90–91, 92–93, 94–96]

President Grant possessed an exceptional ability to meet and mingle with prominent people of his nation and the world. He was known for his ability to

Wilford Wood presents President Grant with some papers, David O. McKay looking on

build good will and to reduce prejudice. He made many friends for the Church.

Missionary Work

His love and tolerance of people made him an able missionary. At age twenty-six, as a newly-appointed member of the Council of the Twelve, he served a mission to the Indians. In 1901, he was called to far-off Japan to open and preside over that mission. While there, he delivered a stirring proclamation.

In company with my associates sent to you from the headquarters of the Church of Jesus Christ of Latter-day Saints, in Salt Lake City, Utah, as an Apostle and minister of the Most High God, I salute you and invite you to consider the important message which we bear. We do not come to you for the purpose of trying to deprive you of any truth in which you believe, or any light that you have been privileged to enjoy. We bring to you greater light, more truth and advanced knowledge, which we offer you freely. We recognize you as the children of our common Father, the Creator of the universe. The spirit of man, the intelligent ego, is the offspring of God; therefore men and women of all races and kindreds and tribes and tongues on the face of the earth are brothers and sisters. It is, then, in the spirit of fraternity that we approach you, desiring your welfare now and hereafter. Our mission is one of duty. We have been commanded of God to proclaim His word and will to the world. It is by His divine authority that we act, and not in our own name or for personal ends. We entreat you to listen to our word. . . .

By His authority we turn the divine key which opens the kingdom of heaven to the inhabitants of Japan. We say to them all, come to the light which has been shed forth from the Son of Righteousness. We offer you blessings that are beyond price. They are not of man, nor do they come by the power of man, but they are from heaven where the true and living God dwells and rules in majesty and glory. That which your ancestors received which was good and which leads to do good, was but as the glimmering of the twilight. We bring to you the truth in all its effulgence, direct from the great Luminary of the day. Come to the light and the truth, and walk in the one way that leads to the divine and eternal presence! Then shall your souls be filled with peace and love and joy, and you shall learn how to unite with the great and pure of all nations and tribes, for the establishment of the grand empire of righteousness on earth, and hereafter you shall dwell with the just, and the redeemed, in the immediate presence of our Eternal Father, and your glory and dominion shall be celestial and everlasting.

Your servant for Christ's sake,

Heber J. Grant. [Quoted in Preston Nibley, *The Presidents of the Church,* 1974 ed., pp. 240–42].

President Grant's absolute conviction of the truthfulness of his message made him a fearless missionary. He said in the October 1907 conference, after having recently returned from presiding over the European Mission, "We acknowledge our weaknesses, but while we acknowledge them we can also proclaim to the world our strength, strength in the knowledge that God lives, that Jesus is the Christ, that Joseph Smith is a Prophet of God, and that we have the truth to proclaim to the world" (in Conference Report, Oct. 1907, p. 25). Such strength of testimony was characteristic of the man throughout his life. Twenty-two new missions were opened during his administration.

It is impossible to measure the impact of Heber J. Grant on the Church he loved and served for more than sixty-three years. He lived as he taught. He understood that the gospel was to save, not to condemn men, and he was always ready to forgive. He had the assurance of his own eternal identity, perhaps seen most clearly in the 1883 Arizona desert. His testimony burns with the confidence born of truth.

STUDY QUESTIONS

1. How can Sister Rachel Grant's relationship with her son Heber help a single parent succeed in raising a family?

2. In what specific ways did Heber J. Grant's life teach the value of complete honesty?

3. How does President Grant's life demonstrate the principle of the dignity of work, which he taught forcefully and often?

4. At the time of his Arizona revelation, what was the only qualification that Heber J. Grant saw in himself for the apostleship?

5. In light of the past thirty years, were President Grant's comments on the Word of Wisdom prophetic?

6. How does the First Presidency's statement concerning war answer questions many people still raise?

Elder Grant in Japan

THE FIRST CENTURY: SOME REFLECTIONS

SUNDAY, 6 April 1930, marked the one-hundredth anniversary of the organization of The Church of Jesus Christ of Latter-day Saints. The decade of the 1920s had already witnessed a series of centennial observances. At the April general conference in 1920, Church leaders marked the one hundredth anniversary of Joseph Smith's vision of the Father and the Son by bearing witness of the authenticity of his testimony and by paying tribute to his work. In 1923 and 1927, Saints and missionaries from the eastern United States together with representatives from Church headquarters gathered at the Hill Cumorah and Sacred Grove near Palmyra, New York, to commemorate the visit of the Angel Moroni directing Joseph Smith to the gold plates of the Book of Mormon, one hundred years earlier. All these celebrations, as they focused on the major highlights of Church history, pointed toward the decade's climax—the centennial of the Church's organization.

HIGHLIGHTS

1919 Nov. 27: President Heber J. Grant dedicates the Hawaii Temple.

1923 The Church purchases part of the Hill Cumorah.

Aug. 26: President Heber J. Grant dedicates the Alberta Temple.

1924 Oct. 3: General conference is broadcast over radio for the first time.

1926 The Church purchases the Peter Whitmer, Sr., farm, where the Church was organized in 1830.

1927 Oct. 23: President Heber J. Grant dedicates the Arizona Temple.

1928 The Church purchases the rest of the Hill Cumorah.

1929 June 15: The Tabernacle Choir and organist begin weekly network radio broadcasts.

1930 Apr. 6: The centennial of the Church organization is observed during general conference.

Elder B.H. Roberts of the First Council of the Seventy presents his *Comprehensive History of the Church,* which was written for the centennial, to the conference.

The Message of the Ages, a special centennial pageant, premieres and runs for thirty nights without interruption.

HISTORICAL SUMMARY

Special Services

As the date of the centennial drew near, many thousands of people poured into Salt Lake City. In order to accommodate all who wanted to attend a conference session in the Tabernacle, Church leaders added one day to the usual three-day general conference format. The opening day, Sunday, 6 April, was to be the highlight. President Heber J. Grant read the First Presidency's centennial message to the peoples of the world, which bore witness to the divine mission of the Savior and to the latter-day restoration of his Church through the Prophet Joseph Smith and challenged Church members to rededicate themselves to the Lord's service.

The First Presidency of the Church of Jesus Christ of Latter-day Saints to our beloved brethren and sisters throughout the world:

On this, the one hundredth anniversary of the organization of the Church, we salute you, and pray that the blessing of God our Father, and the grace and love of Jesus Christ, our Lord, may abide with you forever.

We preface our message to you by reference to the following scripture:

"Behold, I am Jesus Christ, the Son of God. I am the life and the light of the world. I am the light which shineth in darkness, and the darkness comprehendeth it not."

As Moses lifted up the serpent in the wilderness, even so was the Son of God lifted up, that whosoever believeth in him shall not perish, but have eternal life.

The Church of Jesus Christ of Latter-day Saints, through its presidency, reaffirms the truths set forth in the above scripture, and calls upon its members in all parts of the world to rededicate their lives to the service of the Master and the establishment of his kingdom upon earth.

From the beginning of time, as we count it, to the present, God our Father has, at divers times, both by his own voice and the voice of his inspired prophets, declared that he would send to the earth his only Begotten Son, that through him, by means of the resurrection, of which our Lord was the first fruits, mankind might be redeemed from the penalty of death, to which all flesh is heir; and by obedience to the law of righteous living, which he taught and exemplified in his life, be cleansed from personal sin and made heirs to the Kingdom of Heaven. . . .

In humility, and with full consciousness of the responsibility involved, we bear witness to the people of the world that with the appearance of the Father and the Son to the Prophet Joseph Smith, in the early spring of 1820, the greatest gospel dispensation of all time was ushered in, a dispensation of light, radiating from the presence of God, illuminating the minds of men, increasing intelligence and knowledge, which is the glory of God, and by the application of which the past one hundred years have been made the Miracle Century of the ages.

The increase of scientific knowledge, invention, industrial development; the harnessing of the forces of the universe and adapting them to the comfort and convenience of man, have reached a degree of perfection not dreamed of by people who lived when the past century was ushered in. . . .

Undoubtedly the greatest miracle of the century is the acccomplishment by which the human voice, with the personality of the speaker, may be indefinitely preserved and reproduced with every detail of originality. Whether uttered in the frozen arctics, or from the jungles of the tropics, without visible means of conduct, the human voice instantly circles the earth, thus overcoming the hitherto insurmountable barrier of both time and space.

Contemplating these accomplishments of the past century, to which but brief reference has been made, we are led to exclaim:

"Great and marvelous are thy ways, O Lord!

"From eternity Thou art the same!

"Thy purposes fail not, neither are there any who can stay Thy hand!" . . .

The opening of a new Gospel dispensation was not a thing of chance. Jesus Christ, through his messenger, had declared to John while he was upon the isle of Patmos, that an angel would come flying through the midst of heaven, having the everlasting gospel to preach to them that dwell upon the earth, calling them back to the worship of God, who is the Maker of the heavens and the earth, the sea and the fountains of water. [See Revelation 14:6–7] The Redeemer himself had declared that before the time of his glorious appearance, to assume his rightful place among his people, the Gospel of his kingdom should be preached in all the world, for a witness unto all nations, before the coming of the end. [See Matthew 24:14]

As the time of the restoration of the

President Grant at the tabernacle pulpit, 4 April 1929

Gospel was clearly indicated, so was the gathering place of those who would accept the truth definitely declared. The prophet Isaiah had said that it should come to pass in the last days, that the mountain of the Lord's house would be established in the top of the mountains, and be exalted above the hills, and that people from all nations would flow unto it. Many people, he declared, would go and say: "Come ye, and let us go up to the mountains of the Lord, to the house of the God of Jacob." For what purpose? That they might be taught the way of the Lord and learn to walk in his paths. . . .

Prior to his death our father Jacob called his twelve sons to him, blessed them, and defined the future of their posterity, adding little to that which had before been promised, until he laid his hands upon the head of Joseph and not only conferred upon him the blessing and heritage of his fathers, but also declared that his heritage prevailed above that of his progenitors, unto the utmost bounds of the Everlasting Hills, to a land

choice above all other lands, a land rich in the blessings of the earth, of the heavens above, and the sea beneath. . . . [See Genesis 49:22, 26]

It was not by chance that the Puritans left their native land and sailed away to the shores of New England, and that others followed later. They were the advance guard of the army of the Lord, predestined to establish the God-given system of government under which we live, and to make of America, which is the land of Joseph, the gathering place of Ephraim, an asylum for the oppressed of all nations, and prepare the way for the restoration of the Gospel of Christ and the reestablishment of his Church upon earth. It was under these circumstances and others of which the Lord was the author, that the stage was set for the raising of the curtain upon the opening scene of the Dispensation of the Fulness of Times. As the Christian Dispensation was ushered in, the glory of the Lord shone round about the shepherds who kept watch over their flocks by night upon the hills of Judea, while the voice of the angel of the Lord declared the Babe of Bethlehem to be the Savior of the world.

So also the glory of the Lord overshadowed Joseph Smith, and God himself, in the glory and majesty of his person, with his Only Begotten Son, Jehovah, revealed himself in vision, and with his own voice designated Joseph Smith to be the instrument through whom the greatest gospel dispensation of the ages was to be ushered in.

There was nothing of ostentation, pageantry or dramatic display; it was a simple, solemn occasion, superlatively glorious and impressive beyond expression.

The voice of the Lord, which had been silent for ages, was heard again. Again that divine message, so oft repeated, was delivered: "This is My Beloved Son. Hear Him!" The personality of the Father and his Only Begotten Son was again revealed that mankind may know them as they are. . . .

The mountain of the Lord's house has been established in the top of the mountains, and people from all nations have flown unto it. Through the blessings of the Lord upon their labors the desert has been subdued and made to blossom as the rose. Solitary places have been made glad because of them. [Isaiah 35:1] Cities have been established, springs of water have broken out which have given life to the thirsty land, music and the voices of children are heard in the streets where desolation and silence had reigned for ages.

President Grant, other General Authorities, and their wives at the dedication of the Alberta Temple, 26 August 1923

Temples have been erected in which the work of redemption has been done for an innumerable host of the living and the dead.

Many thousands have been brought from the poverty and distress of the old world to this blessed land of Joseph, to become wealthy and be made happy as they have participated in the blessings which the Lord our God has pronounced upon it.

Looking backward to the organization of the Church, which occurred under the most humble and, to the world, obscure circumstances, and following its history through persecution, poverty, and distress, can it be denied that a great and marvelous work has been accomplished, that the promises of the Lord have been fulfilled, and His power to accomplish that to which he sets his hand to do, manifested? . . .

With this glorious vision of the future, to which we look forward, we exhort our brethren and sisters to put their houses in order, that they may be prepared for that which is to come.

Refrain from evil; do that which is good. Visit the sick, comfort those who are in sorrow, clothe the naked, feed the hungry, care for the widow and the fatherless. Observe the laws of health which the Lord has revealed, and keep yourselves unspotted from the sins of the world. Pay your tithes and offerings, and the Lord will open the windows of heaven and pour out blessings until there shall not be room to contain them. Be obedient to the laws of God and the civil laws of the country in which you reside, and uphold and honor those who are chosen to administer them.

To the people of the world we send our blessing, and bear witness to them that God lives, that Jesus Christ is his Only Begotten Son, the Redeemer of the world. We call upon all men to come unto him, that through his grace they may attain to eternal life and an inheritance with him in the kingdom of his Father. [James R. Clark, comp., *Messages of the First Presidency of The Church of Jesus Christ of Latter-day Saints,* 5:274–86]

Church leaders were sustained in the order usually reserved for solemn assemblies, bearers of each priesthood office standing in turn to cast their

Elder B.H. Roberts

vote. The entire congregation then stood and rendered the sacred "Hosanna Shout," three times repeating

Hosanna! Hosanna! Hosanna!
To God and the Lamb
Amen, amen, and amen.

President Grant delivered a concluding address and blessed the people. The Tabernacle Choir closed the session by singing Handel's great "Hallelujah Chorus" from the oratorio "The Messiah."

Anxious to have as many as possible participate in these services, Church leaders arranged for the thousands who could not be accommodated in the Tabernacle to hear the proceedings over loudspeakers on the ground or in an overflow gathering in the nearby Assembly Hall. In addition, a network of radio stations carried the conference to listeners throughout the western United States. For areas that could not be reached by the broadcast, the First Presidency outlined a special service similar to that conducted in the Salt Lake Tabernacle. They instructed the Saints, "the same Address will be read, the same hymns sung, and the same Hosanna Shout [be] given" around the world on this special day. Mission presidents in non-English-speaking areas were to take special care in translating the First Presi-

dency's centennial message (see Clark, *Messages,* 5:272–73).

Additional Events

Other special events also marked the Church's centennial. The seven Latter-day Saint temples were illuminated for the first time during conference week. In Salt Lake, for example, crowds gathered to enjoy the awe-inspiring sight of the temple's brightly lighted spires against the night sky. A centennial pageant, *The Message of the Ages,* presented nightly for a month in the Tabernacle, showed how the latter-

A scene from The Message of the Ages

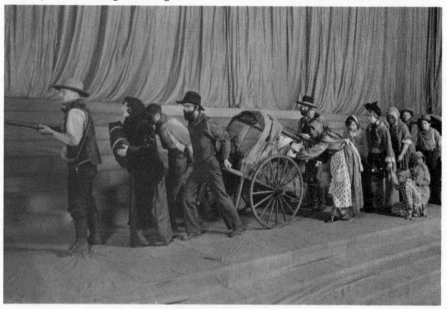

day restoration of the gospel and Church were the culmination of the Lord's work in former dispensations.

The centennial provided Latter-day Saints the opportunity to reflect on the Church's achievements during its first century. This was a dominant theme in many of the talks given during the centennial conference. These accomplishments included the Restoration itself, establishing the Church on a firm foundation, and gathering faithful converts from many lands to build Zion.

In his comments on the growth of the Church, Elder James E. Talmage of the Council of the Twelve observed, "At this major milepost in the course of the history of the Church, it is natural that we indulge in retrospect, and I think a hundred years is a span of sufficient length to give us a fair perspective of that which lies behind us" (in Conference Report, Apr. 1930, p. 95).

Histories of the Church

In preparation for the centennial celebration, the Church Historian's office had been actively collecting, compiling, and preserving a record of the Church's accomplishments. Assistant Historian Andrew Jenson, for example, traveled an estimated one million miles while interviewing early Church leaders and collecting valuable records. He then compiled over eight hundred large manuscript volumes. About half of these were histories of individual stakes, wards, and missions; the

Measure of Church Progress

Statistics reflected the extent of Church growth during its first one hundred years.

	1880	1930
Church membership	160,000*	672,488
Number of stakes	23	104
Number of missions	9†	29†
Temples in service	1	7
Full-time missionaries called during the year	450	2,068

* estimated figure

†not including the European Mission, which was solely administrative

[from statistics provided by the Historical Department, The Church of Jesus Christ of Latter-day Saints, Salt Lake City]

remainder formed a chronological "Journal History" of the Church.

A particularly significant feature of the centennial observance was the publication of Elder Brigham H. Roberts' multi-volume *Comprehensive History of the Church*. In his conference address Elder Roberts declared that this

President David O. McKay in the 1930s

work included the testimony he wished to bear concerning the Church's divine mission and destiny. He laid five completed volumes of the six he had written on the pulpit (the last volume to be published the following month) and prayed: "And now, O God, the Eternal Father! Here as to an altar, I bring this

work of mine, and dedicate it unto thee and to thy cause. If there is any way of excellence in it, I am sure it is of thee, and unto thee belongs all glory and all praise and honor" (in Conference Report, Apr. 1930, p. 49).

Historic Sites

During the early years of the twentieth century the Church had purchased several key sites related to its early history, including Joseph Smith's birthplace in Vermont; the Smith home, the Sacred Grove, and the Hill Cumorah near Palmyra, New York; property surrounding the temple lot in Independence, Missouri; and the Carthage Jail in Illinois. Bureaus of information (visitors' centers) were established at several of these sites to tell the world about the significant events that had happened there. These historic places became focal points of centennial celebrations and helped to broaden the Saints' interest in Church history.

Many individual members became involved in commemorating points of local importance. Youth groups conducted a variety of projects to raise funds to erect historical markers.

As the Saints looked back on their past, they were better able to contemplate what lay ahead. Elder David O. McKay of the Council of the Twelve epitomized the feelings of Church members as they looked from the vantage point of the centennial into the years to come:

The Church, established by divine inspiration to an unlearned youth, offers to the world the solution of all its social problems. It has stood the test of the first century successfully. In the midst of brilliant concepts of men in this twentieth century, who seek conscientiously for social reforms and who peer blindly into the future to read the destiny of man, the Church shines forth as the sun in the heavens, around which other luminaries revolve as satellites of minor importance. Truly it is the creator and preserver of man's highest values. Its real task, the redemption of our human world. "It is the light of truth radiating everywhere in the world, and this light cannot fail to reveal to man, sooner or later, the divine ideals by which man should live."

God help us and qualify us for the mission of carrying to the world this light. May we labor even more zealously than heretofore for the establishment of a social order in which God's will shall be done on earth as it is in heaven—a kingdom of God which shall foster the brotherhood of man and acknowledge the fatherhood of God. May we so live that men seeing our good deeds may be led to glorify our Father in heaven, I pray in the name of Jesus Christ. Amen. [In Conference Report, Apr. 1930, p. 83]

STUDY QUESTIONS

1. What is the main point of the First Presidency's centennial message?

2. What specific counsel did the First Presidency give to the Saints as they commemorated their centennial?

3. In what ways has Satan opposed the Lord's work over the centuries? What have been the results of the adversary's efforts?

4. What were some of the major achievements of the Church during its first century?

5. In what major ways did the Church celebrate its one-hundredth anniversary? What was the value of these celebrations?

6. What contributed to the Latter-day Saints' interest in their history?

7. Of what value is an understanding of history?

THAT THE CHURCH MAY STAND INDEPENDENT

THE 1930s brought severe economic difficulties to most parts of the world. In the boom years following World War I, unwise borrowing and a spirit of speculation had placed most nations' economies on extremely shaky footings. The United States stock market crash of late 1929 ushered in the Great Depression. Around the world, businesses closed or drastically cut back production, throwing a distressingly large number of people out of work. Long lines at employment offices and at public soup kitchens became an all-too-common sight. The Depresion's impact was particularly severe in the western United States where most Latter-day Saints then lived. As prices for crops fell, many farmers were not able to make mortgage payments and so lost their land. Together with the thousands of unemployed city workers, these farmers found the gospel ideals of independence and self-reliance increasingly difficult to maintain. In the midst of these trying economic difficulties, the Lord revealed a plan for the material security and welfare of the Saints. First known as the Church security plan, the welfare plan helped restore thousands to productivity and self-respect while emphasizing self-reliance and the virtues of honest work. Over the years, the welfare plan would become a monument to the industry and vision of the Latter-day Saints.

HIGHLIGHTS

1929 Oct. 29: The stock market crashes: "Black Tuesday."

1933 Sept. 2: The First Presidency encourages bishops to meet the needs of the poor.

1935 Apr. 20: President Grant calls Harold B. Lee to head the welfare program.

1936 Apr. 7: The First Presidency outlines the welfare plan.

Oct. 2: The First Presidency evaluates the achievements to date of the welfare program.

1937 Apr. 6: President Clark stresses the Saints' individual responsibilities, including storing one year's supply of food.

1938 Aug. 12: Deseret Industries is inaugurated.

1942 Oct. 3: President Clark contrasts communism, the united order, and the welfare plan.

HISTORICAL SUMMARY

The Lord's Plan Revealed

On 6 April 1933, J. Reuben Clark, Jr., was sustained as a counselor in the First Presidency. He subsequently played a key role in the development of a Churchwide welfare program.

In September 1933, the First Presidency, recognizing that the government could not carry the entire burden of relief for the needy, and that the

Church should prepare to shoulder part of the load, instructed local Church leaders concerning how this assistance was to be rendered:

Reported conditions in the state and nation suggest that a considerable burden may rest upon our Church relief activities in the near future. While it seems our people may properly look, as heretofore, for relief assistance from governmental and perhaps other sources, it cannot now be certainly foretold either what or how fully sufficient this assistance will be, and we must therefore prepare ourselves to meet the necessities that may fall upon us.

The Lord will not hold us guiltless if we shall permit any of our people to go hungry, or to be cold, unclad, or unhoused during the approaching winter. Particularly He will consider us gravely blameful if those who have heretofore paid their tithes and offerings to the Church when they had employment, shall now be permitted to suffer when the gen-

The Quorum of the Twelve, 1931–33

eral adversity has robbed them of their means of livelihood. Whatever else happens, these faithful persons must not be permitted to come to want or distress now....

The Church organizations set up by the Prophet Joseph in the very early days of the Church, if properly co-ordinated by the bishops and presidents of stakes, are qualified by purpose, jurisdiction, ability of membership, and experience, to carry on adequately, during the coming winter, the work of caring for Church members. Indigent non-Church persons will obviously look to other sources. But no one must be permitted to starve or freeze in our midst.

In rendering assistance to those in need, the Church officers should have one prime consideration in mind, namely: that relief, except to sick, infirm, or disabled, should not be extended as charity. Our faithful Church members are independent, self-respecting, and self-reliant; they do not desire charity. Our able-bodied members must not, except as a last resort, be put under the embarrassment of accepting something for nothing. In recognition of this wholly praiseworthy and admirable attitude of mind, Church officials administering relief must devise ways and means by which all able-bodied Church members who are in need, may make compensation for aid given them by rendering some sort of service. It is believed that private and community enterprise in our wards and stakes can be found or created in sufficient quantities for this purpose. [James R. Clark, comp., *Messages of the First Presidency of The Church of Jesus Christ of Latter-day Saints*, 5:331–32]

These principles were to form an important foundation for the welfare plan that would be developed in coming years.

In the spring of 1935, the First Presidency decided that the time had come to establish a Churchwide welfare organization. Harold B. Lee was called to head this venture. He later recalled:

I had a lesson years ago as to the greatness of priesthood. It had to

do with the call of the First Presidency for me to come to their office on a day that I shall never forget—April 20, 1935.

I was city commissioner in Salt Lake City. I was a stake president. We had been wrestling with this question of welfare....

Harold B. Lee

It was from our humble efforts that the First Presidency, knowing that we had had some experience, called me one morning asking if I would come to their office. It was Saturday morning; there were no calls on their calendar, and for hours in that forenoon they talked with me and told me that they wanted me to resign the city commission, and they would release me from being stake president; that they wished me now to head up the welfare movement to turn the tide from government relief, direct relief, and help to put the Church in a position where it could take care of its own needy.

After that morning I rode in my car (spring was just breaking) up to the head of City Creek Canyon into what was then called Rotary Park; and there, all by myself, I offered one of the most humble prayers of my life.

There I was, just a young man in my thirties. My experience had been limited. I was born in a little country town in Idaho. I had hardly been outside the boundaries of the states of Utah and Idaho. And now to put me in a position where I was to reach out to the entire membership

of the Church, worldwide, was one of the most staggering contemplations that I could imagine. How could I do it with my limited understanding?

As I kneeled down, my petition was, "What kind of an organization should be set up in order to accomplish what the Presidency has assigned?" And there came to me on that glorious morning one of the most heavenly realizations of the power of the priesthood of God. It was as though something were saying to me, "There is no new organization necessary to take care of the needs of this people. All that is necessary is to put the priesthood of God to work. There is nothing else that you need as a substitute." [In Conference Report, Oct. 1972, pp. 123–24; or *Ensign*, Jan. 1973, p. 104]

A survey conducted during the fall of 1935 revealed the extent of the challenge faced by the Church. A total of 88,460 Latter-day Saints, 17.9 percent of the Church's membership, were receiving aid from the government. The Church was assisting only 8,213 persons, 1.6 percent of its members. Furthermore, Church leaders were disappointed to note that from 11,000 to 16,000 of the total 88,460 relief recipients did not deserve this help because they themselves could have been working. (See Clark, *Messages*, 6:10; or *Deseret News*, 7 Apr. 1936, p. 1; or *Improvement Era*, May 1936, pp. 305–6.)

The Welfare Plan Inaugurated

In conjunction with the April 1936 general conference, the First Presidency conducted a special meeting for stake presidents and ward bishops. Here the Presidency outlined the major principles and features of the plan which was now to be implemented Churchwide:

1. Fast offerings must be increased to an amount equalling one dollar per Church member per year. This is an amount within the reach of every head of family and every single person in the Church. Those who can give more should do so.

2. Tithing should be fully paid, where possible in cash and where cash payment is not possible, then payment is to be made in kind.

The general Church welfare committee in the late 1930s

3. The Ward authorities, the Relief Society, and the Priesthood quorum organizations must exert the greatest possible effort to see that fast offerings and tithing are fully paid.

4. Upon Ward teachers and the Relief Society must rest the prime responsibility for discovering and appraising the wants of the needy of the Ward. These wants must be administered to under and in accordance with the regular rules and through the regular organizations of the Church.

5. Every Bishop should aim to have accumulated by next October Conference sufficient food and clothes to provide for every needy family in his Ward during the coming winter. The Relief Society must cooperate in this work by directing and assisting the needy sisters of the Ward in drying and preserving fruits and vegetables, providing clothing and bedding, etc.

6. Every Bishop and every President of a Stake must keep constantly before himself, that other Wards and Stakes may be more needy than his own, and therefore that even though his own Ward or Stake may not need the whole he is to collect on fast offerings, nevertheless he must collect the full sum in order that the sum not needed for the needs of his own Ward or Stake may be passed on to places where it is needed. . . .

7. Relief is not to be normally given as charity; it is to be distributed for work or service rendered. All members of the Church must cooperate to this end.

The Church itself will be prepared to assist to the utmost extent possible in providing work on its own properties for its unemployed members, as also in providing other work in wisely rehabilitating ranches, farms, gardens, and orchards that may be used to furnish foodstuffs for those in need.

No pains must be spared to wipe out all feeling of diffidence, embarrassment, or shame on the part of those receiving relief; the Ward must be one great family of equals. The spiritual welfare of those on relief must receive especial care and be earnestly and prayerfully fostered. A system which gives relief for work or service will go far to reaching these ends.

8. The work of directing and coordinating all this work will be in the hands of the Presiding Bishopric of the Church. The First Presidency will appoint a Church Relief Committee to assist the Presiding Bishopric in their work.

9. It will be observed that the foregoing general principles call only for the operation of regular Ward and Stake organizations. Some supplemental, coordinating and grouping organization may be nec-

essary as the plan is more fully developed. The regular Church organization, set up under revelations from the Lord, was planned by Him to meet every emergency coming to human beings. The Church organization will meet the present grave economic crisis if the members of the Church will but live fully and conscientiously the Gospel.

10. For the present and pending further developments in the working out of the Church plan, all persons engaged in W. P. A. [Works Progress Administration, an agency set up by the U.S. government to employ needy people during the depression] projects should endeavor to retain their positions, being scrupulously careful to do an honest day's work for a day's pay.

11. Whether we shall now take care of our own Church members in need and how fully, depends wholly and solely upon the faith and works of the individual Church members. If each Church member meets his full duty and grasps his full opportunity for blessing, full necessary relief will be extended to all needy Church members; in so far as individual members fail in their duty and opportunity, by that much will the relief fall short. [Clark, *Messages,* 6:10–12; or *Deseret News,* 7 Apr. 1936; or *Improvement Era,* May 1936, pp. 305–6].

Following this announcement, the Church organized a central committee called the General Church Relief Committee under the First Presidency and Presiding Bishop Sylvester Q. Cannon to supervise the implementation of the Church security plan (it became the welfare plan in 1938). The first members of this committee were Harold B. Lee and Mark Austin. By the end of June 1936, Stringham Stevens, Campbell M. Brown, and Henry D. Moyle had been called to the committee with Elder Melvin J. Ballard of the Twelve serving as advisor. During that same month, April 1936, Church leaders organized a series of new regions at various Latter-day Saint centers in the western United States. (This was the beginning of regions that have since become key administrative units in Church government.) Each region, comprising from four to sixteen stakes, was to coordinate production projects in the area, and a regional storehouse was established to receive and distribute the production of these projects. President Heber J. Grant personally attended many of the initial regional meetings. His exhortations to abolish laziness and to keep the commandments brought a spirit of enthusiasm to the program (see "Launching of a Greater Church Objective," *Church News*, 25 Apr. 1936, pp. 1, 4).

At the general conference six months later, 2 October 1936, the First Presidency summarized the accomplishments of the welfare plan to date, and reemphasized the fundamental principles on which the program was being developed: "Our primary purpose was to set up, in so far as it might be possible, a system under which the curse of idleness would be done away with, the evils of a dole abolished, and independence, industry, thrift and self respect be once more established amongst our people. The aim of the Church is to help the people to help themselves. Work is to be re-enthroned as the ruling principle of the lives of our Church membership" (Heber J. Grant, in Conference Report, Oct. 1936, p. 3).

In the April 1937 conference, President J. Reuben Clark, Jr., anticipated the possibility of even harder times than those already experienced during the Depression:

> What may we as a people and as individuals do for ourselves to prepare to meet this oncoming disaster, which God in his wisdom may not turn aside from us?
>
> First, and above and beyond everything else, let us live righteously, fearing God and keeping his commandments, that we may in part claim his blessing as of right, and not as of mercy only. Along this way only lies happiness and salvation. . . .
>
> Let us avoid debt as we would avoid a plague; where we are now in debt let us get out of debt; if not today, then tomorrow.
>
> Let us straitly and strictly live within our incomes, and save a little.

> Let every head of every household see to it that he has on hand enough food and clothing, and, where possible, fuel also, for at least a year ahead. You of small means put your money in foodstuffs and wearing apparel, not in stocks and bonds; you of large means will think you know how to care for yourselves, but I may venture to suggest

President J. Reuben Clark, jr.

> that you do not speculate. Let every head of every household aim to own his own home, free from mortgage. Let every man who has a garden spot, garden it; every man who owns a farm, farm it.
>
> Let us again clothe ourselves with these proved and sterling virtues—honesty, truthfulness, chastity, sobriety, temperance, industry and thrift; let us discard all covetousness and greed. [In Conference Report, Apr. 1937, p. 26]

A welfare canning project

As the welfare program unfolded, stakes throughout the Church organized a wide variety of projects to produce food, clothing, and other needed items. A significant addition occurred on 12 August 1938, when the first Deseret Industries store opened. This branch of the welfare plan created employment for handicapped or older workers by collecting clothing, furniture, and other items to be reconditioned and sold to the public.

As it has expanded in scope, the welfare program has blessed members and nonmembers many times over. It has rendered assistance to thousands at times of floods, earthquakes, and personal crises. As shall be seen in the next chapter, it also enabled the Church to be prepared to provide needed food and clothing to the stricken Saints in Europe immediately following World War II.

Communism and the United Order

During the 1930s communism attracted increasing attention. Some Church members felt that communism would lead to the restoration of the law of consecration and united order. In an important statement issued 3 July 1936, the First Presidency stressed that this was not true:

> To our Church members we say: Communism is not the United Order, and bears only the most superficial resemblance thereto; Communism is based upon intolerance and force, the United Order upon love and freedom of conscience and action; Communism involves force-

ful despoliation and confiscation, the United Order voluntary consecration and sacrifice.

Communists cannot establish the United Order, nor will Communism bring it about. The United Order will be established by the Lord in His own due time and in accordance with the regular prescribed order of the Church.

Furthermore, it is charged by universal report, which is not successfully contradicted or disproved, that Communism undertakes to control, if not indeed to proscribe the religious life of the people living within its jurisdiction, and that it even reaches its hand into the sanctity of the family circle itself, disrupting the normal relationship of parent and child, all in a manner unknown and unsanctioned under the Constitutional guarantees under which we in America live. Such interference would be contrary to the fundamental precepts of the Gospel and to the teachings and order of the Church. [Clark, *Messages,* 6:18; or *Deseret News,* 3 July 1936, p. 1; or *Improvement Era,* Aug. 1936, p. 488]

The Welfare Plan and the United Order

In a related and oft-quoted address given at the October 1942 general conference, President Clark also pointed out that the welfare plan is not the same as communism or the united order, emphasizing that it is instead a preparation for living the law of consecration:

There is a great deal of misapprehension among our people regarding the United Order.

I have not been able to believe that the United Order meant what some people have thought it meant, so within the last months I have spent quite a little time reading the revelations thereon, also reading our history, and at the same time giving some consideration to a dissertation which has been written regarding the Order.

There is a growing—I fear it is growing—sentiment that communism and the United Order are virtually the same thing, communism being merely the forerunner, so to speak, of a reestablishment of the United Order. I am informed that ex-bishops, and indeed, bishops, who belong to communistic organizations, are preaching this doctrine. So I thought that perhaps if I said just a few words to you tonight regarding the way I interpret the revelations that are printed about this in the Doctrine and Covenants (if there are other revelations about the Order, I do not know of them), I thought if I said something about it, it might be helpful. I recommend that you, my brethren, read a few of the Sections of the Doctrine and Covenants which cover this matter, beginning with Sections 42 and 51. (See also Sections 70, 78, 82, 83, 85, 90, 92, 96, and 104.) If you will go over these sections, I feel sure that you will find that my explanation of the United Order will be substantially accurate.

I may say to begin with, that in practice the brethren in Missouri got away, in their attempts to set up the United Order, from the principles set out in the revelations. This is also true of the organizations set up here in Utah after the Saints came to the Valleys. So far as I have seen there has been preserved only one document that purports to be a legal instrument used in connection with the setting up of the United Order, and that document is without date. It is said to have been found among the papers of Bishop Partridge. It was a 'lease-lend' document. You may have heard that phrase before. Under this instrument the Church leased to Titus Billings a certain amount of real estate and loaned him a certain amount of personal property.

This instrument is not in accordance with the principle laid down in the revelations touching upon the United Order.

The basic principle of all the revelations on the United Order is that everything we have belongs to the Lord; therefore, the Lord may call upon us for any and all of the property which we have, because it belongs to Him. This, I repeat, is the basic principle. (D.&C. 104:14–17, 54–57)

One of the places in which some of the brethren are going astray is this: There is continuous reference in the revelations to equality among the brethren, but I think you will find only one place where that equality is really described, though it is referred to in other revelations. That revelation (D.&C. 51:3) affirms that every man is to be "equal according to his family, according to

his circumstances and his wants and needs." (See also D.&C. 82:17; 78:5–6.) Obviously, this is not a case of "dead level" equality. It is "equality" that will vary as much as the man's circumstances, his family, his wants and needs, may vary.

In the next place, under the United Order every man was called to consecrate to the Church all of the property which he had; the real estate was to be conveyed to the Church, as I understand the revelations, by what we would call a deed in fee simple. Thus the man's property became absolutely the property of the Church. (D.&C. 42:30; 72:15) Then the bishop deeded back to the donor by the same kind of deed, that is, in fee simple, and also transferred to him by an equivalent instrument, so far as personal property was concerned, that amount of real and personal property, which, the two being taken together, would be required by the individual for the support of himself and his family "according to his family, according to his circumstances and his wants and needs." [D&C 51:3] This the man held as his own property. (D.&C. 42:32; 51:4–6; 83:3)

In other words, basic to the United Order was the private ownership of property, every man had his own property from which he might secure that which was necessary for the support of himself and his fam-

ily. There is nothing in the revelations that would indicate that this property was not freely alienable at the will of the owner. It was not contemplated that the Church should own everything or that we should become in the Church, with reference to our property and otherwise, the same kind of automaton, manikin, that communism makes out of the individual, with the State standing at the head in place of the Church.

Now, that part of a man's property which was not turned back to him, if he had more than was needed under this rule of "equality" already stated, became the common property of the Church, and that common property was used for the support of the poor of the Church. It is spoken of in the revelations as the "residue" of property. (D.&C. 42:34–36)

Furthermore, it was intended, though apparently it did not work out very well, that the poor coming into Zion, and by Zion I mean, here, Missouri—the poor coming into Zion were to have given to them a "portion" of land, which land was to be either purchased from the Government (and it was planned to purchase large areas from the Government), or purchased from individuals, or received as consecrations from members of the Church. The amount of this "portion" was to be such as would make him equal

to others according to his circumstances, his family, his wants and needs.

The land which you received from the bishop by deed, whether it was part of the land which you, yourself, had deeded to the Church, or whether it came as an out-right gift from the Church as just indicated, and the personal property which you received, were all together sometimes called a "portion" (D.&C. 51:4–6), sometimes a "stewardship" (D.&C. 104:11–12), and sometimes an "inheritance." (D.&C. 83:3)

As just indicated, there were other kinds of inheritances and stewardships than land or mere personal property; for example, the Prophet and others had a stewardship given to them which consisted of the revelations and commandments (D.&C. 70:1–4); others had given to them a stewardship involving the printing house (D.&C. 104:29–30); another stewardship was a mercantile establishment. (D.&C. 104:39–42)

An early stake storehouse and cannery

I repeat that whatever a steward realized from the portion allotted to him over and above that which was necessary in order to keep his family under the standard provided, as already stated above, was turned over by the steward to the bishop, and this amount of surplus, plus the residues to which I have already referred, went into a bishop's storehouse (D.&C. 51:13 and citations above), and the materials of the storehouse were to be used in creating portions, as above indicated, for caring for the poor (D.&C. 78:3), the widows and orphans (D.&C. 83:6), and for the elders of the Church engaged in the ministry, who were to pay for what they received if they could, but if not, their faithful labors should answer their debt to the bishop. (D.&C. 72:11 ff)

Now, as time went on and the system developed, the Lord created two other institutions besides the storehouse: one was known as the Sacred Treasury, into which was put "the avails of the sacred things in the treasurey, for sacred and holy purposes." While it is not clear, it would seem that into this treasury were to be put the surpluses which were derived from the publication of the revelations, the Book of Mormon, the Pearl of Great Price, and other similar things, the stewardship of which had been given to Joseph and others. (D.&C. 104:60–66)

The Lord also provided for the creation of "Another Treasury," and into that other treasury went the general revenues which came to the Church, such as gifts of money and those revenues derived from the improvement of stewardships as distinguished from the residues of the original consecrations and the surpluses which came from the operation of their stewardships. (D.&C. 72:11 ff)

The foregoing is the general outline as it is gathered from the revelations of the law of the United Order which the Lord spoke of as "my law." (D.&C. 44:6; 51:15) There are passages in the revelations which, taken from their context and without having in mind the whole system, might be considered as inconsistent with some of the things which I have set out, but all such passages fall into line if the whole program is looked at as contained in all of the revelations.

The fundamental principle of this system was the private ownership of property. Each man owned his portion, or inheritance, or stewardship, with an absolute title, which he could alienate, or hypothecate, or otherwise treat as his own. The Church did not own all of the property, and the life under the United

Order was not a communal life, as the Prophet Joseph, himself, said (*History of the Church,* Volume III, p. 28). The United Order is an individualistic system, not a communal system.

We have all said that the Welfare Plan is not the United Order and was not intended to be. However, I should like to suggest to you that perhaps, after all, when the Welfare Plan gets thoroughly into operation—it is not so yet—we shall not be so very far from carrying out the great fundamentals of the United Order.

In the first place I repeat again, the United Order recognized and was built upon the principle of private ownership of property; all that a man had and lived upon under the United Order, was his own. Quite obviously, the fundamental principle of our system today is the ownership of private property.

In the next place, in lieu of residues and surpluses which were accumulated and built up under the United Order, we, today, have our fast offerings, our Welfare donations, and our tithing, all of which may be devoted to the care of the poor, as well as for the carrying on of the activities and business of the Church. After all, the United Order was primarily designed to build up a system under which there should be no abjectly poor, and this is the purpose, also, of the Welfare Plan.

In this connection it should be observed that it is clear from these earlier revelations, as well as from our history, that the Lord had very early to tell the people about the wickedness of idleness, and the wickedness of greed, because the brethren who had were not giving properly, and those who had not were evidently intending to live without work on the things which were to be received from those who had property. (D.&C. 56:16–20)

Furthermore, we had under the United Order a bishop's storehouse in which were collected the materials from which to supply the needs and the wants of the poor....

We have now under the Welfare

Plan all over the Church, ward land projects. In some cases the lands are owned by the wards, in others they are leased by the wards or lent to them by private individuals. This land is being farmed for the benefit of the poor, by the poor where you can get the poor to work it.

We have in place of the two treasuries, the "Sacred Treasury" and "Another Treasury," the general funds of the church.

Thus you will see, brethren, that in many of its great essentials, we have, as the Welfare Plan has now developed, the broad essentials of the United Order. Furthermore, having in mind the assistance which is being given from time to time and in various wards to help set people up in business or in farming, we have a plan which is not essentially unlike that which was in the United Order when the poor were given portions from the common fund.

Now, brethren, the Church has made tremendous advances in the Welfare Plan. We shall have to make still greater advances. As the Message of the First Presidency said this morning, we are being told by Government officials that we face what we used to call "hard times." If the Welfare Plan is fully operative, we shall be able to care for every destitute Latter-day Saint wherever he may be. [In Conference Report, Oct. 1942, pp. 54–58]

STUDY QUESTIONS

1. What basic gospel principles guided the formation of the welfare plan? How are these principles reflected in the way the program operates today?

2. What specific organization or procedures instituted during the 1930s are still part of the welfare program today?

3. What responsibilities do families and individuals have as part of the plan?

4. Why was communism not the means of reestablishing the United Order?

5. In what ways is the welfare program a preparation for living the law of consecration?

GEORGE ALBERT SMITH

BLESSED with a noble ancestry, President George Albert Smith led the Church through six transition years that saw the end of the Second World War and the increasing threat of yet another war as some of the nations of Central Europe and the Far East fell behind the curtain of communism and armed conflict broke out in Korea. His own love of mankind helped guide the Church through these troubled times, binding up the spiritual wounds that had been inflicted during the war, and spreading the gospel once again the world over. His creed, formulated over forty years earlier, bore fruit in the outpouring of goods and supplies from the Saints in one country to the Saints and nonmembers in another. In addition, the war, whatever its ill effects, opened countries formerly closed to the Church by hostile governments, and President Smith's vision of missionary work extended far beyond the prospects or methods of the next week or year or decade. In many ways, he planted the seeds for the remarkable Church growth of the next thirty years.

HIGHLIGHTS

1870 Apr. 4: Born in Salt Lake City, Utah.

1883 Begins work in ZCMI's overall factory (13).

1891 Serves a mission in southern Utah for the YMMIA (21).

1892 Marries Lucy Emily Woodruff (22).

1892–94 Serves a mission in the southern states (22–24).

1898 Appointed receiver of United States Land Office and Special Disbursing Agent for Utah by United States President McKinley (28).

1903 Becomes a member of the Quorum of the Twelve (33).

1904 Writes his creed (34).

1909–12 Illness prevents him from being active in the Quorum; has a vision of his grandfather (39–42).

1919–21 Serves as president of the European Mission (49–51).

1922 Elected vice-president of the National Society of the Sons of the American Revolution (52).

1931 Elected a member of the National Executive Board of the Boy Scouts of America (61).

1939 War breaks out in Europe (69).

1941 Japanese attack Pearl Harbor (71).

1943 Becomes President of the Quorum of the Twelve (73).

1945 May 8: War in Europe ends (74).

May 14: Becomes President of the Church (74).

Aug 14: War in the Far East ends (74).

1947 Utah pioneer centennial is celebrated (77).

1951 Apr. 4: Dies in Salt Lake City, Utah (82).

HISTORICAL SUMMARY

Early Ministry

Being born of goodly parents and raised in a religious environment did not automatically destine George Albert Smith to become a great and good person. His ability to respond keenly to his environment, influences, and heritage helped, however, to mold him into the great and good person he became. His ancestry was a noble one. His great grandfather, John Smith, was an uncle of the Prophet Joseph and an early convert to the restored Church, who served as Patriarch to the Church, first president of the Salt Lake Stake, and as an assistant counselor to the First Presidency. George Albert

Young George Albert Smith

Smith's grandfather, George A. Smith, after whom he was named, was one of the youngest men, at twenty-two years of age, called to the Quorum of the Twelve in this dispensation. He later also served in the First Presidency. George Albert Smith had the rare privilege of serving in the Quorum of the Twelve with his own father, John Henry Smith, who also subsequently became a member of the First Presidency. Of him he said, "I have never met a greater man than my father" (quoted in Preston Nibley, *The Presidents of the Church*, p. 270). Young George Albert knew that much was expected of him, and he lived to fulfill these expectations, honorably adding to the accomplishments of his forebearers.

When he was sustained as a member of the Quorum of the Twelve, Elder Smith was taken by surprise. He said of this call, however, "My patriarchal blessing given under the hands of Zebedee Coltrin when I was twelve years of age indicated that I would some day become an Apostle" (quoted in Nibley, *Presidents,* p. 273). Just after becoming a member of the Council of the Twelve, he penned the creed, a list of his most serious goals and aspirations, which would guide him throughout his life:

I would be a friend to the friendless and find joy in ministering to the needs of the poor.

I would visit the sick and afflicted and inspire in them a desire for faith to be healed.

I would teach the truth to the understanding and blessing of all mankind.

I would seek out the erring one and try to win him back to a righteous and a happy life.

I would not seek to force people to live up to my ideals, but rather love them into doing the thing that is right.

I would live with the masses and help to solve their problems that their earth life may be happy.

I would avoid the publicity of high positions and discourage the flattery of thoughtless friends.

I would not knowingly wound the feeling of any, not even one who may have wronged me, but would seek to do him good and make him my friend.

I would overcome the tendency to selfishness and jealousy and rejoice in the success of all the children of my Heavenly Father.

I would not be an enemy to any living soul.

Knowing that the Redeemer of mankind has offered to the world the only plan that will fully develop us and make us really happy here and hereafter, I feel it not only a duty but also a blessed privilege to disseminate this truth. [In Glen R. Stubbs, "A Biography of George Albert Smith, 1870 to 1951," (Ph. D. diss., Brigham Young University, 1974), p. 440]

Vision of Grandfather

Six years later, President Smith suffered a serious illness, which made it impossible for him to actively serve in his calling for more than two years and

Elder George Albert Smith, missionary (third from left)

which weakened him physically for many more years. He moved to St. George, Utah, to take advantage of its warmer climate. While recovering there he had a remarkable dream:

In St. George we arranged for a tent for my health and comfort, with a built-in floor raised about a foot above the ground, and we could roll up the south side of the tent to make the sunshine and fresh air available. I became so weak as to be scarcely able to move. It was a slow and exhausting effort for me even to turn over in bed.

One day, under these conditions, I lost consciousness of my surroundings and thought I had passed to the Other Side. I found myself standing with my back to a large and beautiful lake, facing a great forest of trees.... I realized, or seemed to realize, that I had finished my work in mortality and had gone home....

I began to explore, and soon I found a trail through the woods which seemed to have been used very little, and which was almost obscured by grass. I followed this trail; and after I had walked for some time and had traveled a considerable distance through the forest, I saw a man coming towards me. I became aware that he was a very large man, and I hurried my steps to reach him, because I recog-

nized him as my grandfather. In mortality, he weighed over three hundred pounds, so you may know he was a large man. I remember how happy I was to see him coming. I had been given his name and had always been proud of it.

When Grandfather came within a few feet of me, he stopped. His stopping was an invitation for me to stop. Then—and this I would like the boys and girls and young people never to forget—he looked at me very earnestly and said:

"I would like to know what you have

George Albert Smith, 1870–1951

done with my name."

Everything I had ever done passed before me as though it were a flying picture on a screen—everything I had done. Quickly this vivid retrospect came down to the very time I was standing there. My whole life had passed before me. I smiled and looked at my grandfather and said:

"I have never done anything with your name of which you need be ashamed."

He stepped forward and took me in his arms, and as he did so, I became conscious again of my earthly surroundings. My pillow was as wet as though water had been poured on it—wet with tears of gratitude that I could answer unashamed. [George Albert Smith, *Sharing the Gospel with Others,* pp. 110–12]

Later, he was saddened by the death of his father, with whom he had served in the Quorum of the Twelve for more than five years. He used these trials wisely, however, allowing them to contribute to the development of the love and compassion that characterized his life.

Administration

One of President Smith's outstanding attributes was his capacity to radiate a Christlike love to an uncommon degree. As he said in the October 1921 general conference, "I love my brothers and sisters, and I have affection for my Father's children who are not members of this Church, and inasmuch as he will give me physical strength and mental power, I desire to so order my life that I may be an uplift to all those with whom I come in contact" (in Conference Report, Oct. 1921, p. 43). This was particularly significant as World War II came to an end. With the death of President Grant on 14 May 1945, just six days after the war in Europe had ended, George Alber Smith had the tremendous responsibility to lead the Saints on both sides of the conflict who needed to be reminded that only righteous living could truly solve the world's problems:

We can legislate until doomsday but that will not make men righteous. It will be necessary for people who are in the dark to repent of their sins, correct their lives, and live in such a righteous way that they can enjoy the spirit of our Heavenly Father. [In Conference Report, Oct. 1949, p. 6]

The world is sick. It is not the first time it has been sick. It has had a good many different experiences of that kind. Sometimes nations have had to be wiped out because of the wickedness of the people who live in them. The Lord, all down through the ages, has spoken to his leaders and teachers who are inspired, but when the world refuses to heed after it has been properly taught, it places itself in a position of saying to our Heavenly Father who owns this world—he is our landlord—"We do not need you. We will do just as we please."

Unfortunately, people who think that way do not realize how they are shortening their own experiences in life, and setting the stage for the sorrows that may follow. [In Conference Report, Oct. 1949, p. 167]

A Visit with the President of the United States

Shortly after becoming President of the Church, George Albert Smith initiated actions to relieve the terrible suffering of the Saints in war-torn Europe. He sent Elder Ezra Taft Benson of the Council of the Twelve to assess their needs, and personally visited with United States President Harry Truman to speed up the delivery of that assistance. "Word comes from our people in Europe," he reported in the October 1946 conference.

In many cases they are still having difficult times, but they are faithful, in the main, to God and the Church, and the messages that they send us from time to time in expressing gratitude for food, clothing, and bedding we have sent them warm our hearts.

It may be of interest to you to know that since World War II closed, more than seventy-five major carloads of food and clothing and bedding have been shipped across the sea to those needy people over there, without any expense to them whatsoever.

When the war was over, I went representing the Church, to see the president of the United States. When I called on him, he received me very graciously—I had met him before—and I said: "I have just come to ascertain from you, Mr. President, what your attitude will be if the Latter-day Saints are prepared to ship food and clothing and bedding to Europe."

He smiled and looked at me, and said: "Well, what do you want to ship it over there for? Their money isn't any good."

Elder Ezra Taft Benson in Europe with welfare goods from America

I said: "We don't want their money." He looked at me and asked: "You don't mean you are going to give it to them?"

I said: "Of course, we would give it to them. They are our brothers and sisters and are in distress. God has blessed us with a surplus, and we will be glad to send it if we can have the co-operation of the government."

He said: "You are on the right track," and added, "we will be glad to help you in any way we can."

I have thought of that a good many times. After we had sat there a moment or two, he said again: "How long will it take you to get this ready?"

I said: "It's all ready."

The government you remember had been destroying food and refusing to plant grain during the war, so I said to him:

"Mr. President, while the administration at Washington were advising the destroying of food, we were building elevators and filling them with grain, and increasing our flocks and our herds, and now what we need is the cars and the ships in order to send considerable food, clothing and bedding to the people of Europe who are in distress. We have an organization in the Church that has over two thousand homemade quilts ready."

The group that sang for you this morning, the Singing Mothers of the

Relief Society, represent that organization. They had two thousand quilts made by their own hands ready to ship. The result was that many people received warm clothing and bedding and food without any delay. Just as fast as we could get cars and ships, we had what was necessary to send to Europe. [In Conference Report, Oct. 1947, pp. 5–6]

Church members in several lands co-operated to supply the needs of their suffering brothers and sisters.

In the fall of 1947, the Dutch Saints sent seventy tons of home-grown potatoes to the Saints in Germany; in the fall of 1948, they sent ninety tons of potatoes supplemented by nine tons of herring. And they were not alone in their charity: "That Saints in one country aided Saints in other countries was not unique to the Dutch. Swedes helped Finns. Swiss sent clothes and chocolate to Austrians. Belgian Mormons also sent much of their American welfare supply to German Saints " (William G. Hartley, "War and Peace and Dutch Potatoes," *Ensign,* July 1978, p. 21). They were directed by President Smith, the man who all through his life exemplified concern for all the family of God.

After the initial concern for the European Saints, welfare drives were made in behalf of nonmembers. In December 1947, the Latter-day Saints were called upon to participate in a special fast and to contribute as much as possible for the relief of non-

members in Europe. Over $210,000 was donated.

Missionary Work

With the end of the war came also the opportunity to expand the missionary program. The number of full-time missionaries jumped from 386 in 1945 to 2,297 in 1946. An estimated sixty percent of those who accepted mission calls were war veterans.

Elder Ezra Taft Benson of the Quorum of the Twelve spent a year in Europe supervising the reopening of missionary work as well as the distribution of welfare supplies there. Elder Matthew Cowley received a similar assignment to reestablish missionary work in the Pacific.

President Smith saw clearly the marvelous success that would come to the worldwide missionary work of the Church:

We must preach the gospel to the South American countries which we have scarcely touched. We must preach the gospel to every African section that we haven't been in yet. We must preach the gospel to Asia. And I might go on and say in all parts of the world where we have not yet been permitted to go. I look upon Russia as one of the most fruitful fields for the teaching of the gospel of Jesus Christ. And if I am not mistaken, it will not be long before the people who are there will desire to know something about this work which has reformed the lives of so many people. [In Conference Report, Oct. 1945, p. 119]

Short-wave broadcasting will continue to improve, and it will not be long until, from this pulpit and other places that will be provided, the servants of the Lord will be able to deliver messages to isolated groups who are so far away they cannot be reached. In that way and other ways, the gospel of Jesus Christ our Lord, the only power of God unto salvation in preparation for the celestial kingdom, will be heard in all parts of the world, and many of you who are here will live to see that day. [In Conference Report, Oct. 1946, p. 6]

I have traveled in many lands and climes, and wherever I have gone I

Dutch potatoes bound for German Saints, 1947–48

The First Presidency 1945–51, left to right: J. Reuben Clark, jr., George Albert Smith, and David O. McKay

have found good people, sons and daughters of the living God who are waiting for the gospel of Jesus Christ, and there are thousands, hundreds of thousands, millions of them, who would be accepting the truth if they only knew what we know. [In Conference Report, Oct. 1945, p. 120]

I can think of nobody who has had a fuller life than I have had, and I don't say that boastfully, but gratefully; and I want to say to you that every happiness and every joy that has been worthy of the name has been the result of keeping the commandments of God and observing his advice and counsel. So, as we go forward, each of us, each having an influence with our neighbors and our friends, let us not be too timid. We do not need to annoy people, but let us make them feel and understand that we are interested, not in making them members of the Church for membership, but in bringing them into the Church that they may enjoy the same blessings that we enjoy. [In Conference Report, Apr. 1948, p. 162]

Other Developments

With the end of wartime restrictions, the Church's building program resumed. Scores of new chapels met the needs of growing congregations in many areas. President George Albert Smith dedicated the Idaho Falls Temple, construction of which had been delayed because of the war.

President Smith had a deep compassion for those who had separated from the Church. In 1946 he made a visit to such a group in Mexico. They

were touched by his presence as he shook hands with them, spoke to them, and prayed and wept for them. Feeling the radiant love of Christ reaching out to them through this prophet of the Lord, twelve hundred returned to the Church from which they had strayed, pledging anew their support and allegiance.

The Church witnessed a variety of other important developments. In 1947, as Church membership passed the one-million mark worldwide, the Latter-day Saints commemorated the centennial of the pioneers' arrival in the Salt Lake Valley. President Smith unveiled the impressive "This Is the Place" monument. Priesthood and auxiliary programs were strengthened. Elders quorums were organized in the missions for the first time. Microfilming of vital records was paving the way for the acceleration in genealogy and temple work which was to come in following decades.

World conflicts flared up again toward the end of President Smith's administration. As East-West tensions increased, missionaries were expelled from Czechoslovakia. The Near East Mission was closed. War broke out in Korea. Young men of missionary age were again drafted into military service, and the number of full-time missionaries sent out dropped from 3,014 to 180. To help compensate for this, 1,000 seventies of the Church who were outside the limits of the draft were called to volunteer their services in the mission fields of the world. In December 1950, President Smith said in his last public address: " 'There would be no war in Korea and threats of war everywhere else in the world . . .

if the people accepted and lived the gospel. These wars come solely because the Adversary is able to deceive the bulk of the people. This makes it all the more important that we who have a testimony of the divinity of Jesus should live the gospel and promulgate it" (Nibley, *Presidents*, 1974 ed., p. 302).

President George Albert Smith lived as he taught. "It has been properly suggested that his real name was Love," President J. Reuben Clark, Jr., said at his funeral.

Throughout our association together which has been close and intimate, and under various and trying circumstances, I have never known him even to indicate that he was impatient, that he had lost his temper, or even that he was under the necessity of controlling it.

He was universally kind and considerate of both of us who were privileged and honored to work with him. . . . Evil slunk away from him at all times. It could not abide the presence of his righteous living. I do not know what more I can say in tribute to him than that. ["No Man Had Greater Love for Humanity Than He," *Church News*, 11 Apr. 1951, p. 10]

STUDY QUESTIONS

1. How had George Albert Smith been prepared to lead the Church?

2. If you were to prepare a "creed" by which to live your life, what things would you include? Compare your answer with President Smith's creed.

3. How can we put into action some of the qualities President Smith exemplified and taught throughout his life?

4. What effect do you think the relief given to the Saints and others in Europe had on the image of the Church? What effect could it have had on the lives of the Saints?

5. What is the only lasting solution to war? Why?

6. How can we assure ourselves of peace and safety in this world of ever-increasing wickedness and turmoil?

DAVID O. McKAY

WHEN Brigham Young was yet President of the Church, David O. McKay was born in Huntsville, Utah, to David and Jennette Evans McKay, Mormon immigrants from Scotland and Wales. His mortal life stretched from shortly after the coming of the railroad to Utah to the landing of the first man on the moon. During his sixty-four-year ministry he would serve in the general Sunday School presidency, as Church commissioner of education, and as Second Counselor to two Presidents of the Church. As an Apostle he would be assigned to tour the missions throughout the world, and later, as President, he would again travel worldwide dedicating temples, meeting the Saints, and making friends for the Church among all peoples. During his administration the Church would nearly triple in size, and the gospel would touch the four corners of the Earth through the ever-expanding missionary force and the technological miracles of radio and television.

HIGHLIGHTS

1873 Sept. 8: Born in Huntsville, Weber County, Utah.

1877 President Brigham Young dies (4).

1881–83 Father serves mission in Great Britain (7–9).

1897 Graduates from the University of Utah, where he is president and valedictorian of his class (24).

1897–99 Serves a mission in Great Britain (24–26).

1899 Becomes a faculty member of Weber Stake Academy (26).

1901 Marries Emma Ray Riggs (27).

1906 Becomes a member of the Council of the Twelve; becomes second assistant superintendent of the Sunday School (32).

1907 Becomes a member of the general priesthood and auxiliary correlation committee (33).

1917 Publishes his first book, *Ancient Apostles* (44).

1918–34 Serves as general superintendent of the Sunday School (45–61).

1919–21 Serves as Church commissioner of education (46–48).

1920–21 Tours missions throughout the world (47–48).

1921 May 10: Beholds a vision of the celestial city during world tour (48).

1922–24 Serves as president of the European Mission (49–51).

1934–51 Serves as Second Counselor in the First Presidency, first to Heber J. Grant and then to George Albert Smith (61–78).

1951 Apr. 9: Sustained as President of the Church at the death of President George Albert Smith (78).

1952 Tours the European missions (79).

1954 Tours South Africa, South America, and Central America (81).

1955 Tours Tonga, Tahiti, New Zealand, and Australia; dedicates the Swiss Temple (82).

1956 Dedicates the Los Angeles Temple (83).

1958 Dedicates the New Zealand Temple, the Church College of New Zealand, the London Temple, and the Church College of Hawaii (85).

1961 Announces the members of the First Council of Seventy to be ordained high priests; the Church correlation effort begins (88).

1964 Dedicates the Oakland Temple (91).

1965 Chooses two additional counselors to the First Presidency, Joseph Fielding Smith and Thorpe B. Isaacson (92).

1967 Regional Representatives of the Twelve are first called (94).

1970 Jan. 18: Dies in Salt Lake City, Utah (96).

HISTORICAL SUMMARY

Early Life

"My home life from babyhood to the present time has been the greatest factor in giving me moral and spiritual standards and in shaping the course of my life. Sincerity, courtesy, consistency in word and deed exemplified in the lives of my parents and others . . . have proved a safeguard and guidance" (quoted in F.E. Schulter, *A Convert's Tribute to President David O. McKay,* p. 27).

Such was David O. McKay's home life. As a result, he had great love and respect for his parents. Of his mother he said: "I cannot think of a womanly virtue that my mother did not possess. . . .

"To make home the most pleasant place in the world for her husband and children was her constant aim, which she achieved naturally and supremely.

". . . In tenderness, watchful care, loving patience, loyalty to home and to right, she seemed to me in boyhood, and she seems to me now after these years to have been supreme" (quoted in Bryant S. Hinckley, "David O. McKay," *Improvement Era,* May 1932, p. 391).

President McKay's conviction of the importance of marriage and home and family life, which developed early in his life, deepened as he grew older.

Throughout his ministry as a member of the Twelve, as a counselor in the First Presidency, and as President of the Church, David O. McKay spoke with authority on marriage and the

David O. seated on his father's lap

family. Coupled with his own childhood, his happy marriage to Emma Rae Riggs, stretching over sixty-nine years and becoming a legendary ideal among the Saints, served as a shining example of what he taught.

One of our most precious possessions is our families. The domestic relations precede, and, in our present existence, are worth more than all other social ties. They give the first throb to the heart and unseal the deep fountains of its love. Home is the chief school of human virtues. Its responsibilities, joy, sorrows, smiles, tears, hopes, and solicitudes form the chief interests of human life. . . .

When one puts business or pleasure above his home, he that moment starts on the downgrade to soul-weakness. When the club becomes more attractive to any man than his home, it is time for him to confess in bitter shame that he has failed to measure up to the supreme opportunity of his life and flunked in the final test of true manhood. No other success can compensate for failure in the home. The poorest shack in which love prevails over a united family is of greater value to God and future humanity than any other riches. In such a home God can work miracles and will work miracles.

Pure hearts in a pure home are always in whispering distance of heaven.

In the light of scripture, ancient and modern we are justified in concluding that Christ's ideal pertaining to marriage is the unbroken home, and conditions that cause divorce are violations of his divine teaching. . . .

I know of no other place where happiness abides more securely than in the home. It is possible to make home a bit of heaven. Indeed, I picture heaven as a continuation of the ideal home. [In Conference Report, Apr. 1964, p. 5; or *Improvement Era,* June 1964, pp. 445, 520]

As a child of eight years, he assumed the responsibilities of "man of the house" when his father was called on a mission to the British Isles. Two of his older sisters had just recently died, his mother was expecting another baby, and his father felt that the responsibilities of the farm were too great to be left to David's mother. Under these circumstances Brother McKay told his wife, "Of course it is impossible for me to go." Sister McKay looked at him and said, "Of course you must accept; you need not worry about me. David O. and I will manage things nicely!" (quoted in Llewelyn R. McKay, *Home Memories of President David O. McKay,* pp. 5–6).

Mission, Marriage, and a Career

He began his quest for spiritual development early. As a teenager David prayed fervently for a sure testimony: "I had in mind that there would be some manifestation, that I should receive some transformation that would leave me without doubt" (*Improvement Era,* Sept. 1962, p. 628). The desired manifestation did not come for several years, however, until he served as a missionary. Prior to this he enjoyed a well-rounded college experience. He played the piano for dances, was left guard on the first University of Utah football team, courted his sweetheart, and graduated as president and valedictorian of his class. Just after graduating from the university, David accepted a call to the British Mission even though this represented a financial sacrifice for his family. This was the same mission his father had served in several years earlier.

Here in the mission field great spiritual growth took place, which laid a foundation for his continuing devotion to the gospel and his extraordinary service to the Lord during his life. During a very spiritual and inspirational conference, James McMurrin, his mission president, said to him, " 'Let me say to you, Brother David, Satan hath desired you that he may sift you as wheat, but God is mindful of you.' Then he added, 'If you will keep the faith you will yet sit in the leading counsels of the Church '" ("Two Significant Statements," *Deseret News* Church Section, 27 Oct. 1934).

After returning from his mission, he became an instructor at the Church-

Elder McKay, missionary, in Scotland

owned Weber Academy in Ogden, Utah. One year later, on 2 January 1901, he married his college sweetheart, Emma Rae Riggs, in the Salt Lake Temple. A teacher by profession, he had a lifelong interest in education, feeling it was an important eternal process. He loved to read the scriptures and the works of Shakespeare and other literary masters. His sermons would reflect this love.

David O. and his bride, Emma Ray

During 1901, Elder McKay was called to the Weber Stake Sunday School superintendency with particular responsibility for instruction. There "he introduced features which were destined to find their way into all the Sunday Schools of the Church and which resulted in revolutionizing the teaching throughout the entire organization. For the first time outlines were prepared, preparation meetings held and the lesson work unified and made progressive" (Hinckley, *Improvement Era*, May 1932, p. 443).

In 1906, at the age of thirty-two, David O. McKay became a member of the Quorum of the Twelve Apostles. During this time he served first as a counselor, then as general superintendent of the Sunday Schools, Church commissioner of education, president of the European Mission, and as Second Counselor to both President Heber J. Grant and President George Albert Smith.

World Tour

In 1921 President Grant assigned him to tour the missions of the Church worldwide. This assignment, which took one year to complete, was highlighted by a number of remarkable spiritual experiences. One such experience occurred in Samoa. He noted the following in his diary:

"ON TUESDAY, May 10, 1921, we sailed all day on the smoothest sea of our entire trip. The slightly undulating waves had been so free from even signs of unrest that the slight ripples discernible appeared on the surface like millions of little squares—like plaited cloth with the rich design of the same deep blue material as the body.

Nearing Savali, we could see with the aid of field glasses the "Spouting Horns," which looked like geysers. On our right we caught a glimpse of the little village nestling safely in the mouth of an extinct volcano on the little island of Apolima.

Towards evening, the reflection of the afterglow of a beautiful sunset was most splendid! The sky was tinged with pink, and the clouds lingering around the horizon were fringed with various hues of crimson and orange, while the heavy cloud farther to the west was sombre purple and black. There various colors cast varying shadows on the peaceful surface of the water. Those from the cloud were long and dark, those from the crimson-tinged sky, clear but rose-tinted and fading into a faint pink that merged into the clear blue of the ocean. Gradually, the shadows became deeper and heavier, and then all merged into a beautiful calm twilight that made the sea look like a great mirror upon which fell the faint light of the crescent moon!

Pondering still upon this beautiful scene, I lay in my berth at ten o'clock that night, and thought to myself: Charming as it is, it doesn't stir my soul with emotion as do the innocent lives of children, and the sublime characters of loved ones and friends. Their beauty, unselfishness, and heroism are after all the most glorious!

I then fell asleep, and beheld in vision something infinitely sublime. In the distance I beheld a beautiful white city. Though far away, yet I seemed to realize that trees with luscious fruit, shrubbery with gorgeously-tinted leaves, and flowers in perfect bloom abounded everywhere. The clear sky above seemed to reflect these beautiful shades of color. I then saw a great concourse of people approaching the city. Each one wore a white flowing robe, and a white headdress. Instantly my attention seemed centered upon their Leader, and though I could see only the profile of his features and his

World tour, April 1921: Elder McKay and a group of Maori Saints

body, I recognized him at once as my Savior! The tint and radiance of his countenance were glorious to behold! There was a peace about him which seemed sublime—it was divine!

The city, I understood, was his. It was the City Eternal; and the people following him were to abide there in peace and eternal happiness.

But who were they?

As if the Savior read my thoughts, he answered by pointing to a semi-circle that then appeared above them, and on which were written in gold the words:

"These Are They Who Have Over-come The World—Who Have Truly Been Born Again!"

When I awoke, it was breaking day over Apia harbor. [Claire Middlemiss, comp., *Cherished Experiences from the Writings of President David O. McKay*, pp. 101–2]

Administration

On 9 April 1951, as he was sustained as President of the Church, David O. McKay testified:

No one can preside over this Church without first being in tune with the head of the Church, our Lord and Savior, Jesus Christ. He is our head. This is his Church. With-out his divine guidance and con-stant inspiration, we cannot succeed. With his guidance, with his inspiration, we cannot fail. . . .

I pledge to you that I shall do my best so to live as to merit the com-panionship of the Holy Spirit, and pray here in your presence that my counselors and I may indeed be "partakers of the divine spirit." [In Conference Report, Apr. 1951, p. 157]

President McKay knew that Jesus Christ is the Savior of mankind, and he taught that men find true joy and fulfillment in life only as they make Christ the center of their lives:

An upright character is the result only of continued effort and right thinking, the effect of long-cherished associations with Godlike thoughts.

He approaches nearest the Christ

The First Presidency, 1963–70, left to right: Hugh B. Brown, David O. McKay, and N. Eldon Tanner

spirit who makes God the center of his thoughts; and he who can say in his heart, "Not my will, but thine be done," approaches most nearly the Christ ideal. [In Conference Report, Oct. 1953, p. 10]

Man's chief concern in life should not be the acquiring of gold, or of fame, or of material possessions. It should not be development of physical powers, nor of intellectual strength, but his aim, the highest in life, should be the development of a Christ-like character. . . .

The true purpose in life is perfection of humanity through individual effort, under the guidance of God's inspiration. Real life is response to the best about us. [Quoted in Jeanette McKay Morrell, *Highlights in the Life of President David O. McKay*, p. 240]

The spiritual road has Christ as its goal. The individual lives for some-thing higher than self. He hears the Savior's voice saying: "I am the way, the truth, and the life." [John 14:6.] Following that voice he soon learns that there is no one great thing which he can do to attain happiness or eternal life. He learns that "life is made up not of great sacrifices or duties, but of little things in which smiles and kindness and small obligations given habitually are what win and preserve the heart and secure comfort." [*Relief Society Magazine*, June 1941, p. 366]

During President McKay's twenty-year ministry, the Church truly became a worldwide organization. At the time he was sustained as President, there were one hundred eighty-four stakes, only one of which (Hawaii) was outside of continental North America. At his death, nearly five hundred stakes were organized, and forty-five were then outside the United States and Canada. The Church population had nearly tripled, jumping from 1,111,000 to 2,931,000. In 1950, 90 percent of the Church membership lived in the United States. By the time of his death, that percentage had dropped to 79 percent.

The first temples outside the United States were built, missions were expanded, organizations were correlated and strengthened, regional representatives were called. Under President David O. McKay the Church continued its steady growth and progress toward its destiny of preparing a people for the second coming of the Master. During his sixty-four-year ministry as a General Authority, he traveled over a million miles as an ambassador for Christ and saw the boundaries of the Church stretch to the four corners of the earth. Church expansion had been so great that at his death, half the membership of the Church knew no other prophet as their leader.

President McKay had also become a personal friend of many of the presidents of the United States and leading statesmen from throughout the world. Wherever he traveled he met with top government leaders, expressing the true mission of the Church, correcting misconceptions, and leaving a spirit of friendship that was to bless the progress of the Church many times over. Leading the way, he taught that every member should be a missionary.

> And so with you I say, "We are not ashamed of the gospel of Christ." I am looking upon a segment of the Church of Christ who share the responsibility of preaching this gospel to all the world, for we are part of a world-wide organization. This gospel is not confined to Utah, nor Idaho, nor Wyoming, nor California, nor the United States, nor just to Europe, but it is the power of God to salvation to all who believe, and you and I must share part of the responsibility of declaring it to all the world. [Llewelyn R. McKay, comp., *Stepping Stones to an Abundant Life,* pp. 120–21]

The rapid growth of the Church made communication more challenging. To meet this need, President McKay initiated the use of radio to bring a message to the Saints in the United States, Canada, and Mexico, and over the next few years the use of short-wave radio to broadcast the Church's message to members and non-members worldwide.

Under President McKay's inspired guidance, the work of salvation not only expanded for the living but also for the dead. Temples were dedicated in Bern, Switzerland (1955), Los Angeles, California (1956), New Zealand (1958), London, England (1958), and Oakland, California (1964). With the erection of temples in areas more accessible to Saints in other countries, they now partook of the blessings of temple worship and the work necessary to save their dead that might have been otherwise impossible. The First Presidency also spoke out on such social issues as birth control.

First Presidency Statement on Birth Control

In a circular letter dated 14 April 1969, the First Presidency issued a statement on birth control in response to the growing tendency throughout the world for people to restrict their family size for reasons of personal convenience.

> The First Presidency is being asked from time to time as to what the attitude of the Church is regarding birth control. In order that you may be informed on this subject and that you may be prepared to convey the proper information to the members of the Church under your jurisdiction, we have decided to give you the following statement:
>
> We seriously regret that there should exist a sentiment or feeling among any members of the Church to curtail the birth of their children. We have been commanded to multiply and replenish the earth that we may have joy and rejoicing in our posterity.
>
> Where husband and wife enjoy health and vigor and are free from impurities that would be entailed upon their posterity, it is contrary to the teachings of the Church arti-

ficially to curtail or prevent the birth of children. We believe that those who practice birth control will reap disappointment by and by.

> However, we feel that men must be considerate of their wives who bear the greater responsibility not only of bearing children, but of caring for them through childhood. To this end the mother's health and strength should be conserved and the husband's consideration for his wife is his first duty, and self-control a dominant factor in all their relationships.
>
> It is our further feeling that married couples should seek inspiration and wisdom from the Lord that they may exercise discretion in solving their marital problems, and that they may be permitted to rear their children in accordance with the teachings of the gospel. [Quoted in *Living Prophets for a Living Church,* pp. 126–27]

During this period the Church began what President McKay described as "one of the greatest undertakings that has yet been presented to the Priesthood" (in Conference Report, Oct. 1961, p. 77), with the inauguration of a new Church correlation program.

STUDY QUESTIONS

1. How had David O. McKay been prepared to lead the Church?
2. What does President McKay's family life as a young man and as a married man suggest concerning the practical things we can do to assure ourselves of happiness in our homes?
3. What does the example of President McKay's mother suggest about the major reason for bringing children into the world?
4. What did President McKay's search for spiritual development lead him to?
5. What connection exists between President McKay's teachings on the Christ-centered life and his vision of the celestial city?
6. In what ways was President McKay an ambassador for Christ?
7. In what ways can we become involved in the "Every Member a Missionary" program?

PRIESTHOOD CORRELATION

ONE of the most important developments in the Church during the 1960s was the unfolding of what has come to be known as "priesthood correlation." The first general effort to better coordinate the expanding Church programs began in 1912 when President Joseph F. Smith named Elder David O. McKay of the Quorum of the Twelve chairman of a Church correlation committee, which focused on ending needless duplication of work among the auxiliary organizations. In 1920 an additional study attempted to determine quorum relationships to each other as well as relationships among the auxiliaries, but the First Presidency felt that under existing circumstances it was inadvisable at that time to make the changes recommended in the report. The 1960s, however, saw the introduction of a new correlation program that would not only affect the way of preparing manuals for the Saints in all organizations but introduce a new coordination of priesthood and auxiliary activities throughout the Church.

HIGHLIGHTS

1906 Apr.: Joseph F. Smith foretells the time when all Church programs will be carried on by the priesthood.

1915 Apr.: The First Presidency stresses holding a home evening.

1961 The First Presidency announces a Priesthood Correlation program at fall conference.

1962 June: The First Presidency announces an eight-year curriculum plan of instruction.

Oct.: The First Presidency unveils the priesthood home teaching program.

1963 Apr.: The First Presidency organizes general Church committees for home teaching, welfare, genealogy, and missionary work.

1964 Oct.: The ward priesthood executive committee and ward councils are created.

1965 Oct.: The First Presidency reemphasizes a family home evening program.

1967 Oct.: First Regional Representatives of the Twelve are called.

1971 Jan.: New correlated Church magazines begin publication: the *Ensign,* the *New Era,* and the *Friend.*

1973 Jan.: A Welfare Services Department is created.

1974 Jan.: An Instructional Development Committee is organized as part of the Internal Communications Department.

1975 Jan.: Correlation organizations are formally incorporated into a Correlation Department.

1977 Feb.: The First Presidency defines ecclesiastical and temporal priesthood lines and duties at Church headquarters.

HISTORICAL SUMMARY

Beginnings of Priesthood Correlation

As early as 1906, President Joseph F. Smith looked forward to the time when the priesthood quorums would assume a more vital role in Church activity.

> We expect to see the day, if we live long enough (and if some of us do not live long enough to see it, there are others who will), when every council of the Priesthood in the Church of Jesus Christ of Latter-day Saints will understand its duty, will assume its own responsibility, will magnify its calling, and fill its place in the Church, to the uttermost, according to the intelligence and ability possessed by it. When that day shall come, there will not be so much necessity for work that is now being done by the auxiliary organizations, because it will be done by the regular quorums of the Priesthood. The Lord designed and comprehended it from the beginning, and He has made provision in the Church whereby every need may be met and satisfied through the regular organizations of the Priesthood. It has truly been said that the Church is perfectly organized. The only trouble is that these organizations are not fully alive to the obligations that rest upon them. When they become thoroughly awakened to the requirements made of them, they will fulfill their duties more faithfully, and the work of the Lord will be all the stronger and more powerful and influential in the world. [In Conference Report, Apr. 1906, p. 3]

In 1915 President Smith also urged parents to inaugurate regular home evenings to teach the gospel to their children.

> Dear Brethren and Sisters:
>
> We counsel the Latter-day Saints to observe more closely the command-

ment of the Lord given in the 68th section of the Doctrine and Covenants (25–28):

"And again, inasmuch as parents have children in Zion, or in any of her stakes which are organized, that teach them not to understand the doctrine of repentance, faith in Christ the Son of the living God, and of Baptism and the gift of the Holy Ghost by the laying on of hands when eight years old, the sin be upon the heads of the parents;

"For this shall be a law unto the inhabitants of Zion, or in any of her stakes which are organized;

"And their children shall be baptized for the remission of their sins when eight years old, and receive the laying on of the hands.

"And they shall also teach their children to pray and walk uprightly before the Lord."

The children of Zion should also observe more fully the commandment of the Lord given to ancient Israel, and reiterated to the Latter-day Saints: "Honor thy father and mother: that thy days may be long upon the land which the Lord thy God giveth thee."

These revelations apply with great force to the Latter-day Saints, and it is required of fathers and mothers in this Church that these commandments shall be taught and applied in their homes.

To this end we advise and urge the inauguration of a "Home Evening" throughout the Church, at which time fathers and mothers may gather their boys and girls about them in the home and teach them the word of the Lord. They may thus learn more fully the needs and requirements of their families; at the same time familiarizing themselves and their children more thoroughly with the principles of the Gospel of Jesus Christ. This "Home Evening" should be devoted to prayer, singing hymns, songs, instrumental music, scripture-reading, family topics and specific instruction on the principles of the gospel, and on the ethical problems of life, as well as the duties and obligations of children to parents, the home, the

Church, society and the nation. For the smaller children appropriate recitations, songs, stories and games may be introduced. Light refreshments of such a nature as may be largely prepared in the home might be served.

Formality and stiffness should be studiously avoided, and all the family participate in the exercises.

These gatherings will furnish opportunities for mutual confidence between parents and children, between brothers and sisters, as well as give opportunity for words of warning, counsel and advice by parents to their boys and girls. They will provide opportunity for the boys and girls to honor father and mother, and to show their appreciation of the blessings of home so that the promise of the Lord to them may be literally fulfilled and their lives be prolonged and made happy.

We request that the Presidents of Stakes and Bishops throughout the Church set aside at least one evening each month for this purpose, and that upon such evenings no other Church duties shall be required of the people.

We further request that all the officers of the auxiliary organizations throughout the Church support this movement and encourage

the young people to remain at home that evening and devote their energies to make it instructive, profitable and interesting.

If the Saints obey this counsel, we promise that great blessings will result. Love at home and obedience to parents will increase. Faith will be developed in the hearts of the youth of Israel, and they will gain power to combat the evil influence and temptations which beset them. [James R. Clark, comp., *Messages of the First Presidency of The Church of Jesus Christ of Latter-day Saints*, 4:337–39]

Nevertheless, the auxiliaries continued to occupy the dominant role in Church activities for several decades.

Over the years the General Authorities periodically reviewed the Church's programs to see how adequately they were fulfilling their mission—the perfecting of the Saints—but no program resulted. In 1960, however, the First Presidency wrote to the General Priesthood Committee, chaired by Elder Harold B. Lee of the Quorum of the Twelve:

We of the First Presidency have over the years felt the need of a correlation between and among the courses of study put out by the General Priesthood Committee and by the responsible heads of the other Committees of the General Authorities for the instruction of the Priesthood of the Church.

We have also felt the very urgent need of a correlation of studies among the Auxiliaries of the Church. We have noted what seemed to be a tendency toward a fundamental, guiding concept, particularly among certain of the Auxiliary Organizations, that there must be every year a new course of study for each of the Auxiliary Organizations so moving. We question whether the composite of all of them might not tend away from the development of a given line of study or activity having the ultimate and desired objective of building up a knowledge of the Gospel, a power to promulgate the same, a promotion of the growth, faith, and stronger testimony of the principles of the Gospel among the members of the Church.

We have sometimes been led to wonder whether there was a proper observance of the field of a particular Auxiliary of what might be termed its jurisdiction. The question has not been absent from our minds that there might be a concept entertained by some of them including within their jurisdiction the entire scope of Church activity, and with their members the whole Church membership.

We think that the contemplated study by the Committee now set up, should have the foregoing matters in mind. We feel assured that if the whole Church curricula were viewed from the vantage point of what we might term the total purpose of each and all of these organizations, it would bring about such a collation and limitation of subjects and subject matters elaborated in the various Auxiliary courses as would tend to the building of efficiency in the Auxiliaries themselves in the matter of carrying out the purposes lying behind their creation and function.

We would therefore commend to you Brethren of the General Priesthood Committee the beginning of an exhaustive, prayerful study and consideration of this entire subject, with the co-operative assistance of the Auxiliaries themselves so that the Church might reap the maximum harvest from the devotion of the faith, intelligence, skill and knowledge of our various Auxiliary Organizations and Priesthood Committees.

This is your authority to employ such necessary technical help as you might need to bring this about. We shall await your report. [Quoted in Harold B. Lee, Conference Report, Apr. 1963, pp. 82–83; or *Improvement Era,* June 1963, p. 502]

Announcement of New Correlation Program

On 30 September 1961, in the priesthood session of general conference, Elder Harold B. Lee, chairman of the Melchizedek Priesthood Committee, made the first announcement of the new emphasis on priesthood correlation.

I should like to introduce the thoughts which I shall express by reading a text that to me has particular significance. I quote from the words of the Apostle Paul, speaking of the different organizations of the church within what he called "the body of Chirst," by which he meant the Church:

"For the body is not one member, but many.

"If the foot shall say, Because I am not the hand, I am not the body; is it therefore not of the body?

"And if the ear shall say, Because I am not the eye, I am not of the body; is it therefore not of the body? . . .

Elder Harold B. Lee

"But now hath God set the members every one of them in the body, as it hath pleased him. . . .

"But now *are they* many members, yet but one body.

"And the eye cannot say unto the hand, I have no need of thee: nor again the head to the feet, I have no need of you. . . .

"But God hath tempered the body together, . . .

"That there should be no schism in the body; but *that* the members should have the same care one for another. . . .

"Now ye are the body of Christ, and members in particular.

"And God hath set some in the church, first apostles, secondarily prophets, thirdly teachers, . . . then . . . helps (and) government. . . ." (See 1 Cor. 12:14–28.)

In the great, modern-day revelation on Church government, the Lord concludes with this statement:

"Behold, this is the way that mine apostles, in ancient days, built up my church unto me.

"Therefore, let every man stand in his own office, and labor in his own calling; and let not the head say unto the feet it hath no need of the feet; for without the feet, how shall the body be able to stand?

"Also the body hath need of every member, that all may be edified together, that the system may be kept perfect." (D&C 84:108–110.)

Obviously, as you think about those scriptures, they were given to impress the need for the constant and continued consultations and correlations of the various subdivisions, the priesthood quorums and the auxiliaries and all other units within the kingdom of God for at least four reasons:

First, that each organization was to have its specific function, and it was not to usurp the field of the other, which would be like the eye saying to the hand "I have no need of thee."

Second, that each sub-division is of equal importance in the work of salvation, just as each part of the physical body is essential to a complete human being.

Third, that all may be edified or educated together; and

Fourth, that the system may be kept perfect, or in other words, that within the framework of the Lord's plan of organization for the salvation of his children, the Church will perform as a perfectly organized human body, with every member functioning as it was intended.

Throughout the scriptures there runs a phrase, again and again repeated to remind us of the whole purpose of the Lord's plan. As he told his prophet, his purpose was ". . . to bring to pass the immortality and eternal life of man," (Moses 1:39) or to be more specific and, putting it into the language of our present leaders as they have counseled us, "to plant and to make grow in every member of the Church a testimony of Christ and of the Gospel and of the divinity of the mission of Joseph Smith and the Church and to bring the people to order their lives in accordance with the laws and principles of the restored gospel and priesthood."

The repeated necessity for re-examination of the programs, the activities, and the prescribed courses of study has been apparent over the years to make certain that the original concepts relative to each organization were being adhered to, that each in its field was functioning up to its capacity, that one was not usurping the field of activity designed for the other, and that duplications and overlappings were reduced to a minimum.

I found an apt illustration which illustrates the importance of this periodical re-examination and reappraisal. In history there is found recorded the account of a famed debate known as the Webster-Hayne Debate in Congress in which Daniel Webster made this statement that seems to apply to the point I want to make. Said Daniel Webster:

"Mr. President, when the mariner has been tossed about for many days in thick weather on an unknown sea, he naturally avails himself of the first pause in the storm, the earliest glance of the sun to take his latitude and ascertain how far the elements have driven him from his true course. Let us imitate this prudence and before we float on the waves of this debate refer to the point from which we departed, that we may at least be able to conjecture where we now are." . . .

This whole problem of correlation becomes more acute as the Church grows and develops, if you will just stop to think for a moment what the rapid expansion and growth of the Church entails. . . .

In March of last year, 1960, the First Presidency wrote to the general priesthood committee and called our attention to the need for better correlation between and among the courses of study put out by the general priesthood committee and other responsible heads of other committees of the General Authorities for the instruction of the priesthood of the Church and an urgent need of correlation of studies among the auxiliaries of the Church, to avoid the necessity for new courses of study every year, having the ultimate objective of building up a knowledge of the gospel, a power to promulgate the same, a promotion of the growth, faith, and stronger testimony of the

principles of the gospel among the members of the Church, and expressed the view in that letter to the general priesthood committee that if the whole church curriculum were viewed from the vantage point of what might be termed the total purpose of each and all these organizations, it would bring about such a collation and limitation of subjects and subject-matter elaborated in the various auxiliary courses as would tend to the building of efficiency in the auxiliaries themselves in the matter of carrying out the purposes lying behind their creation and function. . . .

May I say as well, that the key to what now we have to propose and which I will explain to you in a few minutes, and a guide to the educational committee and the research staff, was a communication from the First Presidency in one of these studies some while back when they called attention to the fact that "the home was the basis of a righteous life and that no other instrumentality can take its place nor fulfil its essential functions and that the utmost the auxiliaries can do is to aid the home in its problems, giving special aid and succor where such is necessary, that in aiding the home the auxiliaries may well consider thinking of home-life of the people as having three periods, the first, from birth to twelve years of

The First Presidency, 1959–61, left to right: J. Reuben Clark, jr., David O. McKay, and Henry D. Moyle

age or the childhood period; then the youth period from twelve years up to the early twenties; and then adulthood, from the early twenties on to the end of life."

With that as the key and the letter given from the First Presidency as the blueprint, it is the feeling now of the First Presidency and the Council of Twelve, after reviewing these studies, that there should be presently more coordination and correlation between the activities and programs of the various priesthood quorums and auxiliary organizations and the educational system of the Church. They have decided, therefore, that there should be established an all-Church co-ordinating council and three co-ordinating committees: one for the children, one for the youth, and one for adults. This council and the three committees will correlate and coordinate the total instructional and activity programs of all auxiliaries and priesthood quorums which the brethren have now suggested should include missionary instructions and activities for the entire Church....

The function of the all-Church coordinating council is to formulate policy which will govern the planning, the writing, co-ordination, and implementation of the entire Church curriculum....

In the adoption of such a program, we may possibly and hopefully look forward to the consolidation and simplification of church curricula, church publications, church buildings, church meetings, and many other important aspects of the Lord's work.

With that brief statement, may I conclude with just this one thought. Perhaps one of the most oft-asked questions, as we go about the Church, is "How, with the Church growing to the size that it is, can we hope for the present General Authorities to supervise and keep in contact with the growing Church?" My answer has always been, "I am sure that by the time we arrive at the place where we need more revelations that the Lord will give that light and knowledge to the prophet

whom he has put upon the earth for that purpose."...

Almost imperceptibly we see the hand of the Lord moving to do things, and this I construe to be a consolidation of the forces of the Lord under the direction of the prophet, just as in an army, in order to meet a superior force of the enemy in numbers, the forces of our opposition to the forces of evil must be consolidated in order to give them the most effective possible defense.

We are in a program of defense. The Church of Jesus Christ was set upon this earth in this day "... for a defense, and for a refuge from the storm, and from wrath when it should be poured out without mixture upon the whole earth." (D&C 115:6.) This is a move, which, as I say, has lain close to President McKay's mind and now as the President of the Church he is instructing us to move forward, that we consolidate to make more efficient, and more effective the work of the priesthood, the auxiliaries, and the other units in order that we may conserve our time, our energy, and our efforts toward the prime purpose for which the Church itself has been organized. We must not forget what the Lord said, that he had given a parable to teach us a great lesson, and concluded the parable by saying, "I say unto you, be one; and if ye are not one ye are not mine." (*Ibid.*, 38:27.) [In Conference Report, Oct. 1961, pp. 77–81]

Thus, all Church programs were to be correlated through the priesthood to strengthen the family and individual.

The Unfolding of Priesthood Correlation

The first step in implementing the principles of priesthood correlation was the setting up of a general Church organization. Under the direction of the First Presidency and the Twelve, a coordinating council and age-group committees would plan and write lessons for the Church. By 1962 these committees had outlined a comprehensive curriculum that would soon be the means of teaching the gospel to Church members grouped into three categories: child, youth, and adult. For

example, adult Latter-day Saints are now pursuing an in-depth study of the standard works according to an outline that repeats every eight years.

In 1963 four priesthood committees were added to the all-Church organization to better coordinate direction given to home teaching, missionary, genealogy, and welfare activities.

The correlation organization was extended to the local level in 1964 with the organization of ward correlation councils and priesthood executive committees. In that same year, home teaching consolidated former separate programs of regularly contacting families. Elder Lee explained that "Home Teaching isn't just one of the programs.... Home Teaching is the instrument by which we see to it, through the priesthood, that every program in the Church is made available to parents and their children" (quoted in *Priesthood Home Teaching Handbook* [1967], p. 1). Thus all the resources of the Church were to be made available to the individual to aid him in his efforts to live the gospel and thereby prepare him to reach his maximum potential as a son or daughter of God.

Family Home Evening

In 1964 the Church gave new stress to regularly holding the family home evening that the First Presidency had urged fifty years earlier. In the October 1964 general conference, Elder Harold B. Lee repeated promises made by former prophets to parents who faithfully discharged their responsibility to teach their children.

In all of these [correlation of curricula] studies we have never had absent from our minds the responsibilities the Lord has placed upon the parents in the home in the teaching of our children. You recall what the Lord said:

"And again, inasmuch as parents have children in Zion, or in any of her stakes which are organized, that teach them not to understand the doctrine of repentance, faith in Christ the Son of the living God, and of baptism and the gift of the Holy Ghost by the laying on of hands, when eight years old, the sin be upon the heads of the parents" [D&C 68:25]....

The instructions to which I have made reference and about which President McKay spoke were given about fifty years ago. I read from a letter sent out to the Church in 1915 over the signature of President Joseph F. Smith, Anthon H. Lund, and Charles W. Penrose. But I suppose it is something like Mark Twain said about the weather: "We talk a lot about the weather, but we don't seem to do anything about it." Now we have talked a lot about family home evenings, and this is the announcement which was made. After I have given you this I will make a few comments and then outline the program by which we are now to give strength to the teaching of the family by the parents in the home. This is a quote from the letter.

"We advise and urge the inauguration of a Home Evening throughout the Church, at which time father and mother may gather their boys and girls about them in the home, and teach them the word of the Lord. . . . This Home Evening should be devoted to prayer, singing hymns, songs, instrumental music, scripture reading, family topics, and specific instructions on the principles of the gospel, and on the ethical problems of life, as well as the duties and obligations of children to parents, the home, the Church, society, and the nation."

Then to those who would put this family home hour or evening into practice, the Presidency made this promise:

"If the Saints obey this counsel, we promise that great blessings will result. Love at home and obedience to parents will increase. Faith will be developed in the hearts of the youth of Israel, and they will gain power to combat the evil influences and temptations which beset them." . . .

President Joseph F. Smith, in commenting about the responsibility of parents in teaching their children, said this:

"Do not let your children out to specialists in these things, but teach them by your own precept and example, by your own fireside. Be a specialist yourself in the truth. Let our meetings, schools and organizations, instead of being our only or leading teachers, be supplements to our teachings and training in the home. Not one child in a hundred would go astray, if the home environment, example and training, were in harmony with the truth in the gospel of Christ, as revealed and taught to the Latter-day Saints." (Joseph F. Smith, *Gospel Doctrine*, p. 302.)

About this same matter President Wilford Woodruff said:

"It is one of the greatest blessings that God ever bestowed upon children that they have had parents who were in possession of true principles in relation to their Heavenly Father, salvation, eternal life, and were qualified and capable of teaching and traditionating their children in the same that they may be qualified to fulfil the object of their creation. . . . Ninety-nine out of every hundred children who are taught by their parents the principles of honesty and integrity, truth and virtue, will observe them through life." (*Discourses of Wilford Woodruff*, pp. 266–268.)

And then from President Heber J. Grant:

"I have heard men and women say that they were going to let their sons and daughters grow to maturity before they sought to teach them the principles of the gospel, that they were not going to cram the gospel down them in their childhood, before they were able to comprehend it. When I hear men and women say this, I think they are lacking faith in the principles of the gospel and do not comprehend it as they should. The Lord has said it is our duty to teach our children in their youth, and I prefer to take His word for it rather than the words of those who are not obeying His commandments. It is folly to imagine that our children will grow up with a knowledge of the gospel without teaching. . . . I may know that the gospel is true, and so may my wife; but I want to tell you that our children will not know that the gospel is true, unless they study it and gain a testimony for themselves. Parents are deceiving themselves in imagining that their children will be born with a knowledge of the gospel." (Heber J. Grant, *Gospel Standards*, p. 155.)

This next year will see some definite steps taken to strengthen the hands of the parents in carrying out these great God-given admonitions in placing stress upon the teaching of the gospel in the home. The first step will be to give every parent a set of lessons, one for each week throughout the coming year, for them to teach the gospel to their family in the home. . . .

We have discovered an interesting fact at our Mormon Pavilion at the World's Fair in New York: that the great strength of our pavilion as a missionary project is not in the paintings, not in the sculpture work, not in the film, but in the presentation of the missionaries who have the priesthood of God and in the wonderful spirit which our missionaries have.

As you go out tomorrow look to the east, just underneath the west towers of the great Salt Lake Temple, and see a depiction of the dipper pointing toward the North Star, which Truman O. Angell said in an article in the *Millennial Star* was to symbolize to the Church "that through the priesthood of God, the lost might find their way." May every priesthood holder remember that responsibility.

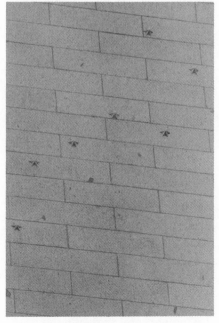

I was at Boston Stake conference a few weeks ago. We installed a young pilot who had served in the Air Force, a fighter pilot, as a coun-

selor in the stake presidency. I was very much impressed by his feeling of responsibility. He said something which I want to impress upon you leaders throughout the entire Church. He said, "I am very fearful of this responsibility now as a member of the stake presidency, because I have come to know that the most dangerous of all traffic aids is a fallen lighthouse, since so many people depend upon it for guidance and for safety."

To have a leader that fails, a "fallen lighthouse" upon whom God depends in a ward or stake or in a general capacity, is the most dangerous thing in the world, because so many are depending on the functioning of that particular man. And so we propose to give out to the Church now these plans which we ask you as stake leaders to be prepared to announce in your stakes as soon as you can after this conference. We will give you materials to help train your ward people and home teachers in order that we may get off at the beginning of the year in this great project of the Lord, that for fifty years has been urged and now is to be strengthened by a set of planned lessons for the parents in the home, actually outlined for the parents to teach their children and

to carry out appropriate activities to aid in the strengthening of the home. As I have thought of home night, I have thought of my own family, and I suppose all of you have as you have been listening.

When our oldest daughter was to be married to a fine Latter-day Saint boy the two mothers were in the corner of the room talking to each other, and the mother of our oldest daughter said, "You know, from the time my little girl was born, I have been praying all my life that somewhere a mother would be preparing a son worthy to marry my daughter." And this other mother smiled and said, "Isn't that strange? This is my only son who is being married to your daughter, and ever since he was born, I, too, have been praying that somewhere there would be a mother preparing a daughter worthy to meet and to marry my son."

It is that kind of home attention—mothers preparing daughters, fathers and mothers, sons—that will make us and our homes stronger today.

One of the hopes we have in this program is that the four standard works will be in the possession of every boy and girl deacons age and older and that on Easter, on birthdays, on Christmas, on New Year's, you make this a part of your family giving to your children, so they may have the joy of personally owning the Bible, the Book of Mormon, the Doctrine and Covenants, and the Pearl of Great Price, and from these precious pages begin to be instructed in the ways of the Lord.

As I thought of what we are doing now and its possible impact, the words of the Prophet Micah came, "But in the last days it shall come to pass, that the mountain of the house of the Lord shall be established in the top of the mountains, and it shall be exalted above the hills; and people shall flow unto it.

"And many nations shall come, and say, Come, and let us go up to the mountain of the Lord, and to the house of the God of Jacob; and he will teach us of his ways, and we will walk in his paths: for the law shall go forth of Zion, and the word of the Lord from Jerusalem." (Micah 4:1–2.)

I say unto you Latter-day Saint mothers and fathers, if you will rise to the responsibility of teaching your children in the home—priesthood quorums preparing the fathers, the Relief Society the mothers—the day will soon be dawning when the whole world will come to our doors and will say, "Show us your way that we may walk in your path." [In Conference Report, Oct. 1964, pp. 83–87; or Improvement Era, Dec. 1964, pp. 1080–81]

In the preface to the first family home evening manual, President David O. McKay wrote:

These lessons for "Teaching and Living the Gospel in the Home" are offered as helps for the weekly home evening. We recommend flexibility in their use, that they be adapted to the age and circumstances of the family, that the parents who have children in Zion recognize their obligation to teach their children "to understand ... and to pray ... and to walk uprightly before the Lord." And again, most urgently we would re-

emphasize that no other success can compensate for failure in the home.

Earnestly we urge parents to gather their families around them, and to instruct them in truth and righteousness, and in family love and loyalty. The home is the basis of a righteous life, and no other instrumentality can take its place nor fulfill its essential functions. The problems of these difficult times cannot better be solved in any other place, by any other agency, by any other means, than by love and righteousness, and precept and example, and devotion to duty in the home.

May you be blessed in teaching and caring for and drawing near to you those whom God has entrusted to you, and in watching over your own. As you do so, love at home and obedience to parents will increase, and faith will develop in the hearts of the youth of Israel, and they will gain power to combat evil influences and temptations, and to choose righteousness and peace, and be assured an eternal place in the family circle of our Father.

God is guiding this church. Be true to it. Be true to our families, loyal to them. Protect your children. Guide them, not arbitrarily, but through the kind example of a father, a loving mother and so contribute to the strength of the Church by magnifying your priesthood in your home and in your lives. [Family Home Evening (manual, 1965), p. iii]

In more recent years, still further steps have been taken to achieve the goals of priesthood correlation. Beginning all Church programs at the same time during the year and standardizing age grouping among the various priesthood and auxiliary organizations has facilitated greater coordination. The three English-language Church magazines, the Ensign, the New Era, and the Friend, as well as a system of magazines for non-English speaking Church members, are published under the direction of the priesthood and correlated with all Church programs serving their respective age groups. General Church correlation review committees, which became part of an

independent department in 1975, have continued to review all Church programs and activities to ensure that they are doctrinally sound and are properly coordinated to give maximum benefit to members of the Church.

Destiny of Priesthood Correlation

In his announcement of priesthood correlation, Elder Harold B. Lee described it as a "program of defense" against the forces of evil, explaining the the Saints needed to consolidate their activities and make them more effective (see Conference Report, Apr. 1963, p. 258). Elder Thomas S. Monson declared: "Today, we are encamped against the greatest array of sin, vice, and evil ever assembled before our eyes. Such formidable enemies may cause lesser hearts to shrink or shun the fight. But the battle plan whereby we fight to save the souls of men is not our own. It was provided to our leader, even President David O. McKay, by the inspiration and revelation of the Lord. Yes, I speak of that plan which will bring us victory, even the Correlation Program of the Church" ("Correlation Brings Blessings," Relief Society Magazine, Apr. 1967, p. 247).

Today members of the Church throughout the world are reaping the benefits of that inspired program.

STUDY QUESTIONS

1. How are we today seeing the fulfillment of President Joseph F. Smith's 1906 prophecy concerning priesthood correlation?

2. When the correlation program was announced in October 1961, what justifications were given for its creation? Are these still valid considerations in our day?

3. What is the overall purpose of priesthood correlation?

4. What remarkable promises have Elder Harold B. Lee and other Church leaders given to Latter-day Saint parents if they would implement the family home evening program?

5. How have you and your family benefited from the correlation program?

JOSEPH FIELDING SMITH

IN 1876 the dusty Salt Lake City streets served as a reminder that although America was then one hundred years old, much of the country remained a frontier. That year Ulysses S. Grant served as president of the United States, and in Salt Lake City, the Saints had just gathered to hear their beloved President Brigham Young in the nine-year-old tabernacle. For Elder Joseph F. Smith the year 1876 brought a new son. On 19 July Julina Lambson Smith gave birth to her first son, who received his father's name and his father's voice, and to an amazing degree, the heritage of his father as a missionary, historian, Apostle, scriptorian, counselor in the First Presidency and President of the Church.

HIGHLIGHTS

1876 July 19: Born in Salt Lake City, a son of the sixth President of the Church.

Young Joseph Fielding

1896 His patriarchal blessing promises, "It shall be thy duty to sit in counsel with thy brethren and to preside among the people" (20).

1898 Marries Louie Emyla Shurtliff (22).

1899 Leaves on a mission to England (22).

1901 Serves as a clerk in the Church historian's office (25).

1906 Becomes assistant Church historian (30).

1908 His first wife, Louie, dies; marries Ethel Georgina Reynolds (32).

1910 Ordained Apostle by his father and becomes a member of the Quorum of the Twelve (33).

1918 Father, President Joseph F. Smith, dies (42).

1919 Called as a counselor in Salt Lake Temple presidency (43).

1921–70 Serves as Church historian (44–94).

1922 Publishes *Essentials in Church History* (45).

1934 Becomes president of the Genealogical Society (57).

1937 His second wife, Ethel, dies (60).

1938 Marries Jessie Ella Evans (61).

1939 Tours Europe prior to World War II, directing evacuation of all missionaries from Europe (63).

1945 Becomes president of the Salt Lake Temple (68).

1951 Becomes President of the Council of the Twelve (74).

1955 Tours the Far East and dedicates four countries for the preaching of the gospel (79).

1965 Becomes a counselor to President David O. McKay in the First Presidency (89).

1970 Sustained as President of the Church (93).

1971 Presides over the first area general conference of the Church, in Manchester, England; His third wife, Jessie Evans, dies.

1972 July 2: Dies in Salt Lake City, Utah (95).

HISTORICAL SUMMARY

Early Life

Joseph Fielding Smith not only bore the name of his father, but also his great-uncle and great-grandfather. He honored his name and never allowed himself to be called by the nickname, *Joe*.

As a boy, Joseph Fielding desired to learn the will of the Lord, prompting him to read the Book of Mormon twice before he was ten years old. When the ball team missed him, they generally found him in the hay loft reading the scriptures. He carried them with him as he walked.

As Joseph rounded the corner on North Temple Street and headed west down along City Creek, he delighted in the sound of the water rippling along over the rocks. He also noted there was a touch of fall in the air now as dusk settled in on the valley. He would have to remember and wear his jacket to work in the morning. Walking along he pulled from his shirt pocket a small copy of the New Testament that he carried with him constantly, reading it during his noon break and while going to and from work, and in fact whenever he had opportunity. He opened it to his marker in the Book of Acts, Chapter 3, and read a few verses, but the light had grown dim, for the days were getting shorter, a thing he disliked, and it was a strain on his eyes to read, especially while walking. So he put the book back in his pocket. His eyes were not too strong anyway, and it would not do to unnecessarily strain them. There was a lot of reading to get done in the days and years ahead. Instead of reading the rest of the way home he would mentally run through some scriptures that he was trying to commit to memory. Matthew, Chapter 11, "Come unto me, all ye that labour and are heavy laden, and I will give you rest. Take my yoke upon you, and learn of me; for I am meek and lowly in heart; and ye shall find rest unto your souls. For my yoke is easy, and my burden light...." [Joseph Fielding Smith, Jr., and John J. Stewart, *The Life of Joseph Fielding Smith*, p. 67]

Reflecting back on these times, he later recalled, "From my earliest recollection, from the time I first could read, I have received more pleasure and greater satisfaction out of the study of the scriptures, and reading of the Lord Jesus Christ, and of the Prophet Joseph Smith, and the work that has been accomplished for the salvation of men, than from anything else in all the world" (in Conference Report, Apr. 1930, p. 91).

Joseph Fielding's quest for knowledge and truth dominated his entire life-style and set the course of his daily habits and practices. Though he worked hard and loved sports and flying, his life revolved around his family and service to his fellowmen.

Early in life he learned responsibility, herding cows near the Jordan river and working with his brothers on the farm in Taylorsville. At age ten he assisted his mother in her responsibilities as a midwife.

Joseph's job was that of stable boy and buggy driver. At all hours of the day or night, when the call came for his mother's services, Joseph was to hitch up the faithful mare "Old Meg" to the buggy and drive his mother to the home of the confinement case. Here he might wait while she delivered the baby, or, if his mother thought the wait would be too long, she would send him home with instructions on when to return for her....

"Sometimes I nearly froze to death. I marveled that so many babies were born in the middle of the night, especially on cold winter nights. I

fervently wished that mothers might time things a little better." [Smith and Stewart, *Life of Joseph Fielding Smith,* pp. 52–53]

At eighteen years of age, Joseph worked as a clerk in the wholesale grocery department in the basement of the ZCMI store at Main and South Temple in Salt Lake City to help support his family. He often worked fifteen or sixteen hours each day. At the end of a long day he liked to stop by the candy counter and purchase a sack of sweets to give to his brothers and sisters after his arrival home.

Strong Self-Discipline

Joseph Fielding never wasted a moment. Following in his father's footsteps, he arose early, which became his formula for getting more work done. He instilled this same habit in the lives of his children. His son recalled, "Somehow it seemed immoral to lie in bed after 6. Of course, I only tried it once. Father saw to that" (quoted in Smith and Stewart, *Life of Joseph Fielding Smith,* p. 3). Joseph managed to develop the habit of using his time wisely. "For years he carried a sack lunch to his office, so he could keep working through the noon hour. 'That gives me an extra 300 hours per year.' One day a sister of his called on him at the office and scolded him for not taking a nap after lunch. She cited by name half a dozen of his associates who had long done so. 'Yes,' he replied, 'and where are they

today? All dead!' " (Smith and Stewart, *Life of Joseph Fielding Smith,* p. 4).

While Joseph Fielding Smith's self-disciplined life-style gave him a stern appearance, his family knew him as a gentle, loving father and husband with a keen sense of humor. Ethel G. Reynolds, whom President Smith

Ethel G. Reynolds, Joseph Fielding's second wife

married in 1908, and who was the mother of nine of his children, described her husband as follows:

I have often thought when he is gone people will say, "He is a very good man, sincere, orthodox, etc." They will speak of him as the public knows him; but the man they have in mind is very different from the man I know. The man I know is a kind, loving husband and father whose greatest ambition in life is to make his family happy, entirely

Elder Smith and his family in 1938 or 1939

forgetful of self in his efforts to do this. He is the man that lulls to sleep the fretful child, who tells bedtime stories to the little ones, who is never too tired or too busy to sit up late at night or to get up early in the morning to help the older children solve perplexing school problems. When illness comes the man I know watches tenderly over the afflicted one and waits upon him. It is their father for whom they cry, feeling his presence a panacea for all ills. It is his hands that bind up the wounds, his arms that give courage to the sufferer, his voice that remonstrates with them gently when they err, until it becomes their happiness to do the thing that will make him happy.

The man I know is most gentle, and if he feels that he has been unjust to anyone the distance is never too far for him to go and, with loving words or kind deeds, erase the hurt. He welcomes gladly the young people to his home and is never happier than when discussing with them topics of the day—sports or whatever interests them most. He enjoys a good story and is quick to see the humor of a situation, to laugh and to be laughed at, always willing to join in any wholesome activity.

The man I know is unselfish, uncomplaining, considerate, thoughtful, sympathetic, doing everything within his power to make life a supreme joy for his loved ones. That is the man I know. [Ethel G. Reynolds Smith, as quoted in Bryant S. Hinckley, "Joseph Fielding Smith," *Improvement Era,* June 1932, p. 459.]

A Defender of Truth

Following a mission to Great Britain from 1899 to 1901, Joseph Fielding Smith became a clerk in the Church historian's office, and in 1906 became assistant Church historian. In 1910, at age thirty-three, he received a call to fill a vacancy in the Quorum of the Twelve Apostles. During the next sixty years as an Apostle, he became an outspoken defender of the truth, of the Church, and of the divine mission of the Prophet Joseph Smith. He spoke and wrote against the evils to which both Church members and nonmembers seemed so easily to succumb.

Elder Smith fought stubbornly against popular scientific theories which made man less than a son of God. Such book titles as *Doctrines of Salvation; Essentials in Church History; Man, His Origin and Destiny; The Progress of Man; Seek Ye Earnestly;* and *The Way to Perfection* are illustrative of his wide range of interests. The creation, the fall of man, the atonement of Jesus Christ, the second coming of the Christ, and the oath and covenant of the priesthood were but a few of the doctrinal themes he treated. He did not aspire to become an author, but desired to see that truth was not misunderstood nor cheapened and that noble leaders were not maligned.

Elder Joseph Fielding Smith, missionary, 1900

During his lifetime, twenty-five volumes were published containing his discourses, letters, and writings. Of his numerous writings, the commentaries on the oath and the covenant of the priesthood (see D&C 84:33–44) and on the fall of Adam and Eve exemplify the logic and power that characterized President Smith's doctrinal explanations to the membership of the Church.

Oath and Covenant of the Melchizedek Priesthood

Summarizing the doctrine of the Oath and Covenant of the priesthood, President Smith pointed out that the covenant is made by man and the oath is sworn by God, and that in it, one finds the keys to exaltation.

There is no exaltation in the kingdom of God without the fullness of the priesthood, and every man who receives the Melchizedek Priesthood does so with an oath and a covenant that he shall be exalted.

The covenant on man's part is that he will magnify his calling in the priesthood, and that he will live by every word that proceedeth forth from the mouth of God, and that he will keep the commandments.

The covenant on the Lord's part is that if man does as he promises, then all that the Father hath shall be given unto him; and this is such a solemn and important promise that the Lord swears with an oath that it shall come to pass. [In Conference Report, Apr. 1970, pp. 58–59; or *Improvement Era,* June 1970, p. 66]

In section 84 of the *Doctrine and Covenants,* the Lord has this to say: "For whoso is faithful unto the obtaining these two priesthoods of which I have spoken, and the magnifying their calling, are sanctified by the Spirit unto the renewing of their bodies. They become the sons of Moses and of Aaron and the seed of Abraham, and the church and kingdom, and the elect of God. And also all they who receive this priesthood receive me, saith the Lord."

And if we receive the Lord, then, surely the Lord receives us, and we are in fellowship with him, "For he that receiveth my servants receiveth me; And he that receiveth me receiveth my Father."

Now, here is the great blessing, which I think many of us have overlooked, and especially these young men when they are called and sustained to be ordained to the office of elder: "And he that receiveth my Father"—and of course we receive the Father through our faithfulness and our obedience—"*receiveth my Father's kingdom; therefore all that my Father hath shall be given unto him.*" [D&C 84:33–38]

Can you think of a greater blessing the Lord could offer to any man holding the priesthood? But this is based upon faithfulness and the magnifying of the calling.

In other revelations, you know, the

Lord says: "And [they] who overcome by faith, and are sealed by the Holy Spirit of promise. . . . They are they into whose hands the Father has given all things—. . . they are gods, even the sons of God." [D&C 76:53–58] [Joseph Fielding Smith, *Doctrines of Salvation*, 3:139–40]

The Fall of Adam and Eve: A Blessing

In the following remarks, President Smith provided one of the clearest explanations of the Fall.

DEATH FOR ALL LIFE CAME BY FALL. President Brigham Young has said: "Some may regret that our first parents sinned. This in nonsense. If we had been there, and they had not sinned, we would have sinned. I will not blame Adam or Eve. Why? Because it was necessary that sin should enter into the world; no man could ever understand the principle of exaltation without its opposite; no one could ever receive an exaltation without being acquainted with its opposite. How did Adam and Eve sin? Did they come out in direct opposition to God and to his government? No. But they transgressed a command of the Lord, and through that transgression sin came into the world.". . .

The fall of man came as a blessing in disguise, and was the means of furthering the purposes of the Lord in the progress of man, rather than a means of hindering them.

"TRANSGRESSION" NOT "SIN" OF ADAM. I never speak of the part Eve took in this fall as a sin, nor do I accuse Adam of a sin. One may say, "Well did they not break a commandment?" Yes. But let us examine the nature of that commandment and the results which came out of it.

In no other commandment the Lord ever gave to man, did he say: "But of the tree of the knowledge of good and evil, thou shalt not eat of it, *nevertheless, thou mayest choose for thyself*." [Moses 3:17]

It is true, the Lord warned Adam and Eve that to partake of the fruit they would transgress a law, and this happened. But it is not always a sin to transgress a law. I will try to illustrate this. The chemist in his laboratory takes different elements and combines them, and the result is that something very different results. He has *changed* the law. As an example in point: hydrogen, two parts, and oxygen, one part, passing through an electric spark will combine and form water. Hydrogen will burn, so will oxygen, but water will put out a fire. This may be subject to some disagreement by the critics who will say it is not transgressing a law. Well, *Adam's transgression was of a similar nature, that is, his transgression was in accordance with law*.

The transgression of Adam did *not* involve sex sin as some falsely believe and teach. Adam and Eve were married by the Lord while they were yet immortal beings in the Garden of Eden and before death entered the world.

ADAM AND EVE REJOICED IN FALL. Before partaking of the fruit Adam could have lived forever; therefore, his status was one of immortality. When he ate, he became subject to death, and therefore he became mortal. This was a transgression of the law, but not a sin in the strict sense, for it was something that Adam and Eve had to do!

I am sure that neither Adam nor Eve looked upon it as a sin, when they learned the consequences, and this is discovered in their words after they learned the consequences.

Adam said: *"Blessed be the name of God, for because of my transgression my eyes are opened, and in this life I shall have joy, and again in the flesh I shall see God."*

Eve said: *"Were it not for our transgression we never should have had*

© LDS

Joseph Fielding Smith, 1876–1972

seed, and never should have known good and evil, and the joy of our redemption, and the eternal life which God giveth unto all the obedient." [Moses 5:10–11]

We can hardly look upon anything resulting in such benefits as being a sin, in the sense in which we consider sin. [*Doctrines of Salvation*, 1:112, 114–15]

A New President Is Sustained

At an age far beyond when most men have retired from an active life, President Smith assumed his greatest responsibility. Following the death of President David O. McKay in January of 1970, Joseph Fielding Smith became President of the Church at age ninety-three. A Church membership of nearly three million members responded to his love and concern for them.

President Smith presided at the first Area Conference of the Church held in 1971 in England, and at the dedicatory services of the Ogden and Provo temples early in 1972. Other developments during his administration included the reorganization of the

Church Educational System and the formation of the Health Services Department, the publication of new church magazines as part of priesthood correlation, and the continued expansion of missionary work around the world.

In evaluating his life, some have seen in President Smith a stern and unbending judge of righteousness. However, if there was sternness, he was stern with the sin, but merciful and kind to the sinner. The only severity in his nature was that severe discipline which he demanded of himself. He allowed himself no flabbiness of character.

Counsel to the Saints

President Smith's last counsel to the world and to the Church, given in his last general conference, shows the wisdom and spiritual power he had acquired through decades of devotion to the truth.

We are the servants of the Lord. We have received light and truth and revelation from him. He has commanded us to proclaim his truths and live his laws. And so now, in

harmony with his mind and will, and as guided by his Holy Spirit, we give counsel and direction to the Saints and to the world.

To the world I say: These are the last days. They are days of trouble and sorrow and desolation. They are days when Satan dwells in the hearts of ungodly men, when iniquity abounds, and when the signs of the times are being shown forth.

And there is no cure for the ills of the world except the gospel of the Lord Jesus Christ. Our hope for peace, for temporal and spiritual prosperity, and for an eventual inheritance in the kingdom of God is found only in and through the restored gospel. There is no work that any of us can engage in that is as important as preaching the gospel and building up the Church and kingdom of God on earth.

And so we invite all our Father's children, everywhere, to believe in Christ, to receive him as he is revealed by living prophets, and to join The Church of Jesus Christ of Latter-day Saints. We call upon the world to repent, to worship that God who made them, and to believe the words of those whom he hath sent in this day to proclaim his gospel.

To the honest in heart in all nations we say: The Lord loves you. He wants you to receive the full blessings of the gospel. He is now inviting you to believe the Book of Mormon, to accept Joseph Smith as

a prophet, and to come into his earthly kingdom and thereby become heirs of eternal life in his heavenly kingdom.

To those who have received the gospel we say: Keep the commandments. Walk in the light. Endure to the end. Be true to every covenant and obligation, and the Lord will bless you beyond your fondest dreams. As it was said by one of old: "Let us hear the conclusion of the whole matter: Fear God, and keep his commandments: for this is the whole duty of man." (Eccles. 12:13.)

To all the families in Israel we say: The family is the most important organization in time or in eternity. Our purpose in life is to create for ourselves eternal family units. There is nothing that will ever come into your family life that is as important as the sealing blessings of the temple and then keeping the covenants made in connection with this order of celestial marriage.

To parents in the Church we say: Love each other with all your hearts. Keep the moral law and live the gospel. Bring up your children in light and truth; teach them the saving truths of the gospel; and make your home a heaven on earth, a place where the Spirit of the Lord may dwell and where righteousness may be enthroned in the heart of each member.

It is the will of the Lord to strengthen and preserve the family unit. We plead with fathers to take their rightful place as the head of the house. We ask mothers to sustain and support their husbands and to be lights to their children.

President Joseph F. Smith said: "Motherhood lies at the foundation of happiness in the home, and of prosperity in the nation. God has laid upon men and women very sacred obligations with respect to motherhood, and they are obligations that cannot be disregarded without invoking divine displeasure." (Gospel Doctrine, p. 288.) Also, "To be a successful father or a successful mother is greater than to be a successful gen-

eral or a successful statesman." (Gospel Doctrine, p. 285.)

To the youth of Zion we say: The Lord bless you and keep you, which most assuredly will be so as you learn his laws and live in harmony with them. Be true to every trust. Honor thy father and thy mother. Dwell together in love and conformity. Be modest in your dress. Overcome the world, and do not be led astray by the fashions and practices of those whose interests are centered upon the things of this world.

Marry in the temple, and live joyous and righteous lives. Remember the words of Alma: "Wickedness never was happiness." (Alma 41:10.) Remember also that our hope for the future and the destiny of the Church and the cause of righteousness rest in your hands.

To those who are called to positions of trust and responsibility in the Church we say: Preach the gospel in plainness and simplicity as it is found in the standard works of the Church. Testify of the truth of the work and the doctrines revealed anew in our day.

Remember the words of the Lord Jesus Christ, who said, "I am among you as he that serveth" (Luke 22:27), and choose to serve with an eye single to the glory of God. Visit the fatherless and the widows in their affliction, and keep yourself unspotted from the sins of the world. [In Conference Report, Apr. 1972, pp. 13–14; or Ensign, July 1972, p. 28]

STUDY QUESTIONS

1. How did Joseph Fielding Smith prepare to fulfill his personal mission in life?

2. How did Joseph Fielding Smith's personal discipline help him live an honorable life? What can we learn from his example?

3. How did his family (wife and children) describe him as a husband and a father?

4. What insights do President Smith's writings give regarding the oath and covenant of the priesthood and the fall of Adam and Eve?

5. What counsel given by President Smith to members of the Church is especially relevant today?

HAROLD B. LEE

IN 1953 Elder Marion G. Romney of the Quorum of the Twelve wrote a tribute to Elder Harold B. Lee which in many respects characterizes his entire life: "Such is Harold B. Lee, who now stands, not at the end of his career but on its threshold. He knows his course, is recognized for what he is, and is on his way. Behind him is a record of high attainment. Before him, 'hills peep o'er hills, and Alps on Alps arise.' Sustained by the conviction that he lives in the shadow of the Almighty, he will not falter. The future must reckon with Harold B. Lee" (Marion G. Romney, "Harold B. Lee, Apostle of the Lord," *Improvement Era,* July 1953, p. 524). Seven years following this statement, Elder Lee was called as chairman of the general priesthood committee, which formulated the Church correlation program. Seventeen years later he was set apart as First Counselor in the First Presidency and President of the Quorum of the Twelve, and in nineteen years he became the President of the Church.

HIGHLIGHTS

1899 Mar. 28: Born at Clifton, Idaho.

1916 Teaches school at Silver Star School, near Weston, Idaho (17).

1917 Becomes principal of the four-room school at Oxford, Idaho (18).

1920 Serves a mission to Western States Mission (21).

1923–28 Becomes a principal in the Granite School District, Salt Lake City (24–29).

1923 Nov. 14: Marries Fern L. Tanner (24).

1929 Becomes president of the Pioneer Stake (31).

1932 Appointed a member of the Salt Lake City Commission (32).

1936 Becomes a member of the first Church security (welfare) committee (37).

1937 Becomes the managing director of the Church security program; tours the Church with Elder Melvin J. Ballard introducing and organizing the program (38).

1941 Becomes a member of the Quorum of the Twelve (42).

1954 Tours the Orient (55).

1959 Visits the missions of Central and South America (60).

1961 As chairman of the general priesthood committee, he helps develop the correlation program (62).

1962 His wife dies (63).

1963 Marries Freda Joan Jensen; becomes a member of the board of directors of the American Red Cross (64).

1970 Set apart as First Counselor to President Joseph Fielding Smith (71).

1971 Speaks at the first area conference of the Church, in England (72).

1972 Dedicates the Provo Temple (72).

July 7: Ordained and set apart as President of the Church (73).

Presides at the second area conference of the Church, in Mexico.

Oct.: Sustained as the President of the Church (73).

Nov.: Announces a new program for the single adults of the Church.

1973 Dec. 26: Dies in Salt Lake City (74).

HISTORICAL SUMMARY

Early Life

The man who eventually became president of a worldwide church that numbered over three million members came from a humble background. His father was one of twelve children born to Margaret McMurrin Lee in a dugout that served for a home. Samuel, the youngest of the twelve, was the only one to survive. Shortly after his birth his mother died. Samuel Lee reared his son Harold on a small farm in Idaho and during his early years Harold did not travel much beyond Denver, Colorado, where he served as a missionary.

His preparation was slow and difficult, but he learned when young to follow the promptings of the Spirit.

I was probably about eight years of age, or younger, when I was taken by my father to a farm some distance away. While he worked I tried to busy myself with things that a young boy would. The day was hot and dusty and I played about until I was tired. Over the fence there was a broken-down shed that looked very interesting to me. In my mind I thought of this broken-down shed as a castle that I would like to explore, so I went to the fence and

Young Harold, age 5

started to climb through to go over to that shed. There came a voice to me that said this very significant thing, "Harold, don't go over there." I looked about to see who was speaking my name. My father was way up at the other end of the field. He could not see what I was doing. There was no speaker in sight. Then I realized that someone that I could not see was warning me not to go over there. What was over there, I shall never know, but I learned early that there are those beyond our sight that could talk to us. [In Conference Report, Mexico Area Conference 1972, pp. 48–49]

This was characteristic the rest of his life; he heard and heeded the whisperings of the still, small voice.

A Polished Shaft

Like other prophets before him, he learned much by the things which he suffered. In his early life he pulled a can of lye in his face, almost blinding him; he severely cut his foot, and nearly lost it to infection; he nearly died of pneumonia at age seventeen; and he nearly froze to death at the same age. In each crisis his mother helped him with appropriate medical attention and with the help of the Lord young Harold's life was saved. Later he experienced the depths of sorrow when he lost his first wife, Fern, and four years later, a daughter, Maurine. All of these experiences, however, helped to prepare Harold B. Lee to become the Lord's chosen prophet.

The day after this appointment [as President], following the passing of our beloved President Smith, my attention was called to a paragraph from a sermon delivered in 1853 in a general conference by Elder Orson Hyde, then a member of the Twelve. This provoked some soul-searching in me also.

The subject of his address was "The Man to Lead God's People," and I quote briefly from his sermon: "...it is invariably the case," he said, "that when an individual is ordained and appointed to lead the people, he has passed through tribulations and trials, and has proven himself before God, and before His people, that he is worthy of the situation which he holds.... that

Active in athletics (far left, standing)

when a person has not been tried, that has not proved himself before God, and before His people, and before the councils of the Most High, to be worthy, he is not going to step in and lead the Church and people of God. It has never been so, but from the beginning some one that understands the Spirit and counsel of the Almighty, that knows the Church, and is known of her, is the character that will lead the Church." (*Journal of Discourses,* vol. 1, p. 123.)

As I have known of the lives of those who have preceded me, I have been made aware that each seemed to have had his special mission for his day and time.

Then, with searching introspection, I thought of myself and my experiences of which Orson Hyde's appraisal had made reference. Then I recalled the words of the Prophet Joseph's characterization of himself, which seemed somewhat analogous to myself. He said:

"I am like a huge rough stone rolling down from a high mountain; and

the only polishing I get is when some corner gets rubbed off by coming in contact with something else, striking with accelerated force against religious bigotry, priestcraft, lawyer-craft, doctor-craft, lying editors, suborned judges and jurors, and the authority of perjured executives, backed by mobs, blasphemers, licentious and corrupt men and women—all hell knocking off a corner here and a corner there. Thus will I become a smooth and polished shaft in the quiver of the Almighty...." (*Teachings of the Prophet Joseph Smith,* p. 304.)

These thoughts now running through my mind begin to give greater meaning to some of the experiences in my life, things that have happened which have been difficult for me to understand. At times it seemed as though I too was like a rough stone rolling down from a high mountainside, being buffeted and polished, I suppose, by experiences, that I too might overcome and become a polished shaft in the quiver of the Almighty.

Maybe it was necessary that I too

must learn obedience by the things that I might have suffered—to give me experiences that were for my good, to see if I could pass some of the various tests of mortality. [Harold B. Lee, in Conference Report, Oct. 1972, pp. 19–20; or *Ensign,* Jan. 1973, pp. 24–25]

Then there came some tests when a loved one was taken from me and my life was crushed. A part of my life was buried in the cemetery, and I wondered. Here I was struggling to help others. Why? Then I theorized that maybe this was a great test, and if I could survive it, maybe there would be no other test that I wouldn't be able to meet. Just as I was recovering from that sorrow a daughter died suddenly, leaving four little children motherless. That was difficult. It is still difficult to understand. But the ways of the Lord are righteous, and sometimes we have to go through experiences like these in order for us to be prepared to face the issues of today's world. [Harold B. Lee, *Ye Are the Light of the World,* pp. 347–48]

May I impose upon you for a moment to express appreciation for something that happened to me some time ago, years ago. I was suffering from an ulcer condition that was becoming worse and worse. We had been touring a mission; my wife, Joan, and I were impressed the next morning that we should get home as quickly as possible, although we had planned to stay for some other meetings.

On the way across the country, we were sitting in the forward section of the airplane. Some of our Church members were in the next section. As we approached a certain point en route, someone laid his hand upon my head. I looked up; I could see no one. That happened again before we arrived home, again with the same experience. Who it was, by what means or what medium, I may never know, except I knew I was receiving a blessing that I came a few hours later to know I needed most desperately.

As soon as we arrived home, my wife very anxiously called the doctor. It was now about 11 o'clock at night. He called me to come to the telephone, and he asked me how I was; and I said, "Well, I am very tired. I think I will be all right." But shortly thereafter, there came massive hemorrhages which, had they occurred while we were in flight, I wouldn't be here today talking about it.

I know that there are powers divine that reach out when all other help is not available. We see that manifest down in the countries we speak of as the underprivileged countries where there is little medical aid and perhaps no hospitals. If you want to hear of great miracles among these humble people with simple faith, you will see it among them when they are left to themselves. Yes, I know that there are such powers. [Harold B. Lee, in Conference Report, Apr. 1973, p. 179; or *Ensign,* July 1973, p. 123]

The Welfare Plan

Harold B. Lee's life was one of decisive direction. He had been a school principal, a member of the Salt Lake City commission, and a stake president by the age of thirty-one. While president of the Pioneer Stake, he was inspired to formulate a program that would later be developed into the worldwide welfare activity of the Church today.

Our goal was to see that none of the children [in the Pioneer Stake] would be without a Christmas. We would see that there was Christmas dinner in all the homes of the 4,800 who, without help, would otherwise not have Christmas dinner.

At that time I was one of the city commissioners. The night before Christmas Eve, we had had a heavy snowstorm, and I had been out all night with the crews getting the streets cleared, knowing that I would be blamed if any of my men fell down on the job. I had then gone home to change my clothes to go to the office.

As I started back to town, I saw a little boy on the roadside, hitchhiking. He stood in the biting cold with no coat, no gloves, no overshoes. I stopped and asked where he was going.

"I'm going uptown to a free picture show," he said.

I told him I was also going uptown and that he could ride with me.

"Son," I said, "are you ready for Christmas?"

"Oh, golly, mister," he replied, "we aren't going to have any Christmas at our home. Daddy died three months ago and left Mama and me and a little brother and sister."

Three children, all under twelve!

I turned up the heat in my car and said, "Now, son, give me your name and address. Somebody will come to your home—you won't be forgotten. And you have a good time; it's Christmas Eve!"

That night I asked each bishop to go with his delivery men and see that each family was cared for, and to report back to me. While waiting for the last bishop to report, I

School principal in Idaho

suddenly, painfully, remembered something. In my haste to see that all my duties at work and my responsibilities in the Church had been taken care of, I had forgotten the little boy and the promise I had made.

When the last bishop reported, I asked, "Bishop, have you enough left to visit one more family?"

"Yes, we have," he replied.

I told him the story about the little boy and gave him the address. Later he called to say that that family too had received some well-filled baskets. Christmas Eve was over at last, and I went to bed.

As I awoke that Christmas morning, I said in my heart, "God grant that I will never let another year pass but that I, as a leader, will truly know my people. I will know their needs. I will be conscious of those who need my leadership most."

My carelessness had meant suffering the first year because I did not know my people, but now I resolved never again to overlook the needs of those around me. [*Ye Are the Light*, pp. 346–47]

For the last five glorious, strenuous years, I have labored, under a call from the First Presidency, with a group of men in the development of and the unfolding of what we have called the Church Welfare Plan. . . . It was on April 20th, 1935, when I was called to the office of the First Presidency. That was a year before official announcement of the Welfare Plan was made in this Tabernacle. There, after an entire

half day session, at which President Grant and President McKay were present, President Clark then being in the East—they had some communications with him, so that all members of the Presidency were in agreement—I was astounded to learn that for years there had been before them, as a result of their thinking and planning and as the result of the inspiration of Almighty God, the genius of the very plan that is being carried out and was in waiting and in preparation for a time when in their judgment the faith of the Latter-day Saints was such that they were willing to follow the counsel of the men who lead and preside in this Church.

My humble place in this program at that time was described. I left there about noon-time. . . . I drove with my car up to the head of City Creek Canyon. I got out, after I had driven as far as I could, and I walked up through the trees. I sought my Heavenly Father. As I sat down to pore over this matter, wondering about an organization to be perfected to carry on this work, I received a testimony, on that beautiful spring afternoon, that God had already revealed the greatest organization that ever could be given to mankind, and that all that was needed now was that that organization be set to work, and the temporal welfare of the Latter-day Saints would be safeguarded. . . .

It was in August of that same year that with Brother Mark Austin of the General Committee, I had driven down to St. George and then back across the mountains to Richfield,

for an early morning meeting. At that time there was an upturn in business, so much so that some were questioning the wisdom of this kind of activity, and why hadn't the Church done it before now? There came to me, in that early morning hour, a distinct impression that was as real as though someone had spoken audibly, and this was the impression that came, and has stayed with me through these years: There is no individual in the Church that knows the real purpose for which the program then launched had been intended, but hardly before the Church has made sufficient preparation, that reason will be made manifest, and when it comes it will challenge every resource of the Church to meet it. I trembled at the feeling that came over me. Since that day that feeling has driven me on, night and day, hardly resting, knowing that this is God's will, this is His plan. The only thing necessary today is that the Latter-day Saints everywhere recognize these men, who sit here on the stand, as the fountainheads of truth, through whom God will reveal His will, that His Saints might be preserved through an evil day. [Harold B. Lee, in Conference Report, Apr. 1941, pp. 120–21]

After demonstrating his great ability to meet the needs of his people in the Pioneer Stake, it was not surprising that in a short time he was called by the Lord to greater responsibilities.

Call to the Apostleship

On 6 April 1941 President Lee was sustained as a member of the Quorum of the Twelve. On 12 April 1941 he gave an address entitled "Easter Morning—A Newness of Life." In the following account he describes the growth he had experienced in just six days and the testimony he had gained of the reality and divinity of Jesus Christ.

As one who is expected to bear solemn testimony, I exercise the opportunity of declaring to you my sacred testimony. When the call to the apostleship came, it was on a Saturday night of general conference. I was called to the front of the Tabernacle to meet the president of the Church [Heber J. Grant], and I walked into the General Authorities' room and found him crying. He put his hands on my shoulders and told me that I had been named to be a member of the Council of the Twelve. I said to him, "Oh, President, do you think I am worthy of that?" As quick as a flash, he said, "If I didn't think so, my boy, you wouldn't be called."

Then I spent a night I shall never forget. There was no sleep that night. All my life seemed to be coming before me, as in a panorama. I could have told you every person who had any ill will toward me. I could have told you every person against whom I had any ill will, and the feeling came that before I was worthy to accept that call as an apostle of the Lord Jesus Christ, I had to love and forgive every soul that walked the earth. Then when I began to fear the experience of standing in the Tabernacle with so many listening, I found the Spirit directed my words. I don't know what I said; it wasn't anything I had prepared.

On the following Thursday I walked into the room where I was to be ordained. There were twelve chairs in a semicircle, with three chairs in front for the First Presidency. As I thought of the men who had sat in those chairs, and I now was being

invited to sit as one in that circle, it was an overwhelming, shattering feeling. Am I worthy, can I measure up, can I reach the goal or attain the spiritual heights that such a position requires?

Well, that day passed, ordination came, and then one of the Twelve came to me and said, "Now we would like you to be the speaker at the Sunday night service. It is for Easter Sunday. As an ordained apostle, you are to be a special witness of the mission and resurrection of the Lord and Savior Jesus Christ." That, I think, was the most startling, the most overwhelming contemplation of all that had happened.

I locked myself in one of the rooms of the Church Office Building and took out the Bible. I read in the four Gospels, particularly the scriptures pertaining to the death, crucifixion, and resurrection of the Lord, and as I read, I suddenly became aware that something strange was happening. It wasn't just a story I was reading, for it seemed as though the events I was reading about were very real as though I were actually living those experiences. On Sunday night I delivered my humble message and said, "And now, I, one of the least of the apostles here on the earth today, bear you witness that I

too know with all my soul that Jesus is the Savior of the world and that he lived and died and was resurrected for us."

I knew because of a special kind of witness that had come to me the preceding week. Then someone asked, "*How* do you know? Have you *seen*?" I can say that more powerful than one's sight is the witness that comes by the power of the Holy Ghost bearing testimony to our spirits that Jesus is the Christ, the Savior of the world. [*Ye Are the Light,* pp. 25–27]

Correlation

Many responsibilities came to Elder Lee to serve the Church as a member of the Quorum of the Twelve, but one of the assignments that had a particularly significant effect was his call to direct the priesthood correlation program of the Church.

President McKay sometime ago in talking to the Presidency and the twelve, urged us to give time for more meditation so that we could tune in with spiritual forces that we had a right to and should expect to direct us in our work. He said, "The best time for me is early in the morning when my mind and body are rested. But when the inspiration comes, and it can come just as clearly as though you were taking down a telephone and dialing in for information; when the Lord tells you what to do, you have to have the courage to do what he instructs you." . . .

I bear you my solemn witness that I know that God is directing this work today and revealing his mind and will. The light is shining through, and if we can get the priesthood now to come alive and to put into full gear the full strength of the priesthood, we shall see some of the most wonderful developments and some of the greatest things happen to the forces which the Lord can set in motion that we have ever known in this dispensation. [Harold B. Lee, in Conference Report, Oct. 1962, pp. 82–83; or *Improvement Era,* Dec. 1962, p. 941]

My mind has been filled with the realization that in 1964 and the year

The resurrected Savior appears to Mary Magdalene

just preceding, we have been receiving as pertinent and important divine direction as has ever been given to the Church in any similar period in its history through the prophet and leader who now presides as the President of this Church. You may recognize it in some of the developments we know as the correlation program. You have seen it being unraveled bit by bit, and you will see and hear more of it. [Harold B. Lee, in Conference Report, Oct. 1964, p. 137; or *Improvement Era,* Dec. 1964, p. 1104]

Again and again has been repeated the statement that the home is the basis of a righteous life. With new and badly needed emphasis on the "how," we must not lose sight of the "why" we are so engaged. The priesthood programs operate in support of the home; the auxiliary programs render valuable assistance. Wise regional leadership can help us to do our share in attaining God's overarching purpose, "to bring to pass the immortality and eternal life of man." (Moses 1:39.) Both the revelations of God and the learning of men tell us how crucial the home is in shaping the individual's total life experience. You must have been impressed that running through all that has been said in this conference has been the urgency of impressing the importance of better teaching and greater parental responsibility in the home. Much of what we do organizationally, then, is scaffolding, as we seek to build the individual, and we must not mistake the scaffolding for the soul. [Harold B. Lee, in Conference Report, Oct. 1967, p. 107; or *Improvement Era,* Jan. 1968, p. 31]

Counselor and President

At the death of President David O. McKay, Joseph Fielding Smith became the President of the Church and selected Elder Harold B. Lee to be his First Counselor. On two occasions President Smith paid high tribute to President Lee: "President Harold B. Lee is a pillar of truth and righteousness, *a true seer* who has great spiritual strength and insight and wisdom, and *whose knowledge and understanding of the Church and its needs is not surpassed by any man*" (in

Conference Report, Apr. 1970, p. 114; or *Improvement Era,* June 1970, p. 27; italics added). "President Harold B. Lee is a spiritual giant with faith like that of Enoch. He has the spirit of revelation and magnifies his calling as a prophet, seer, and revelator" (in Conference Report, Oct. 1971, p. 178; or *Ensign,* Dec. 1971, p. 136).

On 7 July 1972, upon the death of President Joseph Fielding Smith, Harold B. Lee was ordained and set apart as the eleventh President of the Church. He led the Saints for only a short one-and-one-half years, but his impact upon the Church will long be remembered because of his thirty-six years of leadership in the welfare, correlation, and other programs of the Church. One program inaugurated during his administration focused on the single adults of the Church. President Lee showed great concern for the single adult Latter-day Saints, and under his direction a new program especially designed for them, the special interest program, was announced in November 1972 as part of the Melchizedek Priesthood MIA.

> We have found that we have been neglecting some of our adult members—those over eighteen who

have not yet found their companions, or who are perhaps widowed or divorced. They have been saying to us, "But you have no program for us." Instead of our saying, "Sorry, we can't do anything for you except through our existing MIA or Relief Society programs," we have said to them, "We want to find out what you need. It is still the same gospel, but we are endeavoring to reach those for whom we have had no adequate programs. Man wasn't made for the Church, to paraphrase what the Master said, but the Church was made for man"

And so we have become flexible in adapting our methods in order to take care of the needs of our people, wherever they are. But we have built on a foundation laid down by the prophets, and we have not deviated from the principles and teachings of the gospel of Jesus Christ. [Harold B. Lee, *Ye Are the Light,* p. 349]

Now brethren of the priesthood, if you knew the processes by which these new programs came into being, you would know that this just didn't come out of a brainstorm, the figment of somebody's imagination; this was done after some of the

The First Presidency, 1972–73, left to right: N. Eldon Tanner, Harold B. Lee, and Marion G. Romney

most soulful praying and discussing that I believe I have ever experienced. We know, and we have announced when it was given that this came from the Lord. This was an evidence of a thing that the Lord was giving us to do to meet a special need. But it troubles me when I read some of these things where sisters are pleading with us to try to do something to stimulate the activities where the bishops or stake presidents have not caught on to what it is all about.

In the early days of the Welfare Program, everywhere I went people were saying to me, "Brother Lee, how is the Welfare Program going?" And I would answer, "Just as well as the individual bishop of each ward makes it go. In some wards it is an absolute failure. In other wards it is going great guns." And that is exactly what is happening with what we are now launching.

In some places we see the enthusiasm; if you were to start these activities now, you would catch the enthusiasm of the young people and these young widows, divorcees, those who haven't found companions. If we can catch them while their enthusiasm and anticipation are great, great things will come out of it; and we must ask you

brethren now to remember that these things come from a source from which you brethren want to receive instruction. Please, I beg of you, don't let these people down, who are pleading that you listen to your leaders, and follow the counsel that has been given in these Special Interest activities. [Harold B. Lee, in Conference Report, Oct. 1973, p. 117; or *Ensign,* Jan. 1974, p. 99]

The Home and the Family

Like the prophets before him, President Lee knew the importance of the home to the Church and to society. As he saw threats being made upon the home, he issued clarion messages to the world.

I find some of our brethren who are engaged in leadership positions justifying their neglect of their families because they say that they are engaged in the Lord's work. I say to them, "My dear brother, do you realize that the most important part of the Lord's work that you will do is the work that you do within the walls of your own home? That is the most important work of the Lord. Don't get your sense of values mixed up." [Harold B. Lee, *Ye Are the Light,* p. 33]

Don't give up on the boy or girl in that insufferable state of super-ego-

ism through which some teenagers go. I plead with you for those boys and those girls. Don't give up on the boy or girl in that impossible stage of independence and disregard of family discipline. Don't give up on him or her when they show a shocking display of irresponsibility. The know-it-all, self-sufficient person wants nothing of counsel, which to him is just a preachment of an old-timer who has lost step with youth. Knowing is not enough—we must apply. Willingness is not enough—we must do.

A harassed mother was called by a friend who asked her, "What do you think of all the riots going on in all the cities in the country?" And this mother answered, "I'm so busy putting down all the little riots in my own home that I don't have time to worry about riots elsewhere."

We had a missionary grandson in the North British Mission. He hadn't been there very long until he wrote back an interesting letter in which he said the advice of his parents

now comes back to him with great force. It is like a book on a shelf that has been there for nineteen years and he has just begun to take it down and start to read it for the first time. That is your son and your daughter. You may think they are not listening. They may think they are not listening, but one time yours may be the book that they will take down and read again when they need it most. (Harold B. Lee, *Ye Are the Light,* pp. 275–76).

We must call ourselves to new service and new responsibilities, and not stand idly by and let these things go without challenge. Our youth are in danger. Keep your home ties strong, brethren. See to it, as we have all tried to say, and as I have repeated it many times and some have quoted it in this conference, that "the greatest of the Lord's work you brethren will ever do as fathers will be within the walls of your own home." Don't neglect your wives, you brethren. Don't neglect your children. Take time for family home evening. Draw your children around about you. Teach them, guide them, and guard them. There was never a time when we needed so much the strength and the solidarity of the home. If we will do that, this church will grow by leaps and bounds in strength and influence throughout the world. No longer need you be considered as a hiss and byword.

We should stand four-square for the things that are honorable, righteous, pure, virtuous, and true. [Harold B. Lee, in Conference Report, Apr. 1973, p. 130; or *Ensign,* July 1973, pp. 98–99]

Sometimes, as we travel throughout the Church, a husband and wife will come to us and ask if, because they are not compatible in their marriage—they having had a temple marriage—it wouldn't be better if they were to free themselves from each other and then seek more congenial partners. To all such we say, whenever a couple who have been married in the temple say they are tiring of each other, it is an evidence that either one or both are not true to their temple covenants. Any couple married in the temple who are true to their covenants will grow dearer to each other, and love will find a deeper meaning on their golden wedding anniversary than on the day they were married in the house of the Lord. Don't you mistake that. [Harold B. Lee, *Ye Are the Light,* p. 313]

In his teachings concerning family responsibilities President Lee also included counsel to the unmarried man and woman.

Now, there is another matter that I would like to talk about. There are some examples that point up an area of need which applies directly to young men in the past-25-age, who for some reason, and hard to understand, as holders of the priesthood, are shirking their responsibilities as husbands and fathers.... President Joseph F. Smith said... this, which strikes right at the heart of what I want to emphasize: "I desire to emphasize this. I want the young men of Zion to realize that this institution of marriage is not a man-made institution. It is of God. It is honorable, and no man who is of marriageable age is living his religion who remains single. It is not simply devised for the convenience alone of man, to suit his own notions, and his own ideas; to marry and then divorce, to adopt and then to discard, just as he pleases.... Marriage is the preserver of the human race. Without it, the purposes of God would be frustrated; virtue would be destroyed to give place to vice and corruption, and the earth would be void and empty." [In Conference Report, Oct. 1973, p. 117; or *Ensign,* Jan. 1974, p. 99]

You young women advancing in years who have not yet accepted a proposal of marriage, if you make yourselves worthy and ready to go to the house of the Lord and have faith in this sacred principle of celestial marriage for eternity, even though the privilege of marriage does not come to you now in mortality, the Lord will reward you in due time and no blessing will be denied you. You are not under obligation to accept a proposal from someone unworthy of you for fear you will fail of your blessings. Likewise, you young men who may lose your life in early life by accident, or a fatal illness, or in the terrible conflict of war before you have had an opportunity for marriage, the Lord knows the intent of your hearts, and in His own due time He will reward you with opportunities made possible through temple ordinances instituted in the Church for that purpose.

Do all you can to comply with the laws of God pertaining to an exaltation in the kingdom of God. The Lord will judge you too by your works, as well as by the desires of your hearts, and your reward will be assured. [Harold B. Lee, *Ye Are the Light,* pp. 308–9]

Like all prophets before him, President Lee's life was dramatic proof of the power of his testimony of Jesus Christ. "I know that this is the Lord's work, I know that Jesus Christ lives, and that he's closer to this Church and appears more often in holy places than any of us realize excepting sometimes to those to whom he makes personal appearance. I know it and the time is hastening when he shall come again to reign as Lord of Lords and King of Kings" (quoted in *Living Prophets for a Living Church,* p. 119).

STUDY QUESTIONS

1. How had Harold B. Lee been prepared to lead the Church?

2. Harold B. Lee became a "polished shaft in the quiver of the Almighty" by the things he suffered. What implications does that have for every faithful Latter-day Saint?

3. What major programs of the Church came about largely because of President Lee's inspired work both prior to and during his presidency?

4. What do President Lee's insights about the purposes of the welfare program show about following the counsel of the Brethren?

5. What does President Lee's revelation about the Savior while reading the four gospels teach about the importance of scripture study?

6. What do you think President Lee meant when he stated that the correlation program is scaffolding to build the individual?

7. What responsibility did President Harold B. Lee say we have for our single adults?

8. What, according to President Lee, is the major responsibility of family members to each other? What promise did President Lee make to couples who are married in the temple and keep their covenants?

THE EXPANDING WORLDWIDE CHURCH

AS the world reached the mid-twentieth century, many nations struggled to recover from the devastation of World War II. Out of the ashes of that bitter conflict arose much good, however. Many thousands, humbled by their war experience, were better prepared to listen to the Savior's message of peace, hope, and salvation. Many nations previously closed to the Church admitted the missionaries to preach the gospel. Thousands of Latter-day Saint servicemen at the end of the war became messengers of peace as they spread the gospel throughout the world. The worldwide growth that followed was aided in large measure by the era of good will fostered by President George Albert Smith and ably continued upon his death by President David O. Mckay.

HIGHLIGHTS

1947 The membership reaches one million.

Missions open in Uruguay and Finland.

1948 The Japan Mission reopens.

1949 The China Mission opens in Hong Kong.

1950 The Czechoslovak and Near East Missions close.

1955 Sept. 11: The first European temple is dedicated at Berne, Switzerland.

1959 Nov. 1: The Andes Mission is formed in western South America.

1964 Aug. 22: 400th Stake—in Medford, Oregon.

Seventy-five missions are in operation worldwide.

1965 12,585 missionaries are serving.

The Translation Department is organized to more rapidly prepare manuals in major world languages.

1966 May 1: The first stake in South America is organized, in Sao Paulo, Brazil.

Aug. 2: The Italian Mission is reorganized.

Nov. 20: The first stake in Argentina is organized.

1967 Church membership surpasses 2,500,000 (2,614,340).

13,417 missionaries are serving.

Mar.: The unified Church magazine begins publication in nine languages: Danish, Dutch, Finnish, French, German, Norwegian, Portuguese, Spanish, Swedish.

May 21: The first stake in Guatemala is organized.

Nov. 12: The first stake in Uruguay is organized.

1968 Jan. 1: The first Regional Representatives are called to aid the

Twelve in their responsibilities around the world.

Feb. 11: 450th stake—San Jose, California.

Sept. 5: The first stake in Tonga is organized.

1969 June: The first missionaries enter Spain.

June 15: The first stake in American Samoa is organized.

Nov. 1: The Southeast Asian Mission opens (Singapore).

Eighty-six missions are in operation throughout the world.

1970 Jan. 18: 500th stake—in Fallon, Nevada.

Feb. 22: The first stake in Peru is organized.

Mar. 15: The first stake in Asia (Tokyo, Japan) is organized.

Mar. 22: The first stake in Africa is organized.

1971 July: The medical missionary program commences.

Aug. 27–29: The first area general conference (Manchester, England) is held.

Sept. 6: 550th stake—Nuku Alofa East, Tonga.

Church membership exceeds 3,000,000 (3,090,953).

15,205 missionaries are serving.

1972 May 14: The first stake in Tahiti is organized.

Aug. 25–27: The second area general conference (Mexico City, Mexico) is held.

101 missions operate worldwide.

1973 Feb.: The first Church agricultural missionaries go to the Guatemala-El Salvador Mission.

Feb. 11: 600th stake—Southampton, England.

Mar. 8: The first stake on the Asian mainland and third in the Orient is organized—Seoul, Korea.

May 20: The first stake in the Philippine Islands is organized.

June 3: The first stake in El Salvador is organized.

July 1: The Thailand Mission is organized.

Aug. 24–26: The third area general conference (Munich, Germany) is held.

1974 June 16: The Copenhagen Stake, the first in Scandinavia, is organized.

1975 Six General Authorities are assigned to serve as Area Supervisors and to reside in their areas away from Church headquarters.

July 1: Twenty new full-time missions formed, including missions in Utah and Indonesia.

Oct. 3: Elder Charles Didier is the first General Authority called from a non-English-speaking area outside of North America.

Nov. 8–9: Ten new stakes are organized in the Mexico City area.

Nov. 16: The Paris stake, first in France, is organized.

1976 Apr.: The first Chinese stakes are organized in Taipei and Hong Kong.

Oct. 2: Assistants to the Twelve become members of the First Quorum of the Seventy to help administer the worldwide Church.

1977 The Jerusalem branch is placed under local leadership.

The world is divided into eleven zones for strengthened supervision; Presiding Bishopric area supervisors are called.

Jan. 29: 800th stake formed by division of the Vera Cruz, Mexico Stake which had been the 700th stake organized only one year and a half before.

Aug. 9: The Fargo Stake is organized in North Dakota; there is now a stake in every state in the United States.

1978 Membership passes four million.

Feb.: The construction of the Jordan River Temple, the second temple in the Salt Lake Valley and the seventh in Utah, is announced.

June 8: The First Presidency announces priesthood blessings are extended to all worthy male members.

Oct. 30-Nov. 2: The Sao Paulo Temple, first in South America, is dedicated.

HISTORICAL SUMMARY

Phenomenal Growth

The growth in Church membership worldwide has accelerated at an amazing rate. Although proselyting had begun outside the United States in 1833, most Church growth occurred in North America until the administration of President McKay. Then with the passage of little more than a decade, the Church membership expanded dramatically, throughout nearly eighty nations. In 1967, Elder Harold B. Lee discussed projected Church growth.

If one were to paint a picture in broad strokes of just a few features of the future, here are some things that will challenge the Church in the years that lie ahead:

When I came into the Council of the Twelve we had 35 missions. I helped to organize, along with President Joseph Fielding Smith, the 138th stake. We now have 443 stakes.

During the 70 years from 1830 to 1900, the Church grew by 258,000 members. Today, a quarter of a million expansion in membership takes not 70 years, but in only two or three years, we expand by a quarter of a million.

Our Church membership is increasing at about three times the growth rate of the population of the United States. But, just as significantly, the regional distribution of Church membership is also following some clear trends that we must recognize, not only intellectually, but also administratively.

In 1910, Utah and Idaho contained approximately 75 percent of all Church membership. Today, only 40 percent of the Church's members live in these two states. Utah once held two-thirds of all members. Today, even though the number of members in Utah has now risen from 224,000 in 1910 to 714,000, only one-third of all members now live in Utah. Brazil now has 23,000 Latter-day Saints; Australia, 21,000; and Mexico 50,000.

During the last ten years, membership in the southern states has

Church Growth and Distribution, 1920–77

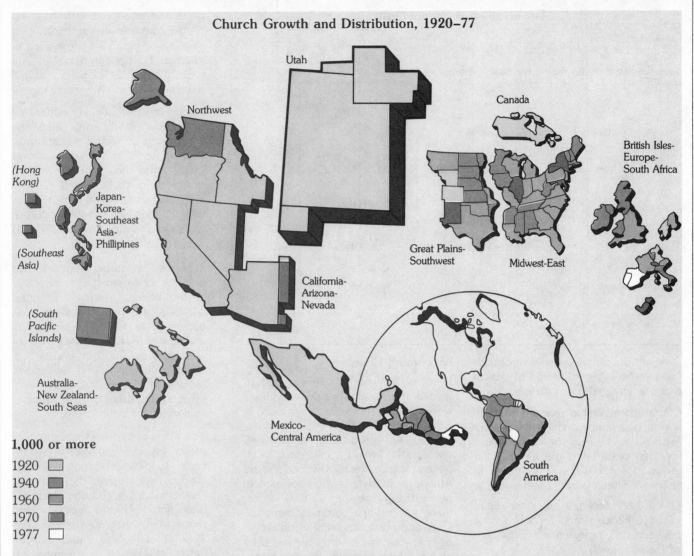

Utah

Northwest

Canada

British Isles-
Europe-
South Africa

(Hong
Kong)

Japan-
Korea-
Southeast
Asia-
Phillipines

(Southeast
Asia)

Great Plains-
Southwest

Midwest-East

(South
Pacific
Islands)

California-
Arizona-
Nevada

Australia-
New Zealand-
South Seas

Mexico-
Central America

South
America

1,000 or more

1920
1940
1960
1970
1977

The relative size of each geographical unit shows the proportion of Church membership residing in that area at the close of 1977.

risen from 72,000 to 170,000; in South America from 6,000 to 67,000; and in Asia from 1,500 to 21,000.

We have no choice but to think regionally.

Research has been done by the department of statistics at the Brigham Young University by Dr. Howard Nielsen, and he estimates the Church membership by 1985, just 17 years from now, will total from 5,700,000 to 7,700,000, depending on the rate of conversions.

By the year 2000 A.D., which means that our children now eight years of age will then be 41-years-old, we could have a total membership of over ten million people. Though this may sound very distant to some of us, it is the year, I repeat, when

these eight-year-olds will become 41, if you get that clearly.

In 1985 there will be more than one million members in Utah, but they will represent only 21 percent of all Church membership. California will have almost a million members by then, and the southern states one-half million. Canada will host 160,000 members, with more than 200,000 in the British Isles, and over one-quarter million in Central and South America.

Today, there are approximately 443 stakes and nearly 4,000 wards and branches. By 1985, depending on our effectiveness and external events, we should have 1,000 stakes and nearly 10,000 wards.

In the calendar year 1985, about 200 new stake presidents will be ap-

pointed to new or existing stakes, and General Authorities will need to direct five stake reorganizations each week. The brethren will then need to clear between 50 and 60 names for the office of bishop each week.

Well, you begin to see something about the growth, and so we could go on with auxiliary organizations.

Now just a word about the missions: It is estimated that in the missions within that 17-year period, in contrast to 77 or 78 missions we have today, we could have as many as 185 missions by then, with probably as many as 30,000 missionaries instead of our 13,000 as of today. [In Conference Report, Oct. 1967, pp. 103–4; or *Improvement Era,* Jan. 1968, p. 29]

The Kingdom Is Rolling Forth

Years	1850	1875	1900	1925	1950	1979
President of the Church	Brigham Young	Brigham Young	Lorenzo Snow	Heber J. Grant	George Albert Smith	Spencer W. Kimball
Number of General Authorities	24	27	26	26	30	68
Total membership	60,000	135,000	268,331	613,653	1,111,314	4,160,000
Stakes	1	10	43	94	180	990
Missions	9	6	18	27	44	166
Temples in service	0	0	4	6	8	16
Missionaries serving	100	400	1,500	1,922	5,156	27,669

Judged from the perspective of Church history, the 1964–78 period of growth was phenomenal. For example:

Church membership reached two million in one hundred thirty-three years (1830–1964). But by 1978, just fourteen years later, the Church had grown to 3,966,019, a 77.5 percent increase in fifteen years.

Of the 1,848,568 new members added in those fifteen years, 1,172,863 were new converts, representing 63 percent of the increase.

In the first one hundred thirty-three years, 389 stakes were organized. Over the next fifteen years, 496 new stakes were added—a growth of 127.5 percent for that brief period.

By 1964, 26 stakes were found in locations outside of the United States and its territories. By 1978, 201 additional stakes were added in international areas—a growth rate of 673.1 percent.

In 1964, 77 missions functioned throughout the world. They grew in number to 157 by 1978, a gain of 104 percent.

More than half of all missionaries set apart since 1830 served between 1964–78.

Church school enrollment (including Seminaries and Institutes) grew from 143,622 in 1964 to 362,000 in 1978, an increase of 152.1 percent.

A Looming Crisis

Even as the growth of the kingdom gained momentum, world conditions worsened. Major military conflicts in Asia, Africa, and the Middle East destroyed the productive lands, freedoms, and lives of millions. Social upheavals spread across Europe and the Americas. In their search for peace, personal fulfillment, and social justice, many ignored the commandments of God, and pornography, abortion, sexual permissiveness, drug abuse, child abuse, and a host of other problems grew each year.

For those who sought to resolve such complex and divisive problems, the prophets clarified the issues and offered remarkably simple, yet highly effective solutions. They proclaimed that only by pursuing personal righteousness, unselfishness, and obedience to the Lord's will could mankind find true happiness and stability.

Elder Spencer W. Kimball plainly testified:

Jesus Christ our Lord is under no obligation to save us, except insofar as we repent. We have ignored him, disbelieved him, and failed to follow him. We have changed the laws and broken the everlasting covenant. We stand at his mercy, which will be extended only if we repent. But to what extent have we repented? Another prophet said, "We call evil good and good evil." We have rationalized ourselves into thinking we are "not so bad." We see evil in our enemies, but none in ourselves. Are we fully ripe? Has the rot of age and flabbiness set in? Will we change?

Apparently we would rather do things the devil's way than the Lord's way. It seems, for instance, that we would rather tax ourselves into slavery than pay our tithing; rather build shelters and missiles and bombs than drop to our knees with our families in solemn prayer, night and morning, to our God who would give us protection.

It seems that, rather than fast and pray, we prefer to gorge ourselves at the banquet tables and drink cocktails. Instead of disciplining ourselves, we yield to physical urges and carnal desires. Instead of investing in building our bodies and beautifying our souls, we spend billions of dollars on liquor and tobacco, and other body-destroying, soul-stultifying concoctions.

Too many of our wives and mothers prefer the added luxuries of two incomes to the satisfactions of seeing children grow up in the fear and love of God. We golf and boat and hunt and fish and watch sports rather than solemnize the Sabbath. Total morality is found neither among the people nor among the leaders of the state and nation. Personal interests and ulterior motives block the way. Old Man "Rationalization" with his long beard is ever present to tell us that we are justified in these deviations, and because we are not vicious enough to be confined in penitentiaries we rationalize that we are not failing to measure up. The masses of the people are perhaps much like those who escaped destruction in the ancient days of this continent. The Lord said to them:

"O all ye that are spared because ye were more righteous than they [the slain ones], will ye not now return unto me, and repent of your sins, and be converted, that I may heal you? (3 Ne. 9:13.)"

"Experience keeps a dear school," said Benjamin Franklin, "but fools will learn in no other." Thus, as a nation we continue in our godlessness. While the iron curtains fall and thicken we eat, drink, and make merry. While armies are marshalled and march and drill and officers teach men how to kill, we continue to drink and carouse as usual. While bombs are detonated and tested, and fallout settles on the already sick world, we continue in idolatry and adultery.

While corridors are threatened and concessions are made, we live riotously, and divorce and marry in cycles, like the seasons. While leaders quarrel and editors write and authorities analyze and prognosticate, we break all the laws in God's catalog. While enemies filter into our nation to subvert and intimidate and soften us, we continue on with our destructive thinking—"It can't happen here."

If we would but believe the prophets! For they have warned that if the inhabitants of this land are ever brought down into captivity and enslaved, "*it shall be because of iniquity; for if iniquity shall abound cursed shall be the land . . .*" (2 Ne. 1:7.) This is a land which the Lord has preserved ". . . *for a righteous people . . .*" (Eth. 2:7. Italics added.)

"And now, we can behold the decrees of God concerning this land, that it is a land of promise; and whatsoever nation shall possess it shall serve God, or they shall be swept off when the fulness of his wrath shall come upon them. And the fulness of his wrath shall come

President Spencer W. Kimball, 1895–

upon them when they are ripened in iniquity. (Eth. 2:9.)"

O that men would listen! Why should there be spiritual blindness in the day of brightest scientific and technological vision? Why must men rely on physical fortifications and armaments when the God of heaven yearns to bless them? One stroke of his omnipotent hand could make powerless all nations who oppose, and save a world even when in its death throes. Yet men shun God and put their trust in weapons of war, in the "arm of flesh."

All this continues despite the lessons of history. The great wall of China, with its 1,500 miles of impenetrable walls, its 25-foot-high impregnableness, its innumerable watchtowers, was breached by the treachery of man. The Maginot Line in France, those forts thought to be so strong and impassable, were bypassed as though they were not there.

The walls of Babylon were too high to be scaled, too thick to be broken, too strong to be crumbled, but not too deep to be undermined when the human element failed. When the protectors sleep and the leaders are incapacitated with banqueting and drunkenness and immorality, an invading enemy can turn a river out of its course and enter through a river bed.

The precipitous walls on the high hills of Jerusalem deflected for a time the arrows and spears of enemies, the catapults and fire-

brands of besieging armies. But even then the wickedness did not lessen; men did not learn lessons. Hunger scaled the walls; thirst broke down the gates; immorality, idolatry, godlessness, even cannibalism stalked about till destruction came.

Will we ever turn wholly to God? Fear envelops the world which could be at ease and peace. In God is protection, peace, safety. He has said, "*I will fight your battles.*" But his commitment is on condition of our faithfulness. He promised to the children of Israel:

"I will give you rain in due season.

"The land shall yield her increase and trees their fruit.

"Granaries and barns will bulge in seed-time and harvest.

"Ye shall eat your bread in abundance.

"Ye shall dwell in your land safely and none shall make you afraid.

"Neither shall the sword go through your land.

"And five of you shall chase an hundred and an hundred of you shall put ten thousand to flight."

In view of the promises God has given respecting America, who can doubt that he would be willing to do the same for us as for ancient Israel? Conversely, should we not expect the same punishments if we fail to serve him? To ancient Israel these were listed.

"The land will be barren (perhaps radioactive or dry from drought).

"The trees will be without fruit and the fields without verdure.

"There will be rationing and scarcity of food, and sore hunger.

"No traffic will jam your desolate highways.

"Famine will stalk rudely through your doors and the ogre of cannibalism will rob you of your children and your remaining virtues will disintegrate.

"There will be pestilence uncontrollable.

"Your dead bodies will be piled upon the materialistic things you sought so hard to accumulate and save.

"I will give no protection against enemies.

"They that hate you shall reign over you.

"There will be faintness of heart, 'and the sound of a shaken leaf' shall chase you into flight, and you will flee when none pursue.

"Your power—your supremacy—your pride in superiority—will be broken.

"Your heaven shall be as iron and your earth as brass. Heaven will not hear your pleadings nor earth bring forth its harvest.

"Your strength will be spent in vain as you plow and plant and cultivate.

"Your cities will be shambles; your churches in ruins.

"Your enemies will be astonished at the barrenness, sterility, desolation of the land they had been told was so choice, so beautiful, so fruitful. Then shall the land enjoy her Sabbaths under compulsion.

"You shall have no power to stand before your enemies.

"Your people will be scattered among the nations as slaves and bondsmen.

"You will pay tribute and bondage, and fetters shall bind you."

What a bleak prediction! Yet "these are the statutes and judgments and laws, which the Lord made between him and the children of Israel in Mount Sinai by the hand of Moses." (Lev. 26:46.) The Israelites failed to heed the warning. They ignored the prophets. They suffered the fulfillment of every dire prophecy.

Do we twentieth-century people have reason to think that we can be immune from the same tragic consequences of sin and debauchery if we ignore the same divine laws?

The outlook is bleak, but the impending tragedy can be averted. Nations, like individuals, must "repent or suffer." There is only one cure for the earth's sick condition. That infallible cure is simply *righteousness, obedience, godliness, honor, integrity*. Nothing else will suffice. [*The Miracle of Forgiveness*, pp. 316–21]

A Time of Gathering

In such troubled times as those in which we live, many Saints wonder if they should flee their homes and gather to Utah for protection. President Harold B. Lee answered that question in the following remarks:

Today we are witnessing the demonstration of the Lord's hand even in the midst of his saints, the members of the Church. Never in this dispensation, and perhaps never before in any single period, has there been such a feeling of urgency among the members of this church as today. Her boundaries are being enlarged, her stakes are being strengthened. In the early years of the Church specific places to which the Saints were to be gathered together were given, and the Lord directed that these gathering places should not be changed, but then he gave one qualification: "Until the day cometh when there is found no more room for them: and then I have other places which I will appoint unto them, and they shall be called stakes, for the curtains or the strength of Zion." (D&C 101:21.)

At the Mexico City Area Conference last August [1972], Elder Bruce R. McConkie of the Council of the Twelve, in a thought-provoking address, made some comments pertinent to this subject, and I quote a few sentences from his address:

"Of this glorious day of restoration and gathering, another Nephite prophet said: 'The Lord . . . has covenanted with all the house of Israel,' that 'the time comes that they shall be restored to the true church and fold of God'; and that 'they shall be gathered home to the lands of their inheritance, and shall be established in all their lands of promise.' (2 Ne. 9:1–2.)

"Now I call your attention to the facts, set forth in these scriptures, that the gathering of Israel consists of joining the true church; of coming to a knowledge of the true God and of his saving truths; and of worshiping him in the congregations of the Saints in all nations and among all peoples. Please note that these revealed words speak of the *folds* of the Lord; of Israel being gathered to the lands of their inheritance; of Israel being *established in all their lands of promise;* and of there being congregations of the convenant people of the Lord in *every nation, speaking every tongue,* and *among every people* when the Lord comes again."

Elder McConkie then concluded with this statement, which certainly emphasizes the great need for the teaching and training of local leadership in order to build up the church within their own native countries:

"The place of gathering for the Mexican Saints is in Mexico; the place of gathering for the Guatemalan Saints is in Guatemala; the place of gathering for the Brazilian Saints is in Brazil; and so it goes throughout the length and breadth of the whole earth. Japan is for the Japanese; Korea is for the Koreans; Australia is for the Australians; every nation is the gathering place for its own people." [In Conference Report, Apr. 1973, p. 6; or *Ensign,* July 1973, pp. 4–5]

STUDY QUESTIONS

1. How does the statistical information concerning Church growth support Daniel's interpretation of Nebuchadnezzar's dream? (Daniel 2:44)

2. What challenges do the Saints as a group face as the Church becomes a worldwide, rapidly expanding kingdom?

3. What challenges does this expansion present for each individual member? Is the challenge for Saints in Utah different from the challenge for Saints in international areas? How and why are these challenges different?

4. Since time began man has tried to solve the ills of the world and failed. Why has he failed? What is the only sure solution?

5. Why do the General Authorities counsel the Saints to remain in their native homelands and build up the Church there?

SPENCER W. KIMBALL

DURING Spencer W. Kimball's thirty-year ministry as a member of the Quorum of the Twelve Apostles, he was actively involved in the tremendous expansion of the kingdom among the nations of the earth. When he became President of the Church in 1973, he could look back to service with five Presidents of the Church. Drawing upon that extensive experience and upon the hidden resources developed in the many trials he has undergone, President Kimball, ever listening to the promptings of the Spirit, has charted a vigorous and demanding course for the Saints. In the brief period he has led the Church, he has directed a dramatic expansion in missionary work worldwide, expanded the First Quorum of the Seventy with the calls of noble men from several nations, announced an unprecedented number of temples for construction, extended the opportunity of priesthood service to all worthy male members of the Church, and given the Latter-day Saints inspired counsel and direction.

HIGHLIGHTS

1895 Mar. 28: Born in Salt Lake City, Utah.

1898 May: The Kimball family moves to Thatcher, Arizona (3).

1906 June 6: Receives patriarchal blessing from Samuel Claridge promising him a great work among the Lamanites.

Oct. 18: His mother, Olive Kimball, dies (11).

1914 Graduates with highest honors from Gila Academy.

June 6: Ordained a priest by his father, Andrew Kimball.

Sept. 15: Ordained an elder.

Oct. 16: Ordained a seventy by his uncle, President J. Golden Kimball of the First Council of the Seventy.

Oct. 16: Called to the Swiss-Austrian Mission, but due to World War I was sent to the Central States Mission (19).

1917 Nov. 16: Marries Camilla Eyring.

1918 Jan. 1: Named stake clerk of the St. Joseph Stake.

Enters banking business (22).

1924 Sept. 8: Called as second counselor in the stake presidency.

Ordained a high priest by President Heber J. Grant (29).

1934 Released as counselor and sustained again as clerk of the St. Joseph Stake (39).

1938 Called as president of the Mount Graham Stake (42).

1943 July 8: President J. Reuben Clark, Jr., telephones to inform him of his call to the apostleship.

Oct. 7: Sustained by the Church as a member of the Quorum of the Twelve (48).

1946 Sept. 13: President George Albert Smith names him chairman of the Church Indian Committee (51).

1951 Loses his voice through a serious throat ailment. His voice is restored following a blessing (56).

1957 Undergoes an operation for cancer of the throat; one and one-half vocal cords are removed (62).

1969 Publishes *The Miracle of Forgiveness* (74).

1972 Undergoes an operation for a heart ailment; doctors implant an artificial aortic valve and graft a coronary artery; publishes *Faith Precedes the Miracle* (77).

1973 Dec. 30: Ordained and set apart as the President of the Church (78).

1974 Apr. 4: Gives a major address to Regional Representatives of the Twelve on expanding missionary work (79).

Nov. 19: Dedicates the Washington D.C. Temple (79).

1975 May 3: General Authority Area Supervisors are assigned outside the United States and Canada (80).

July 24: Dedicates the new Church Office Building (80).

Announces temple construction in Brazil, Japan, Mexico, and Washington state; rededicates the renovated Arizona and St. George temples (80).

1976 Apr. 3: In general conference, the Saints accept Joseph Smith's vision of the celestial kingdom and Joseph F. Smith's vision of the redemption of the dead as part of the standard works of the Church.

Young Spencer

Oct. 2: Assistants to the Twelve become members of the First Quorum of the Seventy (81).

1977 Feb.–Mar.: Conducts area conferences in Mexico, Guatemala, Costa Rica, Peru, Chile, Bolivia, and Columbia (81).

Aug. 24: Dedicates the land of Poland (82).

Dec.: Announces the construction of the second temple in the Salt Lake Valley, the Jordan River Temple (82).

1978 Jun. 8: Announces priesthood blessings are extended to all worthy male members (83).

Sept. 30: In general conference, the Saints accept the revelation on priesthood as the word and will of the Lord. (83).

HISTORICAL SUMMARY

Early Life

The name Spencer Woolley Kimball represents two stalwart families. Spencer's paternal grandfather was Heber C. Kimball, a close associate and counselor to President Brigham Young. His father was a beloved and widely respected stake president. The forebears of his mother, Olive Woolley, were also among the faithful Saints who helped to pioneer the West. These two families passed on to him a rich family heritage.

Heber C. Kimball

Spencer on his father's lap

Spencer W. Kimball was born in Salt Lake City, Utah, but spent his formative years in the Gila Valley of southeastern Arizona. His life was full of character-building experiences.

"[The Lord] was not just preparing a businessman, nor a civic leader, nor a speaker, nor a poet, nor a musician, nor a teacher—though he would be all of these. He was preparing a father, a patriarch for his family, an apostle and prophet, and a president for His church.

"There were testings along the way. Examinations in courage and patience, that few would have passed" (Boyd K. Packer, "President Spencer W. Kimball: No Ordinary Man," *Ensign*, Mar. 1974, p. 3). These trials included a facial paralysis, relieved only by a priesthood blessing; drowning and being revived again; and the death of his mother when he was only eleven years old.

As a young man, Spencer became a community leader as he entered the banking business, real estate, and related enterprises. Church responsibilities also came to him early. These he accepted willingly, and through them enriched the lives of many.

Service in the Quorum of the Twelve

Although he had had excellent preparation, Spencer W. Kimball felt unpre-

pared for the call to the apostleship when it came on 8 July 1943. In his first general conference address, 7 October 1943, he described the eighty-five days and nights of soul-searching self-appraisal through which he passed.

I feel extremely humble in this calling that has come to me. Many people have asked me if I was surprised when it came. That, of course, is a very weak word for this experience. I was completely bewildered and shocked. I did have a premonition that this call was coming, but very brief, however. On the eighth of July, when President Clark called me I was electrified with a strong presentiment that something of this kind was going to happen. As I came home at noon, my boy was answering the telephone and he said, "Daddy, Salt Lake City is calling."

I had had many calls from Salt Lake City. They hadn't ever worried me like this one. I knew that I had no unfinished business in Salt Lake City, and the thought came over me quickly, "You're going to be called to an important position." Then I hurriedly swept it from my mind, because it seemed so unworthy and so presumptuous, and I had convinced myself that such a thing was impossible by the time that I heard President Clark's voice a thousand miles away saying: "Spencer, this is Brother Clark speaking. The brethren have just called you to fill one of the vacancies in the Quorum of the Twelve Apostles."

Like a bolt of lightning it came. I did a great deal of thinking in the brief moments that I was on the wire. There were quite a number of things said about disposing of my business, moving to headquarters, and other things to be expected of me. I couldn't repeat them all, my mind seemed to be traveling many paths all at once—I was dazed, almost numb with the shock; a picture of my life spread out before me. It seemed that I could see all of the people before me whom I had injured, or who had fancied that I had injured them, or to whom I had given offense, and all the small petty things of my life. I sensed immediately my inability and limitations and I cried back, "Not me, Brother Clark! You can't mean that!" I was virtually speechless. My heart pounded fiercely. . . .

I remember reading that Jacob wrestled all night, "until the breaking of the day," for a blessing; and I want to tell you that for eighty-five nights I have gone through that experience, wrestling for a blessing. Eighty-five times, the breaking of the day has found me on my knees praying to the Lord to help me and strengthen me and make me equal to this great responsibility that has come to me. I have not sought positions nor have I been ambitious. Promotions have continued to come faster than I felt I was prepared for them. [In Conference Report, Oct. 1943, pp. 15–16]

Work with the Lamanites

In 1946 Elder Kimball was assigned to head the Church's Lamanite work, a calling that he felt was a fulfillment of a prophetic patriarchal blessing given at the age of nine. As he explained in the April 1947 general conference:

I do not know when I began to love the children of Lehi. It may have come to me at birth, because those years preceding and after I was born, were spent by my father on missions among the Indians in Indian territory. . . . It may have come

from my patriarchal blessing which was given to me by Patriarch Samuel Claridge, when I was nine years of age. One line of the blessing reads:

"You will preach the gospel to many people, but more especially to the Lamanites, for the Lord will bless you with the gift of language and power to portray before that people, the gospel in great plainness. You will see them organized and be prepared to stand as the bulwark 'round this people.' "

Elder Spencer W. Kimball, 1943

I do not know when my appreciation for them came, but I have always had a sympathetic heart for the sons and daughters of Lehi, and so, recently, when President Smith called Brother Cowley, Brother Ivins, and myself to give attention to their problems and ". . . the work of disseminating the gospel among the Indians. . . . not only to the Indians close to us but also over the world, in the islands of the sea and elsewhere. . . ." a great thrill came to me such as I have had few times in my life.

I had waited forty-two years for the fulfilment of this patriarchal blessing! When I was called to the mission field in 1914, my assignment was to the Swiss-German Mission, and then the war broke out and prevented my going there, and I was sent to the Central States Mission. I knew there were no Indians in Switzerland and Germany. I knew also there were Indians in the Cen-

tral States Mission, but in all my two years' mission, I had not seen an Indian. I wondered, "Can I have failed, or did the patriarch err," and now, forty-two years after the promise, President George Albert Smith called me to this mission, and my blessing was fulfilled. . . .

We have about a half-million children of Lehi in the islands of the sea, and about sixty million of them in North and South America, about a third of them perhaps, being pure-blood Indians, and about two-thirds are mixtures, but they have the blood of Jacob in their veins. . . .

Only through us, the "nursing fathers and mothers," may they eventually enjoy a fulfilment of the many promises made to them. Assuming that we do our duty to them, the Indians and other sons of Lehi will yet rise in power and strength. The Lord will remember his covenant to them; his Church will be established among them; the Bible and other scriptures will be made available to them; they will enter into the holy temples for their endowments and do vicarious work; they will come to a knowledge of their fathers and to a perfect knowledge of their Redeemer Jesus Christ; they shall prosper in the land and will, with our help, build up a holy city, even the New Jerusalem, unto their God. . . .

May the Lord assist us all to see our full duty respecting these people and give us the courage and determination to guarantee that they have the education, culture, security, and all other advantages and luxuries that we enjoy. [In Conference Report, Apr. 1947, pp. 143–52]

Over the years Elder Kimball became a most persuasive and much beloved advocate for the Lamanites. In countless sermons he shared his vision of the destiny of this chosen people. At a special Lamanite conference held in Mesa, Arizona, 15 November 1947, he said:

Our vision reveals these people in the tomorrow as free citizens with a vote and the right and the ability to engage in all activities enjoyed by their non-Indian brothers, including holding office, serving as executives and administrators in cities, counties, and other government circles.

The Indians "—shall no more be confounded—" and will be brought "—out of obscurity and out of darkness—" The light of truth will be brought to them both spiritual and temporal as universal education comes to them from their government. The vision shows them engaging in the professions, and in business. No longer the servants, they seek and fill ambitious posts. They become dentists, occulists and physicians, jewelers, merchants and brokers with the public generally to support them, in a day of equality without discrimination. In vision they appear as lawyers, becoming peace makers, taking care of business transactions and sitting as judges in the courts. They are found in legislative halls, helping to make laws for and govern a nation. And should the Gentiles not repent and humble themselves, they as "—a remnant of the seed of Jacob shall go forth among you as a lion." But a softening of the hearts of the Gentiles toward the redman is predicted and the Gentiles "—shall be like unto a father to them." They shall not be "confounded" but may establish themselves in industries, merchan-

dising, and as to homes they may "build and inhabit."

The vision discloses a day of universal education when every child of Lehi may have twelve to sixteen or more years of training and when the Indian will teach in the school room with his white brother and will administer schools the same as non-Indians do, and Indian scientists will be found in the laboratories with their white brothers delving into new worlds....

The vision shows enlightened Indians, no longer "imprisoned" on reservations, but tilling fertile soils in the approved manner, herding their flocks and herds on ample ranges; engaging in all worthy enterprises.

Their larger incomes will enable them to build and occupy commodious and well furnished homes, drive good cars, travel in comfort, and enjoy the blessings afforded other peoples. We see them in vision developing their talents becoming sculptors, painters and musicians to delight the eye with the excellence of their artistic creations, and the ear in oratorio, grand opera and symphony.

But the greatest blessing which will come is that of spiritual light, when

"—their scales of darkness shall begin to fall from their eyes." ...

This Gospel will be taken to them by the Latter-day Saints and they "will receive the Gospel and their endowments and the blessings of God—this Church will fill North and South America—" so we may know that when they hear, they will accept the truths....

The vision reveals the extension of the Lamanite missions, new countries being brought under the missionary system and great numbers of missionaries among them to include the Lamanite youths. It reveals these returned missionaries like their non-Indian brothers, becoming the leaders in branches, quorums, wards, stakes and missions as well as in the auxiliary organizations, the seminaries, and all other phases of the work of the kingdom....

THE DAY OF THE LAMANITE IS DAWNING—THE LORD BE PRAISED! ["Hope Sees a Star for the Sons of Lehi," *Church News,* 20 Dec. 1947, p. 9]

Elder Kimball was confronted almost continually with serious health problems. In 1951 his voice was restored through a special blessing by three General Authority colleagues. Six years later he feared that a throat cancer might rob him of his voice altogether. Following much prayer and fasting, the operation proved to be less radical than had originally been thought necessary, though his voice was reduced to a whisper. "The voice was all but gone, but a new one took its place. A quiet, persuasive, mellow voice, an acquired voice, an appealing voice, a voice that is loved by the Latter-day Saints" (Packer, *Ensign,* Mar. 1974, p. 4). In 1972, after enduring long-standing heart ailments that were threatening to cause chronic congestive heart failure, Elder Kimball underwent a complex open-heart operation to relieve the basic problems. With the faith of many and through the outstanding skill of a devoted Latter-day Saint surgeon, the Lord again spared the life of his chosen servant.

These difficulties did not, however, stop Elder Kimball from setting an ex-

Left to right, Elders Mark E. Petersen, Matthew Cowley, Spencer W. Kimball, Ezra Taft Benson, and Harold B. Lee (seated)

ample of devoting long hours of hard work to his calling. "Prominently displayed on President Kimball's desk," observed Elder Robert L. Simpson, "is a slogan which reads simply, 'DO IT.' With this inspired leader, personal convenience comes second. Everything is done to meet the Lord's convenience. His example for work has become legend and establishes an example for us all to follow" (in Conference Report, Oct. 1975, p. 17; or *Ensign*, Nov. 1975, p. 13). A working schedule of sixteen- to eighteen-hour days was not uncommon for him. Many times while traveling to conferences, he took his portable typewriter in his lap, spread out his papers on the seat beside him, and answered the many letters he received.

Many of Elder Kimball's sermons also reflected his commitment to hard work and to careful and prayerful preparation. He vividly taught gospel principles as he spoke of "hidden wedges," "tragedy or destiny," "love versus lust," or "broken power lines." His teachings on these subjects were collected in two books, *The Miracle of Forgiveness* and *Faith Precedes the Miracle*.

Repentance and Forgiveness

The following teachings on repentance are taken from *Faith Precedes the Miracle:*

Repentance could well fall into five steps:

1. Conviction of and sorrow for sin
2. Abandonment of sin
3. Confession of sin
4. Restitution for sin
5. Doing the will of the Lord

1. *Sorrow for Sin*

To be sorry for our sin, we must know something of its serious implications. When fully convicted, we condition our minds to follow such processes as will rid us of the effects of the sin. We are sorry. We are willing to make amends, pay penalties, to suffer even excommunication, if necessary. Paul wrote: "For godly sorrow worketh repentance to salvation not to be repented of; but the sorrow of the world worketh death." (2 Corinthians 7:10.)

If one is sorry only because his sin was uncovered, his repentance is not complete. Godly sorrow causes one to harness desire and to determine to do right regardless of consequences; this kind of sorrow brings righteousness and will work toward forgiveness.

2. *Abandonment of Sin*

One discontinues his error when he has a full realization of the gravity of his sin and when he is willing to comply with the laws of God. The thief may abandon his evil in prison, but true repentance would have him forsake it before his arrest and

return his booty without enforcement. The sex offender as well as any other transgressor who voluntarily ceases his unholy practices is headed toward forgiveness. Alma said: "... blessed are they who humble themselves without being compelled to be humble...." (Alma 32:16.) And the Lord in our dispensation said: "By this ye may know if a man repenteth of his sins—behold, he will ... forsake them." (D&C 58:43.)

The discontinuance must be a permanent one. True repentance does not permit repetition. Peter said: "For if after they have escaped the pollutions of the world ... they are again entangled therein.... it had been better for them not to have known the way of righteousness, than, after they have known it, to turn from the holy commandment.... [as the] dog is turned to his own vomit again; and the sow that was washed to her wallowing in the mire." (2 Peter 2:20–22.)

Forgiveness is not assured if one reverts to early sins. The Lord said: "... go your ways and sin no more; but unto that soul who sinneth shall the former sins return...." (D&C 82:7.)

3. *Confession of Sin*

The confession of sin is an important element in repentance. Many offenders have seemed to feel that a few prayers to the Lord were sufficient and they have thus justified themselves in hiding their sins. The Proverbs tell us: "He that covereth his sins shall not prosper: but whoso confesseth and forsaketh them shall have mercy." (Proverbs 28:13.) "By this ye may know if a man repenteth of his sins—behold, he will confess them and forsake them." (D&C 58:43.)

Especially grave errors such as sexual sins shall be confessed to the bishop as well as to the Lord. There are two remissions that one might wish to have: first, the forgiveness from the Lord, and second, the forgiveness of the Lord's church through its leaders. As soon as one has an inner conviction of his sins, he should go to the Lord in "mighty prayer," as did Enos, and never cease his supplications until he shall, like Enos, receive the assurance that his sins have been forgiven by the Lord. It is unthinkable that God absolves serious sins upon a few requests. He is likely to wait until there has been long-sustained repentance as evidenced by a willingness to comply with all his other requirements. So far as the Church is concerned, no priest nor elder is authorized by virtue of that calling to perform this act for the Church. The Lord has a consistent, orderly plan. Every soul in the organized stakes is given a bishop who, by the very nature of his calling and his ordination, is a "judge in Israel." In the missions a branch president fills that responsibility. The bishop may be one's best earthly friend. He will hear the problems, judge the seriousness thereof, determine the degree of adjustment, and decide if it warrants an eventual forgiveness. He does this as the earthly representative of God, who is the master physician, the master psychologist, the master psychiatrist. If repentance is sufficient, he may waive penalties, which is tantamount to forgiveness so far as the church organization is concerned. The bishop claims no authority to absolve sins, but he does share the burden, waive penalties, relieve tension and strain, and he may assure a continuation of church activity. He will keep the whole matter most confidential....

4. *Restitution for Sin*

When one is humble in sorrow, has unconditionally abandoned the evil, and confesses to those assigned by the Lord, he should next restore insofar as possible that which was damaged. If he burglarized, he should return to the rightful owner that which was stolen. Perhaps one reason murder is unforgivable is that having taken a life, the murderer cannot restore it. Restitution in full is not always possible. Virginity is impossible to give back.

However, the truly repentant soul will usually find things that can be done to restore to some extent. The true spirit of repentance demands this. Ezekiel taught: "If the wicked...give again that he had

robbed, walk in the statutes of life, without committing iniquity; he shall surely live...." (Ezekiel 33:15.)

Moses taught: "If a man shall steal an ox, or a sheep... he shall restore five oxen for an ox, and four sheep for a sheep." (Exodus 22:1.)

A pleading sinner must also forgive all people of all offenses committed against himself. The Lord is under no obligation to forgive us unless our hearts are fully purged of all hate, bitterness, and accusations against others.

5. *Do the Will of the Father*

The Lord in his preface to modern revelations gave us the fifth and one of the most difficult requirements to forgiveness. He says:

"For I the Lord cannot look upon sin with the least degree of allowance;

"Nevertheless, he that repents and does the commandments of the Lord shall be forgiven." (D&C 1:31–32.)

Under the humiliation of a guilty conscience, with the possibility of detection and consequent scandal and shame, with a striving spirit urging toward adjustment, the first steps of sorrow, abandonment, confession, and restitution must now be followed by the never-ending requirement of doing the commandments. Obviously this can hardly be done in a day, a week, a month, or a year. This is an effort extending through the balance of life. "Unto the end" is an often-used phrase in the scriptures. [pp. 180–83]

Administration

Following the unexpected death of President Harold B. Lee on 26 December 1973, Spencer W. Kimball became the twelfth President of the Church. "We will, in large measure," he humbly announced, "carry forward the same program, which we have helped in a small way to make." He indicated that the First Presidency was especially interested in "the family, work with youth, missionary work, Indian programs, health and education programs, temple work, and church welfare" ("First Presidency Meets with

News Media," *Church News,* 5 Jan. 1974, p. 14). These themes were to be repeated again and again in the coming years.

"When the World Will Be Converted"

Rapid Church growth continued. As President Kimball's administration began, Church membership exceeded three million, having doubled in the previous fourteen years. In his first address as President of the Church, given at the Regional Representatives' seminar, 4 April 1974, he challenged the Church to lengthen their stride in carrying the gospel to *all* the earth.

May I now discuss with you some of the things which have been uppermost in my mind.

Every area of the Church must properly feel that its work is of greatest value, but let me quote the Lord in a revelation to the Prophet Joseph Smith:

"And if it so be that you should labor all your days in crying repentance unto this people, and bring, save it be one soul unto me, how great shall be your joy with him in the kingdom of my Father!" (D&C 18:15.)

If there were no converts, the Church would shrivel and die on the vine. But perhaps the greatest reason for missionary work is to give the world its chance to hear and accept the gospel. The scriptures are replete with commands and promises and calls and rewards for teaching the gospel. I use the word *command* deliberately for it seems to be an insistent directive from which we, singly and collectively, cannot escape.

I ask you, what did he mean when the Lord took his Twelve Apostles to the top of the Mount of Olives and said:

"...And ye shall be witnesses unto me both in Jerusalem, and in all Judea, and in Samaria, and unto the uttermost part of the earth." (Acts 1:8.) ...

... It seems to me that the Lord chose his words when he said "every nation," "every land," "uttermost bounds of the earth," "every

Spencer W. and Camilla Eyring Kimball

tongue," "every people," "every soul," "all the world," "many lands."

Surely there is significance in these words!

Certainly his sheep were not limited to the thousands about him and with whom he rubbed shoulders each day. A universal family! A universal command!

My brethren, I wonder if we are doing all we can. Are we complacent in our approach to teaching all the world? We have been proselyting now 144 years. Are we prepared to lengthen our stride? To enlarge our vision?

Remember, our ally is our God. He is our commander. He made the plans. He gave the commandment. Remember what we have quoted thousands of times as told by Nephi:

"And it came to pass that I, Nephi, said unto my father: I will go and do the things which the Lord hath commanded, for I know that the Lord giveth no commandments unto the children of men, save he shall prepare a way for them that they may accomplish the thing which he commandeth them." (1 Ne. 3:7.)

And as I read the scripture I think of the numerous nations that are still untouched. I know they have curtains, like iron curtains and bamboo curtains. I know how difficult it is because we have made some efforts. Surely the Lord knew what he was doing when he commanded. . . .

And certainly the command to the original apostles of this dispensation followed the command of the others of earlier years, and you Twelve have that same command.

The 112th section of the Doctrine and Covenants was addressed to Thomas B. Marsh, the President of the Twelve in 1837, and concerns the Twelve Apostles. The keys of the kingdom were given to the Presidency and the Twelve. Apparently President Marsh had been praying for his brethren and the Lord listened:

". . . Thine alms have come up as a memorial before me, in behalf of those, thy brethren, who were chosen to bear testimony of my name and to send it abroad among all nations, kindreds, tongues, and people. . . ." (D&C 112:1.)

Further:

". . . Thou shalt bear record of my name, not only unto the Gentiles, but also unto the Jews; and thou shalt send forth my word unto the ends of the earth." (D&C 112:4.)

He was commanded:

". . . Let not the inhabitants of the earth slumber, because of thy speech.

". . . Thy path lieth among the mountains, and among many nations." (D&C 112:5, 7.)

You, the Twelve, today inherited that command. . . .

When I read Church history, I am amazed at the boldness of the early brethren as they went out into the world. They seemed to find a way. Even in persecution and hardship, they went and opened doors which evidently have been allowed to sag on their hinges and many of them to close. I remember that these fearless men were teaching the gospel in Indian lands before the Church was even fully organized. As early as 1837 the Twelve were in England fighting Satan, in Tahiti in 1844, Australia in 1851, Iceland 1853, Italy 1850, and also in Switzerland, Germany, Tonga, Turkey, Mexico, Japan, Czechoslovakia, China, Samoa, New Zealand, South America, France, and Hawaii in 1850. When you look at the progress we have made in some counries, with no progress in many of their nearby countries, it makes us wonder. Much of this early proselyting was done while the leaders were climbing the Rockies and planting the sod and starting their homes. It is faith and super faith.

These men of valor began to walk the earth with dignity and honor, with mantles on their shoulders and keys in their hands and love in their hearts.

To the Twelve the Lord said,

"You have a work to do that no other men can do. . . . There will be times when nothing but the angels of God can deliver you out of their hands...." (*History of the Church,* vol. 2, p. 178.)

Now let me speak of the expansion which I think is necessary and, may I add, which I think is possible....

The Twelve have the keys and those they send have the command to open doors. Today we are blessed with many strong, trained men, in government, in foreign service, and with much prestige and "know-how." Perhaps we can bring to our call men like these who can make new contacts with emperors and kings and rulers and magistrates.

Somehow I believe the Lord meant what he said through the centuries.

Again to the apostles through their president, Thomas B. Marsh:

"Contend thou, therefore, morning by morning; and day after day let thy warning voice go forth; and when night cometh let not the inhabitants of the earth slumber, because of thy speech." (D&C 112:5.)

"For verily the voice of the Lord is unto all men, and there is none to escape; and there is no eye that shall not see, neither ear that shall not hear, neither heart that shall not be penetrated.

"And the voice of warning shall be unto all people, by the mouths of my disciples, whom I have chosen in these last days." (D&C 1:2, 4.)

Somehow, brethren, I feel that when we have done all in our power that the Lord will find a way to open the doors. That is my faith.

"Is any thing too hard for the Lord?" he asked, when Sarah laughed when she was told that she would have a son. When she heard this in the tent door, she knew that both Abraham at 100 years and she at 90 years were past the age of reproduction. She could not bear children. She knew that, as well as it has been known that we could not open doors to many nations.

"And the Lord said unto Abraham, Wherefore did Sarah laugh....

"Is any thing too hard for the Lord? At the time appointed I will return

unto thee, according to the time of life, and Sarah shall have a son." (Gen. 18:13–14.)

Brethren, Sarah did have a son, from Abraham, the father of nations.

"Therefore sprang there even of one, and him as good as dead [and that was Abraham, 100 years old], so many as the stars of the sky in multitude, and as the sand which is by the sea shore innumerable." (Heb. 11:12.)

Is anything too hard for the Lord?

Also to Jeremiah he had said:

"Behold, I am the Lord, the God of all flesh: is there any thing too hard for me?" (Jer. 32:27.)

If he commands, certainly he can fulfill.

We remember the exodus of the children of Israel crossing the uncrossable Red Sea.

We remember Cyrus diverting a river and taking the impregnable city of Babylon.

We remember the Lehites getting to the promised land.

We remember the Revolutionary War and the power of God that gave us triumph.

I believe the Lord can do anything he sets his mind to do.

But I can see no good reason why the Lord would open doors that we are not prepared to enter. Why should he break down the Iron Curtain or the Bamboo Curtain or any other curtain if we are still unprepared to enter?

I believe we have men who could help the apostles to open these doors—statesmen, able and trustworthy—but, when we are ready for them.

Today [1974] we have 18,600 missionaries. We can send more. Many more!...

I believe it was John Taylor who said, "God will hold us responsible to the people we might have saved, had we done our duty."

When I ask for more missionaries, I am not asking for more testimony-barren or unworthy missionaries. I

am asking that we start earlier and train our missionaries better in every branch and every ward in the world. That is another challenge— that the young people will understand that it is a great privilege to go on a mission and that they must be physically well, mentally well, spiritually well, and that "the Lord cannot look upon sin with the least degree of allowance."

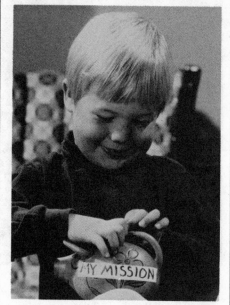

I am asking for missionaries who have been carefully indoctrinated and trained through the family and the organizations of the Church, and who come to the mission with a great desire. I am asking for better interviews, more searching interviews, more sympathetic and understanding interviews, but especially that we train prospective missionaries much better, much earlier, much longer, so that each anticipates his mission with great joy....

The question is frequently asked: Should every young man fill a mission? And the answer has been given by the Lord. It is "Yes." Every young man should fill a mission....

Every man should also pay his tithing. Every man should observe the Sabbath. Every man should attend his meetings. Every man should marry in the temple and properly train his children, and do many other mighty works. Of course he should. He does not always do it....

Yes, we would say, every able worthy man should shoulder the cross. What an army we should have teaching Christ and him crucified! Yes, they should be prepared, usually with saved funds for their missions, and always with a happy heart to serve.

The Lord says:

"And that *every man*"—(Did you catch the words, "every man"?) "should take righteousness in his hands and faithfulness upon his loins, and lift a warning voice unto the inhabitants of the earth: and declare both by word and by flight that desolation shall come upon the wicked." (D&C 63:37.)

Note that he said *every man;* but we must find a way to have *every man* prepared.

Now, how can we do this? We see that there are these elements to be considered: the breaking down of resistance of the nations of the world to receive our missionaries; a greatly increased missionary force (greatly, I emphasize); a better trained missionary army; and better and additional methods and approaches.

Now here we will consider each one in its turn. We need to *enlarge our field of operation.* We will need to make a full, prayerful study of the nations of the world which do not have the gospel at this time, and then bring into play our strongest and most able men to assist the Twelve to move out into the world and to open the doors of every nation as fast as it is ready. I believe we have many men in the Church who can be helpful to us, who are naturally gifted diplomats. I believe we should bring them to our aid and as stated before, I have faith that the Lord will open doors when we have done everything in our power.

Second, I have already discussed and will discuss a little further, an enlarged army of missionaries.

Third, I believe that the Lord is anxious to put into our hands inventions of which we laymen have hardly had a glimpse.

The Prophet Joseph Smith declared: "The truth of God will go forth boldly, till it has penetrated every continent, and sounded in every ear, till the purposes of God shall be accomplished."

A significant revelation states: "For, verily, the sound must go forth from this place into all the world, and unto the uttermost parts of the earth—the gospel must be preached unto every creature. . . ." (D&C 58:64.)

I am confident that the only way we can reach most of these millions of our Father's children is through the spoken word over the airwaves, since so many are illiterate. We have proved the ability of our young men to learn other languages.

President David O. McKay, speaking in the October 1966 conference of the Church, said of the scientific discoveries of recent years which will make possible the preaching of the gospel to every kindred, tongue, and people: "They stagger the imagination."

And further: ". . . discoveries latent with such potent power, either for the blessing or the destruction of human beings as to make men's responsibility in controlling them the most gigantic ever placed in human hands. . . . This age is fraught with limitless perils, as well as untold possibilities." . . .

Our Father in heaven has now provided us mighty towers—radio and television towers with possibilities beyond comprehension—to help fulfill the words of the Lord that "the sound must go forth from this place unto all the world." . . .

Just think what can be accomplished when we broadcast our message in many languages over numerous radio stations, large and small, around the world, and millions of good people listening on their transistors are being indoctrinated with the truth. . . .

With the Lord providing these miracles of communication, and with the increased efforts and devotion of our missionaries and all of us, and all others who are "sent," surely the divine injunction will come to pass: "For, verily, the sound must go forth from this place into all the world, and unto the uttermost parts of the earth—the gospel must be preached unto every creature. . . ." (D&C 58:64.) And we must find a way.

We are happy with the people of Hong Kong, but according to our records only 1,000, or less than 1 percent of the people have accepted the gospel.

We have a stake in South Korea and a mission there, with about 7,500 members. What must be done to reach the other 37,000,000? There must be a way, for the Lord does not talk in riddles. He must have anticipated that something could be done so that his word might be fulfilled.

The millions of people in the Philippines would receive the gospel in large numbers if it were properly presented to them. We have two missions and a stake there. We should use their own young men as missionaries and then every facility that is available to bring them to a knowledge of the true church.

There are 14,000,000 people in Taiwan, 2,000,000 in Singapore, 119,000,000 in Indonesia, 31,000,000 in Korea, 40,000,000 in Thailand, and 103,000,000 in Japan, and all these 300,000,000 people are sons and daughters of God and have a right to hear the gospel, and we have not only the right to give it to them but the obligation to do so.

We mention Australia with its over 13,000,000 people, and we have been doing missionary work there since 1851. Now, after 123 years, we still have only 29,000 members, for which we are grateful, with 13,000,000 yet to touch, and for 123 years we have been sending missionaries from this land to that land and today have more than 600 missionaries in Australia. Of this 600 plus missionaries, only a relatively small handful, about 5.5 percent, are Australians. Where have we failed to help these good people to see their duty in this pivotal matter?

In Mexico we have around 54,000,000 people with about 92,000 members. We have 489 full-time missionaries now serving in that country, only 122 of which are native Mexicans. . . .

There is ample argument that Mexico, with its nine stakes and five missions, should furnish its own missionaries, or the equivalent.

Suppose that South Korea with its 37,000,000 people and its 7,500 members were to take care of its own proselyting needs and thus release to go into North Korea and possibly to Russia the hundreds who now go from the states to Korea.

If Japan could furnish its own 1,000 missionaries and then eventually 10,000 more for Mongolia and China, if Taiwan could furnish its own needed missionaries plus 500 for China and Vietnam and Cambodia, then we would begin to fulfill the vision. Suppose that Hong Kong could furnish its needed missionaries and another 1,000 to go to both of the Chinas; suppose the Philippines could fill its own needs and then provide an additional 1,000 for the limitless islands of southeast Asia; suppose the South Seas and the islands therein and the New Zealanders and the Australians could furnish their own and another several thousand for the numerous islands of south Asia and for Vietnam, Cambodia, Thailand, Burma, Bangladesh, and India.

With this movement of missionaries who would be traveling north and west, the lands of the world could begin to be covered with the gospel as the lowlands of the world are covered with the oceans.

Now in another part of the world, suppose that Mexico and Central America provided far more missionaries than they needed themselves and the people of South America had reached the point where they could export numerous fine missionaries and then suppose that the United States and Canada awakened to their real responsibility, sending thousands of missionaries to join them, going east and north so that Iceland, Scandinavia, southern Europe, Germany, and Europe could be covered. . . .

This would be difficult. It would take some time. Sometimes it might seem impossible but again remember the little stone cut out of the mountain without hands which was destined to roll forth and fill the whole earth. It has gone a long way but it must go farther.

Using all the latest inventions and equipment and paraphenalia already developed and that which will follow, can you see that perhaps the day may come when the world will be converted and covered?

If we do all we can, and I accept my own part of that responsibility, I am sure the Lord will bring more discoveries to our use. He will bring a change of heart into kings and magistrates and emperors, or he will divert rivers or open seas or find ways to touch hearts. He will open the gates and make possible the proselyting. Of that, I have great faith.

Now, we have the promise from the Lord that the evil one will never be able to frustrate totally the work that He has commanded us to do.

"This kingdom will continue to increase and to grow, to spread and to prosper more and more. Every time its enemies undertake to overthrow it, it will become more extensive and powerful; instead of decreasing it will continue to increase; it will spread the more, become more wonderful and conspicuous to the nations, until it fills the whole earth." (President Brigham Young, April conference, 1852.) . . .

You are acquainted with the statement of the Prophet Joseph Smith in the Wentworth Letters written March 1, 1842. (*History of the Church,* vol. 4, p. 536.) I am sure the Prophet Joseph looked ahead and saw many problems with national animosities and fears with war and commotions and jealousies, and I am sure that he saw all these things would happen and yet in spite of everything he said with great boldness and assurance:

"No unhallowed hand can stop the work from progressing; persecutions may rage, mobs may combine, armies may assemble, calumny may defame, but the truth of God will go forth boldly, nobly and independent, till it has penetrated every continent; visited every clime, swept every country and sounded in every ear; till the purposes of God shall be accomplished, and the great Jehovah shall say the work is done."

The immensity of the work before us is emphasized as we consider the population of the world as it approaches the four billion mark.

I am under no delusion, brethren, to think that this will be an easy matter without strain or that it can be done overnight, but I do have this faith that we can move forward and expand much faster than we are now.

As I see this almost impossible demand, I believe that you brethren, our representatives, can immediately accept the challenge and in your stakes and missions explain to the people how they must increase their missionaries, how they can finance their missionaries, how they can indoctrinate and train these additional missionaries, and how, through all the agencies of the Church, they can move ahead. Here is where you come in. . . .

I have stated the problem. I believe there is a solution. I think that if we are all of one mind and one heart and one purpose that we can move forward and change the image which seems to be that "We are doing pretty well. Let's not 'rock the boat.'"

In all the countries I have ever visited I have found many intelligent and qualified people who give leadership in their countries, and I also remember numerous people from deprived countries enjoying benefits from the gospel.

In our stake missionary work at home we have hardly scratched the surface.

Brother T. Bowring Woodbury told us of 93 cooperating families in one Utah stake who were working with 93 non- or part-member families. Clifford Johnson told us of bringing five of 26 nonmembers into the Church in a few months.

It can be done.

We can change the image and approach the ideal set out by President McKay, "Every member a missionary." That was inspired!

I know this message is not new, and we have talked about it before, but I believe the time has come when we must shoulder arms. I think we must

President and Sister Kimball greeting First Lady Betty Ford at the Washington Temple

change our sights and raise our goals.

When we have increased the missionaries from the organized areas of the Church to a number close to their potential, that is, every able and worthy boy in the Church on a mission; when every stake and mission abroad is furnishing enough missionaries for that country; when we have used our qualified men to help the apostles to open these new fields of labor; when we have used the satellite and related discoveries to their greatest potential and all of the media—the papers, magazines, television, radio—all in their greatest power; when we have organized numerous other stakes which will be springboards; when we have recovered from inactivity the numerous young men who are now unordained and unmissioned and unmarried; then, and not until then, shall we approach the insistence of our Lord and Master to go into all the world and preach the gospel to every creature.

Brethren, I am positive that the blessings of the Lord will attend every country which opens its gates to the gospel of Christ. Their blessings will flow in education, and culture, and faith, and love, like Enoch's city of Zion, which was translated, and also will become like the 200 years of peaceful habitation in this country in Nephite days. There will come prosperity to the nations, comfort and luxuries to the people, joy and peace to all recipients, and eternal life to those who

accept and magnify it.

Someone gave us this:

To walk with God, no strength is lost.
Walk on.
To talk with God, no breath is lost.
Talk on.
To wait on God, no time is lost.
Wait on.

I pray the blessings of the Lord will be upon us as we approach our great responsibilities, in the name of the Lord, Jesus Christ. Amen. ["When the World Will Be Converted," *Ensign*, Oct. 1974, pp. 3–14]

This growth was reflected in an acceleration in the number of area conferences held around the world and the discontinuation of annual auxiliary conferences at Salt Lake City. For the first time in Church history, President Kimball called new General Authorities who were not living in North America. The First Quorum of the Seventy was formally organized and expanded to include those who had been serving as Assistants to the Twelve. Several members of this quorum were assigned to reside in and supervise areas throughout the world. In addition the First Presidency appointed David M. Kennedy a diplomatic affairs consultant to assist the internationally expanding Church.

The Importance of Temple Work

President Kimball's administration also has witnessed a period of unprecedented temple activity. In 1974 he dedicated the Washington Temple, the largest built during this dispensation.

During the next three years he announced the construction of six new temples—the most ever to be under construction at one time. These included the Sao Paulo Temple, the first in South America; the Tokyo Temple, the first in Asia; a temple in Samoa; one in Mexico City; one in the state of Washington; and one in the Salt Lake Valley. And this promised to be only the beginning. The Arizona, Idaho Falls, St. George, Logan, and Hawaii temples were modernized to accommodate the performance of a vastly expanded number of ordinances. At the same time, improvements in genealogical procedures were announced, and President Kimball challenged Church members not to neglect this vital work.

I feel the same sense of urgency about temple work for the dead as I do about the missionary work for the living, since they are basically one and the same. I have told my brethren of the General Authorities that this work for the dead is constantly on my mind.

The First Presidency and the Council of the Twelve recently gave careful consideration as to how we can lengthen our stride in this tremendously important responsibility. We announce a twofold emphasis.

First, all members should write a personal history and participate in a family organization. Also, we want to emphasize again and place squarely upon the shoulders of these individuals and their families the obligation to complete the four-generation program. Families may extend their pedigree beyond the four generations if desired.

Secondly, we are introducing a Church-wide program of extracting names from genealogical records. Church members may now render second-mile service through participating in this regard in extracting these names in this program super-vised by the priesthood leaders at the local level, where you will receive further details.

On the bookshelves in my office at home there are thirty-three large, well-filled journal books. In my journal, a year for each book, I have written daily and filed in this library. It records the trips to many of the nations in the world and all around the world and meetings held, people contacted, marriages performed, and all things of interest to my family, and, I hope, someday to the Church.

I urge all of the people of this church to give serious attention to their family histories, to encourage their parents and grandparents to write their journals, and let no family go into eternity without having left their memoirs for their children, their grandchildren, and their posterity. This is a duty and a responsibility, and I urge every person to start the children out writing a personal history and journal. [In Conference Report, Apr. 1978, p. 4; or *Ensign*, May 1978, p. 4]

Priesthood Blessings for All

During President Kimball's administration, the Church took another major step toward bringing the message and the blessings of the gospel to all the peoples of the earth. Since 1974 the Saints had responded to President Kimball's inspired plea for expanded missionary labor, swelling the missionary ranks to 26,000 in late 1978. The First Presidency, in a letter dated 8 June 1978, noting the great growth of the kingdom worldwide and "inspired...with a desire to extend to every worthy member of the Church all of the privileges and blessings which the gospel affords" gave the Lord's will to the Church: the priesthood could now be granted in its fulness to "all worthy male members of the Church...without regard for race or color."

Dear Brethren:

As we have witnessed the expansion of the work of the Lord over the earth, we have been grateful that people of many nations have responded to the message of the restored gospel, and have joined the

The First Presidency, 1973–present, left to right: N. Eldon Tanner, Spencer W. Kimball, and Marion G. Romney

(Reprinted courtesy of Sunstone)

Church in ever-increasing numbers. This, in turn, has inspired us with a desire to extend to every worthy member of the Church all of the privileges and blessings which the gospel affords.

Aware of the promises made by the prophets and presidents of the Church who have preceded us that at some time, in God's eternal plan, all of our brethren who are worthy may receive the priesthood, and witnessing the faithfulness of those from whom the priesthood has been withheld, we have pleaded long and earnestly in behalf of these, our faithful brethren, spending many hours in the Upper Room of the Temple supplicating the Lord for divine guidance.

He has heard our prayers, and by revelation has confirmed that the long-promised day has come when every faithful, worthy man in the Church may receive the holy priesthood, with power to exercise its divine authority, and enjoy with his loved ones every blessing that flows therefrom, including the blessings of the temple. Accordingly, all worthy male members of the Church may be ordained to the priesthood without regard for race or color. Priesthood leaders are instructed to follow the policy of carefully interviewing all candidates for ordination to either the Aaronic or the Melchizedek Priesthood to insure that they meet the established standards for worthiness.

We declare with soberness that the Lord has now made known His will for the blessing of all His children throughout the earth who will hearken to the voice of His authorized servants, and prepare themselves to receive every blessing of the gospel. [*Ensign,* July 1978, p. 75.]

A Warning Voice

Latter-day Saints have listened to President Kimball's warning voice on a variety of contemporary issues. His conference addresses have included counsel on civic involvement, on the family and home, on gardening and family preparedness, on immorality, pornography, drug abuse, homosexuality, divorce, and abortion. In his first conference address as President of the Church, he sought to "reaffirm some vital matters which concern us," turning first to "our civil obligations":

In 1903 President Joseph F. Smith said, "The Church [as such] does not engage in politics; its members belong to the political parties at their own pleasure...." ("The Probable Cause," *Improvement Era,* June 1903, p. 626.)

And in the October conference in 1951, the First Presidency said:

"A threat to our unity derives from unseemly personal antagonisms developed in partisan political controversy. The Church, while reserving the right to advocate principles of good government underlying equity, justice, and liberty, the political integrity of officials, and the active participation of its members, and the fulfillment of their obligations in civic affairs, exercises no constraint on the freedom of individuals to make their own choices and affiliations... any man who makes representation to the contrary does so without authority and justification in fact." (President Stephen L Richards, *Conference Report,* October 1951, pp. 114–15.)

Now these statements we reaffirm as setting forth the position of the Church today concerning civil government and politics....

Along with our unprecedented growth, our next problem is definitely the world—not the high ranges and the wide valleys and the hot deserts and the deep oceans, but the pattern of life to which too many of our people gear their lives....

The encroachment of the world into our lives is threatening! How hard it seems for many of us to live *in* the world and yet not *of* the world....

Now the works of the flesh are many, as given by Paul.... [See 2 Timothy 3:1–3; Romans 1:26–27, 30; James 4:4]...

These ugly transgressions Paul called "doctrines of devils," and their authors "seducing spirits." (See 1 Tim. 4:1.) These distortions of the normal life have not changed in this century, except possibly to grow more vile and permissive and vulgar and degenerate.

And we plead with our people everywhere, "Submit yourselves therefore to God. Resist the devil, and he will flee from you." (James 4:7.)...

You have come here seeking guidance. It is the purpose of your leaders to give that direction. As the brethren speak, you will feel the inspiration of our Lord. The gospel gives purpose in our lives. It is the way to happiness....

Now the family is basic. We are children of our Heavenly Father, and as he loves us, so our souls are bound up in our posterity....

...We call upon all people to accept normal marriage as a basis for true happiness. The Lord did not give sex to man for a plaything. Basically marriage presupposes a family. The psalmist said:

"Lo, children are an heritage of the Lord: and the fruit of the womb is his reward.

"Happy is the man that hath his quiver full of them...." (Ps. 127:3, 5.)

Certainly anyone who purposely denies himself or herself honorable parenthood is to be pitied, for the great joy of parenthood is fundamental in the normal, full life, and we remember the command of God in the beginning, "...Be fruitful, and multiply, and replenish the earth, and subdue it...." (Gen. 1:28.)...

We decry the prevalence of broken homes. Every man should love his wife and cherish and protect her all the days of their lives and she should love, honor, and appreciate her husband....

...When a man gives leadership in his home as Christ gives leadership in his church, little else can be desired.

Analyze the divorces of which you know, and you will find so often self-ishness is in them.

Most divorces are unwarranted and come of weakness and selfishness and often result in great unhappiness for the divorced persons and also almost irreparable damage and frustration to the unfavored children, who are torn and disturbed....

Again, abortion is a growing evil that we speak against....

"Abortion must be considered one of the most revolting and sinful practices in this day, when we are witnessing the frightful evidence of permissiveness leading to sexual immorality." (*Priesthood Bulletin,* February 1973, p. 1.)

As to drugs "...the Church has consistently opposed the improper and harmful use of drugs or similar substances under circumstances which would result in addiction, physical or mental impairment or in lowering moral standards." We reaffirm this positive statement.

Then in the area of one of Satan's most destructive evils, we strongly warn all our people from childhood to old age to beware of the chains of bondage, suffering, and remorse which come from improper use of the body....

We urge, with Peter, "...abstain from fleshly lusts, which war against the soul." (1 Pet. 2:11.) No indecent exposure or pornography or other aberrations to defile the mind and spirit. No fondling of bodies, one's own or that of others, and no sex between persons except in proper marriage relationships. This is positively prohibited by our Creator in all places, at all times, and we reaffirm it. Even in marriage there can be some excesses and dis-

tortions. No amount of rationalization to the contrary can satisfy a disappointed Father in heaven....

We reaffirm again our strong, unalterable stand against unchastity in all of its many manifestations.

Now our mothers have a sacred role. The following is a partial quote from the First Presidency of the Church. We reaffirm it strongly:...

"...To you mothers in Israel we say, God bless and protect you, and give you the strength and courage, the faith and knowledge, the holy love and consecration to duty, that shall enable you to fill to the fullest measure the sacred calling which is yours. To you mothers and mothers-to-be we say: Be chaste, keep pure, live righteously, that your posterity to the last generation may call you blessed." ("Message of the First Presidency," *Deseret News Weekly Church Edition,* October 1942, p. 5.)

This, then, is our program: to reaffirm and boldly carry forward the work of God in cleanliness, uprightness, and to take that gospel of truth to that world that needs so much that godly life.

Eternal life is our goal. It can be reached only by following the path our Lord has marked out for us.

I know this is true and right. I love

our Heavenly Father and I love his Son, and I am proud to be even a weak vessel to push forward their great eternal work. I testify to all this humbly, sincerely, in the name of Jesus Christ. Amen. [In Conference Report, Apr. 1974, pp. 9–10; or *Ensign,* May 1974, pp. 4–8]

STUDY QUESTIONS

1. How did Spencer W. Kimball's earlier experiences prepare him to lead the Church?

2. Who can be called "Lamanites" today? Why should Latter-day Saints feel a special desire to work with these people?

3. Why should forgiveness be called a "miracle"?

4. How is the counsel given by President Kimball related to the Church's basic mission? Which of the themes is particularly relevant to you?

5. How are missionary work and temple work related?

6. What does the latest revelation on the priesthood mean in terms of missionary work and the overcoming of cultural barriers?

7. Why is family stability so important today? According to President Kimball, what can be done, before as well as after marriage, to assure the attainment of this goal?

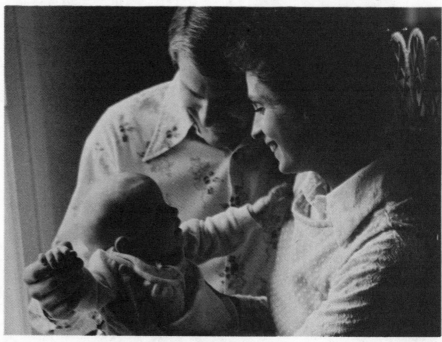

ZION WILL YET ARISE

THE history of the Church is a record, not merely of the deeds of men, but of the Lord's preparations for his millennial reign. As the predictions of both ancient and modern prophets have been fulfilled, they have become history, and such will be the case with prophecies that have yet to be fulfilled. In the last quarter of the twentieth century, the Saints have witnessed prophetic fulfillment in the dramatically accelerating growth of the Church. As the pace of the work hastens and as the faithful Saints prepare to receive the Savior, they come closer to being the kind of people that will inhabit the Zion envisioned and longed for by the prophets.

The building up of Zion is a cause that has interested the people of God in every age; it is a theme upon which prophets, priests and kings have dwelt with peculiar delight; they have looked forward with joyful anticipation to the day in which we live; and fired with heavenly and joyful anticipations they have sung and written and prophesied of this our day; but they died without the sight; we are the favored people that God has made choice of to bring about the Latter-day glory; it is left for us to see, participate in and help to roll forward the Latter-day glory, "the dispensation of the fulness of times, when God will gather together all things that are in heaven, and all things that are upon the earth," "even in one," when the Saints of God will be gathered in one from every nation, and kindred, and people, and tongue, when the Jews will be gathered together into one, the wicked will also be gathered together to be destroyed, as spoken of by the prophets; the Spirit of God will also dwell with His people, and be withdrawn from the rest of the nations, and all things whether in heaven or on earth will be in one,

even in Christ. The heavenly Priesthood will unite with the earthly, to bring about those great purposes; and whilst we are thus united in one common cause, to roll forth the kingdom of God, the heavenly Priesthood are not idle spectators, the Spirit of God will be showered down from above, and it will dwell in our midst. The blessings of the Most High will rest upon our tabernacles, and our name will be handed down to future ages; our chidren will rise up and call us blessed; and generations yet unborn will dwell with peculiar delight upon the scenes that we have passed through, the privations that we have endured; the untiring zeal that we have manifested; the all but insurmountable difficulties that we have overcome in laying the foundation of a work that brought about the glory and blessing which they will realize; a work that God and angels have contemplated with delight for generations past; that fired the souls of the ancient patriarchs and prophets; a work that is destined to bring about the destruction of the powers of darkness, the renovation of the earth, the glory of God, and the salvation of the human family. [Joseph Smith, *History of the Church,* 4:609–10]

HIGHLIGHTS

(This list is not meant to be exhaustive or chronological, but rather to briefly summarize some of the great events to transpire before the return of the Savior.)

— The Church spreads throughout the world.

— The Saints gather out of Babylon.

— Universal warfare occurs.

— The nations of the earth collapse.

— The kingdom of God rises up.

— The Saints gather to Zion and to her stakes.

— The ten tribes return.

— The city of Zion is established.

— The glory and power of Zion increase.

— Babylon falls.

— The Savior comes in glory.

— The paradisaical state is introduced.

— The Millennium begins.

HISTORICAL SUMMARY

The Nature of Zion

It will be during this dispensation that the highest point of spiritual perfection obtainable by mortals will be realized. Only rarely has the earth seen a host of men and women ascend to a pinnacle of spiritual knowledge and personal righteousness that merited the glory of the Lord to dwell in their homes and communities (see Moses 7:17–19 and 4 Nephi 1:15–18). Indeed, it was Zion, for the people were "the pure in heart" (see D&C 97:21). In fact, the people lived lives of such a high degree of purity and godliness that the Lord himself dwelled with them. So, too, will it be in this dispensation.

Zion is both the condition of being pure in heart and the community, or communities, where the pure in heart dwell. The center place of Zion will be located in Jackson County, Missouri (see D&C 57:1–3), where the Garden of Eden was located and where the Lord has revealed that the New Jerusalem will be built. This does not mean, however, that only Jackson County is to be Zion. Joseph Smith taught that all of North and South America constitute the "land of Zion" (see *Teachings of the Prophet Joseph Smith,* p. 362). Today the faithful

Saints, who comprise Zion, gather to stakes of Zion throughout the world.

Zion is more than a city or even a continent. It is a total environment with all its major aspects—cultural, social, economic, political, intellectual, ecological, and spiritual. This society is, however, a reflection of the purity, unity, and holiness of those who make up its membership. Undergirding and overspreading that environment is the glory of God. Indeed, the law of Zion is that of the celestial kingdom (see D&C 105:5). Thus, Zion belongs to the order of the eternities.

Zion is always opposed on the earth by spiritual Babylon. Like Zion, Babylon is a condition of the heart and of the mind with its accompanying environment. The difference, of course, is that Zion is purity and holiness and Babylon is evil and wickedness. Therefore, Babylon is spoken of in the scriptures as "the whore of all the earth" (see Revelation 17:1–5; D&C 29:21; 86:3), who seduces men by the lure of her promise of wealth, prestige, and power, to persecute the Saints and to fight against the Lord and his Church. Although Babylon may pose a real threat to the Church, it can never endanger Zion, once it is established. In the past, when the earth could no longer tolerate the righteousness of Zion (and for other reasons that the Lord has not revealed), Zion was not destroyed but taken: "It came to pass that Zion was not, for God received it up into his own bosom; and from thence went forth the saying, ZION IS FLED" (Moses 7:69).

When the earth, or more accurately the Church, becomes sufficiently pure to receive Zion, God will make it his abode, and "it shall be Zion, which shall come forth out of all the creations which [he has] made" (Moses 7:64). Therefore, "the glory of the Lord shall be there, and the terror of the Lord also shall be there" (D&C 45:67). For this reason it has been said that the latter-day Zion will be "a land of peace, a city of refuge, a place of safety for the saints of the Most High God" (D&C 45:66). Indeed, Zion will be a terror to the wicked because the power and majesty of the Lord will be there. "And it shall be said among the wicked: Let us not go up to battle

against Zion, for the inhabitants of Zion are terrible" (D&C 45:70).

Establishing the Cause of Zion

Through Joseph Smith, the Lord revealed again the keys for the building up of the kingdom of God and the establishment of Zion. Of him the Lord said, "Him I have inspired to move the cause of Zion in mighty power for good" (D&C 21:7). From him, the keys have been passed on from prophet to prophet, each in turn directing the work and moving the kingdom forward in preparation for the glory that is to come. This glory cannot be realized without a constant striving on the part of the Saints, however. Preparing to live in Zion should in fact be the greatest objective of every Saint.

We ought to have the building up of Zion as our greatest object. When wars come, we shall have to flee to Zion. The cry is to make haste. The last revelation says, Ye shall not have time to have gone over the earth, until these things come. It will come as did the cholera, war, fires, and earthquakes; one pestilence

after another, until the Ancient of Days comes, then judgment will be given to the Saints. . . .

The time is soon coming, when no man will have any peace but in Zion and her stakes.

I saw men hunting the lives of their own sons, and brother murdering brother, women killing their own daughters, and daughters seeking the lives of their mothers. I saw armies arrayed against armies. I saw blood, desolation, fires. The Son of Man has said that the mother shall be against the daughter, and the daughter against the mother. These things are at our doors. [Joseph Smith, *History of the Church,* 3:390–91]

The Lord has declared that Zion will not come forth in power until the Saints are properly prepared, taught, and matured in righteous experience, "know more perfectly concerning their duty" and what the Lord requires of them, and, finally, "are endowed with power from on high" (see D&C 105:10–11).

Responsibility to Establish Zion

The Latter-day Saints are the pioneers who must labor to prepare the way for Zion.

We talk and read about Zion, we contemplate upon it, and in our imaginations we reach forth to grasp something that is transcendant in heavenly beauty, excellency, and glory. But while contemplating the future greatness of Zion, do we realize that we are the pioneers of that future greatness and glory? Do we realize that if we enjoy a Zion in time or in eternity, we must make it for ourselves? That all who have a Zion in the eternities of the gods organized, framed, consolidated, and perfected it themselves, and consequently are entitled to enjoy it. [Brigham Young, in *Journal of Discourses,* 9:282]

Only when the Saints are prepared through personal righteousness will the Lord allow them to build up the center place of Zion.

And no man, so far as I know, can foretell the day or the hour, the month or the year when the people of God shall be ready to redeem Zion and build up the center stake. The Lord has not revealed this, so far as I know. But I can tell you, in one sense, when it will come to pass. I will not attempt to point out the day or the year. It will be in the due time of the Lord, when the people of God are prepared to go back, and not before. Whether it be in this generation or in the next generation, it matters not; it will only be when the people have prepared themselves to do it by their faithfulness and obedience to the commands of God. I prophesy to you, in the name of the Lord, that when the Latter-day Saints have prepared themselves through righteousness to redeem Zion, they will accomplish that work, and God will go with them. No power will then be able to prevent them from accomplishing that work; for the Lord has said it shall be done, and it will be done in the due time of the Lord, when the people are prepared for it. But when shall I be prepared to go there? Not while I have in my heart the love of this world more than the love of God. Not while I am possessed of that selfishness and greed that would induce me to cling to the world or my possessions in it, at the sacrifice of principle or truth. But when I am ready to say, "Father, all that I have, myself included, is Thine; my time, my substance, everything that I possess is on the altar, to be used freely, agreeable to Thy holy will, and not my will, but thine, be done," then perhaps I will be prepared to go and help to redeem Zion. ["Discourse by President Joseph F. Smith," *Millennial Star,* June 1894, pp. 385–86]

Zion will not come until the Saints have become pure. Brigham Young, as well as every other prophet, admonished the Saints to build the qualities of Zion into their own lives: "Zion is here. It is in my heart. Peace dwells with me, and good principles will prevail here until all evil is overcome even in all the earth. . . . Now remember this, that we will have Zion when all wickedness is gone. We have got to fight, fight, fight, until we gain the victory over ourselves" (as quoted in Diary of Wilford Woodruff, 20 July 1851, Historical Department, The Church of Jesus Christ of Latter-day Saints, Salt Lake City; spelling and punctuation modernized).

Zion must first be built within the heart, and then must radiate out to purify and prepare the earth.

Whenever we are disposed to give ourselves perfectly to righteousness, to yield all the powers and faculties of the soul (which is the spirit and the body, and it is there where righteousness dwells); when we are swallowed up in the will of Him who has called us; when we enjoy the peace and the smiles of our Father in Heaven, the things of His Spirit, and all the blessings we are capacitated to receive and improve upon, then are we in Zion, *that is Zion. . . .*

If every heart were set upon doing right, we then should have Zion here. I will give you my reason for thinking so. It is because I have had it with me ever since I was baptized into this kingdom. I have not been without it from that day to this. I have therefore a good reason for the assertion I have made. I live and walk in Zion every day, and so do thousands of others in this Church and kingdom, they carry Zion with them, they have one of their own, and it is increasing, growing, and spreading continually. Suppose it spreads from heart to heart, from neighborhood to neighborhood, from city to city, and from nation to nation, how long would it be before the earth would become revolutionized, and the wheat gathered from among the tares. [Brigham Young, in *Journal of Discourses,* 1:3–4]

The Saints are responsible for preparing not only their hearts, but also their homes and communities for the glory of Zion.

I have Zion in my view constantly. We are not going to wait for angels, or for Enoch and his company to come and build up Zion, but we are going to build it. We will raise our wheat, build our houses, fence our farms, plant our vineyards and orchards, and produce everything that will make our bodies comfortable and happy, and in this manner we intend to build up Zion on the earth and purify it and cleanse it from all polutions. Let there be an hallowed influence go from us over all things over which we have any power; over the soil we cultivate, over the houses we build, and over everything we possess; and if we cease to hold fellowship with that

which is corrupt and establish the Zion of God in our hearts, in our own houses, in our cities, and throughout our country, we shall ultimately overcome the earth, for we are the lords of the earth; and, instead of thorns and thistles, every useful plant that is good for the food of man and to beautify and adorn will spring from its bosom. [Brigham Young, in *Journal of Discourses,* 9:284]

The Lord has appointed that Zion become great through the strengthening of her stakes around the world.

Today we are witnessing the demonstration of the Lord's hand even in the midst of his saints, the members of the Church. Never in this dispensation, and perhaps never before in any single period, has there been such a feeling of urgency among the members of this church as today. Her boundaries are being enlarged, her stakes are being strengthened. In the early years of the Church specific places to which the Saints were to be gathered together were given, and the Lord directed that these gathering places should not be changed, but then he gave one qualification:

"Until the day cometh when there is found no more room for them; and then I have other places which I will appoint unto them, and they shall be called stakes, for the curtains or the strength of Zion." (D&C 101:21.)

At the Mexico City Area Conference last August [1972], Elder Bruce R. McConkie of the Council of the Twelve, in a thought-provoking address, made some comments pertinent to this subject, and I quote a few sentences from his address:

"Of this glorious day of restoration and gathering, another Nephite prophet said: 'The Lord . . . has covenanted with all the house of Israel,' that 'the time comes that they shall be restored to the true church and fold of God'; and that 'they shall be gathered home to the lands of their inheritance, and shall be established in all their lands of promise.' (2 Nephi 9:1–2.)

"Now I call your attention to the facts, set forth in these scriptures, that the gathering of Israel consists of joining the true church; of coming to a knowledge of the true God and of his saving truths; and of

worshiping him in the congregations of the Saints in all nations and among all peoples. Please note that these revealed words speak of the *folds* of the Lord; of Israel being gathered to the lands of their inheritance; of Israel being *established in all their lands of promise;* and of there being congregations of the covenant people of the Lord in *every nation, speaking every tongue,* and *among every people* when the Lord comes again."

Elder McConkie then concluded with this statement, which certainly emphasizes the great need for the teaching and training of local leadership in order to build up the church within their own native countries:

"The place of gathering for the Mexican Saints is in Mexico; the place of gathering for the Guatemalan Saints is in Guatemala; the place of gathering for the Brazilian Saints is in Brazil; and so it goes throughout the length and breadth of the whole earth. Japan is for the Japanese; Korea is for the Koreans; Australia is for the Australians; every nation is the gathering place for its own people." [Harold B. Lee, in Conference Report, Apr. 1973, pp. 6–7; or *Ensign,* July 1973, pp. 4–5]

The gathering of the Saints to the stakes of Zion shall be for a defense and a refuge.

In 1847, the Lord revealed, "Let every man use all his influence and

the storm, and from wrath when it shall be poured out without mixture upon the whole earth." (D&C 115:6.) [Spencer W. Kimball, in Conference Report, Stockholm Area Conference 1974, p. 6]

The Church is to arise and shine forth that its light might be a standard to the nations.

As though to impress upon these early struggling members their destiny in the world, the Lord in another revelation told them this:

"Therefore, verily, thus saith the Lord, let Zion rejoice, for this is Zion—THE PURE IN HEART; therefore, let Zion rejoice, while all the wicked shall mourn." (D&C 97:21.)

To be worthy of such a sacred designation as Zion, the Church must think of itself as a bride adorned for her husband, as John the Revelator recorded when he saw in vision the Holy City where the righteous dwelled, adorned as a bride for the Lamb of God as her husband. Here is portrayed the relationship the Lord desires in his people in order to be acceptable to our Lord and Master even as a wife would adorn herself in beautiful garments for her husband.

The rule by which the people of God must live in order to be worthy of acceptance in the sight of God is indicated by the text to which I have made reference. This people must increase in beauty before the world; have an inward loveliness which

property to remove this people to the place where the Lord shall locate a stake of zion." (D&C 136:10.) There is good reason for members of the Church who are isolated from the stakes and their benefits that they may wish to consider moving to central places, where all the blessings of the Church are available. Sometimes, of course, that is not feasible, and so we remain in the outskirts and build up the Church wherever we are.

In January, 1832, the Lord said: "For Zion must increase in beauty, and in holiness; her borders must be enlarged; her stakes must be strengthened; yea, verily I say unto you, Zion must arise and put on her beautiful garment." (D&C 82:14.)

In December 1833, the Lord gave to the Prophet Joseph Smith this order:

"And, behold, there is none other place appointed than that which I have appointed...,

"Until the day cometh when there is found no more room for them; and then I have other places which I will appoint unto them, and they shall be called stakes." (D&C 101:20–21.)...

And again, the Lord speaks of the gathering to centers so that the work may roll on; we are so much stronger in larger groups than in the scattered places. "And that the gathering together upon the land of Zion, and upon her stakes, may be for a defense, and for a refuge from

(NASA photo)

and let us go up to the mountain of the Lord, to the house of the God of Jacob; and he will teach us of his ways, and we will walk in his paths...." (Isa. 2:2–3.) [Harold B. Lee, in Conference Report, Apr. 1973, pp. 4–5; or *Ensign*, July 1973, pp. 3–4]

Zion in This Dispensation

This is the dispensation in which the Saints will become pure. "This is the only dispensation that God has ever established that was foreordained, before the world was made, not to be overcome by wicked men and devils" (Wilford Woodruff, in *Journal of Discourses*, 17:245). Brigham Young said:

> The powers of earth and hell have striven to destroy this kingdom from the earth. The wicked have succeeded in doing so in former ages; but this kingdom they cannot destroy, because it is the last dispensation—because it is the fulness of times. It is the dispensation of all dispensations, and will excel in magnificence and glory every dispensation that has ever been committed to the children of men upon this earth. The Lord will bring again Zion, redeem his Israel, plant his standard upon the earth, and establish the laws of his kingdom, and those laws will prevail. [Brigham Young, in *Journal of Discourses*, 8:36]

With Brigham Young, we should declare: "To me it is the Kingdom of God or nothing upon the earth. Without it I

may be observed by mankind as a reflection in holiness and in those inherent qualities of sanctity. The borders of Zion, where the righteous and pure in heart may dwell, must now begin to be enlarged. The stakes of Zion must be strengthened. All this so that Zion may arise and shine by becoming increasingly diligent in carrying out the plan of salvation throughout the world.

While the Church was in its infancy, the Lord pointed to a time when those earlier gathering places would not have room for all who would be gathered for reasons for which he declared that his church should be united. Here are his words:

"For thus shall my church be called in the last days, even The Church of Jesus Christ of Latter-day Saints." And then this command: "Arise and shine forth, that thy light may be a standard for the nations." (D&C 115:4–5.)

Here is clearly inferred that the coming forth of his Church in these

days was the beginning of the fulfillment of the ancient prophecy when "the mountain of the Lord's house shall be established in the top of the mountains, and shall be exalted about the hills; and all nations shall flow unto it. And many people shall go and say, Come ye,

would not give a farthing for the wealth, glory, prestige and power of all the world combined; for like the dew upon the grass, it passeth away and is forgotten, and like the flower of the grass it withereth, and is not" (*Discourses of Brigham Young,* pp. 444–45).

Zion cannot be fully realized until the central city, the New Jerusalem, has been built and the glory of the Lord rests upon it. However, in terms of possessing the keys, authority, and power to transform the hearts of those willing to receive and, also, of extending and expanding this work over the earth, Zion is on the earth now, for the Church is Zion. Speaking of the task before the Church, President Spencer W. Kimball has stated: "As we speak of Zion, we think of the world, since this now has become a worldwide church.

"The Lord says the stakes must increase in holiness, and must be strengthened, and must arise and put on their beautiful garments" (in Con-ference Report, Stockholm Area Conference 1974, p. 5).

Today, those who discern with spiritual eyes can see that Zion is indeed arising, and that nothing can prevent it from fulfilling its destiny. From its infancy, the prophets, by revelation, have known the path it must follow. The task to which the prophets are now directing the Saints is to spread the vision of truth into every receiving heart, that they may join in the labor until "the earth shall be full of the knowledge of the Lord, as the waters cover the sea" (Isaiah 11:9). Joseph Smith said: "No unhallowed hand can stop the work from progressing; persecutions may rage, mobs may combine, armies may assemble, calumny may defame, but the truth of God will go forth boldly, nobly, and independent, till it has penetrated every continent, visited every clime, swept every country, and sounded in every ear, till the purposes of God shall be accomplished, and the Great Jehovah shall say the work is done" (*History of the Church,* 4:540).

STUDY QUESTIONS

1. What is the nature of Zion? What conditions have allowed Zion to be established in the past?

2. What must take place for Church members to become a Zion-like people? What part can each Saint play in the establishment of Zion?

3. Why must this present dispensation bring forth Zion upon the earth?

4. Since Zion will be established no matter what we do, why should we do anything?

5. For what reasons today should the Saints "gather"?

6. In what way today do the Saints gather?

7. According to the prophets, where are today's designated gathering places?

(From a painting by Carl Bloch, by permission of Globe Photos, Clix Camera Division, New York)

SOURCES CITED AND SUGGESTED READINGS

Anderson, Joseph B. *Prophets I Have Known.* Salt Lake City: Deseret Book Co., 1973.

Clark, James R., comp. *Messages of the First Presidency of The Church of Jesus Christ of Latter-day Saints.* 6 vols. Salt Lake City: Bookcraft, 1965–75.

Cooke, Philip St. George. *The Conquest of New Mexico and California.* New York: G.P. Putnam's Sons, 1878.

Cowley, Matthias F. *Wilford Woodruff: Fourth President of The Church of Jesus Christ of Latter-day Saints.* Salt Lake City: The Deseret News, 1909.

Cracroft, Richard H., and Lambert, Neal E. *A Believing People: Literature of the Latter-day Saints.* Provo, Utah: Brigham Young University Press, 1974.

Doxey, Roy W. *Zion in the Last Days.* Salt Lake City: Bookcraft, 1968.

Gibbons, Francis M. *Joseph Smith, Martyr, Prophet of God.* Salt Lake City: Deseret Book Co., 1977.

Grant, Heber J. *Gospel Standards.* Compiled by G. Homer Durham. Salt Lake City: Improvement Era, 1941.

Hafen, LeRoy F., and Hafen, Ann W. *Handcarts to Zion.* Glendale, California: The Arthur H. Clark Co., 1960.

Hinckley, Bryant S. *Heber J. Grant: Highlights in the Life of a Great Leader.* Salt Lake City: Deseret Book Co., 1951.

Jessee, Dean C., ed. *Letters of Brigham Young to His Sons.* Salt Lake City: Deseret Book Co., 1974.

Journal of Discourses. 26 vols. London: Latter-day Saints' Book Depot, 1854–86.

"Journal of Mary Ann Weston Maughan." *Our Pioneer Heritage,* vol. 2, compiled by Kate B. Carter, pp. 345–420. Salt Lake City: Daughters of Utah Pioneers, 1959.

Kimball, Edward L., and Kimball, Andrew E., Jr. *Spencer W. Kimball.* Salt Lake City: Deseret Book Co., 1977.

Kimball, Spencer W. *Faith Precedes the Miracle.* Salt Lake City: Deseret Book Co., 1972.

———. *Marriage and Divorce.* Salt Lake City: Deseret Book Co., 1976.

———. *The Miracle of Forgiveness.* Salt Lake City: Bookcraft, 1969.

———. *One Silent Sleepless Night.* Salt Lake City: Bookcraft, 1975.

Lee, Harold B. *Ye Are the Light of the World.* Salt Lake City: Deseret Book Co., 1974.

Lyman, Albert R. *Francis Marion Lyman, 1840–1916.* Delta, Utah: Melvin A. Lyman, M.D., 1958.

McKay, David O. *Cherished Experiences from the Writings of President David O. McKay.* Compiled by Clare Middlemiss. Salt Lake City: Deseret Book Co., 1955.

———. *Stepping Stones to an Abundant Life.* Compiled by Llewelyn R. McKay. Salt Lake City: Deseret Book Co., 1971.

McKay, Llewelyn R. *Home Memories of President David O. McKay.* Salt Lake City: Deseret Book Co., 1956.

Morrell, Jeanette McKay. *Highlights in the Life of President David O. McKay.* Salt Lake City: Deseret Book Co., 1966.

Nibley, Preston. *The Presidents of the Church.* Salt Lake City: Deseret Book Co., 1974.

Pratt, Parley P. *Autobiography of Parley P. Pratt.* Salt Lake City: Deseret Book Co., 1938.

Rich, Russell Rogers. *Ensign to the Nations.* Provo, Utah: Brigham Young University Publications, 1972.

Roberts, B.H. *A Comprehensive History of The Church of Jesus Christ of Latter-day Saints, Century One.* 6 vols. Salt Lake City: The Church of Jesus Christ of Latter-day Saints, 1930.

———. *The Life of John Taylor, Third President of The Church of Jesus Christ of Latter-day Saints.* Salt Lake City: Bookcraft, 1963.

Romney, Thomas C. *The Life of Lorenzo Snow, Fifth President of the Church of Jesus Christ of Latter-day Saints.* Salt Lake City: Sugarhouse Press, 1955.

Schulter, F.E. *A Convert's Tribute to President David O. McKay.* Salt Lake City: Deseret Book Co., 1964.

Smith, Eliza R. Snow. *Biography and Family Record of Lorenzo Snow.* Salt Lake City: Deseret News Co., 1884.

Smith, George Albert. *Sharing the Gospel with Others.* Selected and compiled by Preston Nibley. Salt Lake City: Deseret Book Co., 1948.

Smith, Joseph. *History of The Church of Jesus Christ of Latter-day Saints.* 7 vols. 2nd ed., rev. Edited by B.H. Roberts. Salt Lake City: The Church of Jesus Christ of Latter-day Saints, 1932–51.

———. *Teachings of the Prophet Joseph Smith.* Selected by Joseph Fielding Smith. Salt Lake City: Deseret Book Co., 1938.

Smith, Joseph F. *Gospel Doctrine.* 5th ed. Salt Lake City: Deseret Book Co., 1939.

Smith, Joseph Fielding. *Doctrines of Salvation.* 3 vols. Compiled by Bruce R. McConkie. Salt Lake City: Bookcraft, 1954–56.

———. *Life of Joseph F. Smith, Sixth*

President of The Church of Jesus Christ of Latter-day Saints. Salt Lake City: Deseret Book Co., 1969.

Smith, Joseph Fielding, Jr., and Stewart, John J. *The Life of Joseph Fielding Smith.* Salt Lake City: Deseret Book Co., 1972.

Smith, Lucy Mack. *History of Joseph Smith.* 1945. Reprint. Salt Lake City: Bookcraft, 1954.

Spencer, Clarissa Young, with Harmer, Mabel. *Brigham Young at Home.* Salt Lake City: Deseret Book Co., 1940.

West, Emerson R. *Profiles of the Presidents.* Salt Lake City: Deseret Book Co., 1974.

Young, Brigham. *Discourses of Brigham Young.* Selected by John A. Widtsoe. Salt Lake City: Deseret Book Co., 1954.

Young, John R. *Memoirs of John R. Young, Utah Pioneer, 1847.* Salt Lake City: Deseret News Press, 1920.

Young, S. Dilworth. *Here Is Brigham Young . . . the Years to 1844.* Salt Lake City: Bookcraft, 1964.

Comments and Suggestions

Your comments and suggestions about the materials in this manual will be gratefully appreciated. Please submit them to:

Instructional Development
50 East North Temple Street
24th Floor
Salt Lake City, Utah 84150
U.S.A.

Identify yourself by name and address. Then identify the name of the manual, how you used it, your feelings regarding its strengths and weaknesses, and any recommended improvements.

Notes

Notes

Notes

Notes

Notes